Understanding China

More information about this series at http://www.springer.com/series/11772

Silvio Beretta · Axel Berkofsky
Lihong Zhang
Editors

Understanding China Today

An Exploration of Politics, Economics, Society, and International Relations

Springer

Editors
Silvio Beretta
Department of Political and Social Sciences
University of Pavia
Pavia
Italy

Lihong Zhang
East China University of Political Science and Law
Shanghai
China

Axel Berkofsky
Department of Political and Social Sciences
University of Pavia
Pavia
Italy

ISSN 2196-3134 ISSN 2196-3142 (electronic)
Understanding China
ISBN 978-3-319-29624-1 ISBN 978-3-319-29625-8 (eBook)
DOI 10.1007/978-3-319-29625-8

Library of Congress Control Number: 2017937132

Printed on acid-free paper

This Springer imprint is published by Springer Nature
The registered company is Springer International Publishing AG
The registered company address is: Gewerbestrasse 11, 6330 Cham, Switzerland

The editors would like to thank Prof. Giuseppe Iannini for his precious help reviewing the manuscript.

Preface

Already in 1960 the historian and journalist Guy Wint wrote about China's rapid rise and its objective to become a great power in terms of economic and political weight and influence only comparable to the United States and the former Soviet Union: a country, whose policies have an enormous impact on and consequences for the balance of power in Asia, Africa and even Europe.[1] Guy Wint, as it turned out, was right. China, has after its economic opening under Deng Xiaoping in the late 1970, indeed become a great power, the world's second biggest economy and its foreign and security as well as its foreign economic policies in Africa, Asia and Europe have an increasingly visible impact on geopolitical and geo-economic balances in all of the above-mentioned regions.

The analysis of Chinese foreign and security policies, Chinese domestic policies, China's economy and finance, China's judicial system, demography, the so-called 'Chinese Dream', history and culture: all of this is covered by Italian (plus one German and Chinese) Asia and China scholars in this edited volume. Needless to say that the analysis of China presented in this volume is not exhaustive and does not cover all there is to cover on China's domestic, economic, social and foreign policy agendas. However, the volume does nonetheless undertook an ambitious attempt to put together a relatively large group of Italian China and Asia scholars writing on their respective areas of China-related work and research.

The book is divided into four parts: 1. 'China in World Politics', 2. 'China in the International Economy', 3. 'Chinese Politics and Culture' and 4. 'Italian Views on China.' The part 'China in World Politics' starts off with Axel Berkofsky writing on the relations between China and the European Union, which since 2003 refer to each other as 'strategic partners.' His Chapter "The EU and China-Myth Versus Reality of a (not so) 'Strategic Partnership'" provides a (very) critical analysis of relations between the European Union and China and concludes that cooperation in international politics and security takes much more place on paper than in reality.

[1]Guy Wint, *Common Sense about China*, London, Macmillan 1960 (translated into Italian as *La Cina e noi*, Milano, Bompiani 1961).

In fact, the 'strategic partnership' Brussels and Beijing entertain in official EU documents and declarations, Berkofsky concludes, is often neither a 'partnership' nor 'strategic' and there are far more problems and disagreements than achievements and results on the bilateral EU-China political and economic agendas.

Sandro Bordone analyses in his Chapter "The Relations between China and India from Bandung to the 'New Silk Road'" the history of China's bumpy relations with India starting in the 1950s and the Bandung Conference. In Bandung, Bordone explains, it seemed that China and India could join forces and counter the influence and dominance of the two superpowers United States and Soviet Union. However, geopolitical and geo-strategic rivalry, a border war in the early 1960s and Mao Zedong's chaotic and indeed disastrous domestic and foreign policies made sure that Beijing and Delhi never became overly friendly with each other, let alone allies. Today, Bordone explains, there is a lot of talk about 'Chindia' and the idea that China and India could pool their enormous economic resources and benefit from each other's skills and capabilities. Whether or not, the author concludes, the Chinese dragon will tightly embrace the Indian elephant, among other through India's inclusion in China's very ambitious 'New Silk Road' project, however, remains yet to be seen.

Silvana Malle examines in her Chapter "Russia and China: Partners or Competitors? Views from Russia" the state and quality of Sino-Russian relations, providing the reader with a fascinating insight into how Russian policymakers and scholars view Moscow's so-called 'Pivot to China', i.e. Russia's attempt to intensify and expand relations with Beijing on all levels. Russia under President Vladimir Putin has indeed invested enormous resources into expanding relations with Beijing over the last two years in order to render Russia less dependent on Western technology, know-how as well as imports from and exports to the West (which imposed economic onto Russia after Moscow's annexation of Crimea in 2014). Not all Russian policymakers and scholars, Malle explains, are convinced that expanding trade and investment, energy, financial and technology ties with China is the answer to all of Russia's current economic and financial problems and Malle has in her chapter all the details on who says and writes what in Russia on that topic.

Matteo Dian analyses in his Chapter "Sino-Japanese Relations in the Xi-Abe Era. Can Two Tigers Live on the Same Mountain?" the state of fragile and more often than not tense Chinese–Japanese relations. Put bluntly, political relations between Beijing and Tokyo, Dian concludes, are close to as bad as they could be and the prospects for improved relations are very bleak. Both China and Japan, Dian explains, are to blame that bilateral political relations can hardly be referred to as such. China's territorial ambitions in the East and South China Seas, its apparent plan to 're-conquer' the Japanese-controlled Senkaku Islands in the East China Sea continue to alarm Tokyo's policymakers, who will continue to invest significant resources into defending Japan against the perceived Chinese military threat. Beijing—often with the support of an army of Chinese scholars, who complement government-induced anti-Japan propaganda—for its part gives itself concerned about the alleged 'militarization' of Japanese foreign and security policies,[2] Japanese historical revisionism—practiced and propagated by Japan's Prime Minister Shinzo Abe—and (probably most importantly) Tokyo's expansion of regional bilateral and multilateral defence ties, which Beijing fears is part of a US—driven China containment strategy. Indeed, despite enormous bilateral trade and investment ties, China under Xi Jinping and Japan under the (nationalist) Prime Minister Shinzo Abe will continue to invest as many resources into the bilateral geopolitical rivalry, disagreements over the interpretation of World War II history and a territorial dispute in the East China Sea as into expanding their bilateral trade and investment relations. Nationalism and at times historical revisionism in both China and Japan, Dian concludes, will continue to add their share to make sure that bilateral ties will continue to remain prone to conflict and tension.

Prone to conflict are also the ties between Washington and Beijing, writes Giovanni Salvini in his Chapter "The Relations between the People's Republic of China (PRC) and the United States (US)". Salvini analyses the ups and downs of relations between Beijing and Washington since 1949 until today and while the US and China, the author explains, have come a long way since adopting diplomatic relations in 1979, today US—Chinese geopolitical and geo-strategic rivalry is here to stay and indeed is likely to increase in the years ahead. In fact, against the background of China's economic and more importantly military rise, rivalry and indeed military conflict between Washington and Beijing, be it over Taiwan or over territorial disputes in the East and South China Seas, can no longer be completely excluded. What Salvini did not know when he wrote the chapter was that new US President Donald Trump could in the months and indeed years ahead unravel a lot of the achievements on the already difficult and controversial bilateral economic and political US-Chinese agenda. To be sure, by the time of this writing it is too early to tell whether Washington under Trump has embarked on an evitable course of confrontation with China, but what has emerged from the early days of the Trump's China policy agenda does not sound encouraging and points to rough years ahead on the US-Chinese agenda under an unpredictable and indeed erratic US president.

Filippo Fasulo in his Chapter "Coping with the Rising Dragon: Italy–China Relations Beyond Business" analyses Italian ideas and strategies on how to expand old and create new relations with China in geographical regions where Italy and China share interests (e.g. Africa and the Middle East). While Italy, Fasulo concludes, has a lot of catching-up to do with other (Western) countries as regards the scope of relations with Beijing, the potential of intensifying political and security relations is yet untapped and to be developed. Fasulo cites and elaborates on the possibilities of cooperating in areas such as international terrorism, migration, development aid in Africa and elsewhere.

[2]'Alleged' militarization of Japanese foreign and security policies as Beijing is well aware that this is not what is taking place in Tokyo.

Barbara Onnis in her Chapter "China in Africa: Challenges and Opportunities" looks into how Beijing's policies towards Africa have evolved over the decades. China, Onnis concludes, is an actor to reckon with in Africa and rapidly increasing trade and investment ties with African countries—above all with those rich of natural resources China is badly in need of—are evidence that Beijing under Xi Jinping is indeed considering Africa a 'strategic' continent to expand economic and political ties with: while the West accuses Beijing of conducting so-called 'value free diplomacy' and of adopting 'neo-colonial' policies in Africa while at the same providing many African countries with 'no-strings-attached' economic and technical assistance. To be sure, that looks very different from where Beijing is standing: the political leadership in Beijing does not get tired of pointing out that its policies in Africa are all 'win-win-ties', i.e. ties through which both Beijing and its partners and host countries in Africa benefit. While the truth could lie somewhere in the middle, Onnis' chapter presents both sides' arguments and the jury is still out there whether China's policies in and towards Africa exploit Africa and its resources or whether they instead help the continent to develop on a sustainable basis.

In his second Chapter "Enemies, Friends and Comrades-in-Arms. The Awkward Relations between the GDR and China in the 1980s" Axel Berkofsky analyses the relations between China and the German Democratic Republic (GDR) in the 1980s. East Berlin run by the ageing and increasingly senile Erich Honecker, he writes, was obliged to look for 'new friends' in the 1980s when the Socialist world Honecker knew collapsed around him. However, that friendship did not last very long when the GDR was catapulted to the dustbin of history in 1989 without a single shot fired at peacefully demonstrating East German citizens.

Silvia Menegazzi concludes the first part of the volume with her Chapter "China's Foreign Policy and Ideational Narratives: Key Trends and Major Challenges", in which she examines the conceptual and ideological basis shaping Chinese foreign and security policies. While Beijing, Menegazzi concludes, is slowly but surely learning and applying Western-made rules and norms of international politics and security, China under Xi Jinping's has also a few ideas of its own on how to organize or indeed reorganize the international system. Making use of its enormous economic and financial resources and capabilities, Beijing under China's strongman Xi is shaping the nature of global political and economic governance and China's 'One Belt One Road' (OBOR) initiative, Menegazzi explains, is impressive evidence of that. To be sure, the OBOR initiative is still in its very early stages and it remains yet to be seen when and to what extent China—with among others massive funds provided for by the 'Asian Infrastructure Investment Bank' (AIIB)—will be able to realize all of the very ambitious infrastructure projects aimed at connecting China with Europe over land and sea.

Giuseppe Iannini and Silvio Beretta kick off the second part with their Chapter "National Egoism or Cooperation in Providing Global Public Goods? China's Foreign Economic Strategy under Review". The authors critically examine the possibilities and limits of China becoming a sustainable provider of 'global public goods' in the years ahead and conclude that the international community might have to wait a little longer before Beijing and its institutions become a significant provider of such goods. Responsible for that, the authors conclude, are the peculiarities of China's economic and financial system, political and economic governance and its overall stage of economic development.

Patrizia Farina analyses the demographic consequences of Beijing abandoning its infamous 'One-Child Policy' in her Chapter "Chinese Population Policies: Towards a Free Choice". Revising China's 'One-Child Policy', Farina explains, was indeed very necessary against the background of a rapidly shrinking working population. The number of Chinese citizens over 60 years old today has reached 132 million and the number will climb to roughly 400 million in 2040. By the middle of this century, the author writes, China will have one of the oldest populations on the planet with a very high old-age-dependency ratio. As a consequence, the Chinese government has begun experimenting with the 'Two-Child Policy', although it remains yet to be seen whether this new policy can in the years ahead address China's demographic problems quickly and efficiently enough.

Guido Masella takes a critical look at the Chinese banking and finance sectors in his Chapter "The Chinese Banking and Financial System: A Fast-Paced Evolution Journey". A very timely chapter indeed, given the challenges and problems China's banking and financial sectors are currently confronted with. Although accurate and reliable data on China's banking and finance sectors continue to be hard to be come by, analysts warn that the level of non-performing loans (NPL) in China's banking sector could already be very high and indeed unsustainable. Furthermore, the 'Economist' has recently estimated that China's overall debt (private and public) could amount to up to 300 percent of China's GDP.

Vito Amendolagine, Alessia Amighini and Roberta Rabellotti look in their Chapter "Chinese Multinationals in Europe" into how Chinese multinational companies and investors position themselves in Europe. Chinese foreign direct investments (FDIs) in Europe are concentrated in a few European host countries and in only a few strategic sectors such as automotive, communications, electronics, machinery sectors. Chinese investments in Europe, the authors explain, have experienced a boom over the last decade, an increase of Chinese FDIs in Europe much bigger than Chinese FDIs in the US. Chinese multinationals investing in Europe, the authors conclude, is not least motivated by a strategy to acquire strategic assets in Europe, among other through greenfield investments and acquisitions.

Marina Timoteo concludes the second part with her Chapter "Sustainability and Law-Assessing: The New 'Green Rules' for Foreign Companies Doing Business in China", assessing the impact of new Chinese laws and regulations aiming at facilitating Beijing's vision of sustainable economic development. Aware of heavy economic pollution as a result of decade-long rapid economic growth, Beijing, Timoteo explains, has recently begun drafting new norms and legislation related to environmental protection standards by which foreign investors are obliged to abide by. The so-called 'Catalogue for the Guidance of Foreign Investment Industries', the author explains, is aimed at among other encouraging environmental-friendly foreign investments. As part of that process, Timoteo writes, Beijing has introduced market-based instruments, including economic and fiscal incentives for investors whose investments are environmentally friendly in support of sustainable development.

Marina Miranda's Chapter "The Issue of Political Reform and the Evolution of the so-called 'Deng Xiaoping Model' in Hu Jintao and Xi Jinping's China" kicks off the third part of the volume. Miranda examines how China's government led by Xi Jinping responds to ideas and concepts aimed at reforming governance in China suggested by the previous Chinese government led by former President Hu Jintao and Prime Minister Wen Jiabao. Towards the end of his second term as Chinese Prime Minister Wen Jiabao has repeatedly and in various speeches spoken about the necessity to adopt political reforms in China and has even mentioned the 'D-word', i.e. 'democracy', when he elaborated on where Chinese governance should eventually be heading towards. To be sure, today Chinese President Xi Jinping is not—to put it bluntly—having any of that. 'Political reforms' other than pushing ahead with his ruthless anti-corruption campaign aimed at among others politically eliminating opponents and potential challengers to his power, are not on his agenda. 'Democracy' in any shape or form does not get mentioned by Xi either, and those scholars and policymakers outside of China, who thought that Xi would further develop the sort of thinking and concepts of Wen Jiabao-style 'democracy' and 'political reforms' were proven to be too optimistic. Indeed, reading Miranda's chapter one could be tempted to conclude that China's current government under Xi Jinping is (far) less than sympathetic to what former Chinese Prime Minister Wen Jiabao towards the very end of his second term suggested is necessary for China to pursue in the years ahead: 'real' political reforms as opposed to reforms aimed at rendering the rule and governance of the Communist Party more efficient. Indeed, we do not hear anything at all on 'democracy' coming out of Xi's China today, which instead warns Chinese citizens from being 'contaminated' with Western values, including Western-style democracy.

Alessandra Lavagnino analyses the quality and impact of Chinese official slogans setting policy goals and visions in her Chapter "From 'Chinese Characteristics' (*Zhongguo Tese*中国特色) to 'Chinese Dream' (*Zhongguo Meng* 中国梦)-The Chinese Political Discourse Today". China's political leaders have over the decades used and propagated slogans like 'Crossing the river by feeling the stones', 'Socialism with Chinese characteristics' and 'Scientific vision of development' to explain and set policy goals and visions, Lavagnino explains. While all of these slogans had their meaning and impact when they were announced by former Chinese leaders Deng Xiaoping, Jiang Zemin and Hu Jintao, the 'Chinese Dream' as propagated by the country's current leader Xi Jinping since 2013, Lavagnino concludes, marks a fundamental change as regards the quality and impact of Chinese officials slogans. The 'Chinese Dream', the author argues, sets a clear and very optimistic vision for China and reaches the people in a language that is accessible and easily understandable.

Bettina Mottura in her Chapter "'Disclosure Is the Norm, Non-disclosure Is the Exception'. A Genre-Based Analysis on Institutional Discourse on the Government Information Disclosure in China" examines recent developmentsxamines recent developments and procedures of Chinese government information disclosure practices as part of generating a steady and accountable flow of information between the Chinese state and its citizens. From 2007 to 2016, Mottura writes, China's information disclosure policies were codified by a number of official documents providing guidelines on the dos and don'ts of those policies. This, the author explains, has led to a very vivid scholarly debate within China, and both the state's institutions and the citizens, the author concludes, are now considered relevant stakeholders providing input to the process of implementing policies. China's new disclosure system, Mottura further concludes, is also designed as an instrument to consolidate the legitimacy of public institutions governing the country. Riccardo Puglisi for his part provides the reader with an analysis on the quantity and quality of coverage of foreign countries in the Chinese newspaper 'China Daily'. In his Chapter "A Portal or a Mirror? The Reporting of Foreign Countries in 'China Daily'" Puglisi's empirical research concludes that a country is covered more often and more in detail by the 'China Daily' the bigger its economy and the geographically closer it is to China. Puglisi also finds out that—like it is indeed the case for other non-Chinese newspapers too—'bad news' sell better than 'good news': there is more coverage on foreign countries with higher unemployment rates.

Guido Samarani's Chapter "Italy's Policies Towards and Relations with China from 1937 to 1945" is the first chapter of the fourth part of this volume. Samarani analyses Italian–Chinese relations in 1936/1937, at a time when also Rome and Tokyo undertook efforts to improve and indeed expand their bilateral ties. In the second half of the 1930s, Samarani explains, the 'golden years' of relations between Italy and China were *de facto* over as Rome chose Japan over China as ally in the Far East. Italy's adherence to the 'Anti-Comintern' Pact and recognition of *Manzhouguo* at the end of 1937 further confirmed that Rome supported Tokyo's increasingly aggressive and expansionist policies in Asia in general and China in particular. Consequently, after Japan invaded China in 1937, Samarani explains, Italian-Sino relations went from bad to worse. It was only in 1947, the author concludes, that bilateral relations recovered sustainably. Italy and Nationalist China signed a peace treaty in Paris in that year and Italy renounced all former colonial rights and interests in China.

Lihong Zhang's Chapter "Confucianism, Communism and Democracy: A 'Triangular' Struggle in China—Reflections on Italy's Historical Experience with Cultural Reform" argues that Beijing today struggles with how to incorporate three different ideologies and forms of governance into contemporary China: Confucianism, democracy and communism. Confucianism, Zhang explains, has after the demise of Mao Tse-Tung celebrated a 'comeback' in China and goes on to argue that no foreign ideology or form of governance—be it communism or democracy—can survive in China without harmonizing itself with Confucianism. In the second part of his chapter Zhang urges Chinese policymakers to acknowledge and protect individual rights and freedom and suggests that a political order modelled on the Roman Principate, characterized by the centralization of powers in a head of state and the rule by law, could be a realistic *interim* solution for China on its path from totalitarianism to republicanism.

Cristina Bombelli and Alessandro Arduino in their Chapter "Human Resource Management in China: an Italian Perspective" introduce the reader into human resources management (HRM) in China and explain that HRM in China is still fairly different when compared to Europe or the US. Using case studies of Italian businesses operating in China, the authors analyse different phases of Chinese HRM, beginning with HRM during recent Chinese financial and production crises.

Renzo Cavalieri concludes the volume with his Chapter "*Fa* Versus *Guanxi*: Legality with Chinese Characteristics and Implications for Italian Business in China". Cavalieri explains the for foreigners sometimes incomprehensible differences between legal norms and 'alternative' systems of rules and norms: the difference between *fa* (*law*) and *guanxi (personal relations, personal connections)*. The relationship and conflicts between *fa* and *guanxi*, the author explains, have obviously implications for Westerners doing business in China and not all of what is formulated as laws and norms in China gets actually applied and adopted. History, politics and culture are entangled, Cavalieri explains, leading to a notion of a 'fluid' and pragmatic concept of business in China.

Pavia, Italy — Silvio Beretta
Pavia, Italy — Axel Berkofsky
Shanghai, China — Lihong Zhang

Contents

Introduction: China the Rest of the World Between Symmetries and 'Games of Mirrors'

Silvio Beretta

The 'parallel lives' of men and of states—from Plutarch to Toynbee—has become a well-established literary genre. But when the parallel lives of the great socio-political aggregates are recounted through an organised sequence of images of works which have been produced by these empires, the resulting narrative sheds new light, by virtue of being 'illustrated', on the events being compared and on how they evolved over time. Our perceptions of these events, especially when they take place over a large number of centuries, become even clearer, and the analogies, as well as the differences, become easier to understand. The weighty tome that accompanies the exhibition which was on display in the rooms of the Palazzo Reale in Milan in 2010 (De Caro and Scarpari 2010a), is a powerful example of this communicative mode and shows how effective it can be. The works exhibited and illustrated varied enormously. They include statues and bas-reliefs, coins and everyday artefacts in times of war and peace, mosaics and frescoes, bronzes and jewels, urns and work tools, models of buildings and fantastic figures, fabrics and sarcophagi, as well as jades and paintings. The parallel stories that gave life to the superb handmade objects that filled the rooms of the exhibition were, in turn, those of the empire of the Eagle—Rome—and those of the empire of the Dragon—China—respectively in the centuries that span, in the case of Rome, from 753 BC. (the city's traditional foundation date) to the end of the Western empire in 476 AD (the year in which Romulus Augustus was deposed) and, in the case of China, which span from 1045 BC (the date of the beginning of the Zhou dynasty, the last pre-imperial dynasty) to 317 AD (with the end of the reign of the Western Jin dynasty). Wars and social struggles, kingdoms and principalities and dynasties, victories as well as defeats and pillaging mark the history of the Roman eagle in the space of over one thousand two hundred years, in a series of temples, walls, aqueducts, amphitheatres, monuments, arches, poems and, finally, basilicas. On the other

S. Beretta (✉)
Department of Political and Social Sciences, University of Pavia, Pavia, Italy
e-mail: silvio.beretta@unipv.it

S. Beretta et al. (eds.), *Understanding China Today*, Understanding China,
DOI 10.1007/978-3-319-29625-8_1

side of the world revolts and insurrections, defeats and restorations, armies and conquests and, once again, kingdoms and principalities and dynasties, in turn, accompany the history of the Chinese dragon for almost one thousand four hundred years (largely overlapping with those of Rome) in a succession of ceremonies and new styles of writing, philosophers and philosophies, religions and inventions, burnings of books and imperial libraries (De Caro and Scarpari 2010b, pp. 364–367).

In the fifteen centuries which frame both chronologies, approximately between the eleventh century BC and the fifth century AD, the stories of the two empires appear to develop in parallel, i.e. without intersecting, without coming into contact with each other. In truth, however, there seems to have been at least one point of contact. Chinese sources report that in 166 AD a diplomatic mission sent by Andun, king of Da Qin (none other than emperor Marcus Aurelius) reached Luoyang in the province of Henan (one of the ancient capitals of China under various dynasties) from the Southern coasts, that is to say from present-day Vietnam, bearing gifts for the Han rulers. According to the same sources, however, they were in reality merchants exhibiting diplomatic credentials in order to obtain trading privileges. The episode, or rather the fact that at least *that* contact took place,[1] in no way dims, however, the fascination of a comparison 'from a distance' i.e. of comparing the history of civilisations in Toynbee fashion. As Stefano De Caro underlines in his introduction to the exhibition catalogue, this is—despite its many difficulties—a methodologically valid approach, given that the "comparison between two civilisations in the same chronological period is no ordinary one but, more meaningfully, one between civilisations at the same stage of development". More specifically "despite the thousands of kilometres that separate them, at the two ends of the world,…what emerges is the story of a humanity which, with obvious, marked differences in tools and in outcomes, nevertheless tackled similar problems: the production of food for huge numbers of inhabitants, the defence of the borders of the empire against external enemies and against internal threats to the unity of the state, the administration of the *res publica* through specialized bureaucracies and in relation to private interests; the relationship, in the case of religious beliefs, between more archaic polytheisms and monotheisms which were more satisfying for the spiritual needs of man …".[2] The fact that, in the histories of both empires, we can also find narrations of prodigies and of miraculous births that are utterly analogous (the birth of the emperor Liu Bang and that of Augustus, for example, the latter, in turn, recalling that of Alexander the Great) only adds to the fascination of the historiography mentioned above. It also suggests that the caravans which travelled the silk route, from West to East and back to the West, carried with them not only goods but also myths and legends.

[1]The diplomatic mission sent to Rome (Da Qin to the Chinese) by Ban Chao, during the reign of Hedi of the Eastern Han, was forced to interrupt its journey in Persia as Ru Xin recounts in his introductory essay entitled: Le Dinastie Qin e Han e l'Impero romano: due grandi civiltà antiche dell'Oriente e dell'Occidente (in: De Caro and Scarpari, cit., p. 89).

[2]See ibidem.

And as regards their 'parallel stories', it can be noted that the two empires, which both originated from small states situated in peripheral areas of the world, (1) had in common the circumstance of "dominating the most advanced forces of production available in their time" starting with the techniques applied to the production activities prevailing in both regions, i.e. agriculture, the growth of which was fostered—in Rome as in China—by an advanced system of road communications; (2) they both established "relatively well-defined political systems" and "an apparatus complete with laws" so as to "be able to maintain social order, or restore it rapidly"; (3) both promoted the 'accumulation' of 'spiritual' culture in philosophy, science, history and literature, art and religion, based on identifiable foundations, in particular the thought of the pre-Qin period in the case of China and what Ancient Rome inherited from Ancient Greece. If the similarities between the two empires in the material, legal, institutional and spiritual fields are quite clearly not attributable to mutual 'exchanges', of which there are not sufficient testimonies, the histories of *each* of these empires are undoubtedly *also* due to the "contacts and conflicts with the different civilisations that inhabited bordering countries, through an interchange of reciprocal influence, learning from experience, absorbing ideas from them, eventually mixing with them and reciprocally changing each other; gradually, they evolved and became stronger".[3] Moreover, these similarities do not diminish the importance of very important 'specificities'. One need only recall that the feudal system was abolished early on by Qin Shi Huangdi, First Emperor of Qin and founder of the first imperial dynasty in 221 BC in favour of an organisation in prefectures and provinces.[4]

As circumstances changed and as the means of communication improved, and links intensified, and, more generally, with the expansion and dissolution of these empires, the parallel stories ceased being such and entered into contact with each other. Mutual *perceptions* became important, of course, alongside the *exchanges* (economic and otherwise) that these links enabled and fostered. This gave rise to a complex system of mutual references, to a sort of 'game of mirrors' which, due to the peculiar characteristics of the protagonists' historical contexts, would have

[3]The quotation, like those which preceded it, is taken from Ru Xin, cit., *passim*.

[4]In his introductory essay entitled: Qin Shi Huangdi e la fondazione dell'impero cinese (in: De Caro and Scarpari, cit.) Maurizio Scarpari points out in the catalogue mentioned in footnote 1, pp. 46–50, in particular p. 49, that "After the military conquests a system of government was set up to establish imperial authority at the expense of the local aristocracies …To achieve and consolidate centralized power an impressive bureaucratic apparatus was created with the task of exercising complete control over its subjects, the immense territory was divided into governorships and districts administered by salaried officials …. weights and measurements were unified, calligraphic style and monetary system introduced, the length of cart axles was standardised to make them suitable for travelling the roads of the empire, the calendar was reformed, emphasising the birth of a new era. Impressive works of civil engineering were also carried out …giving continuity to pre-existing defensive fortifications to create a single wall thousands of kilometres long …The pillars of a political and administrative order were thus erected as were the general lines of continuity for over two thousand years".

important consequences for the *civilizations* in question. Familiar examples of this, from a European perspective, are 'Orientalism' in all its manifestations, and before it 'Exoticism'. There is obviously a very rich literature on this subject, and the innumerable links have been explored on many occasions, including exhibitions. During a conference entitled: China: challenge or resource?, promoted by the then Faculty of Political Sciences of the University of Pavia in 2007,[5] for example, a bibliographic exhibition was organised of a significant selection of works on China owned by the University's Library. They include the travel reports of the humanist, historian and geographer Giovan Battista Ramusio, Florentine merchant Francesco Carletti's *Ragionamenti*, Matteo Ricci's *De christiana expeditione,* Jesuit Alvaro Semedo's *Relazione*, Jean Bodin's *Six Books of a Republic,* Giovanni Botero's *The Reason of State* and *Relazioni universali*, Montaigne's *Essays*, and finally Montesquieu's *Spirit of the laws*. In describing the content of the exhibition, Paolo C. Pissavino's essay (Pissavino 2007) places the works in the context of the debate on the *outstanding political systems* which flourished in 16th and 17th century Italy and Europe. In that debate, and in that context, China served as a *model* against which to be compared, towards which the 'ought to be' attributed to Europe tends or is in opposition to. The 'Orient' was a kingdom of morality and of wisdom in contrast with a Europe that was in search of new distinctive characteristics after the dissolution of the *respublica christiana* or, on the contrary, the 'symbol' of despotic centralism characteristic of 'Eastern' systems. The first is well described by Federico Chabod who, referring to Europe and the post-Reformation, underlines that "the dissatisfaction with certain forms of European life, and above all the dissatisfaction with political systems and continuous civil wars, drove a number of writers to create the myth of happy worlds, where there are no wars, where men, who are naturally good, have not yet been corrupted by courtly life, by political intrigues and by base national interest, or by the accursed hunger for gold …This led to the birth of the myth of the 'noble savage', which would culminate in the eighteenth century, and would go some way to determining Rousseau's admiration for natural man …Europe is contrasted with what is not Europe (here… China and America amount to one and the same, because China…is the kingdom of wisdom and morality), not as civil with barbarian, but rather bloody inhuman plunderer with gentle human peace-lover. The roles are reversed: here the barbarians, the real barbarians, are the Europeans" (Chabod 1991). The second has as its reference point Chap. 4 of Machiavelli's *The Prince* where, referring to the "principalities of which one has record", he contrasts the despotic ones, governed

[5]A book edited by Iannini et al. (2006) was presented during the conference. Further papers discussed during the conference are collected in 'Il Politico', January–April 2008 (in particular pp. 165–94). Papers covering more specifically economic and practical issues can be found in: Beretta and Pissavino (2009), produced by the 'Forum on the internationalisation of small and medium-sized enterprises' and the Centro Studi Beonio-Brocchieri, both initiatives supported by the Faculty of Political Sciences of the University of Pavia (which today is the Department of Political and Social Sciences).

"by a prince, with a body of servants, who assist him to govern the kingdom as ministers by his favour and permission" with those governed "by a prince and barons, who hold that dignity by antiquity of blood and not by the grace of the prince". The former are examples of the 'Oriental' regimes which Machiavelli personifies in the 'Turk', whose "monarchy…is governed by one lord, the others are his servants… and he shifts and changes them as he chooses"; an example of the latter is France, whose sovereign "is placed in the midst of an ancient body of lords", whose privileges he must take into account.[6]

While these are alternative, quite stylised approaches, they have numerous variants, though all markedly 'Eurocentric', insofar as they served to identify the distinctive characteristics (to be affirmed and/or restored) of the 'West' compared with an 'Orient' that was prevalently mythologized, and while not quite utopian, in any case 'different'. Indeed it was almost a *paradigm* of difference.[7] So, while Carletti exalted the inventions originating in China (printing and gunpowder first and foremost) indeed hazarding the opinion that *all* inventions—and in general all *new ideas*, be they good or bad—hailed from that country, Semedo appears to be quite aware of the dangers that distance and isolation imply for the *truthfulness* of what is written. And while the erudite Tommaso Garzoni corroborated, with reference to China, a 'rhetoric of the marvellous', the nephew of Francesco Guicciardini, Ludovico, from a different perspective, praised the 'excellent systems'. The discourse, in all its political implications, was thus oriented towards the image of a *well-governed system,* which was adopted as a paradigm of comparison by many scholars. Montaigne particularly praised the Chinese political system's method of administering justice and, more generally, the organisation of the state, underlining, with admiration, the fact that it developed *independently* of events in the rest of the world, and indeed *ignorant* of what was happening elsewhere. Jean Bodin, for his part, re-interpreted what news was available on China attributing it to the principle of *sovereignty*. As a result, alongside recognising the superiority of the Chinese—and of the Orientals in general—for their courtesy and cordiality, he praised the rulers of that country who proved themselves able to protect China and its inhabitants from the seductions and plots hatched by foreigners, by removing them from its territory. As for Giovanni Botero, the theorist of the *reason of state* and the ideologue of conservation, his description of China used the rhetorical form of utopian literature.[8] All his works celebrated the glory of that kingdom: from the perfection of the infrastructure to the quality of its crafts, from the fertility of its soil to the industriousness of its inhabitants and the wisdom of its systems; all these

[6]The quotation, like those before it, is taken from Machiavelli N., The Prince, translated by Marriott (1908).

[7]In political thought, moreover, "…Chinese culture and existing forms of politics became the litmus test for any proposed political theory that sought for itself broader horizons than those provided by the inevitable quotations from the classical authors" (Pissavino cit., p. 21).

[8]It was Ludovico Zuccolo, another theorist of the *reason of state*, who used China, and its laws and customs, to construct a utopia known as the 'Repubblica di Evandria'.

made China a "province that is excellently governed". Botero, therefore, turned on its head the affirmation that China's government was—undoubtedly and utterly—*despotic* (but at the same time *peaceful*, i.e. not at all inclined to territorial expansion, unlike the European powers of the time), praising this political system. In other words he praises *conservation* ('peace' and 'conservation of the state' are the goals that Botero attributes to the Chinese form of government), which, naturally, are a founding political value of the *reason of state*.

However, while mutual perceptions tend to emerge out of the parallelisms between distant and almost incommunicable worlds, and the bold analogies on which they are founded, more intense links and exchanges give rise to sets of continually verifiable and updatable *knowledge*. Above all, they are no longer manipulated in order to compare/contrast 'Western' political objectives and/or in order to define new political concepts, but they continue to serve the needs of Europe and its affairs. Globalised links also favour the knowledge of *facts*, to be treated and evaluated as such, to the same extent as their absence—or lack thereof—favour false intellectual castles and mythological constructions.

Chinese civilisation, in its multiple dimensions, has been the subject of a recent systematisation on an 'encyclopaedic' scale in Italy. Both chronological narration and a set of thematic essays, the four volumes entitled *La Cina*, edited by Scarpari (2009),[9] seek to chart events from prehistory to modern times. Of the two published volumes, volume II (Sabattini and Scarpari 2010) encompass a period of over 1600 years starting with the end of the Han empire (the apex of the ancient Chinese civilisation) to the beginning of the 3rd century AD. It is worth noting that, in his *Introduction* to the volume, Mario Sabattini again counterpoints the events of Roman history by describing one of the numerous 'parallel stories', the one between the restoration—albeit short-lived—of the unity of the empire by the Jin dynasty in 280 AD and the attempt, at about the same time, by Diocletian to solve similar difficulties by establishing a tetrarchy, which was also short-lived. He also mentions the subsequent division, in China, between the 'barbarian' North and the South ruled by 'legitimate' Chinese dynasties and, in Rome, the contrast between a West ruled by 'barbarian' kingdoms and an 'imperial Roman' East. Alongside *analogies* there are also *differences*. Indeed Sabattini points out that "…the period of division might well have continued into the present, that there would not have been a united China if the descendents of a 'barbarian' race which had invaded northern China had not succeeded, through the Sui and Tang dynasties, in restoring the unity of the empire, bringing levels of power and wealth that had never been achieved previously, not even in the Han era. In the West things turned out differently because the Germans were unable, for various reasons, to achieve the same unity: the Holy Roman Empire was, on the whole, a colossal failure, and, as Voltaire stated, before Napoleon finally dissolved it in 1806, it was 'neither Holy,

---

[9]Maurizio Scarpari is also the author of: Il confucianesimo. I fondamenti e i testi (2010). François Jullien provides a particularly illuminating analysis of the Chinese 'civilization' from a comparative perspective in his essay *Conférence sur l'efficacité* (2005).

nor Roman, nor an Empire'" (Sabattini 2010, p. XXIX). Vol. III (Samarani and Scarpari 2009) covers events in China from the clash with the West through the First Opium War (1839–1842) and the subsequent 'unequal treaties' towards the end of the first half of the nineteenth century, to the Republic of China and the People's Republic, with the end of the 'century of national humiliation', right up to that most recent 'imperial' event, the Olympics of 2008.[10] The self-centred vision—clearly unaware of its actual power—that China had of itself at the beginning of the 'modern age' is described well by Guido Samarani in his *Introduction* to the volume, when he quotes the truly eloquent letter which Lin Zexu, the imperial official instructed by the court to end the trade in opium, sent to Queen Victoria in August 1839. Lin Zexu writes: "Our Celestial Empire towers over all other countries in virtue and possesses a power great and awesome enough to carry out its wishes." He continues, incredulous and dismayed: "Your country is very far from China. Your ships strive to come here for trade for the purpose of making a great profit. Since the great profit made is all taken from the rightful share of China, by what right do they then in return use the poisonous drug to injure the Chinese people? …I have heard that the smoking of opium is very strictly forbidden by your country; that is because the harm caused by opium is clearly understood. Since it is not permitted to do harm to your own country, then why do you choose to let it be passed on to the harm of other countries such as China? Why?" (Samarani 2009, pp. XXII–XXIII). Amina Crisma discusses similar issues in the same book. At the beginning of her essay, with reference to the cultural interaction between China and the West, she underlines that: "Through the dramatic impact with the technological power of the 'barbarian' West, which first occurred in the Opium Wars (1839–42, 1856–58), the Celestial Empire discovered for the first time, traumatically, its vulnerability and weakness, which led to an unprecedented crisis and irreparably shook Chinese scholars' proud belief in the superiority of their own civilisation. It marked the beginning of China's difficult and tormented path towards modernity…" (Crisma 2009, p. 859).

Alongside the wide ranging works with encyclopaedic ambitions, however, there are also other publishing initiatives in Italy which, though more limited in scope, also seek to promote awareness of contemporary China[11] avoiding not only ancient, but also the most modern stereotypes, in particular those "…of a China that is more 'Westernised' than the West—[which]—have taken the place of the older ones of

[10]At the beginning of his essay (Cina, ventunesimo secolo 2010, p. X) Guido Samarani stresses the links between the venues of major exhibitions and sports events and the global dislocation of power: "We need only recall … the fact—symbolic but with very concrete implications—that between the nineteenth and twentieth centuries the Expo was held in London and Paris while the Olympic Games were hosted in Athens, once again in Paris and Saint Louis. In the last few years the Olympics have been held in Beijing (2008) and the World's Fair in 2010 will be held in Shanghai, shortly after the one held in Japan's Aichi and ahead of the one due to take place in South Korea's Yeosu".

[11]See, for example, Cavalieri and Franceschini (2010) on the forms and modes of participation of Chinese citizenry in public life, with papers ranging from the political and legal spheres to the media, labour relations, as well as environment protection.

an immutable, unfathomable, mysterious China" (Lavagnino 2010, p. VIII). The essays gathered in this book are aimed at divulging the viewpoint of *Italian* scholars (the only non Italian is Lihong Zhang) on China itself from multiple viewpoints: geostrategic and international relations, economic, political and cultural.

As this short collection of essays shows, the ancient 'game of mirrors', i.e. the investigation into mutual *perceptions*, therefore, continues to be of interest to understand—and describe—the behaviours of the 'players' (China-Italy, China-European Union, China-rest of the world). However, these perceptions should not lead us into self-centred temptations (be they *euro*-or *sino*centric) or to neglect to explain the organisations, affairs and institutions from the prevailing perspective of those who (China and the Chinese in our case) have produced, developed and are governing them.

References

Beretta S, Pissavino PC (eds) (2009) Cina e oltre. Piccola e media impresa tra internazionalizzazione e innovazione, Rubbettino ed, Soveria Mannelli

Cavalieri R, Franceschini I (eds) (2010) Germogli di società civile in Cina. Francesco Brioschi Editore, Milano

Chabod F (1991) Storia dell'idea di Europa. Laterza Ed., Roma-Bari, p 63

Crisma A (2009) Interazioni intellettuali tra Cina e Occidente dal 1860 a oggi. In: Samarani G, Scarpari M (eds) La Cina III. Verso la modernità. Giulio Einaudi ed., Torino, cit., p 859

De Caro S, Scarpari M (eds) (2010a) I due imperi. L'aquila e il dragone, Federico Motta Editore, Milano

De Caro S, Scarpari M (2010b) 'Cronologia comparata. In: De Caro S, Scarpari M (eds) I due imperi. L'aquila e il dragone. Federico Motta Editore, Milano, pp 364–367

Jullien F (2005) Conférence sur l'efficacité. Presses Universitaires de France, Paris

Iannini G, Salvini G (eds) (2006) Cina. L'avvio del terzo millennio. Il Politico, Rivista Italiana di Scienze Politiche, Rubbettino ed, Soveria Mannelli

Lavagnino AC (2010) Introduzione. In: Cavalieri R, Franceschini I (eds) Germogli di società civile in Cina. Francesco Brioschi Editore, Milano, p VIII

Machiavelli N (translated by Marriott WK) (1908) The Prince. J. M. Dent & Company, London

Pissavino PC (2007a) Una protostoria attuale. Le immagini della Cina nell'Italia moderna I. Secoli XVI e XVII, Monboso, Pavia

Pissavino PC (2007) Una protostoria attuale. Le immagini della Cina nell'Italia moderna I. Secoli XVI e XVII. Monboso, Pavia, p 21

Ru X (2010) Le Dinastie Qin e Han e l'Impero romano: due grandi civiltà antiche dell'Oriente e dell'Occidente. In: De Caro S, Scarpari M (eds) I due imperi. L'aquila e il dragone. Federico Motta Editore, Milano, p 89

Sabattini M (2010) Introduzione. In: Sabattini M, Scarpari M (eds) 2010 La Cina II. L'età imperiale dai Tre Regni ai Qing. Giulio Einaudi ed, Torino, p XXIX

Sabattini M, Scarpari M (eds) (2010) La Cina II. L'età imperiale dai Tre Regni ai Qing. Giulio Einaudi ed, Torino

Samarani G (2009) Introduzione. In: Samarani G, Scarpari M (eds) La Cina III. Verso la modernità. Giulio Einaudi ed, Torino, pp XXII–XXIII

Samarani G (2010) Cina, ventunesimo secolo. Giulio Einaudi ed,Torino, p. X

Samarani G, Scarpari M (eds) (2009) La Cina III. Verso la modernità. Giulio Einaudi ed, Torino

Scarpari M (ed) (2009) La Cina (four vol.), Giulio Einadi ed, Torino
Scarpari M (2010) Il confucianesimo. I fondamenti e i testi. Giulio Einaudi ed, Torino
Scarpari M (2010) Qin Shi Huangdi e la fondazione dell'impero cinese. In: De Caro S, Scarpari M (eds) I due imperi. L'aquila e il dragone. Federico Motta Editore, Milano, pp 46–50, 49
VVAA (2008), Il Politico, Rivista Italiana di Scienze Politiche, January–April 2008, pp 165–194

Part I
China in World Politics

The EU and China-Myth Versus Reality of a (not so) 'Strategic Partnership'

Axel Berkofsky

Abstract When the European Union (EU) started referring to China as 'strategic partner' in 2003, it announced that the 'strategic partnership' with Beijing would facilitate the adoption of joint regional and global foreign and security policies. More than a decade later, however, that has not taken place as Brussels and Beijing have indeed very little (if anything) in common as regards approaches towards international politics and security. In fact, critical scholars and analysts (like this author) have for years argued that there is no 'strategic dimension' of EU-China ties beyond the expansion of bilateral EU-China trade and commercial ties. The below-mentioned EU-Chinese dialogue on Asian security e.g. has not produced any tangible results and China's current regional foreign and security policies in general and those related to Beijing's territorial disputes in particular are evidence for at least two things: firstly, EU influence on Chinese security policy behaviour remains in spite of a bilateral security dialogue on East Asia de facto non-existent. Secondly, Beijing will continue to completely ignore EU advice and concerns about Chinese regional and global foreign policy behaviour and will continue to pursue regional security policies in general and those related to territorial claims and disputes in particular, which are—to put it bluntly—the very opposite of how the EU approaches and adopts foreign and security policies. Consequently, this chapter concludes that EU-China cooperation in international politics and security will continue to take place largely (if not exclusively) on paper and paper only.

A. Berkofsky (✉)
Department of Political and Social Sciences, University of Pavia, Pavia, Italy
e-mail: Axel.Berkofsky@unipv.it

A. Berkofsky
Istituto per gli Studi di Politica Internazionale (ISPI), Milan, Italy

S. Beretta et al. (eds.), *Understanding China Today*, Understanding China,
DOI 10.1007/978-3-319-29625-8_2

1 Introduction

Since 2003 the EU and China have referred to each other as 'strategic partners.' As an expression of that partnership, Brussels and Beijing have over the last decade established more than 50 bilateral so-called 'sectoral dialogues' covering 24 areas, including competition policy, civil aviation, market access, intellectual property rights, nuclear energy, food safety, environment, regulatory and industrial policy, trade policy etc. While the intense institutional exchanges suggest that Brussels and Beijing both assign great importance above all to bilateral trade investment ties, many of the problems and disagreements covered by many of the 'sectoral dialogues' have been dealt with for years without having produced any progress, not to mention tangible results. The dialogues dealing with issues related to trade and investment, such as the ones on market access, government procurement and intellectual property rights in particular, deal with issues European business investing in China has been complaining about for years. In fact, the list of complaints about the obstacles European investors and investments in China are confronted with has remained—at least as far as the Beijing-based EU Chamber of Commerce is concerned—(very) long and indeed identical over the years.

Numerous and persistently unresolved problems on the bilateral trade and investment agenda notwithstanding, in 2013 the EU and China again confirmed their 'strategic partnership' by adopting the 'EU-China 2020 Strategic Agenda for Cooperation' (European Union External Action Service 2013). Sino-European cooperation in international politics and security (under the headline 'Peace and Security') will—at least according to that policy paper—feature prominently on the EU-China policy agenda in the years ahead (European External Action Service 2013). The areas and issues Brussels and Beijing envision to be jointly dealing with include areas such as nuclear security, the international non-proliferation regime and related export control arrangements, transnational organised crime, cyber-crime, anti-terrorism, maritime security as well Asian security in the framework of the below-cited 'EU-China High Level Strategic Dialogue.' The 'EU-China 2020 Strategic Agenda for Cooperation' also announced that it would "raise the level of EU-China dialogue and cooperation on defence and security, advancing towards more practical cooperation." While this sounds good on paper, the move towards more practical security cooperation (i.e. the adoption of joint security policies) will continue not to take place. The EU and China continue to have very different positions on most (if not all) current issues on the regional and international security agendas, be it the crisis in Ukraine, the Middle East (e.g. Iran or Syria), and the so-called 'rogue regimes' in North Korea or Sudan—hardly the basis for moving towards practical cooperation on security in Asia (or elsewhere). The recent years of EU-Chinese consultations and dialogues on regional and global security have shown that the EU's influence on actual Chinese foreign and security policy behaviour and policies is de facto non-existent and have also shown that Beijing could indeed not care less about European concerns about Chinese foreign and security policy conduct in Asia or elsewhere. In other words, Beijing will realistically not alter the quality of its regional foreign and security policies in response to European advice or requests to do so. China denying others the right to 'interfere' in any of what China refers to as its 'internal affairs' is (very) deeply embedded in Chinese foreign and security policy thinking and making and Beijing will continue to take on board only the kind of advice on its foreign and security policies that comes nowhere near to resembling 'interference.' In fact, when Xi Jinping took power in 2012, Chinese policymakers as well as Chinese scholars interacting with European counterparts have tended to become very defensive and indeed aggressive fairly quickly when perceiving anything that might be in any way interpretable as 'interference' in Chinese domestic affairs from the outside. It is accurate to conclude that China is in a phase of seeking to define its identity, role and reach as regional and global security policy actor and it will only cooperate with the EU on security if such cooperation does not—at least from a Chinese perspective—obstruct the process of developing the kind of foreign and security policy identity endorsed in Beijing (as opposed to in Brussels or Washington).

2 Not Accepting 'Interference'

Even if often-repeated official rhetoric speaking of EU-Chinese 'mutual understanding' and 'common interests' might suggest otherwise, the history of European colonialism in Asia in general and China in particular is still very present in China's historical memory and hence any European opinion on Chinese domestic and foreign policies that could be interpreted as unwanted 'interference' is in today's China almost inevitably associated with European colonialism and China's so-called 'Century of Humiliation', i.e. the roughly 100 years from the first 'Opium War' (1839) to the founding of the People's Republic of China (PRC) in 1949. Furthermore, in order to be able to understand current Chinese foreign policy behaviour, it is necessary to mention that China's President Xi Jinping has over the last two years in his speeches on domestic and foreign policies numerous times called on the Chinese people to remember China's past of European colonialism and imperialism when outlining his vision of the so-called 'China Dream' to the Chinese people. The 'induction' of national self-confidence (accompanied by patriotism and at times strong nationalism) through Xi's 'China Dream' has without a doubt had an impact on how much outside advice and opinions Chinese foreign policymakers are willing to accept. Indeed, an economically rapidly growing China governed by a leadership determined to encourage the Chinese people to exercise Chinese economic and political patriotism probably feels less than ever inclined to endorse outside advice which in turn within China could be interpreted as a sign of weakness. The analysis of China's 'national psyche' taking into account Chinese history of the 18th and 19th centuries have over recent years sought to explain current Chinese foreign policy rhetoric and more importantly foreign policy behaviour. Among others, scholars concluded that Chinese foreign policy approaches and policies are—at least up to a point—the result of a mix between an 'inferiority complex' (as a Chinese 'hangover' of the above-mentioned 'Century of Humiliation') and a growing 'national self-confidence' (as a result of China's phenomenal economic growth and development over the last 30 years) (Zheng 2012). Such—at least from a European perspective—contradictory elements making up and defining China's 'national psyche' produce policies that in the West are perceived as nationalistic and driven by the motivation and determination to conduct policies independent and free from Western pressure and lecturing. The scope and limits of China's cooperation with the EU and Europe in international politics and security have also to be understood and analysed against that background.

States and governments typically only do what they are obliged to do and China is certainly no exception. Giving in to European requests to make its political and governance system more 'European' or more 'Western' is not—put bluntly—one of the things China's policymakers feel that they are obliged to do. China is referring to itself as a 'great power' and Xi Jinping's foreign policy rhetoric and his earlier cited determination to induce the concept of China's so-called 'National Revival' into the Chinese psyche is making sure that China's policymakers in case of doubt opt for 'interference'. In fact, in the current atmosphere and the ongoing phase of Xi's campaigns and policies of consolidating his power in China, opting for categorically referring to any outside opinion on Chinese domestic and foreign policy as unwanted 'interference' has become the 'safe option' as it makes Chinese policymakers less vulnerable to inter-Chinese accusations of being 'too soft' with the West so to speak. To be sure, the jury is still out on whether such an approach is sustainable in the long-term and whether China will—against the background of China's rapidly growing economy and global investments—find out rather soon that the 'principle of non-interference' and the de facto refusal to accept outside advice on its foreign and foreign economic policies could become unsustainable (European Council on Foreign Relations 2013).

According to the American China scholar David Shambaugh, China's determination to insist on the 'principle of non-interference' in defence of Beijing's foreign policy independence from outside pressure has already led to Beijing being short of 'friends' and without any close allies—a 'lonely power' as Shambaugh calls China (Shambaugh 2014). No other countries, Shambaugh argued, are copying China's political and economic model and hence the country is not a 'role model' country for anyone. Almost needless to say that Beijing and numerous Chinese scholars have responded to and strongly disagreed with Shambaugh's argument. Chinese soft power in the form of economic relations and investments in Africa or South America it is e.g. argued in China, have successfully promoted what Beijing argues is an alternative (i.e. non-Western) model of relations and development-a model, it is argued in Beijing, that has been endorsed and welcomed in many countries of the developing world.

Foreign and security policies, however, are not the only areas, in which Beijing does not want the EU (or anybody else for that matter) to 'interfere' in its internal affairs. As regards China's domestic policies and issues and areas such as freedom of speech and expression, the rule of law, governance and other issues, China is indeed determined not to follow European advice and input as regards the level of free speech and expression and the rule of law (as opposed to the rule 'by law'). In fact, Beijing has in January 2016 made it very clear that it is very determined to suppress any European attempts to 'interfere' in what China insists are its internal affairs for nobody to interfere with. In fact, Beijing's determination to 'protect' itself against being 'contaminated'[1] with Western values and influence reached a new level in January 2016 when Chinese authorities arrested and detained a Swedish citizen, the founder of a non-governmental organization (NGO) operating in China. Peter Dahlin, founder of 'China Urgent Action Working Group' was arrested and only deported from China after having obliged to confess his 'wrongdoings', i.e. his work on the promotion of human rights, on Chinese television. Such practice recalled the bad old days of Mao Zedong's notorious forced self-confession sessions in the 1950s and 1960s,[2] leading the EU to express its protest against Beijing's decision to publicly humiliate a European citizen on Chinese state television. "Mr Dahlin's arrest and detention are part of a worrying trend and call into question China's respect for the rule of law and for its international human rights obligations", the EEAS declared in January 2016 (European External Action Service 2016).

3 Not (Fully) Trusting Brussels

Chinese policymakers are undoubtedly aware that the EU and the big EU member states would side with the US on Asian security issues in the case of a US-Chinese controversy if the conflict in question also affects European interests. Beijing has probably very few illusions about European preparedness to side with China and not the US, should Washington's security interests in the region be affected by China's regional security policies. When China in the early 2000s—during Washington's unilateral moment in international politics and the invasion of Iraq in 2003—asked Europe to endorse the concept of a 'multipolar world' to counter US unilateralism, the European reaction (perhaps with the exception of France and Germany, which refused to participate in the invasion and later occupation of Iraq) was not enthusiastic, to say the very least. There are few illusions in Beijing today about the fact that the EU's political and security ties with Washington are much more substantive than the ones with Beijing, which have led Beijing's policymakers

[1]Xi Jinping and his administration have in 2015 launched an official campaign strongly advising the Chinese people (i.e. 'ordering' the Chinese people) to protect themselves against the dangers of being 'contaminated' by Western values such as democracy and human rights, as the attempt to promote and introduce such 'dangerous' of such values are—at least as far as Beijing is concerned—part of a Western conspiracy to weaken and create instability in China.

[2]When Chinese citizens were forced to confess their alleged wrongdoings in public under humiliating circumstances and under enormous pressure.

not to fully trust European counterparts to adopt policies which would run counter to or are fully independent from US policies. In fact, there are numerous scholars and also policymakers in China who argue that high-sounding EU-China statements on the quality and scope of bilateral EU-Chinese security cooperation do not change anything about the fact that Europe continues to be an 'agent' of US interests in the region.

4 Siding with US Containment, Beijing Fears

When the US administration announced its 'pivot to Asia' in 2011, accompanied by increased US involvement in Asian security through the strengthening of existing military alliances with Japan and South Korea and the establishment of new defence ties with countries such as Australia, India, the Philippines, and Vietnam, Beijing concluded that Washington's Asia 'pivot' was aimed at containing China. Beijing policymakers argued then (and still do) that the US 'pivot' and the expansion of US defence ties in the region accompanying it are aimed at 'encircling' China and continuing to ensure US regional military hegemony, deterring China's rapid economic and military rise. While to date Washington continues to argue that its Asia 'pivot' is in no way intended to 'encircle' China, China continues to insist that it is just that. Furthermore, from China's perspective the 'pivot' is a US attempt to convince other Asian countries to join Washington to deter China's economic and political rise and that Europe will—again from a Chinese perspective—sooner or later be pressured into actively supporting China's containment. Some European scholars on the other hand argue that the expansion of the EU's economic and political engagement in Asia in general and with China in particular over the last decade can be referred to as a EU 'pivot' to Asia (Casarini 2013; Parello-Plesner 2012). To be sure, not a 'pivot' with the expansion of military ties and alliances at the centre but instead one with policies aimed at engaging China economically and politically as much as possible. As the last three years of Chinese foreign and security policies under Chinese President Xi Jinping have shown, however, the kind of engagement the EU has in mind is bound to remain very limited, if at all existent. Indeed, the quality of Chinese policies related to territorial claims in the South China Sea has unambiguously demonstrated that Beijing is not willing to accept what it refers to as 'interference' from the outside.

Indeed, over the last two-three years Beijing has created facts on the ground, which have made it very clear that China is indeed in the business of expanding its territories in the South China Sea (to be sure, Beijing argues that it is merely reclaiming land and islands that have always and since ancient history belonged to

China) (Panda 2015; Watkins 2016; The Economist 2015). Through the so-called 'Nine-Dash Line' Beijing has unilaterally decided that more than 90% of the South China Sea belongs to China, thereby de facto rendering other claimants countries' territorial claims as good as obsolete.[3] While such kind of territorial policies must without much doubt be referred to as unilateral territorial expansionism in the South China Sea in 2014[4] and 2015,[5] Beijing in turn pretends not to understand that its territorial policies are in the region perceived as threatening regional peace and stability. Instead, Beijing (wrongly) argues that it is merely claiming and defending territories and islands that have already belonged to China since 'ancient times.'

When in July 2012 Catherine Ashton, then EU High Representative for Foreign Affairs and Security Policy and Hillary Clinton, then US Secretary of State adopted the 'US-EU Statement on the Asia-Pacific Region[6] (US State Department 2012)', EU policymakers found themselves under pressure to explain to Chinese counterparts why the joint US-EU statement on Asian security does not mean that the EU is planning to join alleged US-led China containment policies. Beijing on the other hand maintained back then that the Clinton-Ashton joint statement sounded like the EU is preparing itself to get involved in a US-driven containment policy strategy towards China even if such a conclusion does not at all reflect the realities of EU foreign and security policies towards Asia in general and China in particular.

---

[3]Beijing's 'Nine-Dash Line' stretches several hundreds of miles south and east from China's most southerly province of Hainan. On the basis of that line the Paracel and Spratly Islands are part of Chinese sovereign territory and although largely uninhabited, the Paracel and the Spratly Islands are believed to have reserves of natural resources around them. Beijing claims that its territorial rights in the South China Sea go back centuries to when the Paracel and Spratly island chains were regarded as integral parts of the Imperial China. Vietnam and the Philippines dispute China's historical account, arguing China had never claimed sovereignty over the islands before the 1940s. Vietnam for its part claims that it has ruled over both the Paracels and the Spratlys since the 17th century and also claims to have historical documents to prove its dominion over these groups of islands.

[4]In May 2014, the intrusion of a Chinese drilling rig into waters near the Paracel Islands led to numerous collisions between Vietnamese and Chinese ships. Tensions between Vietnam and China further increased in the same year after China moved a state-owned oil rig, flanked by civilian, coast guard, and military vessels, into waters claimed by Vietnam as part of its exclusive economic zone (EEZ).

[5]In 2015 Beijing has accelerated the construction of facilities on and around disputed islands. After declaring in June 2015 that the process of building seven new islands by moving sediment from the seafloor to reefs was close to completion, Beijing has in the second half of the year 2015 undertaken efforts to build ports, airstrips and radar facilities on disputed islands in the South China Sea. In April 2015, satellite images showed China building an airstrip on reclaimed land in the Spratlys. When announcing naval exercises off the coast of Hainan Island near the disputed Paracel Islands in the South China Sea in July 2015, Beijing issued a statement not allowing other vessels to enter the waters in which the exercises take place.

[6]On the side-lines of the ASEAN Regional Forum (ARF) in Phnom Penh, Cambodia.

5 Nothing in Common

The debate on the scope and quality of EU-Chinese cooperation in international politics tends to neglect the fundamental question of whether and to what extent cooperation between democratic and non-democratic countries in international politics and security beyond informal consultations is at all feasible and able to produce actual results in the form of measurable joint policies. While it is from a policymaker's point of view understandable—understandable since a policymaker is expected to produce on paper commitments from counterparts to demonstrate on paper preparedness to cooperate, regardless of different political systems and forms of governance—to publicly ignore the question of the feasibility and prospects of actual results as regards cooperation, the absence of actual joint EU-Chinese policies provides evidence that entirely different forms and systems of governance do indeed matter a great deal and have an impact on whether joint policies are at all realistic. In fact, it is accurate to conclude that recent Chinese regional and global foreign and security policies have more than anything else demonstrated that Chinese approaches towards regional and global politics and security are fundamentally different from European approaches and policies. Furthermore, EU-Chinese bilateral consultations and dialogues on human rights, governance, democracy, freedom of speech and expression, terrorism and arguably many other issues have made it very clear that Beijing and Brussels often do not even agree on shared definitions of concepts such as human rights, democracy and terrorism. While policymakers in both Europe and China tend—at least on the official record—to play down the differences as regards differing definitions standing in the way of going beyond agreeing to disagree—it can be concluded that the absence of the aforesaid jointly shared definitions a priori limit the possibilities of actual meaningful cooperation.

6 'EU-China High-Level Strategic Dialogue'

Doubts about the potential impact of European concerns and advice on Chinese regional and global security policy notwithstanding, in 2010 the EU and China set up an annual dialogue on Asian security. The last annual 'EU-China High-level Strategic Dialogue' was held in June 2016 and Brussels among others hoped that the dialogue would encourage Beijing to become more transparent about its defence expenditures and military equipment procurement and sales policies. However, that is clearly a case of European wishful-thinking as China will not make any more information on its arms procurement policies available simply because the EU is requesting Beijing to do that in the context of a bilateral dialogue on Asian security. When analysts argue that the EU-China strategic dialogue on Asian security is more than anything else an annual window-dressing event as opposed to a dialogue that produces real results, let alone joint policies related to Asian security,

EU policymakers typically point out that the dialogue's objective is not the adoption of joint policies but rather a platform to informally consult with each other on Asian security issues. While dialogue and consultations are positive as such, the raison d'être of such a dialogue must however be put in doubt if European advice and input on Chinese regional security policy conduct such as Beijing's (very) assertive policies related to territorial claims in the East and South China Seas are quite simply ignored in Beijing. Indeed, as already mentioned above, the reality of Chinese regional security policy conduct and polices has shown that Beijing's preparedness to consult with the EU on security issues which fall under what Beijing refers to as its 'core interests'—the Taiwan and Tibet 'questions' and what Beijing refers to as 'territorial integrity' in Asia's disputed territorial waters—is de facto non-existent. If that is accurate and if European views and advice on Chinese security policies in Asia are only endorsed during official encounters as opposed to in the 'real' world, then it is fair to question whether the dialogue on Asian security with China is an efficient use of EU resources and political capital. China's very assertive and indeed aggressive policies related to territorial claims in the East China Sea and more importantly South China Sea have indeed very clearly and unambiguously demonstrated that the EU does not have any influence on Chinese foreign and security policy behaviour, be it through the above-mentioned 'High-Level Strategic Dialogue' or any other bilateral dialogues and exchanges. To be sure, expectations that a bilateral dialogue on East Asian security with Beijing would inevitably lead to EU influence on Chinese regional policies and Beijing were always very low even if official rhetoric on the purpose and impact of Brussels talking on Asian security with Beijing suggests otherwise. In reality, however, EU officials involved in the bilateral dialogue on Asian security are fully aware that China's preparedness to accept and act upon European advice on how to tackle Asian security issues and issues related to territorial disputes in Asian territorial waters is de facto non-existent.

Brussels' decision not—at least now—to get involved in Asian territorial conflicts that involve China beyond urging involved parties to solve conflicts peacefully, have undoubtedly led Beijing policymakers to conclude that Brussels does not pose a 'danger' in terms of 'interference' in China's regional security policies. While Beijing on the official record complains about Europe's inability to formulate and adopt joint foreign and security policies, such inability makes sure that the EU is probably just the kind of institution China wants the EU to be: an institution with a foreign policy apparatus that is not equipped with the instruments and the authority to formulate policies towards China that cannot be undermined by individual EU member states when and how they see fit. In other words: an European External Action Service (EEAS) that can be ignored if and when it adopts policies towards China which China in turn perceives as threatening its interests or as unwanted 'interference' in its internal affairs. China's above-mentioned (very assertive) policies related to territorial claims in the South China Sea—policies that can indeed be referred to as unilateral territorial expansionism—have arguably further eroded the raison d'etre of the European-Chinese dialogue on East Asian security. Beijing's regional policies related to its territorial claims in the East and

South China Seas are the very opposite of what the EU argues China should do: instead of reclaiming disputed territories in the South China Sea unilaterally, the EU has in 2015 and also 2016 several times called on China and other involved parties to address territorial disputes in the Sough China Sea through multilateral consultations. As recently as March 2016 the EU voiced outspoken concerns about China's policies related to territorial claims in the South China Sea. "The EU is concerned about the deployment of missiles on islands in the South China Sea. The temporary or permanent deployment of military forces or equipment on disputed maritime features which affects regional security and may threaten freedom of navigation and overflight is a major concern", a statement by the European Council read (European Council 2016).[7] To be sure, such statements are due to the reasons elaborated above not likely to lead China to adjust or change its policies related to territorial claims and will most probably not keep Beijing from continuing to build civil and military facilities on disputed islands in the South China Sea. In fact, the opposite is the case: The EU expressing its preoccupations about aggressive Chinese regional territorial policies typically lead Beijing to 'remind' Brussels to mind its own business and not 'interfere' in what it insists are China's 'internal affairs.'

7 Conclusions

It is telling that a significant part of the EU's 'Guidelines on the EU's Foreign and Security Policy in East Asia' adopted in June 2012 deal with China and the limits, problems of EU-China cooperation in regional politics and security (Council of the European Union 2013). Telling because the guidelines display an arguably very critical European assessment of the quality of Chinese domestic and foreign policies by listing a number of (from a EU perspective) very problematic issues on China's domestic and regional foreign and security policy agendas. Such issues obviously include human rights, the—from an EU perspective—insufficiently developed application of the rule of law in China and the complete lack of progress as regards fundamental freedoms in the country. The long list of problematic issues also concern Chinese approaches to the rule of law, governance, international politics and (many) other issues, which indeed suggests that the EU and China have in terms of governance and approaches towards international politics and security as good as nothing in common. To be sure, as elaborated above, China will continue to ignore EU criticism as it seems fit and will certainly not change or adjust any of its domestic and foreign just because Brussels is requesting Beijing to do so.

[7]Although China is not explicitly mentioned in that statement, there is no doubt that China is meant as it is the only country that has in 2016 deployed military installations and facilities on disputed territories in the South China Sea.

China, French scholar François Godement concludes, is a realist power that does not in any way feel obliged to take European foreign policy opinions and criticism into account when implementing its foreign and security policies and Asia and elsewhere. "As a realist power, China has neither the inclination to consider Europe's geopolitical influence at a time when Europe is struggling with an ongoing economic and political crisis, nor the incentive to favour a more united and empowered Europe that would also be a more effective negotiator with China" (Godement 2013). As long as individual EU member states opt for adopting their own China policies when it suits their interests, Godement argues, China will reserve the right to consider the EU a 'support actor' and not a protagonist in international politics and security. "National shortcuts are very tempting, but they will weaken the EU's hand as a whole, and if such an approach is pursued Europe will never receive the kind of recognition from China that a united continent of 500 million people can expect to command." The 'national shortcuts' Godement cites are still and undoubtedly part of European policies towards China and the Union's big member states with strong business interests in and trade ties with China will like in the past also in the future continue to hinder the EU and its EEAS from adopting a coherent set of policies towards China if and when it is against their (business and trade) interests.

A European role promoting European models and modes of security multilateralism, some European scholars and (many) EU policymakers argue on the official record, is endorsed in Asia, including in China (Peyrouse 2012). However, as was sought to show above, such an assessment does not at all reflect the realities of Chinese regional security policies in general and its policies related to territorial claims in the South China Sea in particular. Insisting on the aforesaid 'principle of non-interference,' there is a near-consensus among independent and well-informed China scholars and analysts that Beijing will continue to remain opposed to multilateralizing its regional security policies in any meaningful and sustainable fashion. Indeed, unless there is a fundamental shift in Chinese foreign policy thinking and making (which is very unlikely), Chinese policymakers will continue to pursue what can be referred to as 'multilateralism à la carte' and Beijing will continue to turn to individual EU member states if and when it does not get what it wants from EU institutions. The problem of course does not lie with China alone. The three biggest EU member states—Germany, France and the UK—will for their part continue to formulate and adopt their very own individual policies towards China when they see fit, which will inevitably continue to have a negative impact on the EU's ability to have one set of European economic, political and security policies towards China. Numerous times in the past have the above-mentioned three EU countries adopted their own foreign policies towards China without having felt obliged to consult with the European External Action Service (EEAS). Unless there is a fundamental shift in how the EU's big member states conduct their respective foreign and security policies and unless they are prepared to assign more authority and competencies to the EEAS at the expense of the ability to adopt individual policies towards China (which is as unlikely as it is that Beijing will be fundamentally changing its foreign policy conduct), Beijing will seek to continue to be able to exploit the lack of European foreign and security policy unity for its own benefit. While China is not the only country and actor exploiting insufficient European foreign and security policy coherence, it is—viewed against the background of Europe's trade and investment ties and interests with and in China—probably the country in a position to exploit the lack of inner-EU unity most successfully.

Finally, it is accurate to conclude that China's policies related to territorial claims in the East and South China Seas have over the last three years under President Xi become increasingly assertive and aggressive and indeed and from a non-Chinese perspective expansionist.[8] As mentioned above, what China does as regards its territorial claims in the East and South China Seas does not have anything to do with EU approaches towards international politics and security and for the sake of EU credibility in international politics and security, Brussels' policymakers are advised to point out just that to their counterparts in Beijing. The trouble is that they don't and won't.

References

Callahan WA (2012) China: the pessoptimist nation. Oxford University Press, New York

Casarini N (2013) The european 'pivot'. European Institute for Security Studies, Paris, March 2013, http://www.iss.europa.eu/uploads/media/Alert_Asia.pdf

Council of the European Union, General Secretariat (2012) Guidelines on the EU's foreign and security policy in East Asia, http://eeas.europa.eu/asia/docs/guidelines_eu_foreign_sec_pol_east_asia_en.pdf

Godement F (2013) Key issues of China's leadership succession. In: Casarini N (ed) Brussels-Beijing: changing the game, Report No. 14, European Institute for Security Studies, Paris, February 2013, http://www.iss.europa.eu/uploads/media/Report__14.pdf

European Council, Council of the European Union (2016) Declaration by the high representative on behalf of the EU on recent developments in the South China Sea, March 11, http://www.consilium.europa.eu/en/press/press-releases/2016/03/11-hr-declaration-on-bealf-of-eu-recent-developments-south-china-sea/?utm_source=dsms-auto&utm_medium=email&utm_campaign=Declaration+by+the+High+Representative+on+behalf+of+the+EU+on+Recent+Developments+in+the+South+China+Sea

European Council on Foreign Relations (2013) The end of non-interference, http://www.ecfr.eu/page/-/China_Analysis_The_End_of_Non_interference_October2013.pdf

European Union External Action Service (2016). Statement by the spokesperson on the arrest and detention of EU Citizen Peter Dahlin, January 22, http://eeas.europa.eu/statements-eeas/2016/160122_02_en.htm

European External Action Service (2013) EU-China 2020 strategic agenda for cooperation, http://www.eeas.europa.eu/china/docs/20131123_agenda_2020__en.pdf

Panda A (2015) Vietnam slams Chinese Naval Drill in South China Sea, The Diplomat, July 27, http://thediplomat.com/2015/07/vietnam-slams-chinese-naval-drill-in-south-china-sea/

Parello-Plesner J (2012) Europe's Pivot to Asia, East Asia Forum, November 12, www.eastasiaforum.org/2012/11/12/europes-pivot-to-Asia/

[8]Obviously a conclusion that is not shared in China.

Peyrouse S (2012) Europe's involvement in East Asian security-how to engage China, Fride Analysis, October, http://www.fride.org/publication/1058/europe's-involvement-in-east-asian-security
Shambaugh D (2014) The illusion of Chinese power. Brookings Institution, Washington D.C, http://www.brookings.edu/research/opinions/2014/06/23-chinese-power-shambaugh
The Economist (2015) Who rules the waves, October 17, http://www.economist.com/news/international/21674648-china-no-longer-accepts-america-should-be-asia-pacifics-dominant-naval-power-who-rules
US Department of State (2012) US-EU Statement on the Asia-Pacific region, July 12, http://www.state.gov/r/pa/prs/ps/2012/07/194896.htm
Watkins D (2016) What China has been building in the South China Sea, New York Times, February 29, http://www.nytimes.com/interactive/2015/07/30/world/asia/what-china-has-been-building-in-the-south-china-sea-2016.html?_r=0
Zheng W (2012) Never forget national humiliation. Columbia University Press, New York

The Relations Between China and India from Bandung to the 'New Silk Road'

Sandro Bordone

Abstract A few years after their national emancipation, the Bandung Conference in 1955 facilitated the establishment of relations between the Republic of India and the People's Republic of China. Having repelled Western colonialism, each of these two new states has given itself a new political order and is establishing new relations at the international level. Over the course of history, the continuous changes and evolution in the global balance of powers have made new needs arise in terms of self-assertion, defence and preservation. *Chindia* is quite a recent concept, which is mainly perceived as an economic one, as the vision of a 'magical land' where the economies of China and India could merge and unleash unprecedented wealth. The hope (or forecast) of *Chindia* and the impressive economic development of these two countries, however, are not enough to make these two 'state-civilisations' merge peacefully, nor to disengage the economy from the reality of political power and balance. *Chindia* means a strategy. What will the effects be of the embrace between the dragon and the elephant?

1 Introduction

In the jargon of financial markets, *Chindia*, a term coined by former Indian Environment Minister Jairam Namesh to describe his vision of close cooperation between India and China, in support of each other's economic development, would be a magical land where the economies of China and India could merge and unleash unprecedented wealth.

This intriguing scenario had made headway after Hu Jintao's visit to India in November 2006, the first by a General Secretary of the Chinese Communist Party and President of the People's Republic of China in the last decade, reciprocated by Indian prime Minister Manmohan Singh's visit to Beijing on 14 January 2008, after both parties' grand-sounding commitments to put aside past disputes and march

S. Bordone (✉)
Department of Political and Social Sciences, University of Pavia, Pavia, Italy
e-mail: sandro.bordone@unipv.it

S. Beretta et al. (eds.), *Understanding China Today*, Understanding China,
DOI 10.1007/978-3-319-29625-8_3

together toward a bright future. It was to be based on a strategic partnership between New Delhi and Beijing with the slogan 'Asia to the Asians.' Although the economies of the two countries could be complementary since India is the 'office of the world' as China is its 'factory,' their deep rivalry feeds reciprocal suspicions of encirclement; China is wary of India's ties with the United States and Japan and its growing presence in ASEAN and the South China Sea, which Beijing sees as a sort of 'mare nostrum' in which it allows itself to exercise its full sovereignty.

The only obvious similarities between the two countries are that they both occupy a large part of the Asian continent, they are both populous (over two and a half billion people combined), are poor and are growing at a rapid pace (India faster than China at present)—according to some forecasts, China's GDP will be equal to or greater than that of the United States by 2040, and about ten years before that, India's will have surpassed Japan's (Balcet and Valli 2012)—and both are hungry for natural resources. In many other ways, they are the opposite of each other. China is a communist autocracy whose authoritarian political model appears inscrutable and unpredictable in its long-term evolution; it started wide-ranging economic reforms, including open economy policies at the end of the 1970s, and mobilised vast resources for development, becoming the world's second largest economy despite a recent slowdown. India's democratic system is branded by chaos and elephantiasis, "anarchy that works," as described by the economist J.K. Galbraith, US ambassador to India in the early 1960s. India's economic reforms date back to 1992 and were forced by a financial crisis; its liberalisation was subsequently politically deadlocked and, up until now, it has not yet been able to mobilise significant resources to finance an investment strategy for social and public services, but it can count on strong democratic and electoral institutions, freedom of the press and the rule of law. China has been prospering thanks to the policies established by the government; India on the other hand has been thriving despite state intervention and policies.

In addition, there is only marginal integration of the two economies. Bilateral trade has grown rapidly, but the Chinese market accounts for only 8% of Indian exports, which consist mostly of low value-added goods, iron ore and other raw materials. Unfortunately for Delhi, the trade flow in the other direction is dominated by industrial products. Investments are hard to come by in either direction and each side complains about the difficulties of operating in the other's market. According to almost all economic parameters, today's China is more economically integrated with the United States than with India.

However, both countries want to keep old rivalries, disputes and suspicions from interfering with their race to development, while continuing to take separate roads toward that goal. Furthermore, both countries face major political uncertainties. If Indian politicians do not go ahead with economic and social reforms, open the doors to foreign direct investment and begin to address structural obstacles to growth, the economy will grow less than it potentially can and the growth momentum will eventually weaken. China's most pressing problem in the short run is whether its authoritarian regime will continue to be able to handle the challenges created by the country's tumultuous and poorly controlled growth, the factor on which its fragile legitimacy depends. Furthermore, the global recession of recent years, and the problems posed by growing inequality, corruption, riots and perhaps also demands for political emancipation could lead the system to the breaking point.

Indian democracy, despite all its faults, is famous for its stamina, but it developed during an era of rigid social structures, where everyone was resigned to their place in the hierarchy. India's accelerated growth is challenging the old order, offering hope to many, but is also exacerbating disparities between the rich urban elites and the poor masses. Catering to these aspirations while maintaining social stability is a very important test for India's national political system. At least in this respect, China and India have something in common, but they have a long history of difficult relations, political conflicts, border disputes and even a war.

2 A Past Marred by Conflicts

Let's go back in time. In 1938, during a visit to China, Pandit Jawaharlal Nehru said to Chiang Kai-shek: "I am increasingly convinced that China and India will cooperate in the future" (Thant 2011). At the time, Nehru was one of the leaders of the Indian National Congress, and he would later become the head of India's first independent government. He considered China a friendly country and an ally of choice in the leadership of postcolonial Asia, and not even the communists taking power could change his mind about close cooperation between the two countries.

On 15 August 1947, India became independent. The People's Republic of China was proclaimed on 1 October 1949. India arose from a large non-violent mass movement ruled by a strong pluralistic democracy; modern China from a great revolutionary movement ruled by a one-party dictatorship. The differences were obvious and deep, but for almost a decade (1949–1957) Sino-Indian relations were excellent. Even before India's independence, Nehru and the Congress Party had maintained good relations with Chiang Kai-shek's nationalist China; however, when Chiang fled to Taiwan and China fell into the hands of the communists and Mao Zedong, the pre-existing good relations with Chiang did not prevent Nehru from reaching the logical conclusion that communist China was now a real global power. For this reason, he championed the transfer of the permanent UN Security Council seat from nationalist to Communist China. Sino-Indian relations became even closer in June 1954, when Prime Minister and Foreign Minister Zhou Enlai, taking advantage of a break during the Geneva conference, stopped in New Delhi on his way back to Beijing and had a series of talks with Nehru, at the end of which a joint statement reaffirmed the validity of the foreign policy based on Nehru's *Panche Shila*, the 'Five principles of peaceful coexistence,' which was to lead to a historic change in the relationship of forces in Asia and guide relations between the two countries. China was—at the insistence of Burmese Prime Minister U Nu and Nehru—invited to the Bandung Conference in 1955. Nehru justified the invitation in the following terms, "We all want to understand what China wants and the next conference will at least allow it to express its point of view" (Bordone 2007). The Bandung Conference was for the Indian Prime Minister a highly visible and prestigious platform from which to set forth his theories on non-alignment aimed at Third World countries that did not identify themselves the two opposing blocs, while at the same time, for Beijing it meant returning to the international scene with a policy that was taking a more peaceful turn, as well as a more extensive and determined one. It was in Bandung that the Indian Prime Minister illustrated the above-mentioned 'five principles' that were to be the basis of relations between non-aligned nations: respect for the territorial integrity of states, non-aggression, non-interference, development of relationships based on equality and mutual benefits and, finally, peaceful coexistence. On that same occasion, he reiterated the Gandhian principle that any disputes between non-aligned nations should be resolved peacefully, through negotiations without preconditions. In Bandung, he was the main figure together with Zhou Enlai, although the Chinese Prime Minister's popularity, determined by his personal charisma as much as his political dynamism, led to the Indian Prime Minister's irritation: "…Not only did he invite to Beijing that fool Kotelawala, the Sri Lankan Prime Minister, but also Jamali, the Iraqi Foreign Minister, the most anti-communist at the conference… He invited anyone, as long as he is an anti-communist or a son of Allah." In some ways, Bandung represented the apogee of Indian diplomacy, but it was also the starting point of a Chinese diplomatic activism that would lead to many achievements in the following years, especially as far as Third World countries were concerned. Nehru's dream of Sino-Indian cooperation faded, and then disappeared entirely with the 1962 war, which marked forever the minds of both parties and originated from an underlying problem, the British Empire's legacy.

In 1914, the British, Tibetan and Chinese representatives met in Simla, which was British Raj territory at that time, to sign an agreement in principle on their respective territorial borders on the sides of Kashmir and Assam. The Simla Agreement was the basis of what is today known as the 'McMahon Line', which has since then defined the borders of that region of the world. But the Chinese government neither recognised nor ratified what its delegate signed in Simla, claiming 90,000 square kilometres of territory located south of the line, 2000 km^2 in the central sector of the border and 33,000 km^2 in the uninhabited region of Ladakh. In other words, the McMahon Line was never recognised by the Beijing government as the official border with the then Anglo-Indian Empire (Maxwell 1973). Neither Chiang Kai-shek nor the Communists agreed to that colonialist imposition, but at the beginning of their history as independent countries neither Beijing nor New Delhi raised the issue. Indeed, Nehru was eager to establish good relations with the difficult neighbour; after independence, he appointed Sardar Panikkar, one of his most skilled diplomats, as ambassador in Beijing, and began to make extensive use of the slogan *Hindi-Chini Bhai-Bhai* (Indians and Chinese are brothers).

When India became independent, Tibet was an autonomous region ruled by a theocracy; although formally under Chinese authority, its inhabitants had little in common with the Chinese from an ethnic and cultural point of view. However, immediately after coming to power, the new communist regime decided to give substance to the Chinese sovereignty over Tibet inherited from the Nationalist government and the imperial government before that. Consequently, the People's Liberation Army (PLA) of China occupied the region in 1950, although Beijing kept the existing government formally in place for the time being. The Indian government not only accepted the legitimacy of the Chinese military occupation by recognising the correctness of Beijing's claim that Tibet was part of China, but also voluntarily gave up the right to maintain garrisons in Tibetan territory, a right inherited from the colonial government. China's position on Tibet was then implicitly recognised in 1954 by a Sino-Indian treaty that confirmed the pre-existing Indian rights to trade with the region through a number of border passes (Guillermaz 1973a).

New Delhi's decision to recognise Chinese claims over Tibet was the result of a realistic acknowledgement of its weak political and military situation and its attempt to handle it in the best possible way. However, this did not stop Nehru from acting in a preventative manner and declaring in parliament on November 20, 1950, that the McMahon Line was the border between Tibet and India established by the Simla Convention of 1914. At the same time, he began a policy of containment toward China, by extending the Indian defence perimeter in Nepal, Bhutan and Sikkim, the Himalayan kingdoms then nestled between Tibet and India (now India and China) and at that time strategically placed in a key position, while continuing to keep a low profile on the issue of Tibet and proposing a solution based on Tibetan autonomy from Beijing. However, the Indian negotiators failed in their attempt to convince the Chinese about the benefits of this solution. Relations between the two countries began to deteriorate.

At the end of the 1950s, a rebellion broke out in Tibet against the Chinese presence. On 31 March 1959, the Dalai Lama fled from Lhasa and took refuge in India. Nehru decided to welcome him in the city of Dharamsala, provoking a harsh Chinese response. Beijing accused the United States and India of plotting a covert anti-Chinese operation, and openly attacked the CIA's role in the affair. To Chinese eyes, Nehru's action had been an open provocation against Beijing. Sino-Indian relations worsened significantly.

Three years later (in 1962), the inevitable happened: war broke out in the eastern sector of the border, to the north of the McMahon Line, after the Indians had attempted to occupy the Thagla mountain range (in June 1962). China responded with its troops on 20 October by attacking along the disputed McMahon Line and breaking through the Indian defences. The Chinese would stop a month later (21 November), observing a unilateral truce, when Zhou Enlai turned personally to Nehru offering him a ceasefire and the withdrawal of Chinese troops behind the McMahon Line. In exchange, he asked the cessation of India's *forward policy* enunciated and implemented since November 1960, which consisted in sending patrols deep into areas that India claimed as its own. This forward thrust had been meant to create stable border posts that, in the Indian government's view, would prevent by their mere presence any further Chinese advances, and lead to the opening of negotiations aimed at "finding an amicable solution of the Sino-Indian border matter."

Nehru refused the proposal immediately. After waiting patiently for three weeks, the Chinese broke through the inertia and unleashed a new offensive along the borderline. Within three days, they annihilated the Indian troops, occupied Ladakh and reached the gates of Assam. In these catastrophic circumstances, Nehru's non-alignment policy displayed all its inconsistency. Not one of the non-aligned countries, which the Indian leader thought he was leading after Bandung, moved in its favour, not even at the diplomatic level. Nehru, who now expected the occupation of Assam and feared an aerial attack on Delhi, lost his head and, terrified, turned to the United States, asking for military aid that was promptly granted. However, his actions ended up having no relevance as on 22 November 1962, the Chinese government declared a unilateral cease-fire and, a month later, withdrew its troops to 20 km behind the McMahon Line, maintaining its occupation of the Ladakh territory. In Zhou Enlai's last letter to the Indian Prime Minister (April 1963), while accusing him of a "dishonest approach" to the whole border question aimed at masking total unavailability to a diplomatic solution, Zhou Enlai maintained that, "if the Indian government, because of internal and external political conditioning, is not ready to deal with the Chinese government, the Chinese government is willing to wait patiently" (Guillermaz 1973b). The time of waiting would be much longer than the years the two opponents had still left to live.

The trauma in New Delhi was immense. India realised its military weakness, lost border territories and any ability to exercise a decisive international role, basically limiting its de facto foreign policy to South Asia from that point on; it was also beset by further political and military crises (Kashmir border war with Pakistan in 1965) and finally, a few years later, it even discovered that it had a nuclear neighbour. China exploded its first atomic bomb on 16 October 1964, thus becoming a member of the planet's nuclear club.

The only positive factor for India was the UN condemnation of the Chinese policy of aggression. Where Moscow continued to support China both economically and diplomatically while the United States, with the Kennedy administration and with the presence of John Kenneth Galbraith in New Delhi, took a softer position toward the Indian government, while still continuing to consider (until the mid-1980s) the non-alignment "immoral or, at the very least, amoral" and Nehru a sort of 'crypto-communist'. But the trauma was still huge and the defeat and humiliation were reinforced by a surprise move from the emerging Zulfikar Ali Bhutto, Foreign Minister of Pakistan at the time, who, a few months after the end of the war, relinquished a portion of Pakistani-controlled Kashmir to Beijing. This was the last straw for Nehru. The Indian leader would die on 24 May 1964, never having recovered from the disappointment and humiliation of heavy military defeat at the hands of a country that he believed to be a friend. What the Chinese and Indian historians call 'the Sino-Indian Cold War' had begun.

3 The Sino-Indian Cold War

However, the new Sino-Indian animosity was not limited to a strictly bilateral context. After the Twentieth Congress of the CPSU (Communist Party of the Soviet Union) (1956), China broke up relations with the Soviet Union at all levels, political, ideological and state, thus initiating the 'Sino-Soviet split conflict', which only ended with conclusion in Mikhail Gorbachev's trip to Beijing (15–18 May 1989), in conjunction with the Tiananmen Square events (Bergère 2000). India in turn had a historical enemy to its western and eastern borders: Pakistan. It was therefore inevitable that India would strengthen its alliance with the USSR and that China would find a natural political and military ally in Pakistan. The Sino-Indian crisis thus became part of Asia's larger strategic context; a context that became even more important and complex thanks to Kissinger's strategy. At the end of the 1960s, President Nixon's influential National Security Advisor was working on a rapprochement between the United States and the People's Republic of China. The Pakistanis acted as the middlemen for Kissinger when Nixon went to Beijing in February 1972 (Kissinger 2011). The China-Pakistan axis became the strategic axis China-Pakistan-United States.

The India-Soviet Union relationship grew even closer with the Bangladeshi war of independence of 1971, when East Pakistan (present day Bangladesh) proclaimed itself independent and Indian troops entered the territory of the future republic to defend it from Pakistani occupation forces. New Delhi was able to do this thanks to the *Treaty of Peace and Friendship* signed with Moscow in August 1971 (renewed for another twenty years in August 1991), which gave India the certainty that balance had been restored with respect to the strategic partnership of the United States with China and Pakistan. In the early 1970s, Sino-Indian relations became for the most part one aspect of the broader strategic confrontation between Washington and Moscow, with somewhat heterodox alliances and friendships.

Those covenants and friendships were exactly the same as a few years later during the Afghan war: Chinese, Americans and Pakistanis against the Russians in support of the Afghan resistance, including the Taliban, against the Kabul government backed by the Soviet Union.

4 The Turning Point

It wasn't until 1976 that the situation started to change (Indira Gandhi's previous attempt made in 1969 to improve relations with Beijing had failed). China and India resumed diplomatic relations when Beijing asked Romanian President Ceausescu to convey a message to the Indian leadership in which it stated its willingness to initiate talks about the border issues. The Chinese message was welcomed by the then Indian Prime Minister Morarji Desai of the Janata Party, which for the first time in independent India's history had sent the Congress party into opposition.

The new government in New Delhi was beginning to distance itself from the USSR and had therefore every interest to resume the dialogue with China. The post-Mao Chinese leadership showed similar political interests. Three years later (February 1979), these converging interests brought Indian Prime Minister Atal Vajpayee to Beijing, which spelled the end of the Sino-Indian Cold War. At the time, Vajpayee was an exponent of the Hindu fundamentalist right-wing and the leader of a composite coalition. A few months later, Chinese paramount leader Deng Xiaoping, who was implementing policies of openness and modernisation, launched a proposal in an interview with an Indian newspaper for the resolution of the border dispute that divided the two countries; following what had been Zhou Enlai's position, India and China would essentially have to ratify the status quo, with India accepting China's control over Aksai Chin (the Chinese name for Ladakh) and China accepting India's control over Assam.

A slow process thus began, made of small concrete steps toward normalising relations. The first step was Rajiv Gandhi's visit to Beijing in 1988, during which he stated that "India recognises Tibet as part of China and will not allow anti-Chinese activities by the Tibetan government in exile". Further steps were taken by subsequent governments. In December 1991, confirming the changed political climate, Chinese Prime Minister Li Peng arrived in the Indian capital. It was the first visit by a Chinese political leader since 1960. The joint statement by Li Peng and Narasimha Rao stressed their will for rapprochement and criticised "the military dominance of the West in the post-Cold War world" and "the emergence of an oligarchy of countries that manipulate international affairs practicing power politics" (15–16 December 1991). However, the two governments simply set as a concrete goal to "create an atmosphere that would lead to an agreement on the borders at a later time" (21 December 1991). A year later (May 1992), during Indian President Ramaswamy Venkataraman's visit to Beijing, his counterpart Yang Shangkun declared that, "cooperation between China and India is essential to avoid being left behind" in the new world order. A direct result of the visit was the reopening in July of direct communications along the land border between the two countries, for the first time since the Sino-Indo border war of 1962. This was accompanied by the reduction of the forces deployed along the LAC ('Line of Actual Control', the de facto border between India and China) and the implementation of a further series of measures to reduce the danger of incidents along the border. Nevertheless in May 1998 India conducted a series of five nuclear tests, which derailed the fragile normalisation process.

In India, the nuclear weapons debate had begun immediately after the Chinese atomic test of 1964. India's first test took place in 1974 and, in many ways, it had been a delayed response to China's nuclearisation. However, a feature of Indian nuclear policy has always been its reluctance to assign military significance to the nuclear option, the 1974 test notwithstanding. This may have been largely determined by its military alliance with the Soviet Union, enshrined in the above-mentioned treaty of 1971. India's intense economic, military and political cooperation with Moscow had probably reduced its incentive to acquire its own nuclear arsenal, despite the fact that China, its rival in the region and in the Third

World in general, was a fully recognised nuclear power. It was after the collapse of the Soviet Union, the end of the Cold War and the global rebalancing when internal pressures grew stronger for India to exercise the nuclear option. Having lost its only great partner and ally and main source of military equipment, having to come to terms with a rising China and unable to create a new partnership with the only remaining superpower, India was forced to redesign its strategic framework in the 1990s. The decision to become a nuclear power taken in 1998 had been a consequence of the underlying change in the balance of power around the country, which was not willing to accept a regional security order based on the supremacy of Beijing, despite the now extensive economic ties with China (Perkovich 2000). The Pakistani nuclear arms race was not a classic response to India's acquisition of nuclear weapons, rather a response after having been unable to protect its own territorial integrity in 1971. We now have enough clues to support the conclusion that the Pakistani nuclear program did not really come as a consequence of the Indian nuclear tests of 1974, but was due to the fact that New Delhi had been capable of successfully 'dissecting' Pakistan. When India, with the support of the Soviet Union, undertook the project of dividing Pakistan, the US and China were unable to counter that. Acknowledging that without a nuclear arsenal Pakistan would not have been able to defend itself against Indian conventional military capabilities, Zulfiqar Ali Bhutto gave top priority to Pakistan's nuclear program in early 1972. It was not important whether India had nuclear weapons - rather Pakistan believed it needed them to balance India and preserve itself as a nation. In his letter from May 13, 1998 to US President Clinton, as an attempt to justify India's position and choices in the eyes of the US, the then Prime Minister Atal Vajpayee stated, "We have an overtly nuclear State on our borders, a State that launched an armed aggression against us in 1962. An atmosphere of mistrust persists, mainly due to the unresolved border issues. To top it all, that country gave material aid to another neighbour of ours (Pakistan) so that it might become a nuclear state". As an American analyst ironically put it, it was as if Clinton had justified a possible resumption of US nuclear testing, "because of residual tensions with Russia linked to the Cuban missile crisis of 1962!" (IT 25 May 1998). Vajpayee's justifications, which ended up immediately in the New York Times (3 June 1998) despite the fact that they had been stated in a private letter, not only did not improve India's image in Washington's eyes, but also had the effect of leading to a drastic worsening of regional relations. The *Pokhran II* tests of 11 and 13 May would put an end to negotiations with Pakistan, which responded in kind by completing six nuclear tests on 28 and 30 May (evidently, five for the five of *Pokhran II* plus one for the one of *Pokhran I* in 1974).

The deterioration of relations between India and China was definitely more serious than what had happened between India and Pakistan. In this case, it was India's justification, rather than the tests, that wrought the most damage. However, despite relations between the two countries reaching one of the lowest points since the 1962 war, Beijing and Delhi were able to overcome this crisis quite quickly, especially because, despite pressure from Islamabad, China maintained a neutral stance during the *Kargil War* of June 1999 (a military confrontation in the Kashmir valley between India and Pakistan that had brought the subcontinent to the brink of a possible nuclear war), which favoured the defusion of that crisis and was obviously appreciated by the Indian government (Borsa and Torri 1999).

5 New Relations

On 9 April 2005, then Chinese Prime Minister Wen Jiabao landed in New Delhi for a summit with Manmohan Singh; with him, he brought a suitcase full of hypotheses for agreements and cooperation with an India blessed by very impressive economic growth rates. It was the embrace between the dragon and the elephant, as emphasised by Beijing's official press release at the time. New Delhi was not Wen's first stop; he had begun his tour in Bangalore, the capital of the state of Karnataka, known as India's Silicon Valley. His choice was extremely significant, as China owned the hardware, while India had become the software capital of the world. Wen wanted to emphasise the complementarity between the Chinese and Indian economy, which could revolutionise the global economy based on information and communications. The Chinese Premier launched a slogan from Bangalore that would have seemed unrealistic not long ago, "Together we can make the twenty-first century the era of Asia's technological leadership", Wen declared. At the same time, the Indian media placed a strong emphasis on the 'free zones', an experiment that the Indian prime minister wanted to introduce to attract investments from large companies; it was a clear reference to the SEZs (Special Economic Zones) established since the early 1990s by Deng Xiaoping, the architect of China's opening to capitalism.

The Delhi summit was not only the prelude to a potential new era for the world economy, but also a political breakthrough toward a closer partnership "for global and strategic cooperation to ensure peace and stability" as it was put. They were not just standing on ceremony. Singh declared that the two countries could "redesign the world order" and Wen added that, "a trilateral cooperation between Russia, India and China will contribute to democratising international relations" i.e., to overcoming US dominance and building a multipolar world. Based on the priority directive for relations between the two countries, i.e., increasing economic relations, and the profound changes in the regional and international situation, New Delhi and Beijing recognised the strategic priority of their mutual effort to improve bilateral relations (the official statement emphasised 'friendly closeness, not rivalry'), but did not go beyond statements of good will on the borders issue, where deep differences still remained, despite Singh's stated determination "to solve the issues we inherited from history".

This interest in cooperation, encompassing potentially all areas, would lead to the signing of twelve agreements, protocols and memoranda that not only dealt with commercial and customs aspects (trade increase from 14 to 40 billion dollars by 2010, achieved in 2007), but also extended to matters of financial and economic development, scientific and technological cooperation in strategic areas such as research of non-renewable energy sources in other countries, cooperation in the field of oceanography and even went as far as the proclamation of the 'year of friendship between China and India' in 2006. All of this took place in a context in which the two countries were putting up with American unilateralism with increasingly undisguised annoyance and asserting the common goal of a new multipolar international economic and political order that would be, "fair, rational, equal and mutually beneficial… and capable of fighting poverty and reducing the gap between North and South". The importance of the UN was therefore emphasised, and UN reform was advocated by both countries. India aspired to a permanent seat with veto power on the Security Council and Wen Jiabao declared that he, "acknowledged and supported India's aspirations to play a greater role within the United Nations" as well as its increased importance in the international arena (this support to Indian aspirations was reaffirmed in the Joint Statement *A Shared Vision for the 21st Century* released on 14 January 2008 during Manmohan Singh's visit to Beijing).

Progress beyond diplomatic niceties was made on the road to peace between the two countries during the four-day visit by the Chinese Prime Minister. A kind of *roadmap* was agreed upon that showed the way to follow in order to resolve the border dispute, which was to "refuse to let problems left over from history create mistrust or impede the development of our relations" as Wen Jiabao stated before departing for India. The *roadmap* stipulated that the dispute had to be resolved without recourse to force (art. 1), taking into account respective strategic interests and security (art. 4), historical experience, national sentiment, practical difficulties, reasonable concerns on both sides and the current situation of the borders (art. 5) and that the special representatives on the border issue should continue consultations to arrive at an agreed framework on which to base the next joint delineation and demarcation (art. 9–10).

The joint document of 14 January 2008 reiterated the same points referring extensively and explicitly to the *Agreement on the Political Parameters and Guiding Principles for the Settlement of the Boundary Question* signed in April 2005. As an Indian diplomat commented, "the approach accepted by the prime ministers is that the border issues can only be addressed in a long-term context". In a highly symbolic move, the historic pass of Nathu La was reopened to frontier trade after 45 years in June 2006, along with the Silk Road, between Sikkim and Tibet (4000 meters high and halfway between the capital of Tibet, Lhasa and the port of Calcutta), which as the two countries intended was to become, 'the new channel for Sino-Indian commercial relations', the centre of a large communication network that would connect China to the Bay of Bengal, and the strategic point for the consolidation of the development policy of China's western and Indian's eastern regions. The opening of the pass gave substance to what the Indian Prime Minister had earlier described as a new strategic partnership between China and India, which have a shared border extending for more than 3.000 kilometres.

In November of that same year, Hu Jintao went to India on an official visit, which was the first visit after the 1997 visit of his predecessor Jiang Zemin. It was a visit replete with meaning, to "make efforts to revive the *Hindi-Chini Bhai-Bhai* spirit of the 1950s". The visit was also intended to make it clear to the world that the two countries had put aside any rivalries and had returned to being partners, despite the inexplicit but ever-present issue of China's close alliance with Pakistan, India's eternal enemy, which in recent years had strengthened, after the US-led attack on Taliban-ruled Afghanistan. The Sino-Indian partnership continued to be based on their shared vision of a multipolar world. It was certainly no coincidence that, upon his arrival in India, Hu Jintao had expressed his hope that the two countries would develop a "multilateral cooperation to create a multipolar world" (The Hindu 2006). Besides the symbolic value of the visit, its concrete results included the signing of a wide range of economic and cooperation agreements in various fields, including civil nuclear technology. "Every nation has the right to develop energy in any form, including nuclear energy, to meet its development needs" stressed the Chinese leader. It was a historic declaration that foreshadowed the non-opposition of China to the American project to promote India's free access to the resources of the NSG (Nuclear Suppliers Group) countries, the organisation that brings together the signatories of the NPT (Nuclear Non-Proliferation Treaty), producers of nuclear technology or fuel, promoted by Nixon in the aftermath of India's first nuclear test with the purpose of putting under embargo any country, beginning with India, that had not adhered to the principles set by the NPT.

In August 2009, the illusion of the forthcoming birth of a formidable bloc formed by China and India was quickly replaced with terrifying hypothesis of a military confrontation between the two Asian giants. The Indian media began to report regularly on Chinese military violations along the dividing line between the two countries, along most of the Indo-Chinese Himalayan border. Beijing had wasted no time in responding in kind to the accusations of the Indian press and the Chinese newspaper *Renmin Ribao* (People's Daily) had shot point-blank against the neighbouring country, publishing two editorials in November, while at the same time a meeting was taking place in Bengaluru between the foreign ministers of India, China and Russia, aimed at an improbable strengthening of ties between the three countries, which included the following statements: "The Indians have become more narrow-minded and intolerant of any criticism (…), India pursues a policy of "being friends with those who are far and enemies with those who are near" (…), India should look to pursue relations with its neighbours and abandon reckless and arrogant attitudes (…), If India considers itself the legitimate heir to the British Empire, China's government considers itself the heir to the imperial Qing Dynasty that was overthrown by Sun Yat-sen's revolutionaries" (Natale 2009). Mutual distrust was so strong that the two governments—both guided by pragmatic economists like Wen Jiabao and Manmohan Singh—had not hesitated to jeopardise the future of trade between the two countries, which was expected to exceed 60 billion dollars by the end of that year, a 30 fold increase compared to 2000 levels, and to cause relations between the two countries to fall, as former Indian diplomat M.K. Bhadrakumar had declared to the online newspaper *Asia Times*, "into a deep frozen abyss from which it will take a long time to get out" (Asia Times 2009).

Despite the tensions between the two countries, Chinese Premier Wen Jiabao flew to New Delhi on December 2010. There, he and his counterpart Manmohan Singh signed economic cooperation agreements worth 20 billion dollars, showing once again that economic relations prevailed over political tensions. India received Beijing's support in its request for a permanent seat on the UN Security Council, but political talks had carefully avoided the issues on which disagreements persisted, from the border dispute to the use of water from the Brahmaputra River, which originates in China and runs across the whole of India. Nor was any reference made to the close relations that Beijing entertained with Pakistan—India's traditional rival, with which it has fought three wars and has an on-going quarrel over Kashmir—to which it was giving weapons and technology without imposing conditions on their use.

As Sino-Pakistani relations were becoming increasingly close, an anti-Chinese axis between India and the United States was gaining strength. This encompassed the nuclear deal between Washington and New Delhi signed by George W. Bush on 18 July 2005 in addition to an increasingly evident investiture of India as a bulwark against Chinese expansionism in South and East Asia. President Obama also sent several signals in this direction. During his Asian tour in June 2010, he went to India, Japan, South Korea and Indonesia, visiting those he called, "the nations that show the Asian way to democracy". China was not mentioned in any official speech, a sign that Washington made no mystery of an agreement that was being increasingly consolidated. To be sure, India felt encircled by China not only because of the support that Beijing gave to Pakistan, but also because it had to deal with the growing Chinese influence in the continent and feared that the Chinese *string of pearls* strategy was aimed at removing its control of the Indian Ocean. This strategy consisted in China's construction of a chain of ports and airports, supporting points along the crucial trade route between the Suez Canal and the Strait of Malacca, involving about 40% of the global trade and more than 80% of Chinese oil imports. The port of Gwadar in Pakistan's Balochistan, from which a system of roads and pipelines is planned to be built to import energy sources from the Middle East and Africa directly into the Chinese provinces of Xinjiang and Yunnan; the ports of Hambantota in Sri Lanka, of Akyab, Cheduba and Bassein in Myammar, Chittagong in Bangladesh, the two electronic espionage bases created in the archipelago of the Coco Islands in the Bay of Bengal and the railway and gas and oil pipeline project that is to connect the island of Ramree to Kunming on the coast of Myanmar (Wang 2013) represent a considerable advantage for the Chinese in the race for the control of shipping lanes in Asia.

6 The New Silk Road

'A handshake across the Himalayas' was the title of Chinese Premier Li Keqiang's article published on 20 May 2013, by the English-language Indian daily *The Hindu* on the second day of his first visit to India, a few days after a tentative agreement reached between the armies of the two neighbouring countries following the umpteenth clash caused by the unresolved border dispute in the Himalayan region. 'Friendship' and 'cooperation' were the key words of the text, in which Beijing's number two official referred to China and India as, "the two pillars of Eastern civilisation" and pointed out how the Himalayas had never prevented the cultural exchange between the two countries. Li at the time assured the intensification of bilateral efforts to resolve the border issue through dialogue as, "world peace and regional stability cannot be guaranteed without a relationship of mutual trust between China and India. We have worked together to maintain peace on the border, we have to improve the mechanism defining the boundaries and properly manage and resolve the differences between us," Li said and offered "a handshake across the Himalayas so as to facilitate the transformation of the two countries into the 'new global economic engine'".

Although relatively lower than in previous years, bilateral trade relations had reached 66 billion US dollars, and both countries announced to reach a bilateral trade volume of 100 billion US dollars in 2015. But according to observers as well as members of the two governments, this potential was hampered by disputes such as the outstanding border dispute. Although the focus of the talks was economic issues—of particular importance to India, which was confronted with a 30 billion US dollar trade deficit in China's favour (higher than the trade deficits with the US, Germany and Japan), the border dispute controversy had occupied the front pages of the two countries' newspapers. The Chinese press, in particular, launched conciliatory signals suggesting a possible acceleration of negotiations to solve the problem. In an editorial on the Chinese premier's visit, the official Chinese news agency *Xinhua* said that, "hostile relations between the two neighbouring countries penalise the interests of both" and went on to address indirectly the role of the US in fuelling, or at least exploiting, tensions between China and India, so as to isolate Beijing as part of the *Pivot to Asia*, announced by the Obama administration in 2009 (Xinhua 2013): "Those in the West who tend to define the relations between China and India through territorial disputes" the article went on "forget the fact that their issue with boundaries is largely a legacy of Western colonialism" since "for thousands of years these two ancient civilisations rarely clashed because of territorial issues."

The US attempt to capitalise on its solid relations with New Delhi to strengthen the anti-Chinese front in Asia was then denounced even more clearly when it was argued that China, "has never sought to strengthen ties with any country at the expense of its relations with India" and that the latter, "will pursue its policy towards China according to its own will, without being part of projects by other powers." The reference to Washington's role in the evolution of Sino-Indian relations confirmed how rising tensions in recent years around the Himalayan border were to be connected, at least in part, to the aforementioned US *Pivot to Asia* strategy, which sets India as a key partner in the implementation of its agenda aimed at curbing China's economic and military rise, producing an inevitable confrontation with Beijing, despite the strong trade relations between the two giants on the Asian continent.

Despite the endless stream of border incidents, occurring as late as September 2014, the Chinese President Xi Jinping and Indian Prime Minister Narendra Modi met for a second time (14–16 May 2015), trying to make use of their personal friendship and relationship as the nail on which to hang a renewed diplomatic phase. According to international media, the two are considered the strongest leaders the two countries have produced in recent decades. During his official visit to India in September 2014, in an effort to build a relationship of at least apparent personal trust between them, Xi Jinping travelled to the state of Gujarat, the Indian equivalent of the Chinese province Guangdong, to pay tribute to his host's native land. Modi began his trip to Xian, Shanxi, Mao's region of birth and cultural heart of the former *Celestial Empire*. A particular choice,—referred to as 'original' by the Chinese media to a region that is not used host important foreign visitors. The meaning of the visit, followed closely in Washington, had been anticipated by Modi himself, when he said that "The 21st century belongs to Asia". What was not said, however, was even more decisive: India was warning China that if it was trying to establish a hegemony, India would be there to counter Chinese hegemony. Beyond symbolic gestures, aimed at presenting Asia as a unified bloc, the India-China Summit had agendas replete with economic and political terms and was geared toward a forced political pragmatism. If we really live in an *Asian century*, the two countries may disagree but not oppose each other. India suffers the explosive emergence of China's global influence and, as previously discussed, is linked along with Japan and South Korea to the strategic alliance with the United States. Landing in Xian at the time, Modi admitted to not being able to do without "increasingly closer relations" with the cumbersome neighbour, whom he would not ask for an immediate definition of the disputed Himalayan borders. Beijing continues to be New Delhi's first commercial partner; trade has recently reached 70 billion US dollars, with an Indian deficit of about 38 billion. Nor can China underestimate so important a customer, one that is influential throughout the Pacific, rapidly developing, and that promises to become the second super-power of the century, not least due to its young population. Although there remained solid grounds for conflict, the reasons to overcome mistrust and rivalry prevailed; in addition to signing commercial agreements for 22 billion US dollars in contracts, Modi aimed at establishing smoother relations.

Apart from Xi Jinping, Modi also met the Premier Li Keqiang and the Shanghai business community, seeking to increase economic cooperation. The two richest international projects initiated after the global financial crisis of 2009 were on the agenda: the *Silk Road Economic Belt*, the new Silk Road that would connect the East with Europe, and the Chinese-led *Asian Infrastructure Investment Bank* (AIIB), wanted by Beijing as a sort of 'counter-organization' to the World Bank dominated by the US and Japan.

India has for the time been bypassed by the new *Silk Road* proposed by President Xi Jinping, the economic version of the *Chinese dream* and what Beijing refers to as "new type of relations between the great powers," which is designed to follow the trade routes that once linked China with Europe and is both terrestrial and maritime, with roads and railways crossing Central Asia and Russia and maritime routes that, will reach the Mediterranean. Modi did not hide his irritation about being bypassed, and was concerned about the *string of pearls* trade route, designed to marginalize Indian interests and increase trade and ties with Pakistan,

Bangladesh, Myanmar, Afghanistan, Nepal, Indonesia and Russia to Beijing. Mori reacted by initiating the *Mausam project*, which is aimed at making India the hub of maritime trade in the Indian Ocean, involving the countries of Eastern Africa, the Arabian Peninsula and Southeast Asia. Historically, in order to travel more quickly over this route, ships would set sail during monsoon season (*mausam* in Hindi), stopping in India between the end of one and the start of another monsoon. Details of the project are not yet completely understood, but it appears that New Delhi wants to expand its presence in these waters not only for economic reasons, but also to earn a role of regional importance. Beijing had tried to minimise the impact of the Indian initiative by saying that it "wanted to take advantage of the Indian prime minister's visit to raise China-India relations to a new level" while at the same time saying that "no power can expect to dominate Asia." (a conclusion not only addressed at the Indian interlocutor but also at Western leaders such (the recently ceased US president) Barack Obama, the Japanese leader Shinzo Abe and European political leaders).

While Modi fears "an 18th century style Chinese expansionist mentality," as he put it, Xi Jinping is wary of India's close ties with the West in general and the US in particular. Beijing is the symbol of success of state-driven capitalism, New Delhi is the icon of growing liberal capitalist democracies in Asia. The two leaders, united by business interests and divided geopolitical rivalry, are not, as we read in an Italian newspaper, yet in a position to divide power and influence in Asia among themselves. Instead, they are aware of playing a game for the control of Asia and influence on the rest of the planet" (Il Sole 24 Ore 2015).

7 Conclusions

Interaction between the US, India and China appear to take place according to the assumptions of geopolitical realism while the balance of power is still in favour of the US. However, the threat that the Delhi-Beijing axis will become less dependent on Washington in the medium term is real and an Asia with *Chindia* at its centre is a very real American concern. However, *Chindia* is not yet a reality. It is not conceivable for two *states-civilisations* of that size to merge to create a joint and common front against Western interests. However, a temporary marriage of interests is quite possible, which will strengthen both countries in their relations with the United States. For now, the two countries pursue a common strategic goal: to get rid of, within a few years, the burden of poverty and backwardness. China has undoubtedly made more rapid progress in that respect, expanding its economic, scientific and technological frontiers over the last three decades. China and India proceed at their respective pace, each with their competitive advantages: more law than order in India, more order than law in China. China for its part is moreover testing a new development model full of unknowns, including questions about the current leadership's ability to efficiently govern 1.3 billion people. Their complementarities do not end there. To support growth, China and India need to diversify energy sources and make sure they will have access to sufficient energy and energy sources. The less they will step on each other's feet and collaborate, as they are already doing in Sudan and Iran, the more they will emerge as leading collaborators on the global energy markets. Again, the integration of Indian software with Chinese hardware opens promising horizons to both, as was already suggested by former premier Zhu Rongji at the end of the last decade. China and India could become the leading proponents of a Pan-Asian economic architecture, encompassing three central markets: Japan, South Korea and the ASEAN countries.

But will economic interests and economic complementarities and integration prevail over geopolitical and geostrategic Chinese-Indian rivalries? This is not only a crucial question for the political leaders of the world's two most populous nations, but also for the United States and Europe. As the centre of global economic growth and prosperity is moving towards Asia, the relationship between China and India will become increasingly important. If China and India work together and learn from each other's successes, *Chindia* could become inevitable, even if in the very far future. That could become reality if Beijing were to do away with the lack of transparency and authoritarianism and accept injections of Indian democracy and tolerance as ingredients for a complete transition to modernity. India's democratic model for its part must demonstrate its effectiveness. However, if the Indian ruling class instead chose the Chinese way of economic growth, based on state-driven capitalism and authoritarian governance, the whole of Asia and perhaps other parts of the world would slide towards Chinese-style socio-political authoritarianism. Finally, if the Chinese-Indian rivalry and quest hegemony in Asia resulted into armed conflict between the two countries, as it happened in 1962, the outcome would be apocalyptic, and not only for the Asian continent.

References

Bhadrakumar MK (2009), Times, November 28

Balcet G, Valli V (eds) (2012) Potenze economiche emergenti. Cina e India a confronto. il Mulino, Bologna, pp 11–37

Bordone S (2007) La partecipazione straordinaria della Repubblica popolare cinese. In: Calchi Novati G (ed) Terzo Mondo Addio. La Conferenza afro-asiatica di Bandung in una prospettiva storica, Carocci, Roma, pp 41–54

Bergère MC (2000) La Cina dal 1949 ai giorni nostri. il Mulino, Bologna, pp 313–315

Borsa G, Torri M (eds) (1999) L'incerta vigilia del nuovo secolo in Asia. il Mulino, Bologna, pp 164–167

Guillermaz J (1973a) Il Partito comunista cinese al potere 1949/1972. Feltrinelli, Milano, p 199

Guillermaz J (1973b) Il Partito comunista cinese al potere 1949/1972. Feltrinelli, Milano, pp 285–294

Il Sole 24 Ore (2015) 16 Maggio. http://www.quotidiano.ilsole24ore.com

Kissinger H (2011) On China. Penguin Press, New York

Maxwell N (1973) L'India e la Cina: storia di un conflitto. Mazzotta, Milano, pp 74–93

Natale B (2009) La fine di Cindia: venti di guerra sul confine indo-cinese. Limes, n. 6:163–167

New York Times (1998), June 3

Perkovich G (2000) India's nuclear bomb: the impact on global proliferation. Oxford University Press, New Delhi, pp 181–183
Thant Myint-U (2011) Where China meets India. Farrar Straus & Giroux, New York, Burma and the New Crossroad of Asia, p 301
The Hindu (2006), November 23
The Hindu (2013), May 20
Wang Y (2013) Creative Involvement. The Evolution of China's Global Role. Peking University Press, p. 216
Xinhua (2013), May 22, http://news.xinhuanet.com/english/china/2013-05/22/c_124744742.htm

Russia and China: Partners or Competitors? Views from Russia

Silvana Malle

Abstract Russia's interest for the East can be dated back to the aftermath of the 2008/09 global economic and financial crisis. The effects of the crisis revealed Russia's dramatic exposure to Western developments. Until then the economic potential of fast growing China had been neglected. Developments in 2013–14 were crucial, since Russia finally turned to the East when international tensions linked to conflicts in Ukraine erupted, making her weak- oil price-dependent—economic recovery even more problematic. Building a new Sino-Russian partnership, however, entails risks, since competitive pressures could derail a mutually profitable venture. The challenge for Russia and China is to strengthen their cooperation through dialogue.

1 Introduction

Russia neglected China's economic potential as long as oil prices remained high, sustaining strong economic growth. After the 2008–2009 global economic and financial crisis Moscow's authorities became aware of Russia's excessive exposure to Western economies. When Russia's antagonism with the West strengthened following events in Ukraine, Russia's strategy of turning to the East gained importance. Among the priorities set out by Vladimir Putin in his 7 May 2012 presidential edicts (to be translated from the Russian word term 'ukaz', corresponding to the concept of 'presidential decree'), was assigning a major focus to the Far East, hoping to turn this region into a springboard of economic and commercial relations with China, and possibly other dynamic Asian countries. High-profile Russian economic experts were put in charge of development in the Far East while particular focus fell on the newly-established Eurasian Economic Union (EAEU). Through this entity Russia seeks to foster regional economic integration, strengthen its partnership with Kazakhstan and create a security buffer against possible attacks from enemies and/or terrorist activities following increasing unrest in the Middle East and adjacent

S. Malle (✉)
Department of Economics, University of Verona, Verona, Italy
e-mail: silvana.malle@univr.it

S. Beretta et al. (eds.), *Understanding China Today*, Understanding China,
DOI 10.1007/978-3-319-29625-8_4

countries. At the same time, that new strategy created opportunities for closer cooperation with China, that would bring about foreign investment and joint ventures in the underdeveloped Far East but also the problem of having to compete with an economically stronger partner in the EAEU and Eurasia at large that China considers as important transits towards European markets and a larger area of economic cooperation per se. This chapters deals with the people and institutions in charge of economic development in the Asiatic territories of Russia, discusses the terms of the debate that a sudden change in strategy provoked among experts and federal agencies and investigates the challenges confronting two major world powers of which China is becoming a world economic giant. Russia, it is argued, should not—despite her economic difficulties—be underestimated as the country continues to retain command as a strong military power in the region. It is argued that the Western policies of containment vis-à-vis China and Russia will help to strengthen their cooperation while Western economic sanctions will inevitably push Russia to the East. A number of important deals that go beyond trade in oil and energy have been signed. Others are being worked out through a complex framework for cooperation to be defined in a longer term. Competition versus cooperation is discussed in particular with regard to Eurasia and the recent Chinese project of resuscitating and technically upgrading the ancient Silk Road. Finally, the issue of economic cooperation eventually evolving from common security concerns towards some form of alliance in front of the challenges of a changing and increasingly confrontational western world is explored.

2 Russia Turning Eastwards: People in Charge, Challenges and Opportunities

Putin's above-mentioned May 2012 presidential edicts put a major focus on the Far East, hoping to turn this region into a springboard of economic and commercial relations with China, and possibly other dynamic Asian countries. Two high-profile and experienced individuals were put in charge to combine administrative with managerial skills: Yuri Petrovich Trutnev (born in 1956) with long experience as an advisor to Putin in the Presidential Administration and Aleksandr Sergeyevich Galushka (born in 1975), former head of Delovaya Rossiya (Association of Small and Medium Enterprises (SMEs) and co-chairman of the All-Russian National Front's executive board, an organisation was created in 2011 by Putin. In 2012, Trutnev was appointed Deputy Prime Minister of Russia and presidential envoy to the Far Eastern Federal District, a position he still holds. Galushka is Minister of the Development of the Russian Far East in Dmitri Medvedev's cabinet from September 11, 2013. Since then these two figures have been working hand in hand with a fairly large degree of autonomy compared to other ministries taking part in high-level international meetings with the corresponding leaders of Asian countries and others in the business community. It was Trutnev, out of six deputy Prime Ministers, who was with 'muscular' enthusiasm asked to head of Russian delegation to the 2016 World Economic Forum (WEF) instead of first deputy minister Igor Ivanovich Shuvalov (Lenta 2016a; kremlin 2016a).[1] While Galushka is less prominent in the media compared to Trutnev, his managerial skills have been crucial in laying down plans, gaining support among regional authorities and, finally, getting the Duma's approval for appropriate legislation.

Russia's new strategy has raised conflicting sentiments among ordinary citizens and intellectuals. The former are puzzled since the Far East is not attractive for workers who move towards the western parts of Russia as soon as possible and regional backwardness is ascribed more to local habits than unfriendly geo-physics. Among intellectuals the fear is that going eastwards may further distract Russia from adopting market-enhancing reforms and harm, perhaps destroy, the germs of democracy, introduced from Europe from the early 1990s after the collapse of the Soviet Union. Some academics with close links with Western scholars have decided to take long leaves of absence in Western Europe or the Americas; some remain in Russia from where they continue to observe, comment, and critically react to, questionable economic and political developments. An intellectual diaspora is on the way, solicited by domestic and foreign developments, whose impact on Russian domestic affairs may increase or abate over time depending on the geopolitical context. There are ferments among a rising generation of private businessmen who look for profound changes in economic policy, albeit not identical with liberal principles and policies. The government is blamed for inertia vis-à-vis falling oil prices and punitive Western financial sanctions. Concerns voiced by Russian business leaders are increasingly discussed within the Presidential Administration and with the President himself (Forbes 2016; Vedomosti 2016).[2]

Among resident scholars, one can identify a more nuanced approach toward Russia's eastward policies, although opinions can differ sharply depending on the topics. This is understandable in the present geopolitical context. Despite criticism at home and abroad, international developments nowadays suggest that the turn to the East is well engrained and likely to consolidate further in the future. Ambiguous relations with Western countries and commercially targeted ostracism enshrined in the politics of sanctions militate in this direction (Malle 2015). While the overall support for the leadership remains robust, specific policies, however, do not always find peoples' complacency. A monitoring of people's attitudes toward different countries/regional groupings carried out by the Levada Centre in January 2016 shows that neither hostility vis-à-vis the West nor sympathy for China can be taken for granted. Events related to Ukraine and the rise of antagonism with the West brought about a Russian re-orientation towards China. However, China's economic slowdown from late 2015 has contributed to a significant fall of attraction for China. Simultaneously, sentiments towards Europe and the US improved somewhat (albeit staying comparatively low) (Levada Centre 2016a).

---

[1]Putin advised Trutnev at the time to be careful not to exaggerate with the saber-rattling.

[2]These concerns were expressed by Boris Titov, the presidential ombudsman for business, who founded a right-wing party in view of elections in 2016.

Exogenous developments play a definitive role in peoples' perceptions on China. Cultural diversity may be more difficult to overcome than internal obstacles, such as economic backwardness and lack of domestic and international infrastructure in the East. All throughout her modern history, Russia felt closer to Europe than to Asia. Europe was the continent Russia looked to when the impetus for modernization abruptly emerged by virtue or necessity. Stolypin's forward-looking ambitions to modernize the Far East in a couple of decades turned out to be too costly and, in the end, ineffective (Porter and Seregny 2004). The Stalinist resettlement of people to Siberia and some regions in the Far East during World War II led to one-company towns specialized in military equipment but did not bring about developmental gains. Many company-towns survived even after the transformation of Russia's economy to a market economy and the country's demilitarization in the 1990s, albeit under enormous difficulties and practically no economic prospects. Outmigration has characterized the region from the 1990s onwards.

Developing eastwards takes nowadays place under the pressure of antagonism with Europe and in the hope of turning punitive Western sanctions into an engine of growth in earlier neglected sectors. The chance of success, however, is low. Consolidated backwardness and unfavorable demographic trends remain important obstacles. Nonetheless, prospects are not all bleak. Despite a cumbersome heritage, modern technology and mutually favorable cross-country linkages may facilitate the establishment of large-scale joint projects and nurture corresponding private business incentives.

Russia's culture is also more open to be influenced from abroad. While legends, memories and the brunt of personal experience may feed discouragement and inertia, generational change and opportunities created through interstate agreements may inject confidence in joint ventures. Versatile technologies may be used to speed up change. Transport infrastructure may help overcome previously insurmountable obstacles. On a positive note Russia may take inspiration from other countries. Self-feeding development and growth in countries where climatic/natural conditions were far from favourable, such as Canada, Australia and Israel, where a combination of state guidance, individual liberties and business commitment has proven to be successful. Market-driven development in Japan after the II World War and robust economic and social growth in South Korea are also valuable examples from the East, which Russia could benefit from, if prejudice gave way to an interest in deepening knowledge and curiosity to learn from other cultures.

Russia should also learn from China and its incredibly difficult path to modernity against the background of many obstacles, including a political system that is not always able to swiftly adapt adopt to changes. China's path toward a market economy, the development of its regions and its openness to trade and investment has been extraordinarily successful: indeed, China's success exceeded expectations at home and abroad (OECD 2002).[3] Current difficulties suggest that China has still

[3]The difficulty of the process of China's accession to WTO in 2001 was discussed by this author with Chinese high-level representatives at the time.

a long way to go to improve and master market fundamentals. But there is no reason to believe that China will not be able to tackle the current difficulties in the years ahead. There are reasons, indeed, to believe that Russia could benefit from China's experience comparatively more than from the advanced APR (Asian Pacific Rim) economies, whose economic take-off occurred under very different circumstances and geopolitical contexts. Russia may benefit from China's experience in building dynamic foreign funded areas that supported economic growth in the 1990s, also thanks to the improvement of procedures to allow private businesses to establish themselves and flourish. The Russian authorities in charge are aware of such benefits. Some steps into this direction have been taken, but progress is slow.

3 Turning Eastwards: The Intellectual and Political Divide

Russian scholars and experts are divided on new development strategies. It is often difficult to separate their political allegiances and preferences from the veracity of their arguments. What follows is therefore an attempt to categorize different approaches while acknowledging that each approach would be worth of further investigation. Different views rest on fundamentally different paradigms. Political allegiance matters but may not be determinant. Scientific backgrounds of the people in question also play a role. The economists are more prone to argue against Russia's turning away from Europe than the country's foreign policy experts. Among the critical commentators are well-known Vladislav Inozemtsev, Sergey Guriev and Konstantin Sonin (Ryzhkov et al. 2012; Guriev 2015; Inozemtsev 2014a; Sonin 2014). Other reform-minded scholars take inspiration from a similar analytical approach. Inozemtsev continues to reside in Russia. Some economists have left for different reasons accepting prestigious job offers from abroad. Guriev, the former rector of the Higher School of economics in Moscow e.g. moved to the university Sciences Po in Paris in 2014—a move that turned out to have facilitated his appointment to chief economist at the EBRD (European Bank for Reconstruction and Development) in 2015. Konstantin Sonin, former vice-rector of the Higher School of Economics in Moscow, became professor at the University Of Chicago Harris School Of Public Policy in September 2015 (Harris School 2015). The intellectuals of this group are concerned that turning to the East will hamper Russia's modernization and become an obstacle to European-style democracy. Furthermore, they support European antagonistic policies towards Russia. Inozemtsev, however, does not dismiss the potential of eastward policies, provided they are accompanied by the expansion of relations with technologically advanced countries such as Japan and South Korea rather than only developing China. A separate school of thought is pursued by Aleksei Maslov (from The Oriental School of the Higher School of Economics in Moscow), who warns against China's expansionism and also challenges the idea of cheap labour/low tax economy if compared with developing countries such as Vietnam and India (Maslov 2015). Being by and large dismissive of the Far East's economic potential, liberal economists do not conduct research in the field, but intervene occasionally against specific policies aimed at developing the Far East. Some of their views will be analyzed below when discussing policies and plans.

No matter how sound such arguments are from an economic point of view, one cannot avoid noting that the political implications are significant and not acceptable to the Russian government in the current geopolitical context. Clearly, the consequence of Russia reverting to Europe away from the East would entail accommodating to Western interests, including the expansion of NATO to the Western borders of Russia. It would also entail Russia bowing to a number of demands presently under negotiation within the so-called 'Minsk Agreements' conducted by four powers—Ukraine, France, Germany and Russia: to find a settlement between different forces in Ukraine and possibly the return of Crimea to Ukraine, which Russia annexed after a referendum in March 2014. Moreover, with the unfolding of developments in Syria and Russia's military support for the Syrian government, a change in Russia's strategic plans and cooperation with Asian countries would also have implications for her foreign relations in the Middle East and beyond, i.e. in Asia and North Africa. In respect to such issues, opposing, rightly or wrongly, the turn to the East mirrors Western interests, leaving little room for a more pragmatic search for compromise on thorny issues and policies at home.

Opposite to liberal views, well-known foreign policy experts close to the Russian government such as Fyodor Lukyanov, Sergey Karaganov and Oleg Barabanov argue in favour of Russia's turn to the East, and China in particular (Lukyanov 2015a, b; Karaganov 2016a; Barabanov and Bordachev 2012). Dmitri Trenin's approach, based on a deep knowledge not only of Russian but also of Western policies and goals, is similar. Fyodor Lukyanov, editor-in-chief of Russia in Global Affairs, chairman of the Presidium of the Council on Foreign and Defense Policy and research director of the Valdai International Discussion Club; Sergey Karaganov, honorary chairman of the Presidium of the Council on Foreign and Defense Policy and dean of the School of World Economics and World Politics at the National Research University–Higher School of Economics; Oleg Barabanov, head of Department of EU Politics at the MGIMO-University and professor at the School of World Economics and Global Politics of the National Research University–Higher School of Economics and senior research fellow at the Valdai Club Foundation; Dmitri Trenin, Director of the Carnegie Endowment Centre in Moscow, a regional affiliate of the US-based Carnegie Endowment for International Peace (before joining Carnegie some twenty years ago, Trenin served in the Soviet army and Russian ground forces for 21 years and retired as a colonel: he has a long experience conducting research abroad before being appointed director of the Moscow Carnegie Centre).

Moving from a pragmatic approach to Russia's strategies, they do not conceal the difficulties that changing partnerships would carry along in the absence of adequate administrative measures in bordering territories (Malle 2014). Their advice is not always taken on board, as it happened with the idea of a second capital in the East to better coordinate with regional authorities. Despite the Kremlin's dismissal of this option, the need for more autonomy was understood, facilitating the creation of semi-autonomous territorial organizations (Territories of Accelerated Development—TORs). This idea led to broader autonomy for the Ministry for the Far East compared to the former agencies in charge. Foreign policy experts try to assess Russia's relative strengths and weaknesses in comparison to China. It is not clear how relevant their advice is in shaping Russia's strategies, but it is unlikely the government does not take note. Lukyanov criticizes the policy of containment pursued by the United States vis-à-vis both China and Russia as the main cause of strategic reversals. Similarly Vasiliy Kashin, expert on China and the Chinese military at the 'Centre of Analysis of Strategies and Technologies' (CAST) argues that by waging an economic war against Russia, accompanied by the ousting of Russia from the G8 and the use of sanctions, Western powers impaired any chance of a Russian partnership with Europe, thereby favouring the expansion of Russia's ties in East Asia (Kashin 2014a). For Russian foreign policy experts it would be naïve to expect that Russia will revert to former alliances under the current circumstances, regardless of the duration of economic sanctions and European efforts to broker a joint agreement on Ukraine's separatist regions. They predict long-standing antagonism with the West.

Sergey Karaganov, while critical of the lack of reforms that turned the country into a rent-seeking economy, supports Russia's (costly) action in Ukraine and Moscow's direct involvement in Syria. He also believes that China is ready to invest in Russia when economic growth resumes. "China is turning into a first-tier superpower and may well become number one in the world in terms of aggregate power during the next decade". However, Russia's military strength will prevent domination by China (Karaganov 2016b, c). Owing to his long working experience abroad, the above-mentioned Trenin deserves special attention. Trenin takes into account Russian and Chinese security perceptions in the light of both US foreign policy and the different trajectories of the two countries. While China needs Russia as a fellow non-Western partner and a provider of raw materials, in support of her overall growth and strategy reclaiming what is referred to as a "rightful place in the world", Russia's needs to strengthen her role as a second-tier player in a globalized world. Adopting a defensive strategy, Russia does not try to control other countries, but struggles not to fall prey of dominant players, i.e. the US and China. Before waking up to the importance of China in the aftermath of the 2008–09 global crisis and before the crisis in Ukraine, Russia was relaxed about NATO and "adamant that the alliance should not engage further to the east (of Europe)…and not deploy weapon systems in Europe" (Trenin 2012). Subsequently from 2014, Russia's pivot to Asia that predated the Ukrainian crisis has become more pronounced. Relations with China have turned from a marriage of convenience into a much closer partnership and cooperation on energy, infrastructure and defense. But, contrary to Karaganov's confidence in the future of Sino-Russian relations, Trenin warns about the negative effects of nationalism on the rise not just in Russia but also in China (Trenin 2015a). Interestingly,

Kashin also points to rising nationalism in China, but he interprets this development as a socially cohesive factor that will help the economy to withstand penetration from the West. Nationalism will militate against intrigues aiming at regime change and strengthen military capacity on land and sea (Kashin 2015a, b). It is too early to speculate about the controversial effects of autochthonous nationalism on Sino-Russian relations. But one cannot ignore this development.

Nationalist movements are not very well organized in Russia, although their presence is nonetheless visible. Interestingly, their approach to Russia's turn to the East diverges more from the one of foreign policy experts than the one from liberals. Nationalist political groups and politicians who for some time have been practically without influence (although still vocal in the media) are worth of attention since, like in China, they have strong potential to increase their influence and impact. Among them, there are fervid nationalists on the far right anchored to traditional values and self-propelled patriotism. Hard line patriots observe new strategies with a mix of suspicion and apprehension (Khramchikhin 2015; Manifesto of Nationalists 2014; Dugin 2005).[4] They fear that China may exploit Russia's weaknesses letting her bear the costs of economic deals. Some speculate that over the long term difficulties and conflicts will be overcome while bilateral business ties will create mutually beneficial opportunities (Bordachev 2015). Some nationalists are idealists, others are pragmatic. Ideology is used to stress Russia's unique values and question cross-country cultural compatibility. From a pragmatic point of view, common to the military, the risks of tighter partnership is China's supremacy (Ivashov 2016; Zabelina 2015; Fenenko 2015).[5] China could condition Russian policy not only with regard to the Asian continent, but also Eurasia, which should from a Russian perspective remain under Russia's control (Ingram 2001).[6] This is not the position of the Russian authorities despite claims to the contrary abroad (Krickovic 2014). There was no illusion in Russia that the FSU (Former Soviet Union) would resuscitate, when Russian authorities worked through a series of agreements and compromises to define the pillars of the EAEU (Eurasian Economic Union), an economic community also aimed at stabilizing Russia's borders. The Eurasian Union, a supranational body that entered into force on 1 January 2015 comprises Belarus, Kazakhstan, Armenia, Kyrgyzstan and Russia. Its development went through internal and exogenous strains all through many procedural steps and particularly after 2008 when detailed schedules of economic integration were approved. So far

[4]Aleksandr Khramchikhin, deputy director of the Institute of political and military analysis stresses that compared to an irresolute China, India would be a better ally. A nationalist manifesto warns against China's takeover of the Far East and well-known nationalist Aleksandr Dugin warns that China could become a serious competitor to Russia.

[5]Zabelina notes that China's interest in investing in Russia collapsed after the developments in Ukraine; Fenenko A. claims that close relations with China could create problems for Russia's other partnerships in Asia.

[6]The most forceful description of the dangers to Russia of an Eurasian space subtracted from Russian control is that of philosopher Aleksandr I. Dugin, a hard core Russian nationalist (by some in Russia referred to as fascist).

there is little doubt that Russia is bearing the costs of that union as opposed to economically benefitting from it (Dragneva and Wolczuk 2013). Nonetheless, the geographical area it comprises is of primary importance for Russian security, especially in the light of fighting in the Middle East and risks of expanding terrorism. The EAEU's membership may not expand in a foreseeable future, but will resist outside pressure to dismember. As will be discussed further below, China will have to take the existence and interests of the Eurasian Union into account when threading for a new Silk Road through the region.

Finally, as regards Eastern strategies, the government and its agencies assume an important role. Among the most tormented are the economic ministries—the Ministry of Finance (MOF) and the ministry of economic development (MED)—ministries which are pulled to all sides to deliver 'according to needs' rather than budget revenues. Both agencies are accused of resisting presidential policies for the Far East—defined as priorities in the above-mentioned 2012 Presidential Edicts. Most often under attack from a diverse or opposite approach is finance minister Siluanov whose main concern is to maintain control over fiscal balances and the sovereign stabilization funds (TASS 2016).[7] The Ministry of Economic Development having transferred planning for the Far East to the competent Ministry still checks its spending while trying to avoid interregional feuds for funds. The Ministry of the Far East, on the other hand, needs to prove to be a vital and parsimonious agency capable of delivering results against the background of increasingly scarce resources. The ministry is urged to improve the business environment by streamlining regulatory procedures, create incentives for investment and attract investors from abroad, in particular from China. Its tasks are demanding. All projects are based on public-private partnerships, in which the share of private businesses is expected to be bigger than that of the state. Expected revenues to the federal budget from each particular investment must be provided for. While the initial steps have been difficult, the Ministry of the Far East seems to have been able to increase its capacities and the respect it enjoys in Russian politics.

4 Modernisation of Russia's Far East: The Institutional Approach

Given the backwardness of the territory bordering China, preferential investment conditions were envisaged with the establishment of 'Territories of Accelerated Socio-economic Development' (TORs) that entered into force in 2015.[8]

---

[7]Rumours that Siluanov will exit the party of power, United Russia whose congress at the beginning of 2016—the year of Duma elections—militated for higher social spending, may not be accidental.

[8]This section borrows from Malle (2014) Militant Russia Moving to the East, Il Politico, LXXIX (3), pp. 15–40.

The approach to TORs bears a non-coincidental resemblance to the successful Chinese foreign investment districts promoted in the 1990s (OECD 2002). Experience of APR countries has also been taken into account. TORs are expected to foster export-aimed production. The project was backed by only 42 billion rubles from the Federal Budget based on the understanding that the TORs's privileged status would be able to attract investment amounting up to 2.5 trillion rubles. Despite Moscow's skepticism, Galushka managed to get approval for preferential treatment of Far East investment: a 10% profit tax like in South Korea, electricity cost equal to that of the US per unit of consumption, building license obtained within 26 days like in Singapore (Ministry of the Far East, slide 9 2014). To pre-empt interference from supervisory bodies and put the premises for capital acquisition in place, a so-called 'shareholding managing company' with 100% of shares owned by the Russian Federation and/or its subsidiaries was instituted. Equities can now be listed and exchanged in the market. Individual entrepreneurs submit their application for investment in any TOR to this agency. The agency has the right to negotiate the provision of municipal services to TORs at a discount. The Ministry for the Far East remains in charge of deliberating on, and assigning real estate to industrial purposes. Expropriation is mandatory, only prices may be contested in court. Deadlines are fixed for issuing licenses and responding to applications (Sherbakov 2014; Law on TORs 2014). The assignment of small plots of land free of charge to Russian citizens with the requirement that it should be productively exploited, as well as conditional leasing of land to domestic and foreign production entities have been worked out. The relevant provisions are submitted to the Duma for approval (RG 2016a). How effective such regulations can be is a question that probably only time can answer. Opposition from federal bodies and vested interests is high (Kremlin 2014; FINMARKET 2014). Nonetheless, a new dynamism has been put in place the results of which are slow to materialize in the short-term despite targeted institutional changes. In the medium-term a more complicated picture emerges with an uneven balance of challenges and opportunities whose outcome is still uncertain. When plans for the accelerated development of the Far East were approved, Russia's GDP rate of growth and the economic outlook were positive. However, after the 3.4% growth in 2012 the outlook rapidly deteriorated to 1.3 (2013), 0.6 (2014) to then turn even negative in 2015 (−3.7). The World Economic Outlook does not bode well for China whose economy has been projected to grow in the near future at roughly half the rate of growth of 2010 (IMF 2016).[9] Russia's trade and investment expectations vis-à-vis China are bound to suffer. While Chinese exports remain by and large competitive, total

[9]The IMF Economic Outlook trims growth rates for the world economy to 3.4 (2016) and 3.6% (2017) with a more negative outlook for the emerging market economies.

imports have been rapidly falling (Barclays 2015, Bloomberg 2015a, b and China National Statistics 2016).[10] One could speculate on the intuitively positive impact for EMEs (Emerging Market Economies) of the fall in oil and commodities prices bringing about a rise in purchasing power, better current account balances and more room for accommodative policies thanks to lower inflation. But unless the world economy recovers, it is unlikely that either Russia may benefit from a comparatively higher demand for energy and other raw materials, or China recovers from the impact of the speculative capital outflow to the US and from own systemic problems.

In a longer perspective, one needs to take into account the effects of a regime of import substitution forced from 2014 on Russian producers through sanctions from abroad and security-linked embargoes and/or restrictions introduced by Russia. Whether under such a regime plans for a so-called 'competitive' Russian Far East will retain their special status is doubtful, as fight for access to state resources are on the increase in the country. Nonetheless, in the light of negotiations and agreements to date, stimulated in part by containment policies by the US and their allies against both China and Russia, bilateral cooperation could receive an unexpected impulse. As far as the economy is concerned, the policy of containment was reflected in two maxi Free Trade Area agreements initially meant to economically marginalize both Russia and China. Such agreements may not be pursued in the foreseeable future, due both to changes of US global trade policies and due to reservations by many actors in the respective regions.[11] There were obviously broader confrontational political strategies underlying such developments of which both Russia and China are perfectly aware (Karaganov 2016b; Fenenko 2016; Medvedev 2016; Goldstein 2014; Lee 2015).[12]

[10]Barclays' data refer to projections published on 13 January, 2015. Chinese official statistics indicate that while exports fell 1.8% imports decreased by 13.2% in 2015.

[11]The two agreements, both propelled by the US, are the Trans-Pacific Free Trade Agreement (TPP-FTA), already signed with 12 nations around the Pacific (with a combined GDP of $28.5 trillion), and the Trans-Atlantic Trade and Investment Partnership (TA-TPP) to be negotiated with the EU. The TPP-FTA was from global: the countries which signed the agreement are: Singapore, Brunei, Vietnam, Malaysia, Japan, New Zealand on one side of the Pacific, Australia, Chile, Peru, Mexico and Canada on the other side of the Pacific. Neither South Korea nor India are members. Regarding the EU, negotiations with the US met strong reservations on the part of many countries.

[12]Both Karaganov and Fenenko argue that the stalemate between Russia and the US to date is much more dangerous than during the Cold War. Russia's Prime Minister echoed these sentiments with irritation about in his view Western irrational and repeated claims and policies against Russia at the 2016 Munich Security Conference.

5 Away from Europe Towards Asia: A Tortuous Path Against Western Containment Policies

Eastward strategies, as discussed above, have become a top priority for Moscow after the global financial turmoil and the Ukrainian crisis. Russia's strategic turn-around reveals both heightened security concerns and increasing focus on economic sovereignty. The need for economic sovereignty had been evoked by Putin after the adoption of Western sanctions in 2014. Sovereignty and independence are also prominent in Russia's new security strategy (Ukaz N. 683 2015; TASS 2015a). The approach to import-substitution is twofold as it entails (i) replacing foreign with domestic products in strategic areas of industry and agriculture and (ii) the search for alternative partnerships, primarily in Asia, to lessen dependence from the West in defence and other priority areas. From this perspective, Russia's turn to Asia is of a great significance and may durably effect not only the strategic allocation of resources, but also long standing partnerships in trade and investment and joint defence agreements, as noted by Russian and foreign experts (Karaganov 2013; Ivanter 2013; Inozemtsev 2014a, b, c; Sakhuja Vijay 2014; Fattibene 2015).[13] While the earlier idea of Russia bridging Europe with Asia seemed in the past feasible for the medium to long term for both the West and Russia, this idea is now all but dead (Trenin 2012; Malle and Cooper 2014).

Moving eastwards entails Russia turning away from Europe to give pre-eminence to Asian countries and China (Malle 2014). Many Asian countries manifested interest. The first free trade agreement in Asia—between Vietnam and the Eurasian Economic Union—was approved by the Russian government on 25 May 2015 (Izvestiya 2015a; Government 2015a). Rather than eastwards plus westwards, as conceived earlier, this is a continental shift in cooperation and investment of dramatic dimensions for Russia's EU partners (Ria.ru 2016a).[14] Putin and Xi Jinping standing side by side at the 9 May 2015 Moscow parade for the celebration of victory in World War II with the glaring absence of all Western leaders and/or high-level representative officials is a striking image of currently ongoing changing foreign relations and global power constellations. According to a Chinese expert, this is a reaction to containment strategies adopted by the US, their disrespect of other countries' sovereignty and NATO's expansion to Eastern Europe (Li 2013; Trenin 2015b).[15] The participation of Xi Jinping, along with other representatives from G20 countries, to the ceremonies in Moscow showed the end of Western powers' dominance (Kirillov 2015). The joint declaration signed in

[13]Today's "Asia is a continent looking to the future like no other", concludes Inozemtsev.

[14]There are several estimates of the costs to EU member countries of import-substitution. Estimates cover both the cost of foregone exports and the number of jobs lost. By the end of 2015 these losses amounted for Germany to about €30 billion and half a million jobs; for Italy €16.3 billion and 300,000 jobs. Comparatively less wealthy economies, such as Poland, also suffered with an estimated loss of €5.4 billion and 303,000 jobs.

[15]"Sino-Russo Entente is more than an Axis of Convenience" was what Trenin called it.

Moscow at the time underlines that: "States should respect each other's sovereignty, independence and territorial integrity, choice of social and political structure and ways of development. Interference in the internal affairs of the state and imposition of other parties' will is unacceptable. We express our rejection of attempts at regime change from the outside, and administration and the imposition of unilateral sanctions on the basis of national legislation of individual states" (TASS 2015b).

While there is room for more imaginative narratives (Kaplan 2016)[16] not discussed here, the antagonistic crescendo from the West should be traced back before events in Ukraine 2014. One is the condemnation of the Eurasian Customs Union (ECU) as an alleged revanchist attempt to recreate the Soviet Union, for which no evidence was ever provided (Krickovic 2014).[17] Another is the ostensible disinclination to attend the Sochi Olympics by most Western leaders before the ousting of Ukraine's legitimate government. Finally, NATO's maneuvering against the Eurasian integration project can hardly be separated from the logic of containment described above (Mukhin 2014). This logic, as noted by Kissinger, has replaced diplomatic networking and skillful negotiations that marked decades of peaceful post II World War period helping China to develop into a market economy, millions of people to escape poverty and malnutrition and finally bringing the Cold War with Russia to an end (Kissinger 2014).

To put Russia's integration policies in perspective, one should compare them with regional economic integration pursued by many countries earlier, starting with the EU in the late fifties. The US concluded NAFTA with its neighbors Canada and Mexico in 1994: a less stringent, but also politically-orientated agreement linked to the entry of Mexico in the OECD. Mercosur is also an economic integration project still incomplete after decades of interstate negotiations. The ECU (Eurasian Customs Union) project was largely based on the EU model and regulatory framework. The Eurasian Union (EAEU) is a supranational entity with equal rights for all members. Decisions are taken by consensus at the Highest Council body (Treaty 2014). To date there is no sign that Russia prevailed over other members' interests, including the accession of Armenia and Kyrgyzstan that was reached after laborious negotiations with the existing ECU partners. On the other hand, occasional nationalist overtones in Moscow causing eyebrows to rise should also be put in perspective. First, they are milder than in other EMEs (Emerging Market Economies) among which the NATO member Turkey stands out nowadays as a disquieting Western partner. Secondly, patriotic exuberance may simply reflect pride for robust economic growth during most of 2000s. Economic growth and improvement of welfare were practically achieved by Russia on her own, after a decade of pains from systemic change that heroic, but unprepared, young leaders carried under pressure from the international community and its major international

[16]For Kaplan, containment is "also about engaging in calculated aggression and consistently reassuring allies".

[17]Krickovich provides evidence to the contrary.

organizations. Oil prices mattered for growth, but policies were crucial for welfare. Both the Sochi Olympics and ECU (Eurasian Customs Union) initiatives had been conceived at the time of high GDP growth before the 2008–09 crisis. Steps to strengthen the ECU (limited to Russia, Belarus and Kazakhstan until mid-2014) were gradually undertaken in the aftermath of the crisis by a laborious process of tightening regulations on trade, technical/sanitary product specifications and compromises on customs' barriers and transit. Enlarging the association to poor partners such as Kyrgyzstan and Tajikistan was too costly and postponed to better times, as explicitly reiterated by the authorities in charge of ECU, instead of rushing to implement an allegedly expansionist strategy. The whole process of Eurasian Integration, originally proposed by Nazarbaev in the early 1990s, was slow, marred by stop and go, difficulties in negotiating with weaker but demanding partners and eventually also very costly for Russia.

A coveted potential member of the EAEU (Eurasian Economic Union) was Ukraine with which Russia has strong economic and commercial relations. But Ukraine, despite a number of promises and privileges from Russia declined the offer after anti-government protests erupted in 2013. Unrest in Western Ukraine unleashed the breakdown of government structures and separatist movements in South-Eastern industrialized regions linked to Russia along the ancient Ukrainian West- East civilization fracture. Russia did not expect the burst of pro—EU passions in Kiev. Improvised opposition leaders were hailed by high profile European politicians standing arm in arm against the legitimate government. These developments occurred after the EU had repeatedly fended off Ukraine's demands for membership (Dragneva and Wolczuk 2013). In return, Russia's swift annexation of Crimea backed by a well-organized pro-Russia referendum (but also authentic enthusiasm among people in Russia and Crimea) fomented hopes in the Donbass that their territories, too, could split from Ukraine (Levada Centre 2014). While providing military and humanitarian assistance to the separatists, however, Russia refrained from direct military intervention. Russian analysts agree that the frozen armed conflict in south-eastern Ukraine may become a permanent source of tensions in Europe compelling Russia not to disengage from the region (Trenin 2015c; Ishchenko 2015; Karaganov 2015; Lukyanov 2014a). This chapter cannot discuss further developments in Ukraine. The consequence for Russia is that military expenditures will need to grow to assure stability at her western flank, and Crimea in particular, on the one hand, and the south-eastern borders in Asia (Vz.ru 2015a; Rg.ru 2016b).[18] The turn to Asia will become comparatively more costly while resources are shrinking. While economic and commercial interests were at the fore of Russia's earlier turn eastwards, security concerns are growing. Despite recurrent claims of Russian aggressiveness, her approach is defensive and attentive to the

[18]Russia has stationed a permanent battalion in Crimea, while, according to Security Chief Nikolai Patrushev, security concerns are mounting in the Artic.

potential of spontaneous or organized terrorism in Central Asia and Russia's southern regions (Malle 2013).

Containment policies have been counterproductive. On the one hand, organizations such as the CSTO (Collective Security Treaty Organisation) until now of minor relevance for defence, may develop faster in membership and tasks against the background of security concerns. On the other hand, such policies may help cement ties with China that is not exempted from similar preoccupations. While the EAEU may become an area of contention with China, a serendipitous outcome of containment against both Russia and China could enhance regional cooperation against potential intruders, or, at least more attention for attempts at regime change instigated from the outside. Both issues are discussed below.

6 Networking New Partnerships. The Narrow Scope for the EAU's Enlargement and Powers

Acrimonious relations with the EU and the US after the imposition of sanctions in 2014 have prompted Russia to speed up the enlargement of the Eurasian Union by striving to accommodate recurrent grievances from incumbent members.

Armenia joined Eurasian integration faster than other Central Asian partners. On 4 December 2014 the Armenian parliament approved entry into the EAEU knowing that the country will face a number of problems with integration, not having completed all the necessary formal steps for accession (with eight years of transition period accorded to fully adapt), and will have to bear the cost of no borders with the associated countries (TASS 2015c; Gazeta 2014a, b, 2015a). Thanks to a preferential lane for accession worked out by Russia, on 2 January 2015 Armenia formally acceded to the EAEU at an estimated cost of €5.2bn for the Russian budget due to a number of concessions including a conspicuous gas price rebate for cubic meter from $270 to $180 (Eurasian Commission 2015a, b; Gazeta 2015b; Izvestiya 2014).[19] From 1 February 2016 (by a decision taken mid-October 2015 in view of the proximate conclusion of Viktor Khristenko's mandate) Tigran Sarkisian, Prime Minister of the Republic of Armenia, was elected Chairman of the Council of the Eurasian Economic Commission (Kazinform 2016). That represented a victory for Russia against foreign pressures on Armenia to renounce accession to the EAEU. Fast track accession of Kyrgyzstan was simultaneously pursued by Russia. On 8 May 2015 at the meeting of the Supreme Eurasian economic Council, the Heads of State of the member countries signed a number of protocols relative to the accession of Kyrgyzstan to the Treaty on the EAEU. Amendments to the agreement on the EAEU and to selected international treaties pertaining to the Union were also signed. A protocol on conditions and transitional provisions for membership was

[19]Both the EU (as usual arriving later) and the US tried to deter Armenia from its association with the EAEU. The US also put pressure onto Armenia to join the sanctions imposed by the West.

drafted for approval by EAEU member countries (Interfax 2015a; Kommersant' 2015a). Among the thorny issues discussed by the council were migration, visa conditions and treatment of imports from China, although problems with sanitary requirements for agricultural products had also been raised (Kazinform 2015; Prime 2015). Presumably, like for Armenia earlier, Russia's security interests were determinant for accelerated Kyrgyzstan's membership (Tengrinews 2015).[20]

The accession of Tajikistan, subject to US concerns, looks more problematic (Ng.ru 2015).[21] The closing of the Manas airbase in Kyrgyzstan makes access to Tajikistan's airbases crucial for British and American military convoys (Ng.ru 2014). Political killings and unrest at the time of elections suggest that there can be efforts at regime change by a silenced opposition. President Rahmon remains a contested—and for many odious—figure (Newtimes 2015). But parliamentary elections have been held, marred by violations of electoral rules, and Rahmon's ruling party has won with a large majority (Rferl 2015). Russia may not distance herself from the standing powers under sparks of unrest, but will have to thread diplomatically between contrasting positions on joint defence also depending on the relative power of each country in Central Asia. A case in point is the contrast between Tajikistan and Kazakhstan. At the informal summit of the CIS nations that brought together the Heads of Belarus, Kazakhstan, Kyrgyzstan, Russia, Tajikistan, and Uzbekistan, Tajik President Rahmon called on his CIS counterparts to take immediate measures to strengthen the CIS southern borders and jointly address threats and challenges emanating from Afghanistan, "since the appearance of Islamic State militants pose threats to all in CIS" (News tj 2015; Rbth 2016). This call remained isolated. Earlier, Kazakhstan's President Nazarbaev, in the aftermath of annexation of Crimea, had made forcefully the point that the country will not cede its sovereignty to anyone (The Moscow Times 2014). The EAEU, indeed, has no military/security obligations towards its members. Nonetheless one cannot rule out that the threat of Islamic fundamentalists in the region may help coalesce around common security concerns Russia's more reticent allies. The fact that attack helicopters were sent to a Russian military base in Tajikistan immediately after clashes erupted at the Tajik-Afghan border in October 2015 may prelude to broader military plans and action against terrorist attacks in the region (Expert 2015a).

[20]Kazakhstan was not very supportive. A Kazakh expert compared the two countries to Greece in the EU.

[21]The US objects to Russia's intention of modernising the Tadjik army and see with suspicion its integration into the EAEU.

7 Moving Beyond the EAU: Economic Partnership with China

Russia's eastward turn has been met with scepticism in the West (Lo 2014; Galeotti 2015). Russian observers are as mentioned above critical (Inozemtsev 2014a, b; Karaganov 2013; Strokan 2015; Lukyanov 2015c; Gabuev 2015). Sceptical comments were raised on the gas deal with China as soon as it was announced. After the conclusion of the contract and the publication of some details, some scholars and observers focused on the apparently high price Russia was to pay for the deal. Projects concerning pipelines to be built from Far East to China also provoked acid comments. After the signing of the gas deal with China, the announcement that (a) Russia will halt gas supply to the EU through Ukraine from 2019, (b) will retreat from the never started South Stream project and (c) will shift to projects that became known as the Turkish Stream, which also produced a set of negative comments (Malle 2014; Lukyanov 2014b). Diversification out of Europe—though symmetrical with EU's efforts to minimise oil dependence from Russia—was met immediately with warnings by EU's officials that supply of gas from Turkey to Europe via Greece would not be viable and led to the EU's desperate search for alternative gas routes and allegedly reliable partners in Turkmenistan and Azerbaijan. Turbulence in the Middle East, where Russia engaged in the war on the side of the Syrian government, and problematic relations with Turkey raise strong doubts about the feasibility of the Turk Stream project. Another complication in this field is the project of building a second North Stream to Germany bypassing Ukraine (Vedomosti 2015a; Rbc 2016a; Utro 2016; Ng.ru 2016).[22] The analysis issues, explored by experts, however go beyond the scope of this chapter (Keun Wook Paik 2015).

Two remarks are instrumental to this chapter: (a) ex-ante, striking a 'take or pay' deal with China in May 2014 for an estimated total of $400 billion over 30 years at a price of $350 for thousand cubic meters of gas (Gazeta 2014a), possibly disadvantageous for Russia when factoring in the cost of new pipelines, was a major strategic breakthrough and (b) ex-post, on the score of hydrocarbons' falling price and an ambiguous EU energy strategy, the deal may prove to be crucial for the diversification of energy outlets towards fast growing Asia also increasing the negotiating power of Gazprom vis-à-vis other customers (Bradshaw 2014).[23] The gas deal between Russia and China represents a serious commitment to long-term cooperation. Both parties engage to take all steps necessary to bring the project into fruition and companies have started looking forward to further economic and commercial partnership. A $2 billion

[22] This project aroused contrasting sentiments and hopes as it was seen as a Russo-German initiative bypassing Ukraine. Italy protested, even if an important Italian company was indicated as a possible contributor to the construction. Finland instead welcomed the idea, while the EU, after some confusion on the issue, eventually gave its approval.

[23] According to Bradshaw, the current Russian energy strategy is to increase the volumes of oil and gas sold to the Asia-Pacific from 12% on total exports today to 23% by 2035.

credit from the Bank of China obtained by Gazprom in early 2016 for a period of five years seems to confirm this view (Oilcapital 2015; Mineral 2015; Levada Centre 2014; Rbc 2016b).[24] A number of other deals have followed and/or are in the pipeline despite persisting critical comments (Kaczmarski and Kardas 2015).[25] The most important are large infrastructural projects. Expensive projects need an adequate horizon. That of the gas deal—thirty years from now—can be taken as a benchmark. In the meantime a number of unforeseen difficulties may exert a negative impact. Geophysical obstacles, problems with financing and technical supervision may delay implementation as is already the case with new gas deposits. The following description is revealing. Gazprom's special and particularly skill-intensive seismic survey at Chayanda gas condensate field could be completed, beyond schedule, only by March 2015. Before laying down the pipelines the project entails that seven exploration wells are put in place with drilling of more than 15,000 m of rock. Deposits estimates need to be approved by the State Commission for Mineral Resources. Unsurprisingly while the construction of the Sila Sibiri gas route was inaugurated on 1st September 2014, it took Putin other eight months to ratify the project (Gazprom 2015a; Ngy 2015; Lenta 2015; Vz.ru 2014b). The original 2012 project's deadline for completion of the first 3.200 km tranche of Sila Sibiri—Yakutia, Khabarosvk, Vladivostok—was 2017. Three years later, 2018 or 2019 have been discussed as possible targets (Ampravda 2015; TASS 2015d; Eurodialogue 2015). Delays are inevitable and may even become longer. But there is no evidence to date that the project will be halted. Gas transport to China should become accessible from nearby Blagoveshchensk. This town is located 583 kilometres away from Khabarosvk that lies in the middle of the existing pipeline from Okha (Sakhalin) and Vladivostok (Gazprom 2015b; Sdela 2015). The capacity of Sila Sibiri is 38 billion m^3 per year with a potential of 64 billion m^3. However, while committing to collaborate with China, Moscow may also look beyond. Its three Far East pipelines—including Transneft-run Eastern Siberia-Pacific Ocean oil pipeline—could feed a LNG plant (that is under construction) with a volume of liquefied gas for Japan as well (Nikkei 2015).[26] With the falling oil price, Russia may also increase available oil supply to China. It will be up to China to select her suppliers. In 2014, with lower oil price offsetting part of transport cost from the Middle East, China's oil imports from

[24]Despite widespread skepticism the gas deal is being implemented. The first 15 km of Sila Sibiri pipelines have been laid down. Despite sanctions Gazprom seems to have a relatively easier access to funds in Asia. The population reacted altogether positively to the strengthening of Sino-Russian relations, while at the same time becoming more hostile against the EU and the US.

[25]From the above-cited meeting in Moscow, it was reported that the two countries intended to strengthen cooperation in the railways, banking, energy, innovation and industry sectors. China was invited to join gas exploration in the Artic and Sakhalin. Cooperation in the production of microelectronic components to be used for space projects by Glonass and Beidou and joint production of a large civilian helicopter were also discussed.

[26]Although interested, Japan remains concerned about Gazprom's lack of funding and commitment to the project.

Russia increased from 9 to 11% of total oil imports at the expense of Saudi Arabia's that fell by 8% (War and Peace 2015).

Among other long-term plans one of the most interesting is the high speed rail-link Beijing—Moscow through the Kazakhstan route, which could be subject to problematic regional geopolitical developments (Bloomberg 2015b).[27] China promised to finance the Moscow-Kazan section with $6 billion looking also to Chinese investors' interest (TASS 2015e, 2015f; Kommersant' 2015b). With the slowdown in the world economy badly affecting EMEs, work on the infrastructure may be delayed. A wave of worldwide currency wars from 2013 to 14 exacerbated exchange rate instability in both Russia and China instilling further uncertainty. Nonetheless, a number of cooperation agreements are reported to have been signed during the visit of Putin to Beijing, his 13th, on 2 September, 2015 (Kremlin 2015a, b). They deal with cooperation on energy (oil, coal and atomic stations) on the basis of the May 2014 Sino-Russian deal on gas supply, criteria for joint financing of the 1 trillion rubles estimated cost of the Moscow-Kazan high speed transport route scheduled for 2020 and joint ventures in aircraft and rocket/cosmic branches. During his visit some 30 agreements are reportedly to have been signed. A number of additional Sino-Russian deals were signed. SMEs on both sides start being active. In Primore some 31 contracts were signed for a total of $13.5 billion in 2015 adding to the large $2 billion deal relative to the Yamal LNG concluded between Novatek and the Silk Road Fund (Infoshos 2016a, b). This deal is of strategic importance for China. At present Yamal LNG's major shareholders are Novatek with 60% and CNPS (Chinese National Petroleum Corporation) and Total with a 20% share. With additional funding from the Silk Road Fund, the Chinese shareholding could surpass the 25% threshold formerly enshrined into Russia's provisions in such fields. Some 109 large scale projects are on the way in the Far East—some already completed, some still in the process—taking advantage of TORs. Investors are not only Chinese but also from Japan and South Korea. There are investments from Virgin Islands and Bahama—where Russian offshore companies are nested—but also from the US on shelf gas in Sakhalin. However, two trillion rubles promised by the government did not materialize (Lenta 2016b).

8 From Partnership to Competition, and Perhaps to Alliance? Challenges Ahead

Economic slowdown complicates the present picture and speculations about the future. Hopes to soon reach $100 billion in bilateral trade by 2015 remain improbable in the near future as well. Foreign trade fell by 27.8% to $64.2 billion in

[27]The original project was planned to take 10 years to be realised. 7.000 km of railways were estimated to cost $242 billion, cutting a ten days journey to only two. The cost of the Russian section to the border was estimated to be $60 billion.

2015 with Chinese exports falling comparatively more than Russia's (The Moscow Times 2016).[28] While exports from China, mostly manufactured goods, suffered from the fall in Russian disposable incomes, the need for resources remains robust in China. The volume of investment from China was also subdued compared to expectations: it amounted to $8.7 billion in the first half of 2015 (slightly higher than in the recent past), while Russian investment to China did not even amount to $1 billion (Minecom 2015a).

Both countries have a long way to go to even approach a modest degree of regional economic integration. While China's economic take off in the 1990s had been favoured by its booming coastal regions benefiting from trade and investment with wealthy investors and the Chinese diaspora in the region, the 4.000 km long Chinese-Russia separate the least developed areas in both countries. Focus on developing their respective backward territories will need decades to bring fruit. In the meantime, commercial ventures, which in principle could be mutually beneficial may turn against Russia, if competition from Chinese companies prevails. Chinese ability to rapidly learn and master advanced techniques is factored into any projection. Trutnev's citation of how a Chinese company operated, a short time before construction could be completed on the side of the Russian counterpart, in order to get hold of precious metals put by Russians as collateral against breach of the contract, shows that mutual trust is still largely absent (Lenta 2016b).[29]

Another case in point, regarding competition versus partnership, is aviation where Russia is still clearly more competitive. Against Russian hopes to become a major exporter of civilian aircrafts to China, evidence shows that China could jump ahead taking advantage of learning by doing with Russia) to develop into an aircraft production maker herself (Expert 2015b; Sputnik 2015a, b; China Daily 2015a).[30] The Chinese model of growth, earlier exploited by Japan and South Korea, is indeed, based on strong motivations to master foreign know-how and develop independent production. China may easily turn from partner into competitor and eventually a winner taking into accounts her comparably favourable manufacturing skills, wealth and demography. Some in Moscow are afraid that Russia will be subjugated sooner than later also because of immigration from China (Mir-politika 2015a, b).[31] Eventually, however, the authorities are less concerned and prone to expand economic relations despite cultural gaps. On the one side, Russian businessmen are deterred by a business culture they do not understand and by poor

[28]Chinese exports fell by 34.4 and Russian exports by 19.1% respectively.

[29]In the end, the Russian party rushed to meet the deadlines under pressure from Russian authorities not to breach contractual provisions.

[30]Bilateral negotiations from 2014 aimed at delivering a few years SSJ 100 aircraft worth a total of $3 billion to China and Southeast Asia. Russia hoped this agreement would help maximize capacity utilization of the Komsomol'sk-na-Amure plant, where SSJ are manufactured. However, the final agreement signed on 8 May, 2015 includes a joint leasing company located in China where works on repair/components will be carried out, possibly leading in a not so distant future to the development of a Chinese civilian aviation manufacturing plant.

[31]There are reportedly 250.000 Chinese migrate to come to Russia along the borders with China.

information regarding the Chinese market. On the other side, Chinese get often lost in Russia's bureaucratic procedures and tax regulations. Nonetheless, joint projects in the car industry, woodworking, construction, extraction industry and infrastructure are slowly taking place. Investment plans may clash against unexpected obstacles: for instance smelting of ferromanganese alloys of Krasnoyarsk started long after initial projects, after winning over ecological concerns. Using the local currencies makes commercial deals easier in border regions (Ria.ru 2015). Currency swaps are also taking place to finance major projects, such as energy deals and trade (War and Peace 2015). However, according to Viktor Danilov- Danil'yan, director of the Institute of Water Problems of Russian Academy of Sciences, cooperation with China may succeed only if Russia grasps China's weaknesses and possible odds in working together (ria.ru 2014) (Expert 2015c). At the current stage, indeed, the two countries are inspecting each other with a mix of curiosity and wariness (Ng 2015).[32]

Negotiations and projects are on the way also in the military field—on different levels—raising the issues of whether defence structures could develop hand in hand with progress in the economic partnership. While it is far too early to envisage a full-fledged alliance between the two countries, it would be unwise to outright reject the idea that, under the impulse of confrontational policies from the West, a broader strategic approach develops channelling competition and rivalry towards mutually beneficial cooperative action. According to Feng Shaolei, Director of the Centre for Russian Studies at Chinese the Ministry of Education, Sino-Russian cooperation should help in achieving a balanced stance, as advocated by Henry Kissinger, to maintain mutual respect and tolerance during dramatic changes the countries are undergoing. While conceding that transition countries still look to Western economies for inspiration, his remark that "It is clear that the West does not have moral superiority, and that its priority in each area is, to varying degrees, sharply or slowly changing" (Feng Shaolei 2015)[33] sounds more definitive than the occasional finger pointing towards the West by Russians. Fu Ying, chairman of the Foreign Affairs Committee of the China's National People's Congress, notes that (against US' wishes) the Renminbi was finally included into the IMF system of special drawing rights of the and institutions such as the Asian Infrastructure Investment Bank initiated by China "will compensate for the inadequacy of the existing international mechanism" (Fu 2016). From a different perspective, Kashin points to common interests in defence against indiscriminate Western action aimed at regime change. He rules out that Russia could succumb to China, on the ground of the latter's dependence on Russian advanced military technology and weaponry. China will, indeed, sustain Russia's high tech defence industry (aircraft and submarines in particular) for quite a while. Moreover, after losing more than $16 billion in

[32]China sent a mission from the National Statistical Office to Russia to study the economic situation from Rosstat's statistics and get acquainted with different methodologies.

[33]Feng Shaolei is also the Dean of the School of Advanced International and Regional Studies at East China Normal University in Shanghai.

investment from war in Libya, China is now well placed to discriminate among the pros and cons of existing alliances (Kashin 2014, 2016).[34] In fact, despite military-to-military dialogue and exchanges agreed with the US, sentiments in China towards the US remain cool, as reflected in the assertion that "Beijing has more ways to respond than before when the US tries to hamper China's legal interests" (China Daily 2015b).

Developments in military cooperation reflect traditional prudence and separate concerns (Ivanov 1994).[35] There are, however, signs of change. In May 2014, Russia and China agreed to expand cooperation in security, as well as in the military-technical fields (Security Committee 2015). Beijing expressed its interest in Moscow's aircraft technologies—engines, avionics, and missile air-based weapons (Vz.ru 2014a, Business insider 2015; Kommersant' 2015c).[36] If successfully pursued, access to Russian weaponry may help strengthening China's military capacity faster than expected (ISN 2015). One may also note the acceleration and expansion of joint military exercises. The presence of Fan Chanlun, Deputy Head of the Chinese Central Military Council at the Victory Parade in Moscow on 9 May 2014 gave the opportunity to Russian Minister of Defence Sergey Shoigu to stress the strategic character of Russian-Sino intergovernmental relations. Joint naval exercises, carried out in the Pacific from 2012, took place for the first time in the Mediterranean on 17–21 May 2015 (TASS 2015g; Vz 2015b).

Russia has many arenas for policy dialogue on defence and security cooperation in Asia: the CSTO ('Collective Security Treaty Organisation' among Russia, Armenia, Belarus, Kazakhstan, Kyrgyzstan and Tajikistan), (Periscope 2016a, b; kremlin.ru)[37] and the 'Shanghai Cooperation Organisation' (SCO) with China and other Central Asian countries. Russia may be invited to become a member of the Common ASEAN Community (Association of South-East Asia) created at the meeting of the ASEAN group in Kuala Lumpur in November 2015 (Ria.ru 2015;

[34]According to Kashin the current revision of the model of growth in China towards less dependence on foreign markets, more concerns for income fairness and dramatic changes in the approach to foreign policy will weaken China's potential dominance in the future.

[35]As noted by Ivanov in the early 1990s "The Asia-Pacific region is an area of possible cooperation, as well as conflict between Russia and China".

[36]Kostantin Sivkov, first deputy Head of the Academy of Geopolitical problems, noted that China was particularly interested in missiles type 'Kalibr' (high precision rockets recently used in Syria—author's note) and reportedly quietest submarines launched by Russia in 2015. A $2 billion contract for the supply of Su-35 aircraft was signed in November 2015.

[37]The CSTO has formed groups of regional and interregional armies, up to 20,000 men, which includes 5000 military and 10 battalions, aircrafts and helicopters. Exercises take place regularly to raise the standards up to NATO—Allied Rapid reaction Corps. Mobilisation plans were among the principal matters of discussion at the CSTO meeting in Moscow on 15 September 2015.

Izvestiya 2015b).[38] This group may also develop some forms of military cooperation in the future. A meeting of the Ministers of Defence of the member countries, with the participation a Russian Delegation, took place in February 2016 (Military 2016)[39] From this point of view, Russia is better placed than China in threading defence alliances. However, the SCO may fast develop into a more important organization for both China and Russia on security matters. Indeed, with the participation of Afghanistan in the Shanghai organisation as an observer from 2012, attention is increasingly focused on joint measures against terrorism (SCO 2014; Infoshos 2015).[40] Moreover, ties are developing between the CSTO and China. The issue of a possible merger between the CSTO and the SCO was raised at the SCO Dushanbe meeting in June 2014. Military drills with China and other non-Asian CSTO members were planned by CSTO in 2015 (CACI Analyst 2014; Sputnik 2014, 2015a). At the CSTO summit in September 2015 in Dushanbe, together with the approval of the CSTO's budget, cooperation was agreed among members regarding the transit of military formations and military goods; readiness inspections for carrying out the 'Collective Rapid Reaction Forces' objectives, their composition and deployment (Kremlin 2015a). Measures to secure oil pipelines through the region are also being discussed. (Infoshos 2016c). All these measures involve participation and agreement by the EAEU and CSTO member countries. Putin's unexpected proposal of building a Free Trade Area (FTA) with China at the Victory Parade May 2014 where Chinese and Indian contingents marched together with Russian armies was probably launched with a view to Eurasia and its increasingly crowded economic space.

9 Joint or Competing Projects in Eurasia?

Chinese plans to revive the Silk Road from Asia to Europe underpin Putin's FTA proposals. In December 2014, before facing a sharp economic slowdown and an incipient financial crisis, China instituted a Silk Road Fund worth $40 billion to back infrastructural projects, primarily in transport, for a total of $371 billion envisioned to be financed by private investors (Silkroadfund 2015; Expert 2015d). The opportunity of linking Eurasia's economic integration with the Silk Road project was promptly seized by foreign policy experts and officials afraid of foreseeable unrest and conflict in Central Asia (Periscope 2016a). Economic

[38]Members of the Shanghai Organisation for Cooperation are Russia, China, Kazakhstan, Kyrgyzstan Tajikistan, and Uzbekistan. Observers status have Afghanistan, India, Iran, Mongolia and Pakistan. Members of the ASEAN are Brunei, Vietnam, Indonesia, Cambodia, Laos, Malaysia, Myanmar, Singapore, Thailand and Philippines.

[39]The discussion focused on stability and security cooperation in the region, including cooperation in combating terrorism.

[40]Officially, the SCO is considered as a preferential arena for policy, rather than economic, dialogue.

cooperation together with security plans will need the shaping of a broader strategic approach in/with Asia, which cannot be taken for granted. A FTA with China could serve this purpose, but interests do not fully coincide. The 'Silk Road' project is pursued by China in the aim of deepening its economic expansion to Central Asia while at the same time looking towards Europe. It would need policy dialogue with some EAEU member countries. Putin stressed that a FTA would imply a common economic space on the continent. China's penetration in Central Asia with little or no dialogue with Russia would cause bilateral potential strains. While bilateral agreements with central Asian countries suit China, for Russia the EAEU provides a less risky arena for policy dialogue. However, even if the highest EAEU bodies promote framework meetings, specialized EAEU structures/working groups would be needed to negotiate operational details. China has already established a specialized agency (Eurasian Commission 2015a; Bordachev 2015).[41] Rushing not to be left behind, the EAEU managed to convene the first meeting of a joint working group on infrastructure for the Silk Road in February 2016 at the 'Eurasian Economic Commission' (Izvestiya 2016).[42]

To date there are few relevant initiatives indicating that actual cooperation has started. Igor' Shuvalov, first Deputy Premier, and Chinese deputy premier Zhan Gao Li are in charge of a commission dealing with joint projects, out of which 58 have already reportedly been agreed. While the construction of high speed Moscow Kazan track appears to be making good progress, the participation of China of the modernization of the BAM and Transib as well as port infrastructure is still under negotiation (Minecom 2015b). Progress is slow indicating different interests. While China, on its way to Europe, networks separately with a number of countries, Russia starts looking beyond China to reach other partners in Asia. Both the Silk Road and the FTA with China sound fanciful in the present context. The Silk Road project is at its very beginning and the effective route has not yet been decided. China is also mulling the idea of a revised Maritime Silk Road that would help her economic expansion into the ASEAN (Tiezzi 2014; Diplomat 2015). Critical comments have been raised from a number of opinion makers. Trying to link EAEU with China's Silk Road does not make sense to Inomentzev, first because China's merchandise transport by sea is more advantageous, and second, because Chinese investments in Kazakhstan, Turkmenistan and Uzbekistan are already ten times bigger than in Russia, showing that the latter's comparative disadvantages are overwhelming. Contrary to hopes, the 'Silk Road' may turn into a strong competitor of the EAEU, all the more so that any route circumventing Russia would be shorter and cheaper (Inozemtsev 2015). Why China would engage on a land-based route when more capacity for cargoes by the less expensive maritime route is available disconcerts Kashin too. His view is that the 'Silk Road' is a costly reserve

[41]A joint statement on the start of negotiations for an Agreement on Trade and Cooperation between China and the EAEU was signed in May 2015.

[42]As reported by Dmitri Pankin, the head of Eurasian Investment Bank.

route for China if maritime transit problems arise (Kashin 2015a).[43] The issue for China is neither ideological nor political but instead strategic. Thus, Russia should not disengage but rather seek its own benefits by linking with other partners in Asia (Kashin 2015b). Finally, terrorist attacks and high transit costs from crossing several customs borders must be factored in if the route to Europe circumvents Russia. Maritime routes are not becoming safer either in the light of insecure transit through Malacca and the Suez Canal, both exposed to risk arising from bloody conflicts in the region. Contrary to Kashin's arguments, hard line nationalists boast against China's self-concerned strategy and implicit support of forces hostile to Russia (Popov 2016).

Despite the apparently eccentric character of Sino-Russian integration projects, a FTA framework cooperation agreement remains attractive for Chinese state-supported investors. Russian officials argue that a trade and cooperation agreement between the 'Eurasian Economic Commission' and China would make trade flows more transparent facilitating the establishment of a FTA in the future (Vedomosti 2015b; TASS 2015h). This approach is incorporated into government economic guidelines to 2018, which prioritize APR export- orientated projects. The hope is also that EAEU projects in Central Asia could benefit from the Silk Road Fund and the recently established Asian Bank for Investment in Infrastructure of which Russia is one of the major partners (Government 2015b). All in all, however, the FTA is not attainable before 2025-30 (Kommersant 2015d). In the long run, an even better option for Russia, according to Aleksandr' Knobel's estimates, would be to pursue a EAEU FTA with the SCO including China and India that could bring considerable trade benefits to Russia as well as other in Central Asia (Knobel 2016). What is at stake is long-term feasibility. Although ambitious and far-reaching, these plans seem to confirm Luk'yanov's view that "Both Russia and China are looking for ways to protect their own sovereignty from external influence and prevent political autarky to turn into economic autarky, for a liberal approach to internal development is precluded" (Lukyanov 2015d; Kashin 2014b).[44] Together, he predicts, Russia and China will win their fight against international isolation. A comprehensive economic and military partnership is not foreseeable in the short to medium term. Both Russia and China look beyond their joint partnership initiative. Russia looks to Japan and South Korea, and further to Vietnam and India in Asia, but also to other continents. China banks on ASEAN and Europe. The interests of Russia and China do not overlap, and may even diverge in time (Akopov 2015).[45] For some decades to come, however, both will focus on Asia. In a world of tumultuous changes, Europe and the US remain in the shade.

[43]60% of China's foreign trade is shipped through the Straits of Malacca (80% in case of Japan).

[44]Sharing Lukyanov's view, Kashin cites the memorandum of understanding on construction of a floating nuclear power station between Rosatom and the Chinese Atomic Energy Agency as a major breakthrough. Talks on that project have been suspended for two years.

[45]This is a nationalist view, calling for prudence in approaching China.

10 Conclusions

Russia is engaged in a process that is aimed to lead to 'economic sovereignty' and less dependence on Western markets. This process has been put in motion by what in Russia is perceived as containment policies pursued against both Russia and China by Western powers. Some chancelleries got alarmed by Russia's allegedly aggressive economic expansion in Eurasia and China's economic boom after its entry into the WTO in 2001. Both Russia and China started demanding more influence in the international arena than Western powers were prepared to grant. After the events in Ukraine, Western economic and political ostracism accused Russia of aggression, which in turn made Moscow look for alternative partnerships in the East. Russia applies a selective approach towards partnerships vis-à-vis Asia in an effort to find reliable partners. Before the exacerbation of confrontational East-West policies, Russia envisaged to bridge the East and West by fostering the development of Russia's Far East. Upgrading transport and logistics infrastructure was expected to attract foreign investors from both Europe and Asia. The current Russian strategy is focused on expanding ties with Asia by re-orienting trade and developing joint economic projects with a number of Asian countries, China in primis. The US in the meantime pursued free trade agreements with both Europe and a number of Asian countries-FTAs, which excluded both Russia and China. The draft agreements align economic strategies with defence strategies.

Against this background, Russia and China could be encouraged to deepen ties beyond economic, trade and investment. Indeed, such ties have been developing across the Eastern borders of Russia and are currently being negotiated in Central Asia. Both countries are networking with—and try to possibly attract into their sphere of influence—other Asian countries disturbed by what is often perceived as excessive pressure against domestic policies and governing structures. Regional organisations such as the CSTO and SCO so far inoffensive and by and large without real power, may evolve into better equipped defensive alliances. Russia's abrupt turn from Europe to Asia needs to be sustained by appropriate strategies. Territories of accelerated development (TORy) enjoying fiscal and business privileges have been designed and gradually put in place in Russia's Far East in the hope of attracting foreign investment and joint ventures. While there is interest, activity is slow to get off the ground.

The global economic slowdown with repercussions in both Russia and China is not propitious to investment and growth. Experts are divided on enhanced Sino-Russian relations and, even within government not all agencies march in the same direction. Some fear a waste of resources under plans largely run by state authorities, others warn of the possible subjugation of Russia to wealthy China. A few look forward to the medium-long term to reap the benefits of economic cooperation. Nonetheless, steps to facilitate trade and joint ventures with China have already been taken, despite caveats at home and abroad. The most important is the diversification eastwards of gas and oil supply. This is carried out despite delays due to a number of geological, technical and financial obstacles. Many deals are in their early stages of memorandum of understandings or framework agreements. Progress is slow, but cooperation with China in transport, infrastructure, aviation, banking, innovation and industry is reported to be on the way. In neighbouring regions, SMEs start also trading and engaging in joint projects. Some military cooperation has also been taking place and advanced military aircraft sold to China. But more time is needed to assess how far this form of cooperation can go in the years ahead.

A Free Trade Area (FTA) has been proposed to China by Russia and is currently being discussed between high-level Russian and Chinese officials. The idea emerged when China evoked the revival of the ancient Silk Road along multimodal transport routes that include railways, motorways and their interconnections to facilitate merchandise exports to the European market. While in principle the Silk Road project backed by Chinese funding could also help the EAEU to develop and better integrate, Russian and Chinese interests may not coincide and diverge in time. China prefers to strike bilateral deals, Russia, on the other hand, is interested in preserving the Eurasian space under its control. The EAEU may turn into an area of conflicting pressures and economic competition if single members find cooperation with China more attractive.

While other Asian countries were expected to join the 5-member EAEU, the organization's appeal may decrease under alternative, comparatively advantageous, offers. A Silk Road that cuts off Russia may also cause further frictions. In proposing a Eurasian FTA with China, Russia may have wished to stem seeds of antagonism as soon as possible. A Russian FTA open only to other Asian countries could be seen by China as a potentially unfriendly competitive regional framework. Among the Pacific Asian countries, Vietnam has been the first to sign a FTA agreement with Russia. These developments will take time and some of the agreements could turn to be controversial or counterproductive if policy dialogue with China is not maintained. However, ceteris paribus, in the current geopolitical context the reasons for Sino-Russian cooperation are stronger than any disagreement regarding specific projects. In a long-term perspective, Moscow's partnership with China will need to be supported by a common approach to security and defence. A comprehensive alliance is not for tomorrow. Nonetheless, the perception of any new threat or effort to regime change can only reinforce this pursuit.

References

Akopov P (2015) Rossii i Kitaiu vygodno ostavat'sia 'parternami, no ne siuznikami', http://www.vz.ru/politics/2015/5/19/745927.print.html http://www.vz.ru/politics/2015/5/19/745927.html

Ampravda (2015) http://www.ampravda.ru/2014/12/26/054115.html

Barabanov O, Bordachev T (2012) Realism Instead of Utopia, Russian in Global Affairs, No. 4, http://eng.globalaffairs.ru/number/Realism-Instead-of-Utopia-15821

Barclays (2015) https://live.barcap.com/PRC/servlets/dv.search?contentPubID=FC2101617&bcllink=decode

Bloomberg (2015a) http://www.bloomberg.com/news/commodities/

Bloomberg (2015b) http://www.bloomberg.com/news/print/2015-01-22/china-russia-plan-242-billion-beijing-moscow-rail-link.html

Bordachev T (2015) New Eurasian momentum, Russia in Global Affairs, http://eng.globalaffairs.ru/number/New-Eurasian-Momentum-17886

Bradshaw M (2014) Russia's energy shift to the east: should Europe be worried, http://www.isn.ethz.ch/Digital-Library/Articles/Detail/?lng=en&id=184112

Business insider (2015) http://uk.businessinsider.com/kremlin-launched-quietest-submarine-in-the-world-2015-4?r=US&IR=T

CACI Analyst (2014) http://www.cacianalyst.org/publications/field-reports/item/12983-sco-csto-merger-raised-at-dushanbe-conference.htm accessed 4 June 2014

China Daily (2015a) http://www.chinadaily.com.cn/china/2015-05/11/content_20686619.htm

China Daily (2015b) http://www.chinadaily.com.cn/world/2015-06/15/content_21001723.htm

China National Statistics, http://www.stats.gov.cn/english/PressRelease/201601/t20160119_1306072.html

Diplomat (2015) http://thediplomat.com/2015/03/where-is-chinas-silk-road-actually-going/, respectively accessed 9 May 2014 and 30 March

Dugin' A (2005) Rossiya i Kitay: soyuzniki, partnery, konkurenty? Perspektivy sotrudnichestva, http://uchebnik-online.com/129/1614.html

Dragneva R, Kolczuk K (eds) (2013) Eurasian economic integration. Edward Elgar, Cheltenham (UK)-Northampton(MA USA)

Eurasian Commission (2015a) http://www.eurasiancommission.org/ru/nae/news/Pages/16-10-2015-2.aspx

Eurasian Commission (2015b) http://www.eurasiancommission.org/ru/Documents/EEC_ar2015_preview.pdf

European Bank for Reconstruction and Development (2015) http://www.ebrd.com/news/2015/ebrd-names-sergei-guriev-as-new-chief-economist.html

Eurodialogue (2015) http://eurodialogue.eu/Western%20Priority%20in%20Turning%20to%20China

Expert (2015a) http://expert.ru/2015/10/10/zachem-spasat-rahmona/

Expert (2015b) http://expert.ru/expert/2015/20/ognennyie-ob_yatiya-drakona/

Expert (2015c) http://expert.ru/expert/2015/42/drakon-zakashlyal-kak-ne-zarazitsya/

Expert (2015d) http://expert.ru/expert/2015/42/drakon-zakashlyal-kak-ne-zarazitsya/

Fattibene D (2015) Russia's Pivot to Asia. Myths and realities. Istituto Affari Internazionali, Working Paper 15/44 November, http://www.iai.it/sites/default/files/iaiwp1544.pdf

Fenenko A (2015) China looms large above Russian-Asean partnership, http://valdaiclub.com/news/china-looms-large-above-russian-asean-partnership-/?print=y

Fenenko A (2016) Khuzhe, chem v kholodnuyu voynu. Rossiya v global'noi politike, http://www.globalaffairs.ru/print/global-processes/Khuzhe-chem-v-kholodnuyu-voinu-17994

Feng S (2015) What is the purpose of closer ties between China and Russia, http://valdaiclub.com/asia/80720/print_edition/

FINMARKET (2014) http://www.finmarket.ru/main/article/3698805

Forbes (2016) Kak vernut' rossiyskuyu ekonomiku k rostu, http://www.forbes.ru/mneniya-column/gosplan/312671-kak-vernut-rossiiskuyu-ekonomiku-k-rostu

Fu Y (2016) The American world order is a suit that no longer fits. Financial Times, 7 January

Gabuev A (2015) Udybaensiia i mashem: chto Si Tzsinypin uvez iz Moskvy, http://carnegie.ru/2015/05/12/ru-60047/i8f3

Galeotti M (2015) Moscow is playing second fiddle to Beijing, http://www.themoscowtimes.com/opinion/article/moscow-is-playing-second-fiddle-to-beijing/520216.html

Gazeta (2014a) http://www.gazeta.ru/business/2014/05/21/6042329.shtml

Gazeta (2014b) http://www.gazeta.ru/politics/news/2014/12/04/n_6712641.shtml

Gazeta (2015a) http://www.gazeta.ru/business/2015/01/16/6377985.shtml

Gazeta (2015b) http://www.gazeta.ru/business/2015/01/16/6377985.shtml. Accessed 19 Jan 2015

Gazprom (2015a) http://www.gazprom.ru/press/news/2015/march/article220413/

Gazprom (2015b) http://www.gazprom.ru/about/production/projects/pipelines/ykv/

Goldstein L (2014) How China sees America's moves in Asia: worse than containment, The National Interest, 29 October, http://nationalinterest.org/feature/how-china-sees-americas-moves-asia-worse-containment-11560
Government (2015a) http://government.ru/en/docs/18216/
Government (2015b) http://government.ru/media/files/QTqv2SI5qYEuu2zOHkOAwguydbKD9Ckf.pdf
Guryev S (2015) Deglobalizing Russia. Carnegie Endowment for International Peace, http://carnegieendowment.org/2015/12/16/deglobalizing-russia/in6c, Accessed 16 Dec 2015
Harris School (2015) http://harris.uchicago.edu/directory/faculty/konstantin_sonin
IMF (2016) World economic outlook, http://www.imf.org/external/pubs/ft/survey/so/2016/RES011916A.htm
Infoshos (2016a) http://infoshos.ru/ru/?idn=15241
Infoshos (2016b) http://infoshos.ru/ru/?idn=15133
Infoshos (2016c) http://infoshos.ru/ru/?idn=15239
Infoshos (2015) Rasshireniye SHOS uslozhnit politicheskiy dialog v ramkakh organizatsii, http://infoshos.ru/ru/?idn=14547
Ingram A (2001) Alexander Dugin: geopolitics and neo-fascism in post-Soviet Russia. Polit Geogr 20(8), 1029–106, http://www.sciencedirect.com/science/article/pii/S0962629801000439
Inozemtsev V (2014) Novoazia, http://www.mk.ru/print/article/1107670/
Inozemtsev V (2014a) Mnenie: spaset li Rossiiu razvorot na Vostok, http://rbcdaily.ru/economy/562949991273154
Inozemtsev V (2014b) Shekovyi put' kak zashchita ot sanktsii SShA, http://www.ng.ru/economics/2014-04-21/4_silkway.html?print=Y
Inozemtsev V (2015) Propustit' povorot, http://www.gazeta.ru/column/vladislav_inozemcev/7659597.shtml
Interfax (2015a) http://www.interfax.ru/russia/440813
Ishchenko R (2015) Deescalating the conflict in Ukraine, http://valdaiclub.com/near_abroad/76060.html
ISN (2015) http://www.isn.ethz.ch/Digital-Library/Articles/Detail/?Ing=en&id=19o841
Ivanov V (1994) Russian in the Pacific. Prospects for Partnership with China. In: Chung IY, Chung E (eds) Russia in the Far East and Pacific Region. The Sejong Institute, Seul, pp 294–295
Ivanter A (2013) Vostochnaia chrezvychaika 547, http://expert.ru/expert/2013/44/vostochnaya-chrezvyichajka/
Izvestiya (2014) http://izvestia.ru/news/574746
Ivashov L (2016) Kitay i Rossiya, http://www.zavtra.ru/content/view/kitaj-6/, Accessed 4 Feb 2016
Izvestiya (2015a) http://izvestia.ru/news/586678
Izvestiya (2015b) http://izvestia.ru/news/596732
Izvestiya (2016) http://izvestia.ru/news/604520
Kaczmarski M, Kardas S (2015) Russia-China- ritual demonstrations against the West? http://www.osw.waw.pl/en/publikacje/analyses/2015-05-13/russia-china-ritual-demonstrations-against-west
Kaplan R (2016) Eurasia's coming to anarchy. The Risks of Chinese and Russian weakness, Foreign Affairs, 15 February
Karaganov S (2013) Strategiia XXI: Odnobokaia derzhava. Vedomosti, December 4, n. 225
Karaganov S (2015) Interview—Ukraiinskii krizis nanes moshchnyi udar po evropeiskomu proektu. Politolog Sergei Karaganov o prichinakh i putiakh vykhoda iz mezhdunardnogo krizisa sprovotsirovannogo sobytiiami na Ukraine, http://lenta.ru/articles/2015/02/25/karaganov/
Karaganov S (2016a) A turn to Asia: the history of a political idea, http://eng.globalaffairs.ru/pubcol/A-turn-to-Asia-the-history-of-the-political-idea-17926
Karaganov S (2016b) 2015: Global Tendencies and Russian Policies. Russia in Global Affairs, http://eng.globalaffairs.ru/number/2015-Global-Tendencies-and-Russian-Policies-17976

Karaganov S (2016c) Mir nakhoditsya v predvoyennom sostoyanii. Russia in Global Affairs, http://www.globalaffairs.ru/pubcol/Mir-nakhoditsya-v-predvoennom-sostoyanii-17999
Kazinform (2015) http://www.kazinform.kz/rus/article/2772993
Kazinform (2016) http://www.kazinform.kz/rus/article/2866066
Khramchikhin A (2015) V poiskakh novogo soyuznika Moskva riskuyet poteryat' strategicheskogo partnera, http://nvo.ng.ru/gpolit/2015-08-07/5_soyuznik.html
Kashin V (interview) (2014) Prognozy pro ugrozy: riski i perspektivy rossiysko-kitayskikh otnosheniy, http://www.aif.ru/onlineconf/1392888
Kashin V (2014a) Povorot na Kitay: kak kompensirovat' na Vostoke poteri ot zapadnykh sanktsiy, http://www.forbes.ru/print/node/252849
Kashin V (2014b) Rossiia nachala protsess uskorennogo sblizheniia c Kitaem, http://www.vedomosti.ru/opinion/news/26810471/rossiya-nachala-process-uskorennogo-sblizheniya-s-kitaem?full%23cut
Kashin V (2015) Zamedleniye Kitaya: pochemu eto vazhno i chem eto grozit, http://www.rbc.ru/opinions/politics/06/02/2015/54d378009a7947750cfabb96
Kashin V (2015a) Pochemu opyat' kipit Yuzhno-Kitayskoye more, http://carnegie.ru/2015/10/29/ru-61801/ikkx
Kashin V (2015b) Rossiya i Kitay: gde my nakhodimsya, http://www.vedomosti.ru/opinion/articles/2015/09/10/608214-rossiya-i-kitai-gde-mi-nahodimsya?from=newsletter-editor-choice&utm_source=newsletter&utm_medium=content&utm_campaign=editor-choice&utm_term=news23
Kashin V (2016) Bol'shaya kitayskaya chistka, http://www.vedomosti.ru/opinion/articles/2016/02/18/630151-bolshaya-kitaiskaya-chistka
Keun Wook Paik (2015) Sino-Russian gas and oil cooperation—entering a new era of strategic partnership? https://www.oxfordenergy.org/2015/04/sino-russian-gas-and-oil-cooperation-entering-a-new-era-of-strategic-partnership/
Kirillov A (2015) Paradnaya diplomatiya, http://www.kommersant.ru/doc/2729615
Kissinger H (2014) The world order. Penguin, 2014
Kommersant (2015a) http://www.kommersant.ru/doc/2724492
Kommersant (2015b) http://www.kommersant.ru/doc/2857309
Kommersant (2015c) http://www.kommersant.ru/doc/2723633
Kommersant (2015d) http://www.kommersant.ru/doc/2724437
Knobel A (2016) Yevraziyskiy soyuz i SHOS: v poiskakh istochnikov rosta, http://www.vedomosti.ru/opinion/articles/2016/02/19/630669-evraziiskii-soyuz-rosta
Krickovic A (2014) Imperial nostalgia or prudent geopolitics? Russia's efforts to reintegrate the post-Soviet space in geopolitical perspective. Post-Soviet Affairs 30(6):503–528
Kremlin (2014) http://news.kremlin.ru/news/46522/printon
Kremlin (2015a) http://www.kremlin.ru/events/president/news/50207
Kremlin (2015b) http://en.kremlin.ru/catalog/keywords/18/events/50291
Kremlin (2016) Soveshchaniye s chlenami Pravitel'stva, http://www.kremlin.ru/events/president/news/51214
Law, Policy and Politics. Edward Elgar, Cheltenham (UK)-Northampton(MA,USA), Chapter 6
Law on TORy (2014) O territoriakh operezhaiushchego sotsialno-ekonomicheskogo razvitiia v Rossiiskoi Federatsii, http://www.pravo.gov.ru. 29.12.2014, N 0001201412290024
Lee P (2015) It's official: America has a China-containment policy, 17 June. Asia Times, http://atimes.com/2015/06/its-official-america-has-a-china-containment-policy/
Lenta (2015) http://lenta.ru/news/2015/05/02/gasforchina/
Lenta (2016a) Putin posovetoval vitse-prem'yeru Trutnevu ostorozhneye kichit'sya muskulami, http://lenta.ru/news/2016/01/27/putin/
Lenta (2016b) http://lenta.ru/articles/2016/03/01/trutnev/
Levada Centre (2014) http://www.levada.ru/eng/crimea
Levada Centre (2016a) Monitoring vospriyatiya drugikh stran. Rossiya i Zapad, http://www.levada.ru/2016/02/04/monitoring-vospriyatiya-drugih-stran-rossiya-i-zapad/print/

Li J (2013) Sino-Russian Strategic Partnership Cooperative Relations and the US Factor, http://www.theasanforum.org/sino-russian-strategic-partnership-cooperative-relations-and-the-us-factor/
Lo Bobo (2014) Russia's Eastern Direction-Distinguishing the Real from the Virtual-. Institut Français des Rélations Internationales, http://www.ifri.org/?page=detail-contribution&id=7952&id_provenance=97F
Lukyanov F (2014a) Perestroika 2014—Chast vtoraia, http://www.gazeta.ru/comments/column/lukyanov/6108737.shtml
Lukyanov F (2014b) Russia's Ostpolitik, http://valdaiclub.com/russia_and_the_world/74500.html
Lukyanov F (2015a) Fyodor Lukyanov o tom, chto budet proiskhodit' v novom politicheskom sezone, http://www.gazeta.ru/comments/column/lukyanov/7720847.shtml
Lukyanov F (2015b) Stalin v protsentnom sootnoshenii, http://www.gazeta.ru/comments/column/lukyanov/6671709.shtml, Accessed 7 May 2015
Lukyanov F (2015c) China will win the war over, http://rbth.com/opinion/2015/03/19/china_will_win_the_war_over_ukraine_44623.html
Lukyanov F (2015d) Stalin v protsentnom sootnoshenii, http://www.gazeta.ru/comments/column/lukyanov/6671709.shtml
Malle S (2013) Eurasian economic integration. In: Dragneva R, Wolczuk K (eds) Eurasian economic integration
Malle S (2014) Militant Russia moving to the East. Il Politico, Anno LXXIX 3:15–40
Malle S (2015) Znakom'tsev': Voindsvennaya Rossiya Rossiya in Global'noi Politike. Russia in Global Affairs, November-December, p 2015
Malle S, Cooper J (2014) The pendulum moves from Europe to Asia. Modernising Siberia and the Far East. Economic and Security Issues, Journal of Eurasian Studies (1), January
Manifesto of nationalists (2014) Natsionalisty nachnut kampaniyu protiv peredachi Dal'nego Vostoka Kitayu, http://rusnsn.info/vazhnoe/natsionalisty-nachinayut-kampaniyu-protiv-peredachi-dal-nego-vostoka-kitajtsam.html
Maslov A (2015) Igry v lyubov' » s Kitayem ne vygoden Rossii, http://www.opec.ru/1840417.html
Medvedev D (2016) http://government.ru/news/21784/
Ministry of the Far East (2014) http://minvostokrazvitia.ru/upload/iblock/319/Презентация итогов деятельности Мин....pdf
Military (2016) http://function.mil.ru/news_page/country/more.htm?id=12079218@egNews
Minecom (2015a) http://economy.gov.ru/minec/press/news/2015020910
Minecom (2015b) Stanislav Voskresenskiy: shelkovyy put' soyedinyayet Rossiyu i KNR, http://economy.gov.ru/minec/press/interview/2015082704
Mineral (2015) http://www.mineral.ru/News/74138.html
Mir-politika (2015a) http://mir-politika.ru/4236-suschestvuet-li-ugroza-rossii-so-storony-kitaya-nachalo.html
Mir-politika (2015b) http://mir-politika.ru/4310-suschestvuet-li-ugroza-rossii-so-storony-kitaya-okonchanie.html%23UcnkZ1365489986
Mukhin V (2014) NATO neitralizuet soiuznikov Rossii, http://www.ng.ru/armies/2014-04-23/1_nato.html?print=Y
Newtimes (2015) http://www.newtimes.ru/articles/print/95721/
News tj (2015) http://news.tj/en/news/tajik-president-calls-cis-heads-state-strengthen-security-csi-southern-borders
Ng (2014) http://www.ng.ru/cis/2014-07-03/6_tajikistan.html?print=Y
Ng (2015) http://www.ng.ru/cis/2015-02-06/8_gosdep.html?print=Y
Ng (2016) http://www.ng.ru/economics/2015-09-17/1_china.html?print=Y
Ng.ru (2016) http://www.ng.ru/economics/2016-02-15/1_nordstrread.html?print=Y
Ngy (2015) http://www.ngv.ru/news/gazprom_zavershil_3d_seysmiku_na_chayandinskom_mestorozhdenii/?sphrase_id=884705
Nikkei (2015) http://asia.nikkei.com/Politics-Economy/International-Relations/Uncertainty-engulfs-Russia-Japan-gas-project-in-Vladivostok

OECD (2002) China in the World Economy. The Domestic Policy Challenges
Oilcapital (2015) http://www.oilcapital.ru/transport/267938.html
Periscope (2016a) http://periscope2.ru/2016/02/16/8520/
Periscope (2016b) http://periscope2.ru/2016/02/16/8520/
Popov A (2016) Shelkovaya kitayskaya udavka dlya Rossii, http://newsland.com/community/7044/content/4969971
Porter T, Seregny S (2004) The Zemstvo Reconsidered. In: Evans AB Jr, Gel'man V (eds) The politics of local Governments in Russia, Rhoman and Littlefield Publishers, Oxford
Prime (2015) http://www.1prime.ru/state_regulation/20150425/808615891-print.html
Rbth (2016) http://rbth.com/international/2016/02/18/tajiks-fear-weaker-russian-presence-will-open-the-way-for-isis_569041
Rbc (2016a) http://www.rbc.ru/business/12/01/2016/56952bb19a794756125a7a4a
Rbc (2016b), http://www.rbc.ru/business/03/03/2016/56d809049a79477167e8cb4a?from=main
Ria.ru (2014) http://ria.ru/east/20141120/1034251404.html
Ria.ru (2015) http://ria.ru/infografika/20150708/1120666045.html#ixzz415xytAA5
Ria.ru (2016) http://ria.ru/economy/20160212/1373310802.html
Rferl (2015) http://www.rferl.org/content/tajik-elections-rahmon-party-victory/26877105.html
Rg.ru (2016a) http://www.rg.ru/printable/2016/02/15/reg-dfo/rossiiane-poluchat-besplatno-bolee-140-mln-ga-na-dalnem-vostoke.htm
Rg.ru (2016b) http://www.rg.ru/2016/02/24/reg-dfo/nikolaj-patrushev-rasskazal-rg-o-sozdanii-arkticheskogo-flota.html
Ryzhkov V, Inozemtsev V, Ponomarev I (2012) Continent Siberia, Russia in Global Affairs, http://eng.globalaffairs.ru/number/Continent-Siberia-15820
Sakhuja V (2014) Russia and China: Icy Latitudes for Cooperation and Competition, http://valdaiclub.com/asia/66640.html
SCO (2014) http://www.sectsco.org/EN123/show.asp?id=501
Security Committee (2015) http://www.scrf.gov.ru/news/904.html
Sherbakov D (2014) Operezhenie v zakone, Zakonodatelstvo, http://www.kommersant.ru/doc/2604142, Accessed 6 Nov 2014
Silkroadfund (2015) http://www.silkroadfund.com.cn/enwap/27363/index.html
Sdela (2015) http://sdelanounas.ru/blogs/60589/
Sonin K (2014) Russia can never be like China. RUSBASE, http://archive.rusbase.com/news/author/benhopkins/oil-wont-save-russia/
Sputnik (2014) http://in.sputniknews.com/indian.ruvr.ru/2014_04_04/CSTO-cooperation-China/
Sputnik (2015a) http://sputniknews.com/military/20150513/1022108139.html
Sputnik (2015b) http://sputniknews.com/world/20150508/1021864975.html, Accessed 8 May 2015
Strokan S (2015) Primirenie Indii i Kitaia uskorit' rossiiskii povorot k Azii, http://www.kommersant.ru/doc/2725653
TASS (2015a) http://tass.ru/politika/2568006
TASS (2015b) http://tass.ru/politika/1993006
TASS (2015c) http://tass.ru/ekonomika/1862740
TASS (2015d) http://tass.ru/en/russia/733044
TASS (2015e) http://tass.ru/ekonomika/1956815
TASS (2015f) http://tass.ru/ekonomika/1956881
TASS (2015g) http://tass.ru/armiya-i-opk/1960566
TASS (2015h) http://tass.ru/ekonomika/1957292
TASS (2016) http://tass.ru/politika/2644918
Tengrinews (2015) http://tengrinews.kz/kazakhstan_news/plyusyi-minusyi-vstupleniya-kyirgyizstana-eaes-nazvali-279152/, Accessed 12 Aug 2015
Tiezzi S (2014) China "new silk road" vision revealed and where is China's silk road actually going, http://thediplomat.com/2014/05/chinas-new-silk-road-vision-revealed/
Treaty, http://www.eaeunion.org/files/history/2014/2014_2.pdf

Trenin D (2012) True partners? How Russia and China see each other. Centre for European Reform, February, http://docplayer.net/77651-Centre-for-european-reform-true-partners-how-russia-and-china-see-each-other-dmitri-trenin.html

Trenin D (2015a) From Greater Europe to Greater Asia? The Sino-Russian Entente. Carnegie Moscow Centre, http://carnegieendowment.org/files/CP_Trenin_To_Asia_WEB_2015Eng.pdf

Trenin D (2015b) Russia's victory day celebration: much more than just a Parade, http://nationalinterest.org/print/feature/russias-victory-day-celebration-much-more-just-parade-12860

Trenin D (2015c) Europe's Nightmare: Ukraine's Massive Meltdown, http://nationalinterest.org/feature/europes-nightmare-ukraines-massive-meltdown-12597

The Moscow Times (2014) http://www.themoscowtimes.com/news/article/as-kiev-looks-west-putin-turns-east-to-build-eurasian-dream/496967.html

The Moscow Times (2016) http://www.themoscowtimes.com/business/article/russian-chinese-trade-plummets-in-2015/555632.html

Utro (2016) http://www.utro.ru/news/2016/01/29/1269109.shtml, Accessed 29 Jan 2016

Ukaz Prezidenta RF ot 31 dekabrya 2015g. N 683, http://www.scrf.gov.ru/documents/1/133.html

Vedomosti (2016) Boris Titov sozdayet partiyu biznesa dlya uchastiya v dumskikh vyborakh na baze "Pravogo dela", http://www.vedomosti.ru/politics/articles/2016/02/12/628712-boris-titov-sozdaet-partiyu-biznesa-dlya-uchastiya-dumskih-viborah-baze-pravogo-dela

Vedomosti (2015a) http://www.vedomosti.ru/business/articles/2015/12/16/621202-italiya-nord-stream-2

Vedomosti (2015b) http://www.vedomosti.ru/economics/articles/2015/05/12/kitai-i-evraziiskii-ekonomicheskii-soyuz-mogut-sozdat-zonu-svobodnoi-torgovli

Vz.ru (2014a) http://www.vz.ru/news/2014/9/30/708157.html

Vz.ru (2014b) http://vz.ru/politics/2014/5/21/687567.html

Vz.ru (2015a) http://www.vz.ru/news/2016/2/18/795063.print.html, Accessed 1 Feb 2015

Vz.ru (2015b) http://www.vz.ru/news/2015/5/11/744684.html

War and Peace (2015) http://www.warandpeace.ru/ru/news/view/97731/

Wcam (2014) http://www.wcarn.com/news/39/39860.html

Zabelina N (2015) Rossiya zashla v strategicheskiy tupik, http://www.ng.ru/economics/2015-12-18/1_tupik.html?print=Y, Accessed 18 Dec 2015

Sino-Japanese Relations in the Xi-Abe Era. Can Two Tigers Live on the Same Mountain?

Matteo Dian

Abstract This chapter explores the evolution of Sino-Japanese relations in the Xi-Abe era, considering three different areas: security and defence, economic regionalism, and 'history issues.' Bilateral relations, despite high levels of economic interdependence, remain constrained by an ongoing security dilemma and by the lack of reconciliation over 'history issues.' Moreover, China and Japan are starting to diverge also on how to promote institutionalization in the realm of economic governance.

1 Introduction

An old Chinese proverb suggests that two tigers cannot live on the same mountain. This proverb is often quoted to describe the state of East Asian international politics, alluding to the fact that, historically, the two main powers in East Asia never neither shared leadership in the region, nor have been prosperous and powerful during the same period. Before the *Opium Wars* and the era of Western colonization, the East Asian regional order was based on a Sino-centric structure. China as *The Middle Kingdom* and its Emperor were recognized as politically superior, and other East Asian states recognized its superiority through the tribute system. (Fairbank and Chen 1968; Kang 2010; Zhang 2011). The advent of European colonization reversed this equilibrium. After the *Opium Wars*, China plumbed into a long phase of political stagnation and economic decline, which led it to lose great part of its sovereignty and the control of its coastal areas. On the contrary Japan reacted to the rising tide of European colonialism fundamentally changing its political, social and economic systems (Gluck 1985; Pyle 1969). The Meiji leadership promoted a profound process of modernization of the country through the adoption of Western technology, economic and constitutional models. The ultimate

M. Dian (✉)
Department of Political and Social Studies, School of Political Sciences, University of Bologna, Bologna, Italy
e-mail: matteo.dian2@unibo.it

S. Beretta et al. (eds.), *Understanding China Today*, Understanding China,
DOI 10.1007/978-3-319-29625-8_5

objective of the Japanese leadership at the time was to create a 'Rich Nation with a Strong Army', able to compete with the West and shield itself from the *Hobbesian* nature of international politics in the age of European colonialism in Asia (Wilson 1992). The *Meiji Period* coincided with the decline of the *Qing Empire* in China and the long process of political instability in China up to the instauration of the People's Republic of China in 1949.

Japan showed itself very interested in applying the lessons of the new *Hobbesian* international system, imposing its political superiority during the first Sino-Japanese war in 1894/1895, forcing China to accept an *Unequal Treaty* in 1915, occupying the region of Manchuria in 1931 and finally promoting a war of aggression aimed at completely subjugating the entire China between 1937 and 1945 (Pyle 2008; Mitter 2013). The brutal encounter of the first part of the 20th century turned into mutual isolation in the Cold War period. The *Chinese Revolution* and the Cold War erected a political, ideological and economic barrier between the two states. Japan looked at the West and at the United States to recover from the ashes of the war. China firstly turned first to the Soviet Union in the 1950s, and then isolated itself from the rest of the world during the *Cultural Revolution* (MacFarquhar 1997; Westad 1998).

Japan and China rebuilt diplomatic relations in 1972 and signed the *Treaty of Amity and Cooperation* in 1978. The Sino-Japanese rapprochement was made possible by the Chinese necessity to balance the increasingly competitive relations with the USSR and the American opening to Beijing. The period between 1972 and 1989 is generally remembered as the 'honeymoon period' of Sino-Japanese relations. During this period Beijing and Tokyo had strong incentives to cooperate in all the three realms dealt with here, security, economic-institutional cooperation, memory and history (He 2009).

China's diplomatic revolution of the 1970s created strong incentives for cooperation with Japan. In the 1970s China considered the former Soviet 'comrades in arms' as the main threats to its national security. As a consequence it progressively aligned with the United States against the Soviet threat. During the early phases of the Cold War Japan had always considered the Soviet Union, more than China, its main security threat. Moreover, China's opening in the late 1970s allowed Japan to finally escape the constraints imposed by the Cold War system, which prevented any form of diplomatic, political and commercial relations with China, considered a necessary economic partner, its regime notwithstanding (Radchenko 2009).

Economically the re-opening of bilateral relations was mutually beneficial. China needed Japan's help to pursue its objective of realizing the so-called *Four Modernizations*' by acquiring advanced technologies Japan was able to provide China with. Japan found in China a potentially unlimited market for its products and an attractive destination for overseas investments (Vogel 2011). During this period the Chinese authorities managed to control, or at least did not politically exploit, the issue of collective memory. The narrative of the war time period and the role of Japan in the Chinese collective memory underwent a process of transformation in the 1980s. Deng Xiaoping and his close aides such as Hu Yaobang and Zhao Ziyang maintained the same narrative promoted during the Maoist period as regards the memory of the Sino-Japanese war, which suggested that Japan had conducted a war of aggression against the Chinese people. However, that narrative also suggested that the war was promoted by the Japanese militarists and by the *zaibatsu*, the Japanese capitalist elites. Ordinary Japanese soldiers as well as common Japanese citizens were—like their Chinese counterparts—hence to be considered victims not perpetrators of the war. As a consequence, Deng and his followers argued, Chinese relations with Japan should not be defined by anti-Japanese feelings. At the same time, however, Deng and the Chinese at the time also started to aliment a more distinctively nationalist reading of Chinese history, in order to compensate China's legitimacy crisis after the *Cultural Revolution*. This second trend, even if already clearly present in the 1980s, had a major impact on bilateral relations mainly since the 1990s. Incidents such as the 1982 textbook crisis and the 1985 diplomatic crisis after Nakasone's visit to the Yasukuni Shrine in Tokyo, already showed how the history issue would become a fundamental hurdle for bilateral Sino-Japanese relations (Mitter 2003; Coble 2007; Nozaki 2002).

Overall, however, the Sino-Japanese honeymoon period of the late 1970s and early 1980s constituted probably the most friendly and mutually beneficial period of the history of the Sino-Japanese relations. The relations that emerged during this period were nonetheless substantially asymmetric. In the 1980s, Japan had reached its economic and technological apogee, while China needed Japan's cooperation in technological and economic terms (Kraus et al. 2014). As Ezra Vogel recently stated "During Deng's years at the helm, no country played a greater role in assisting China build its industry and infrastructure than Japan" (Vogel 2011).

2 Security Relations After 1989

This asymmetric equilibrium ended at the end of the Cold War. The demise of the USSR deprived the alignment between Beijing and Washington as well as the Sino-Japanese cooperation of its main strategic rationale. Since the early 1990s Beijing embarked on a process of modernization, accompanied by annual double-digit military budget growth rates. Moreover, the repression of Tiananmen Square in June 1989 demonstrated all the limits of the Chinese reforms (Miles 1997; He and Link 2014).

Since the early 1990s Japan has expressed concern about Chinese efforts to modernise its armed forces, even if referring to China as a 'threat' remained a taboo subject in the Japanese public discourse up until the 2000s. However, since the late 1990s many Japanese analysts and policymakers started to regard the possibility of China seeking regional hegemony as the paramount threat to their security (Christensen 1999; Mochizuki 2007). In the post-Cold War era Japan responded to the Chinese military ascendency and modernization in two distinct ways. Firstly, Japan started the process of 'normalization' of its security policies, abandoning great parts of the self-imposed limits that limited Tokyo's contributions to global security in the post war period: Tokyo began deploying its *Self-Defence Forces*

(JSDF) abroad for UN-mandated peace keeping operations, it relaxed the three principles of arms export(up until then it did not allow the country to export weapons and weapons technology), it started to use space for defence purposes and it added military deterrence to the role of the JSDF. Up until then, the JSDF's role was limited to what is referred to as 'exclusively defensive defence policies', (i.e. the JSDF's role was limited to the defence of Japanese national territory in the case of an attack). Moreover, Japan and the United States renewed and strengthened their security relations. The main initiative in that context was the revision of the *US–Japan Guidelines for Defense Cooperation* in 1997. These guidelines created an improved structure and policy guidelines for US–Japan military cooperation aiming at a higher degree of coordination, both in peacetime and in the case of a military contingency. Another relevant initiative as regards the redefinition of the alliance took place in 2005: the adoption of the *US–Japan Alliance: Transformation and Realignment for the Future.* That document highlighted the envisioned evolution of the role and competencies of Japan's armed forces, away from exclusively defending Japanese national territory towards a progressively more proactive role dealing with so-called 'Far East contingencies' and US–Japan military cooperation beyond the geographical boundaries of the Far East (Dian 2014; Samuels 2007; Hughes 2005). The renewal of the alliance created a significant shift in the Chinese perception of Japan. While during the Cold War the alliance was considered the 'cork in the bottle' of Japanese militarism, since the late 1990s Beijing started to consider the normalization of the Japanese security strategy directly threatening to its security interests (Manning and Przystup 2015).

3 Economic Regionalism After the Cold War

This emerging rivalry in the security realm, however, was coupled with several attempts to cooperate in the realm of regional economic governance and by increasing levels of economic and commercial interdependence. Since the late 1980s, Tokyo began promoting a number of initiatives aimed at strengthening the level of regional economic integration through fora such as the *Japan-ASEAN Ministerial Meeting* and the *Asia Pacific Economic Cooperation Finance Ministers Process* (FMP). However, the achievements of those fora were limited, since they were not able to create binding mechanisms in the realm of financial and trade governance.

The 1997 Asian financial crisis stood for the most important turning point for the regional economic order in the post-Cold War period, creating new incentives for cooperation, opening the way for the establishment of new institutions as well as altering the perceptions of key states' interests. Firstly, the crisis embodied a first and significant moment of decline of American influence in East Asia. In the wake of the crisis the US was criticized for doing too little to prevent the crisis from causing enormous economic losses for Asian states, contributing to the imposition of harsh IMF conditions (Kang 2003; Goh 2013). The United States were particularly criticized for their opposition to the creation of an Asian Monetary Found, proposed by Japan in 1997 (Searight 2010). America's perceived abandonment of the South East Asian states in the moment of need and the imposition of what it was considered US particular economic and ideological interests greatly contributed to spreading the idea that East Asian countries had to look for alternative institutional settings and had to promote a 'close' East Asian form of regionalism that could potentially isolate them from American pressure (Beeson 2006). The decade after the crisis was marked by the creation of a number of new institutional mechanisms, supported both by Japan and China, within the framework of the ASEAN+3. The most relevant are probably the *Chiang Mai Initiative* (CMI), a framework to provide liquidity to the countries affected by speculative attacks, and the ASEAN+3*'s Asian Bond Markets Initiative* (ABMI), aimed at improving local-currency bond markets and creating region-wide bond markets (Grimes 2011). The CMI and the ABMI stood for a first relevant attempt to promote a system to provide public economic goods in the region, while partially isolating it from the American intervention and the financial orthodoxy of the IMF. Overall, these initiatives demonstrated that cooperation between Japan and China can unleash a great potential in terms of creating common prosperity and jointly addressing the most pressing problems in the region, at least in the economic and financial realms.

4 Memory and History After the Cold War

The post-Cold War period was characterized by the rise of the so-called 'memory issue' in East Asia and what is referred to as the 'correct vision of history.' These issues would become a major problem for bilateral relations and both China and Japan undertook a fundamental revision of their historical narratives. In Japan, the early 1990s were marked by an intense process of contestation as regards the issue of the country's collective memory. During the postwar period, conservative and progressive groups in the country promoted two distinct sets of beliefs on Japanese wartime policies. Conservatives argued that Japan did not fight a war of aggression. Rather, it was dragged into the war, because of the brutal and *Hobbesian* nature of international politics in East Asia after European colonialism. Moreover, conservatives tended to negate or downplay the atrocities committed by the Japanese army during World War II, arguing that brutality and excesses are part of every conflict (Wakayama 1999). Progressive groups, on the contrary, recognized the Japanese war crimes and the aggressive nature of the war, and promoted pacifism rejecting the legitimacy of the US–Japan alliance, which they feared could Japan entangle into US wars.

Progressive and conservative groups, however, shared a common belief: Japan too was a 'victim' during World War II. Progressive forces emphasized the role of the Japanese people as victims of American bombings and the brutality of the war. Conservatives highlighted the role of the wartime generation and its sacrifice, as the ultimate foundation of post war prosperity (Orr 2000). That assessment started to be contested in the post-Cold War period. Progressive forces, led by leftist parties and grass-root associations started to promote the idea that Japan had to face its wartime responsibilities, explicitly apologize to its former victims, and promote reconciliation. A momentary political setback in 1993–1994 of the ruling *Liberal Democratic Party (*LDP*)*, allowed progressives to promote a policy of apologizing to the victims of Japanese World War militarism. This culminated in the *Murayama Statement*, the most explicit and politically significant recognition of the Japanese aggression and wartime crimes to date (Szczepanska 2014; Togo 2012).

This attempt to promote reconciliation through apologies generated a long-term backlash. Conservatives mobilized to contest what they considered a masochistic vision of history and to promote their values and beliefs about history. This culminated into the campaign to revise history textbooks, promoted by the *Society for History Textbook Reform* (*Tsukuru Kai*), and was accompanied by repeated visits of former Prime Minister Koizumi Junichiro to the Yasukuni Shrine in Tokyo (Inozuka 2013; Cave 2013).

The Chinese historical narrative also evolved significantly. In the aftermath of Beijing's decision to end students' demonstrations with military force on Tiananmen Square in June 1989 the Chinese government started to promote the so-called *Campaign for Patriotic Education* with the aim of rebuilding its legitimacy. As William Callahan has argued, the CPC started to promote a "Very deliberate celebration of a national insecurity", in order to rebuild the foundations of its political legitimacy and historical necessity (Callahan 2004). The new Chinese narrative is based on the idea of *wuwang guochi* (*Never Forget National Humiliation*). Chinese students and the population in general are constantly reminded of the existential necessity of the Communist Party, which guided the country to overcoming the *Century of Humiliation*, which started with the Opium Wars and culminated with the Sino-Japanese war. This new narrative abandons the dualism people-elite typical of the Maoist period. On the contrary, it identifies and stresses European colonialism and Japanese militarism China suffered from in the past while at the same time warning of possible future aggressions China will suffer from in the future. The Sino-Japanese war and the atrocities perpetrated by the Japanese became the focal point of the Chinese nationalist narrative (Zhao 1998; Wang 2014). This led to the rise of anti-Japanese feeling among the Chinese population, and to widespread anti-Japanese riots, during which Chinese nationalists damaged Japanese property and threatened Japanese citizens in China. While it is not clear how much the Chinese government is able to control such anti-Japan riots, it appears that Beijing actions are increasingly taking into account nationalism and anti-Japan feelings of its population when dealing with Japan-in essence the same feelings that Chinese political leaders promoted through the above-mentioned *Campaign for Patriotic Education* since the early 1990s (Weiss 2014).

It was sought to briefly highlight the long-term trends characterizing Sino-Japanese relations in the realms of security, historical memory and regional economic governance. Next, I will seek to examine the most recent developments in the same three realms since Abe Shinzo took over power and Xi Jinping and China respectively.

5 Sino Japanese Relations in the Xi-Abe Era

Sino-Japanese security relations in the Xi-Abe era have been characterized by two different trends. Under the leadership of Abe Shinzo, Japan accelerated the process of the above-mentioned 'normalization' of its foreign and security posture. Abe promoted several key reforms aimed at overcoming the country's postwar pacifist limits, and strengthening Japan's capacity to protect its security, autonomously and in cooperation with the United States. The most significant initiatives promoted by the Abe administration were the establishment of a *National Security Council*, the adoption of Japan's first *National Security Strategy* and the adoption of Japan's first law on state secrets aimed at facilitating intelligence sharing. The most relevant initiative, however, was probably the re-interpretation of war-renouncing Article 9 of the Japanese constitution. The new interpretation of Article 9 adopted in 2015 allows the Japanese Self Defence Forces to execute the right to collective self-defence as formulated in Chapter VII of the UN Charta. The re-interpretation states that: "The Government has reached a conclusion that not only when an armed attack against Japan occurs but also when an armed attack against a foreign country that is in a close relationship with Japan occurs and as a result threatens Japan's survival and poses a clear danger to fundamentally overturn people's right to life, liberty and pursuit of happiness, and when there is no other appropriate means available to repel the attack and ensure Japan's survival and protect its people, use of force to the minimum extent necessary should be interpreted to be permitted under the Constitution as measures for self-defence in accordance with the basic logic of the Government's view to date" (Sasakawa Foundation 2015). This interpretation significantly enlarges the scope and the competencies of Japan's military. During the post-war era the *JSDFs'* task was the repelling of a direct attack on Japanese soil. The above-mentioned 1997 US–Japan defence guidelines introduced the concept of US–Japanese military cooperation in so-called 'Areas Surrounding Japan.' In 2010, Japan's *National Defense Program Guidelines* introduced the concept of 'dynamic deterrence' as one of the basic tasks of Japan's armed forces. Finally, authorizing Japan's military to execute the right to collective self-defense, enables the military to defend US military in the case of a direct attack on a US military base in Japan or on US forward deployed troops in the region (Dian 2014).

The other fundamental development regards the further deepening of the US–Japan security alliance with the adoption of revised bilateral defence guidelines in 2015. The most important concept in the new guidelines is the idea of what is referred to as 'seamless cooperation.' The 1997 US–Japan defence guidelines stipulated that the US–Japan alliance operated substantially in a binary way. It mainly considered peacetime and war-time scenarios. The Chinese military modernization, in particular the development of Chinese A2AD capabilities, coupled with the emergence of maritime and island disputes in East and Southeast Asia have led both Japan and the US to rethink their approach to deterrence in the alliance, underlining the increasing importance of crafting a strategy aimed at dealing with the emergence of the so-called 'grey zones scenarios.' Since 2015 and the adoption of the above-mentioned defence guidelines, the US and Japan can actively cooperate to deter China from threatening their security with hostile acts shorts of war such as building facilities on contested islands or denying freedom of navigation in contested waters in the East and South China Seas. The above-mentioned upgrades to the bilateral US–Japan alliance in turn were motivated by the continuing expansion and modernization of the Chinese armed forces and the perceived aggressiveness of recent Chinese policies, such as unilaterally establishing a so-called *Air Defense Identification Zone* (ADIZ) over parts of the East and South China Sea and the re-affirmation of the so-called *Nine-Dash Line* around the South China Sea, through which Beijing claims more than 90% of the South China as its sovereign territory (Dittmer and Weissmann 2015). China strongly criticized the revision of the US–Japan defence guidelines in 2015, claiming that they reflect an out-dated hegemonic model, rooted in a Cold War mentality, which does not reflect the current international environment. Moreover, a spokesperson of the Chinese Foreign Ministry stated that the renewal of the alliance represents an attempt to contain China's rise (Tiezzi 2015). As was sought to demonstrate above, Asia's two main powers are—together with the United States—confronted with a security dilemma in East Asia. While none of the actors have offensive intentions, they perceive each other's actions as threatening, which in turn leads to leading to military rivalry, coupled with increasing tensions and growing possibilities for miscalculation or unwanted escalations.

6 Economic Governance: Competitive and Regionalization

China under Xi Jinping has increased its activism in the realm of regional economic governance. Beijing's two noteworthy and main initiatives are the *Asia Infrastructure and Investment Bank* (AIIB) and the *One Belt, One Road* (OBOR) initiative. The AIIB is the more relevant for current Sino-Japanese relations. The political value of the AIIB and its possible consequences for the regional economic order have been widely debated. The current Chinese leadership has made efforts to portray the bank as an entirely cooperative initiative, not aimed at undermining the current regional or global economic and financial institutions. Chinese President Xi defined the AIIB as an "open and inclusive multilateral development agency" during his last visit to the United States. Xi furthermore affirmed that in order to confront major global challenges, the global governance system and its mechanisms and instruments are in need of adjustments and reforms. In his view, "Such reforms are not about dismantling the existing system and creating a new one to replace it. Rather, they aim at improving the global governance system in an innovative way" (Wall Street Journal September 2015). In Beijing's view, China's financial and economic strategies in East Asia, and especially, those in the framework of the

AIIB, are neither driven by the intention of imposing Chinese values and norms onto the region nor by the objective of undermining the existing regional multilateral institutions, but rather by the alleged need to set up a new institution more apt to represent the interests of East Asian states. China has presented the AIIB as an institution of cross-regional financial cooperation based on the principles of openness and inclusion, and would in the Chinese view be a beneficial supplement of the *World Bank*, the *Asian Development Bank* (ADB) and the US-led global financial system rather than a rival to existing institutions. Both in the United States and in Japan, however, the AIIB has been described as a result of China's new regional and global economic and foreign policy activism. Among others it is feared that the bank is aimed at undermining existing international aid and financial institutions, seeking replace the post-World War II international architecture. Moreover, the participation of several European states led some commentators to fear a possible decoupling between United States and European states as regards the approaches to China and global economic governance in general (Dian 2015a, b).

Japan declined the invitation to become a founding member of the AIIB, due to two reasons. Firstly, Tokyo is the main player in the *Asian Development Bank* (ADB), which has a function and a structure similar to the AIIB. Secondly, Tokyo followed Washington's request not to get in involved in the AIIB. Officially, the United States complained about regulatory standards, arguing that the AIIB is likely to lead to a lowering of international standards when it comes to transparency, competitiveness in bidding procedures, and political intervention in bidding processes. Such criticism, however, reflected a broader concern regarding the rise of the Chinese regional and global influence.

At the centre of the Abe government's approach toward is Japan's adhesion to the *Trans-Pacific Partnership* (TPP). The Abe government considers the TPP both a fundamental part of its foreign policy strategy and an instrument to promote structural reforms domestically. The TPP is relevant for Japan because it contributes to the redefinition of East Asian regionalism both geographically and in terms of definition of what is referred to as the 'rules of the game' of economic integration. The TPP arguably aims at including as many countries as possible in economic governance in the Asia-Pacific, including not just the US, but also Canada and Latin American countries. The other crucial point regards the rules of economic regionalism. The TPP opposes the challenge of the Chinese version of 'state capitalism.' In fact, one of the agreement's chapters of the agreement explicitly deals with *State Owned Enterprises* (*SOEs*). The TPP regulates and limits the role of *SOEs* and will limit the preferential treatments they can receive from governments (Szamosszegi and Kyle 2011). Indeed, the part in the agreement dedicated to *SOEs* clearly demonstrates a political nature of the TPP: the Obama administration has aimed at shaping the process of integration in terms favourable to the United States, their interests and their values and, at the same time, creating a less hospitable environment for Chinese *SOEs* and for the Chinese model of development. Ultimately, that chapter reveals how the United States and like-minded partners aim at fostering a version of Pacific-wide economic regionalism rooted in liberal market capitalism and American centrality as opposed to an Asia economic order based on the Chinese model of state capitalism (Solis 2015). The fact that the Abe government considers the TPP and the creation of what it calls 'trans-pacific' form of regionalism the centre of its economic foreign policy constitutes a relevant discontinuity with the past. Since the end of the 1980s and particularly in the aftermath of the Asian financial crisis, Japan had tried to promote East Asian institutional arrangements under Japanese leadership and on models that were rooted on the idea that the creation of institutions including only Asian states and excluding the United States could better serve its interests and the economic stability of the region. These attempts were often promoted in cooperation with Beijing as it was in the case of the ASEAN+3 framework. The current emphasis on the TPP, as well as the refusal to participate to the AIIB highlights an increasing degree of 'securitization' of economic governance as well as the trend toward 'competitive regionalization.

7 History and Memory in the Xi-Abe Era

The return to power of Abe Shinzo and the LDP in Japan in 2012 was accompanied by both the process of contestation of the Japanese collective memory and the most radical attempt to promote a new narrative based on a distinctively conservative vision of the Japanese identity and the country's past (Dian 2015a, b). Abe has been a staunch opponent of progressive attempts to reshape the national narrative through a more apologetic stance. In the mid-1990s he was the secretary of the *Diet Members' League for a Bright Japan* (*Akarui Nihon Kokkai Giin Renmei*), which opposed the above-mentioned *Murayama Statement* and the Diet resolution adopted during the 50th anniversary of the end of World War II. Moreover, he founded the *Japanese Rebirth* (*Sōsei Nihon*), a group of Diet members dedicated to the objective of the "Rethinking the postwar order and establishing a new political order under the fundamental values of conservatism and to make Japan a respected country in the international society" (Hughes 2015).

Abe has always considered war-renouncing Article 9 a fundamental limit for the country's independence and its right to behave as a sovereign nation, independent from political and military subordination to the United States. Consequently, he repeatedly declared that the Japanese *Self Defence Forces* should be re-named as *National Defence Forces*, and that Japan's ability and right to provide for its own security should be recognized. The constitution's pacifist clause however is by no means the only limit of the postwar regime. Abe and his like-minded followers argue that the Japanese educational system is responsible for the above-mentioned 'masochistic view of history.' Therefore, he promoted educational reforms aimed at transmitting to the new generations love for the country as well as respect to patriotic symbols such as the flag and the national anthem (Yoshida 2012).

Since his return to power in December 2012, Abe promoted his agenda in various ways. Abe and his main advisor, Chief Cabinet Secretary Suga Yoshihide, initially proposed the idea that both the *Kono Statement* and the *Murayama*

Statement could be substituted by what they called 'future-oriented' statement. Moreover, Abe visited Yasukuni Shrine in December 2013. However, Abe's bold vision of changing the article 9 has been constrained by political limits and by the necessity to deal with more practical issues, such as the implementation of economic reforms and the management of key issues in foreign affairs, such as the deepening of the US–Japan alliance. Moreover, Abe has made significant progress on the issue of the so-called *Comfort Women* with South Korea.

During the 70th anniversary of the end of the war Abe offered China an apology for Japanese World War II militarism, recognizing Japanese aggression and the suffering of the Chinese people. However, he also stressed how Japan has to face straightforwardly the past today, in order to avoid that "Our children, grandchildren, and even further generations to come, who have nothing to do with the war, be predestined to apologize" (Wall Street Journal 2015). This statement has been criticized in China, because it did not repeat the contents of the *Murayama Statement* and did not add anything new to previous statements. The Chinese criticism however, is also a reflection of Beijing's narrative of history and memory. The Chinese Communist Party increasingly needs to aliment anti-Japanese feelings to justify its legitimacy. This impedes to recognize the political value of Japanese apologies and Tokyo's efforts to exercise restraint as regards its historical narrative.

Xi Jinping has contributed to aliment the Chinese narrative based on victimization and the centrality of the *Century of Humiliation*, which has led to the radical re-interpretation of the role of Japan in Chinese collective memory. Xi's narrative is underpinned by the perception of Japan as aggressor and victimizer. This led to the re-naming of the Sino-Japanese War to the *War of the Chinese People's Resistance Against Japanese Aggression*, with an even stronger emphasis of the Japanese role in the *Century of Humiliation* (Kaufmann 2015). Indeed, the war against Japan increasingly represents a crucial important turning point for contemporary Chinese collective memory. One the one hand it represents the darker moment of the entire national collective experience. On the other hand it represents the first fundamental moment of redemption. From the ashes and the humiliation of the Japanese invasion the Chinese nation would rise to finally achieve national salvation and the first military victory against a foreign power since the *Opium Wars* (Mitter 2003; Reilly 2011). Moreover, the new Chinese narrative stresses the importance of China as a crucial member of the *Anti-Fascist Alliance* that defeated the *Axis Powers* (Gluck et al. 2015). For the contemporary Chinese leadership the global recognition of the Chinese role in World War II represents an important part of China's global recognition of the as great power. As President Xi himself recently stated during his speech in commemoration of the Seventieth Anniversary of the end of World War 2:

> During the war, with huge national sacrifice, the Chinese people held ground in the main theatre in the East of the World Anti-Fascist War, thus making major contribution to its victory. […]The victory of the Chinese People's War of Resistance against Japanese Aggression is the first complete victory won by China in its resistance against foreign aggression in modern times (Xi 2015).

Overall, the 70th anniversary of the end of the war has offered a telling picture of the current state of the role of collective memory in the realm of Sino-Japanese relations. Japan continues to be divided. Progressives aim at building reconciliation through a more apologetic stance. Conservatives momentarily accept the need to apologize, for political convenience, while trying to craft a more patriotic and what they call "less masochistic vision of history." The Chinese leadership continues to exploit anti-Japanese feelings to build a narrative that legitimizes both the historical necessity of the Communist rule and the Chinese role as a great power. This situation highlights how the two countries are far away from achieving substantial reconciliation when it comes to memory and history. Consequently, the history issue remains a main obstacle for stable relations and an issue, which could be the subject of bilateral crisis, similar to the one under former Japanese Prime Minister Koizumi Junichiro.

8 Conclusions

This chapter sought to respond to the question whether China and Japan, the two tigers of the above-mentioned proverb, can co-exist in the same region as powerful and prosperous nations. It can be concluded that they can, but bilateral relations are likely to remain of mixed quality and indeed highly volatile in the foreseeable future. On the one hand economic and institutional cooperation can unleash a tremendous potential for economic growth and development. The two countries are highly interdependent in term of trade, production chains and foreign direct investments. Similarly people exchanges are increasingly significant. Elements of cooperation however co-exist with security competition, recurring bilateral crises, accompanied by disputes over history and memory.

The realm of history remains particularly worrisome. On the Chinese side it has become clear that anti-Japanese feelings and propaganda are increasingly necessary to nurture the current history narrative based on the *Century of Humiliation* and the *Rejuvenation of the Country*. On the Japanese side, the conservative elites accept the necessity of promoting an apologetic stance, but increasingly display what is referred to as 'apology fatigue.' In this situation, a return to tensions similar to those that marked the Koizumi period does not appear completely improbable.

The Xi-Abe era has produced somehow concerning signs also in the realm of economic governance. While in the aftermath of the Asian financial crisis at the end of the 1990s, Tokyo and Beijing tried to find joint and mutually agreeable solutions, more recently their relationship has above all been characterized by rivalry and competition. Japan has sided the US in trying to promote TPP and Asia-Pacific regionalization. China on the other hand has promoted its own initiatives, such as AIIB, aiming at the promotion of a Sino-centric form of regionalization.

Finally, the realm of security remains subject to concerns. On the one hand recent steps toward the Japanese normalization and the upgrade of the alliance with the US are likely to contribute to the peace and stability of the region, sending a clear message that both Washington and Tokyo are committed to jointly exercise military deterrence. However, the regional arms race, China's ongoing military modernization, territorial disputes and grey zones scenarios entail risks of military clashes and conflicts. Moreover, the region lacks shared dispute settlement mechanisms, able to control and reduce the risk of unwanted escalation or the failure of deterrence.

References

Beeson M (2006) American hegemony and regionalism: the rise of East Asia and the end of the Asia-Pacific. Geopolitics 11:541–560

Callahan WA (2004) National insecurities: humiliation, salvation, and Chinese nationalism. Altern Glob Local Political 29:199–218

Cave P (2013) Japanese colonialism and the Asia-Pacific War in Japan's History textbooks: changing representations and their causes. Mod Asian Stud 47:542–580

Christensen TJ (1999) China, the US–Japan alliance, and the security dilemma in East Asia. Int Secur 23:49–80

Coble PM (2007) China's "new remembering" of the anti-Japanese war of resistance, 1937–1945. China Quart 190:394–410

Dian M (2014) The evolution of the US–Japan alliance: the eagle and the Chrysanthemum. Chandos Publishing, Oxford

Dian M (2015a) Interpreting Japan's contested memory: conservative and progressive traditions. Int Relat 29:363–377

Dian M (2015b) La banca Asiatica a guida cinese e i rapport trans-atlantici. Aspenia online: http://www.aspeninstitute.it/aspenia-online/article/la-banca-asiatica-guida-cinese-e-i-rapporti-transatlantici

Dittmer L, Weissmann M (2015) China's maritime embroilments. Asian Surv 55(3):447–454

Fairbank JK (1968) The Chinese world order: traditional China's foreign relations. Harvard University Press, Cambridge

Gluck C (1985) Japan's modern myths: ideology in the late Meiji period. Princeton University Press, Princeton

Gluck C et al (2015) The seventieth anniversary of World War II's end in Asia: three perspectives. J Asian Stud 74:531–537

Goh E (2013) The struggle for order: hegemony, hierarchy, and transition in post-cold war East Asia. Oxford University Press, Oxford

Grimes WW (2011) The Asian monetary fund reborn?: Implications of Chiang Mai initiative multilateralization. Asia Policy 11:79–104

He Y (2009) The search for reconciliation: Sino-Japanese and German–Polish relations since World War II. Cambridge University Press, Cambridge

He RX (2014) Tiananmen exiles: voices of the struggle for democracy in China. Palgrave Macmillan, London

Hughes CW (2005) Japanese military modernization: in search of a 'normal' security role. In: Ashley JT, Wills M (eds) Strategic Asia 2005–06. National Bureau of Asian Research, Seattle

Hughes CW (2015) Japan's foreign and security policy under the 'Abe Doctrine': new dynamism or new dead end? Palgrave Macmillan, New York

Inuzuka A (2013) Remembering Japanese militarism through the Fusosha textbook: the collective memory of the Asian-Pacific War in Japan. Commun Quart 61:131–150

Kang D (2003) Getting Asia wrong: the need for new analytical frameworks. Int Secur 27:57–85

Kang DC (2010) East Asia before the west: five centuries of trade and tribute. Columbia University Press, New York, p 2010

Kaufman A (2015) Xi Jinping as historian: marxist, Chinese, nationalist, global. The ASAN Forum, October
Kraus C et al (2014) More friends than foes: Sino-Japanese relations in 1984. Wilson Centre CWIHP e-Dossier, 48, https://www.wilsoncenter.org/publication/more-friends-foes-sino-japanese-relations-1984
MacFarquhar R (1997) The origins of the cultural revolution, vol 3. Oxford University Press, Oxford
Manning RA, Przystup J (2015) Asian stability hangs in the balance of Japan–China relations. East Asia Forum. http://www.eastasiaforum.org/2015/10/12/asian-stability-hangs-in-the-balance-of-japan-china-relations/ (12 Oct)
Miles JA (1997) The legacy of Tiananmen: China in disarray. University of Michigan Press, Ann Harbour
Mitter R (2003) Old ghosts, new memories: China's changing war history in the era of post-Mao politics. J Contemp Hist 38:117–131
Mitter R (2013) China's war with Japan, 1937–1945: the struggle for survival. Penguin, London
Mochizuki MM (2007) Japan's shifting strategy toward the rise of China. J Strat Stud 30:739–776
Nozaki Y (2002) Japanese politics and the history textbook controversy, 1982–2001. Int J Educ Res 37:603–622
Orr JJ (2000) Victims as a hero. In: Ideologies of peace and national identity in post war Japan. University of Hawaii Press, Honolulu
Pyle KB (1969) The new generation in Meiji Japan: problems of cultural identity, 1885–1895. Stanford University Press, Stanford
Pyle KB (2008) Japan rising: the resurgence of Japanese power and purpose. Public Affairs, New York
Radchenko S (2009) Two suns in the heavens: the Sino-Soviet struggle for supremacy, 1962–1967. Woodrow Wilson Center Press, Washington
Reilly J (2011) Remember history, not hatred: collective remembrance of China's war of resistance to Japan. Mod Asian Stud 45:463–490
Samuels RJ (2007) Securing Japan: Tokyo's grand strategy and the future of East Asia. Cornell University Press, Ithaca
Sasakawa Foundation (2015) Collective self defence. http://spfusa.org/research/collective-self-defense/ (28 Oct)
Searight A (2010) United States and Asian regionalism: the politics of reactive leadership. In: Aggarwal VK, Lee S (eds) Evolution of East Asian regionalism: ideas, interests, and domestic institutions. Springer, New York
Solís M (2015) The geopolitical importance of the Trans Pacific partnership: at stake the liberal economic order. Brookings Institution. http://www.brookings.edu/blogs/order-from-chaos/posts/2015/03/13-geopolitical-importance-transpacific-partnership (1 Mar 13)
Szamosszegi A, Kyle C (2011) An analysis of state-owned enterprises and state capitalism in China. US-China Economic and Security Review Commission, Washington, DC
Szczepanska K (2014) The politics of war memory in Japan: progressive civil society groups and contestation of memory of the Asia-Pacific war. Routledge, London
Tiezzi S (2015) China decries new US–Japan defense guidelines. The diplomat, 1 May
Togo K (2012) Japan and reconciliation in post-war Asia: the Murayama statement and its implications. Palgrave Macmillan, London
Vogel E (2011) Deng and the modernization of China. In: Ezra Vogel, Deng Xiaoping and the transformation of China. The Belknap Press of Harvard University Press, Cambridge
Wakamiya Y (1999) The postwar conservative view of Asia. In: How the political right has delayed Japan's Coming to terms with its history of aggression in Asia. LTC International Library Foundation, Tokyo
Wang Z (2014) Never forget national humiliation: historical memory in Chinese politics and foreign relations. Columbia University Press, New York

Warnock E (2015) Japanese prime minister Shinzo Abe's World War II statement. Wall Street J. http://blogs.wsj.com/japanrealtime/2015/08/14/full-text-japanese-prime-minister-shinzo-abes-world-war-ii-statement/ (15 Aug)
Weiss JC (2014) Powerful patriots: nationalist protest in China's foreign relations. Oxford University Press, New York
Westad O (ed) (1998) Brothers in arms: the rise and fall of the Sino-Soviet alliance, 1945–1963. Stanford University Press, Stanford
Wilson GM (1992) Patriots and redeemers in Japan: motives in the Meiji restoration. University of Chicago Press, Chicago
Yoshida Reiji (2012) Formed in childhood, roots of Abe's conservatism go deep. The Japan Times. http://www.japantimes.co.jp/news/2012/12/26/national/formed-in-childhood-roots-of-abes-conservatism-go-deep/#.WKQQbm81_cs (26 Dec)
Zhang X (2011) China in the conception of international society. the english school: engagements with China. Rev Int Stud 37:763–786
Zhao S (1998) A state-led nationalism: the patriotic education campaign in post-Tiananmen China. Commu Post Commu Stud 31:287–302

The Relations Between the People's Republic of China (PRC) and the United States (US)

Giovanni Salvini

Abstract The quality of the relationship between the United States of America (USA) and the People's Republic of China (PRC) has undergone significant changes over the past decades. This chapter analyses three different phases of bilateral relations, characterized by competition (from 1949 to 1976), cooperation (from 1977 to 2008) and the current phase of 'competitive coexistence.' A common view is that the quality of the bilateral relationship will be characterized by a mixture of cooperation, competition and conflict. To be sure, both Washington and Beijing have acknowledged the problem of mutual mistrust, but have yet to develop sustainable ways of reducing them. That said, the US and China are not necessarily doomed to maintain relations prone to conflict if they are able to increase collaboration and limit the differences of how they define and pursue their respective interests.

1 Introduction

In the framework of relations between the People's Republic of China (PRC) and the United States (US), economic and financial cooperation on the one hand and strategic rivalry on the other are closely interwoven. Therefore, the two countries are like a tangle of contradictions where rifts and cooperation, interdependence and mistrust alternate and intertwine so tightly that it becomes difficult to separate them. This chapter seeks to analyze the most important trends and developments of Sino–US relations from 1949 to the present day. After the first phase of US containment, which was marked by among others the Korean War (1950–1953) and ended with the death of Mao (1976), we move onto the phase of US–Sino engagement. During that phase China experienced a 'second revolution' launched by Deng Xiaoping. Fundamental economic reforms led to unprecedented economic growth, which made China the world's second biggest economy. Today and in the future China

G. Salvini (✉)
Department of Political and Social Sciences, University of Pavia, Pavia, Italy
e-mail: giovanni.salvini3@tin.it

S. Beretta et al. (eds.), *Understanding China Today*, Understanding China,
DOI 10.1007/978-3-319-29625-8_6

aims at presenting itself as a cooperative and responsible power in the international order while at the same time making sure that cooperation with others does not reduce its individual global power and influence.

In the wake of the 2008/2009 global economic and financial crises Washington adds the policy of 'hedging' towards China to a policy of cooperating with and engaging China (Guidetti 2015).

In fact, since 2005 economic cooperation co-existed alongside US–Chinese strategic competition, leading to uncertainties and tensions, which in turn increased reciprocal mistrust.

2 Containment: 1949–1993

The People's Republic of China (PRC) was founded in 1949, and it was immediately recognized by all the socialist countries and the most important Western countries except for the United States. Washington's non-recognition was to last more than twenty years and the US decision to recognize Beijing diplomatically in the 1970s was considered a radical change of policy towards a non-democratic regime. Until then it was the American policy of 'containment' towards Beijing, which stood in the way of any kind of diplomatic, economic or cultural relations with the PRC. It was part of a myth in which the US was leading a sacred mission to contain the Chinese strategy of conducting a revolution against what China under Mao referred to as 'global imperialism.' The US policy of containment leads to the conflict in Korea (1950–1953), when American troops—with the UN mandate to ward off the invasion of North Korea by South Korea—and Chinese volunteers in the North Korean army fight a harsh battle: this 'cleansing operation' is extremely expensive in terms of human lives: millions of Korean soldiers and civilians, almost 1 million Chinese soldiers and 36,000 American soldiers. In the late 1950s and early 1960s relations between the PRC and the Soviet Union deteriorated and Beijing saw itself confronted with what was perceived as be a twofold opposition: 'American imperialism' and 'Soviet revisionism.' During that period Mao launched two radical and disastrous campaigns, resulting in millions of casualties: the 'Great Leap Forward' (1985–1962): the attempt to create an extremely decentralized economy, collectivize agricultural production and the abolition of private land plots) and the 'Cultural Revolution' (1969–1976).

The radicalism of the 'Cultural Revolution' led Mao's China to develop a bipolar vision of the world: industrialized countries against the poor and exploited countryside. The 'Cultural Revolution' led to China's international isolation and its economy was in shambles. Furthermore, Beijing was concerned about US–Soviet Union rapprochement and its further marginalization in a world dominated by the US and Soviet Union. As a result, China decided to consider opening up to some Western countries in general and the US in particular in the early 1970s. That change of policy enabled—with the support of the US–Beijing to become a member of the United Nations (UN) in 1971. In February 1972 then US President Nixon's visited

Beijing, a visit brokered by Henry Kissinger. Washington recognized the government in Beijing as representing all Chinese people including those living in Taiwan. The US acknowledged that Taiwan was 'part of China' and also agreed to withdraw all US military from Taiwan. That marked the end of the period of US containment towards China and also the end of the US economic embargo imposed onto China.

Zhou Enlai's death in January 1976 and Mao Zedong's in September of the same year marked the end of China's revolutionary period, and after two years of battles among internal party factions, the reformist leader Deng Xiaoping was able to claim victory. China under Deng launched China's 'second revolution', which aimed at reforming China's institutions and prioritizing pragmatism over ideology. At the core of these reforms were the so-called 'Four Modernizations' together with the recognition of basic fundamental civil rights (for example, the right to education and housing). In December 1978, a joint Sino–American statement announced the complete normalization of bilateral relations accompanied by Washington's recognition of the PRC as the only legal government of China. Since 1979, the US began providing China with technology, including technology for military use. With these new relations between the United States and the PRC from 1972 to 1981, the US–Soviet 'détente' policies became less relevant as US–Sino relations improved significantly, to the state of a 'quasi-alliance', as Zbigniew Brzezinski, US President Carter's security advisor argued at the time. To be sure, US–Sino relations also improved because Washington took advantage of tense Sino–Soviet Union relations. (Brzezinski 1998).

As China emerged from its international isolation it was able to speed its economic reforms and modernization. Kissinger recalls that after 1972 consultations between both countries reached a rare intensity even for formal allies. A member of the CIA was officially stationed in Beijing and military-to-military and defense ties were established. Washington bought Russian-made MIGs from China to train its pilots and in return sold Beijing technology for fighter aircraft. Exchanges intensify after the Soviet invasion of Afghanistan (1979) and the construction, in the west of China, of a spy station to watch out for the Soviet Union. When Ronald Reagan became US President in 1981, Sino–US relations entered into a period of what is also referred to as the 'golden years of Sino–American relations.' Bilateral relations deteriorated when the US decided to increase weapons sales to Taiwan in order to maintain the military balance between Taiwan and Beijing.

The US was completely unprepared for what happened on Tiananmen Square in June 1989. The US (like Europe) imposed economic sanctions onto China and political relations were temporarily suspended after Beijing decided to violently end students' demonstrations on Tiananmen Square on June 4, 1989. However, Washington's message to Beijing at the time was very clear: the public declarations of the American officials are one thing, but the desire to continue cooperation quite another (Kissinger 2011). In fact, in 1991 US investments in China once again reached the levels of 1989 and during Bill Clinton's presidency (1993–2001) bilateral economic and trade relations were further and significantly increased.

3 Engagement (1993–2005/2010)

In 1979 China officially launched its 'reform and opening up' policy. The economic central planning was replaced by a system with market mechanisms and (partially) capitalist structures. Chinese economic reforms were promoted and launched by Deng Xiaoping, who came to power in 1978. His reform policies were continued by his successors Jiang Zemin and Hu Jintao. So-called 'gradualism' and 'pragmatism' became the two distinctive characteristics of the reform process pursued by Jiang and Hu. 'Gradual' and 'pragmatic' also in order to avoid clashes with the more conservative and less reform-minded factions within the Communist Party. In the countryside the communes were abolished and the farming household was given the right to rent a plot of land. The end of the collectivization of land in China turned out to be successful as agricultural production increased enormously: from 1975 to 1984 agricultural production experienced an annual increase of 8.8% compared to 2.6% from 1952 to 1977. This guaranteed China's food self-sufficiency, which in turn allowed Deng Xiaoping to continue pursue more reforms overcoming the resistance from within the PCC. In addition to agricultural reforms a dense network of small village firms emerged. The contribution of the village firms to Chinese industrial production increased from 9.9% in 1980 to 47.8% in 2001. China's key to success was exports and indeed the country—like other developing countries before—became an export-oriented economy. Many small companies were set up with Chinese capital from abroad and the transfer of financial resources and managerial skills increased the competitiveness and efficiency of Chinese companies. This in turn opened up new channels of sales and distribution on international markets. The results of this economic opening were extraordinary: China's export-oriented economy grew at an average annual rate of 15% from 1980 to 2001.

In 2001, after 15 years of negotiations, China became a member of the World Trade Organization (WTO). China's entry into the WTO was also the result of previous agreements between the PRC and the United States, which concerned trade rules and regulations. The Chinese authorities had to make enormous efforts to adapt their legislative, commercial and financial policies to meet the requirements of the members of the WTO and in particular those of the United States. For example, in 2008 the PRC was subject to numerous investigations regarding forms of dumping and financing from Chinese industries. Chinese law had to adapt to the juridical principles of international commerce. With its entry into the WTO the Chinese government was obliged to speed up the harmonization between domestic and international norms and regulations.

There were important results. There was a significant increase in Chinese exports in new sectors (household appliances, electronic equipment), which accounted for 10–15% of world exports. Since 2004, China has become the third trading power in the world—after Germany and the United States. Foreign trade, which reached $780 billion in 2006, amounted to 60% of China's GDP (it was only 10% in 1978). Exports are the engine behind this growth. Foreign markets provide vital new markets for Chinese industrial products, which are produced thanks to the transfer of capitals, technology and know-how. The offshoring of American, European and Asian industries has made China 'the factory of the world.' Foreign direct investments (FDI) are the main route to access international capital and foreign funds accumulated in China in 2006 reached the sum of 691 billion dollars, which in turn resulted in an enormous commercial and structural surplus. Beijing has become the largest holder of the US government debt (US Treasury Bonds). In 2009, the Chinese currency reserves were over $2 trillion. Essentially, Chinese economic growth mainly depends on the vitality of the American market and consequently the political stability of the Chinese regime indirectly depends on American domestic consumption. The economic historian Niall Ferguson calls this reciprocal dependence 'Chimerica' which he defines as the symbiotic relationship between the American economy 'grasshopper' (low savings rate and high level of spending) and the Chinese economy 'the ant' (high level of savings and a frugal life style). The competitive nature of Chinese production strengthens this symbiosis (Ferguson and Schularick 2009). Therefore, during the period of the above-mentioned US engagement, there was a growing constructive cooperation in the economic field, which coexisted alongside US–Sino strategic rivalry (Shambaugh 2014). In 2005 Robert Zoellick, then US Assistant Secretary of State, urged China to take an active role in international politics and security and become a 'responsible stakeholder' in global affairs honoring international treaties and agreements. Some Chinese policymakers think that the time has come for China to become more involved in international politics and leave its former passive approach towards global affairs behind. The majority of Chinese policymakers, however, continue to emphasize economic growth and development as priorities and the base of their legitimacy. To reach this objective they opt for stability. The Chinese 2002 'White Paper' on defense affirms that China needs a peaceful international regional and global environment to develop and become stronger (Information Office of the State Council of the People's Republic of China 2002). Eventually, the US asking China to become the above-mentioned 'responsible stakeholder' was met with suspicion in Beijing.

4 Engaging and Hedging (2008)

American policy towards China over recent years has been characterized by a dual approach: 'engagement' (involvement, cooperation) and 'hedging' (covering risks and defense). The goal of engagement is to make China a so-called 'responsible stakeholder' within the Western system of world order developed after the Second World War. Parallel to this, the Unites States follow a policy of hedging with the intention of consolidating their position in the Pacific Ocean particularly within their network of security alliances. The interlacing of policies re-emerges again after the period of engagement (1993–2005/2010), when a series of international events spark off new tensions. Particularly important are: (1) The 2008/2009 financial crisis in the

US, (2) the United States' decision to withdraw troops from Iraq and Afghanistan, (3) China becoming the world's second biggest economy and the prediction that Chinese economy will overtake the US economy by 2020. In this new situation—in a context that is also referred to as a 'decline' in the West in general and the US in particular—China reconfirms its pre-eminence regarding its alleged rights in the Strait of Taiwan, the South China Sea and in the East China Sea where it seems that it is beginning to adopt its own 'Monroe Doctrine.' Since 2008, the increasing number of more or less serious incidents caused by Beijing in this area has created tensions in the relations between China and its neighbors—Japan, Vietnam, the Philippines, Malaysia, South Korea—all of which see their security threatened since their economic future depends on their relations with China. However, they refuse to deal with conflicts with China bilaterally because their contractual position is obviously inferior and so they try to redress the balance by looking for support from the United States.

The United States took a stand in 2011 with a strong-worded article by then Secretary of State Hillary Clinton called *America's Pacific Century* published by the magazine *Foreign Policy* (in November 2011). From a strategic point of view she affirmed that the United States intend to keep the peace and security in the entire Asian–Pacific region, insofar that means defending the right of navigation in the South China Sea, curbing nuclear ambitions or ensuring transparency in the military activities of the region's key players. In all these cases, which are defined as being 'of vital interest' to the US, China is never specifically mentioned, but is clear that China is the country the US is most concerned about. At the same period, Washington announced the strategy of 'America's return to Asia.' US President Obama addressed the Australian parliament in November 2011: "As President, I have, therefore, made a deliberate and strategic decision: as a Pacific nation, the United States will play a larger and long-term role in shaping this region and its future, by upholding core principles and in close partnership with our allies and friends [...] I have directed my national security team to make our presence and mission in the Asia Pacific a top priority. As a result, reductions in US defense spending will not—I repeat, will not—come at the expense of the Asia Pacific" (The White House 2011). Barack Obama followed up on this announcement with the stationing of 2500 US marines on the Australian island of Darwin, the most outward defense position of the United States in relative proximity to the South China Sea. The new US focus towards Asia introduced by Washington in 2011 is not only military but also economic. Obama suggests a pact for free commercial exchanges, the Trans-Pacific Partnership (TPP), to twelve countries of the Pacific Ocean—including Australia, Japan, Canada and Vietnam (excluding China). The TPP is aimed at strengthening US economic and trade relations with Asia in order to contain China. All of this takes place within the context of the so-called US 'Pivot Asia.' The TPP is important both because it removes the 18,000 tariffs and tariff barriers in an area accounting for 40% of world trade and because it establishes rules and transparent standards concerning investments, environment and labour. It is aimed at boosting economic growth and create new jobs. It also has an important geopolitical and geostrategic dimension in a political-economic system created by the United States in the Pacific area since 1945. Finally, the TPP is a response to US–Sino economic and geopolitical competition and to Washington deterring China from terminating 'Pax Americana' on its terms.

5 Xi Jinping (Since 2012)

With the arrival of Xi Jinping as China's political leader Chinese politics underwent significant changes. Xi's rise to power was fast and uncontested: He became Secretary-General of the PCC (November 2012), President of the PRC (March 2013), President of the Central Commission for Discipline (2014) and Commander-in-Chief of the People's Liberation Army (April 2016). In the PCC he concentrated all forms of power.[1] The policy Xi follows replaces the 'low profile policy' followed by Deng Xiaoping and the 'Harmonious World' followed by Hu Jintao with the so-called 'China Dream' policy. The 'China Dream' is aimed at restoring China's past 'glory' and will be—at least according to Xi—accompanied by what is referred to as the 'rejuvenation' of China. Military modernization and defending security and territorial interests in Asia are, according to Chinese policymakers, part of restoring China's past glory and status. Following the logic and Chinese arguments of the 'China Dream' China no longer considers itself a developing country but instead a big 'important power with Chinese characteristics', able to set up a 'new type (model) of relations' with the other great powers, including the US. According to Xi, relations with the United States must be based on mutual respect and the understanding of their reciprocal basic interests, avoiding confrontation between the rising power China and the established power United States. The goal pursued by the Chinese leadership is reciprocal respect, avoiding zero-sum competition (Bader 2016).

Under US President Obama Washington proposed to establish a global so-called G2 structure (US and China), in the framework of which Washington and China would cooperate with each other. However, Beijing rejected that proposal, fearing that it was part of US containment strategy and Washington's plan to 'control' China. Despite the reciprocal mistrust, some progress was made between the two countries over recent years. The US and China maintain numerous so-called sectoral dialogues (over 90 in total, among which one between military forces) and have adopted agreements in two important sectors (climate change and industrial espionage agreements). To be sure, the agreements are in essence general declarations of principles as opposed to legally binding agreements. It was agree in principle to jointly deal with illegal computer hacking activities and to reduce CO_2 emissions by a third by the year 2025.

[1]The concentration of power in the hand of Xi Jinping is impressive and can be explained by the nature and instruments of China's national political system. On this subject see Li (2016).

As well as pursuing an intensification of relations with the US, China has adopted its so-called 'neighboring policy'/'neighboring diplomacy', supported by regional economic and infrastructure projects (which in turn also have a geopolitical value).

China's 'Silk Road' project (adopted in 2013) is a complex, multidimensional and multifunctional project, which consists of a myriad of projects that are economically and strategically interconnected and spread across three continents with implications on a global scale. The project attempts to economically connect 4.4 billion people in 60 countries, from Beijing to Europe across Central Asia, the Middle East and Africa in a 'mythical' vision of the ancient 'Silk Road', across land and sea. Some describe the project as a Chinese version of the former US 'Marshall Plan', which attempts to build new road and railway networks, energy connections, new infrastructures across Europe and ports connected to Chinese seas. Over the next decade China plans to invest no less than $900 billion of its reserves in the creation of new financial institutions or to strengthen existing ones: the new Asian Infrastructure Investment Bank (AIIB) will be at the center of financial activities and it will directly or indirectly involve 25–30 countries. Washington sees the initiative of the new 'Silk Road', and in particular, its financial institutions, as a potential threat to the international order since they are—at least for the US perspective—a copy of the existing financial institutions (such as the World Bank, which has close ties with the United States and the Asia Development Bank which has close ties with Japan). Furthermore, it will contribute to weakening the financial system based on the dollar by strengthening the Chinese currency. It is obvious that new institutions such as the AIIB can influence the present global economic and financial order, simply because their existence is by no means purely symbolic (the AIIB has a capital amounting to $100 billion, 30% of which is held by China with a voting quota of 27% followed by India: 8% of capital, Russia: 7% and includes 57 member countries). In addition to China's 'Silk Road' project and the launch of the AIIB, Beijing also sought to expand relations with Russia over recent year. In 2014, Beijing and Moscow adopted a massive gas contract, conducted joint military maneuvers in East and Central Asia, and Beijing expanded its weapons purchases from Russia, among others surface-to-air missiles. Expanding military ties with Moscow is undoubtedly understood to be part of a Chinese strategy to counter what Beijing claims are US containment policies towards China (in Asia and beyond).

The Chinese response to the United States' above-mentioned 're-balancing towards Asia' in 2011 concludes with the publication of China's 2015 *White Paper* (Cordesman and Colley 2015), which defines general guidelines and China's military priorities. The fundamental points are:

(1) China aims at becoming a maritime military power. This marks a radical change with the past, during which China referred to itself as a 'continental' as opposed to 'maritime' power.
(2) China has an 'active defense' policy. Unlike in the past, where military strategy adapted to external situations, China's military strategy today must be active in

order to achieve the goals of the above-mentioned 'China dream' aimed at 'renewing the Chinese nation' and enabling China to 're-emerge as rich and powerful nation.'

(3) Although not specifically stated, the Chinese 'White Paper' criticizes the United States, for its 'interference' in the South China Sea. China, the defense strategy paper argues, must ignore the United States' request to stop building Chinese facilities on disputed islands in the South China Sea. The South China Sea is one of the most thwarted areas on the Asian coast of the Pacific. Through the so-called 'Nine–Dash Line' marking the borders of Chinese territorial waters according to ancient Chinese maps, Beijing claims sovereignty over more than 90% of the South China Sea. The 'Nine-Dash Line' stretches several hundreds of miles south and east from China's province of Hainan. At present Beijing's territorial disputes include: the Paracel Islands (also claimed by the Philippines and Taiwan), the Spratly Islands (claimed also by Taiwan, Vietnam, the Philippines, Malaysia and Brunei), the Scarborough Shoal (also claimed by the Philippines and Taiwan). Furthermore, in the East China Sea China disputes Japanese control over the Senkaku Islands (Beijing calls them 'Diaoyu Islands'). The United States do not take a position on sovereignty in these disputes and instead urge all involved parties to solve the disputes through international arbitration. However, China does not embrace the concept of international arbitration and instead is using its increasing power on the seas through sea patrols, to intrude into the waters of other claimants and more recently to create seven artificial islands equipped with listening points and takeoff strips, which can be quickly transformed for military use.[2]

Beyond the legal aspects, Beijing has a well-defined strategy: to permit its fleet—the atomic submarines stationed on the island of Hainan and its aircraft carrier—to sail beyond the 'first chain' of islands controlled by the United States (which stretch from the south of Japan to Malaysia) to freely emerge in the ocean. Consequently, the objective is to push the United States towards the 'second islands chain', which ranges from Japan to New Guinea with its most important defense centers in Guam and Okinawa. We can identify the classic geopolitical conflict between a continental power (China) and a 'thalassocratic' power (the United Sates). In other words: either the US acknowledges China a power with the same rights as the United States in the Asia–Pacific area or China accepts the *Pax Americana* (in force since 1945).

Since Deng Xiaoping took over power in China in the late 1970s, China has become a contributor to the international trade system. As a member of the United

[2]The Permanent Court of Arbitration in The Hague ruled on July 12, 2016: "Within the exclusive economic zone of the Philippines, because those areas are not overlapped by any possible entitlement of China". The tribunal furthermore found that China had violated the Philippines' sovereign rights in those waters by interfering with its fishing and petroleum exploration and by constructing artificial islands (Holmes and Phillips 2016).

Nations (UN), the World Trade Organization (WTO), the World Bank, the Atomic Energy Agency and the International Monetary Fund (IMF) China makes increasingly valid contributions.

Chinese trade with the United States has increased from $2.7 billion in 1980 to $10.4 billion in 1990 and today amounts to roughly $650 billion. China is the biggest trading nation and it continues to be one of the most attractive destinations for foreign investments. Furthermore, China's foreign currency reserves amount to roughly $3.5 trillion. In the first five months of 2016, Chinese investments in Western companies rose to $111 billion compared to $107 billion in 2015, five times more than in 2006. Furthermore, China consolidates its position as a dominant actor in East Asia with the Asia Infrastructure Investment Bank (AIIB), which—as leader of 56 member countries—challenges the role of the World Bank and that of the Asian Development Bank (ADB) in Asia.

The dynamism of the Chinese economy has led to a debate on Chinese ambitions to pursue a dominant position in Asia to challenge the *Pax Americana*. China's growing influence in Asia is a concern for the US: Chinese assertive regional policies are, from a US perspective, challenging the geo-strategic balance in the region.

6 Defence

In absolute figures, the US defense spending cannot be matched. American spending on defense in 2016 reached $597 billion. China 'only' spent $145 billion in the same year. To match the American figure it is necessary to sum up the spending of the first 14 countries in the world. However, according to reports published by the London-based International Institute of Strategic Studies (IISS) the Western military powers' technological supremacy is no longer a certainty. Western dominance in terms of technological superiority has over the last two decades diminished. China's goal is to catch up with Western technology accompanied by efforts to modernize and professionalize the People's Liberation Army (PLA) (2.2 million soldiers in arms) and improve its nuclear and ballistic capacities. The first effort consists in reducing the number of ground forces in favor of increasing navy and air forces. Until now, China's defense budget assigned 60% to the ground forces, 20% to the navy and 20% to the air force. In the years ahead this proportion will change to 50–25–25.

If we take into account that China's long-term military strategy is aimed at matching US military capabilities—together with securing the control of its coast lines in the short-term—we understand why China invests enormous resources into the modernization of its navy. Evidence of the modernization of the Chinese military naval fleet is the construction of its first nuclear submarine, able to launch new generation missiles and strategic missiles with a range of 800 km. Furthermore, Beijing is currently building its first aircraft carrier. The entire Chinese fleet can only count on five nuclear attack submarines and one submarine able to carry 12–16 nuclear missiles with a range of 3500 km; 20 new submarines are currently being built and there is great anticipation for a new Chinese anti-naval missile. China's naval fleet should act as a deterrent for the Seventh American US naval fleet, which among others guarantees the autonomy of Taiwan from its bases in Guam, Japan and South Korea. The US navy has 53 modern attack submarines—double the amount of other world fleets—and 12 of the 15 aircraft carriers in the world with an unequalled air force fleet.

China has also achieved important results in the process of technological modernization in other fields: the destruction of a satellite (2007) which demonstrated that China has 'second hit' capacity. While China is working towards seeking to match US military capabilities, it is trying to avoid any form of direct conflict and it is trying to exploit every possible occasion to counter American supremacy with asymmetric means (the submarines and the anti-naval missiles already are). In terms of military hard power the US is evidently superior even if China is rapidly catching up, among others developing a so-called 'high-tech asymmetric self-defense strategy.' The objective of the US is to maintain supremacy in the oceans, in the ultra-atmospheric space and in cyberspace. Furthermore, Washington aims at countering Chinese so-called 'anti-access'/'area-denial' strategies with conventional weapons. In terms of 'soft power' too the US has an edge. Despite enormous Chinese efforts to portray itself as 'soft power', it has—unlike in the developing world—little persuasive power in the West. China is, as David Shambaugh argues, a 'partial power' and not—at least not in the near future—able to match US hard or soft power.

7 Chinese Schools of Thought

The following chapter provides a short overview of the various schools of thoughts in China, which reveals that there is indeed a wide-ranging spectrum of opinions and views on China's role and position in international politics. We start with the so-called 'nationalists', a group which believes in Chinese 'isolationism.' This school does not trust the West and pursues complete Chinese autonomy. It is suspicious of international institutions and any kind of Chinese involvement in them. This group has a strong Marxist influence, from e.g. the Marxist Institute of the Chinese Academy for Social Sciences (CASS). This group includes populists and nationalists, who are all very critical of the West in general and the United States in particular. In internal politics the isolationists team up the so-called 'new left' and believe that the politics of 'reform and opening up' over the past 30 years has corroded socialist integrity and weakened China's autonomy and sovereignty in the international politics. They also claim that internal reform has inevitably led to the restoration of capitalism in China and the 'peaceful evolution' has become the main threat for the country. Chinese policymakers believe that the present system of international politics is unfair and favors the rich and what they refer to as 'imperial' countries since 'globalization' is a process of internationalization of capital as suggested by Lenin. The global financial crisis (2008–2010), it is argued in this context, is evidence of the 'State Capitalist monopoly' which brought the world economy to the brink of disaster as Lenin had predicted already in 1917.

According to Fang Ning, director of the CASS (Chinese Academy for Social Sciences), the war in Iraq in 2003 marks the beginning of an era of 'new imperialism' and the coming to an end of Deng Xiaoping's era of 'peace and development' (Nau and Ollapally 2012). China's policy towards the United States is criticized for being too soft and a Sino–American 'strategic partnership' is an illusion. Within this group anti-Americanism is on the rise, as e.g. documented by the book *Unrestricted Warfare, China's Master Plan to Destroy America*, written by two colonels of China's armed forces (Lang and Wang 2002). According to the authors, the Gulf War, which is seen as a punitive operation conducted by the US against Saddam Hussein, radically changed China's strategic equation: from a military point of view China is, in terms of military technology and capabilities, inferior to the US and, from a strategic point of view, it is isolated because the US have enough political capital and influence to convince the international community to carry out military interventions in the defense of democracy. Therefore the authors believe it is necessary for China to identify alternative ways of competing and indeed defeating the US. The theory of the so-called 'war beyond the boundaries' is mentioned and propagated in this context. That sort of war is fought using all means and instruments in the so-called post-modern, post-industrial period: military, economic and technological means.

The nationalists' arguments are explained well in two books, which became bestsellers in China. The first book is called *The Unhappy China*. The author, Song Xiaojun, starts off from the idea that even in the present circumstances the United States and the West are dangerous forces and China's enemies. The second book too warns of the US as China's rival and indeed enemy: *The Chinese Dream*, written by Colonel Liu Mingfu, Director of the Institute of Military Development of the University for National Defense (Saunders 2010). Liu explicitly supports the idea that China should follow a new strategy of development to a position of global leadership in the military field, able to compete with the United States. In his analysis a hegemonic conflict is inevitable. While a majority of Chinese leaders and public intellectuals might not agree with Liu's ideas, his views are nonetheless endorsed by many scholars of international relations and opinion leaders. In his book Liu explicitly states that the general objective of the modernization of China is to become the 'most powerful country in the world'. Already in 1911 Sun Yat-sen said his dream was for China to become the richest and strongest country in the world. Mao's 'Great Leap Forward', according to Liu, was nothing else than an attempt to overtake the United States and Deng Xiaoping's strategy of 'keeping a low profile' was an effort to rapidly modernize China's economy in order for China to become a strong country. According to Liu, the replacement of the US with China as a superpower, which he calls 'the succession of the superpower', is not far off in the future. He urges the Chinese leaders and the people to have no 'illusion' about the coexistence between the superpower and the emerging superpower: in his view the United States are determined to contain China from an economic, a political and in particular military point of view.

The above-mentioned 'China Dream' entails the objective to transform China into the modern version of the 'glorious' country it used to be. To achieve this, it will be necessary to replace the United States' dominance (Liu Mingfu 2015). Liu predicts that the rise of China will inaugurate a golden age of Asian prosperity, an era in which the products, the culture and Chinese values will become the global standard. The world will be harmonious because the Chinese leadership is 'wiser' and more 'humble' than US leaders and because China will avoid pursuing hegemony, and limit itself to exerting a *primus inter pares* role among the nations of the world (Liu looks favorably towards the role played by traditional Chinese businessmen who, as he argues, behave like benevolent 'older brothers' when dealing with counterparts in smaller and weaker countries).

The second school is the realist school of thought, arguably still the dominant school in international relations. According to the realist school, the sovereignty of the nation state must be defended at all costs. Realists tend to see the external world as anarchic and unpredictable, hence the need for a strong state, which is able to resist external pressures. Against this background, China's realists argue that Deng's theory of a 'peaceful development' is dangerous and out of date because it gives the idea that China is not prepared to protect its national sovereignty and interests. As a result, they are in favor of a more assertive policy towards the United States, more in line with the nationalist school, which argues that China's engagement in structures and institutions of global governance is a dangerous trap, which is wasting resources needed for China's development.

The third school is that of the 'great powers'. This school believes that priority in relations with the outside world must be given to the great powers—the United States, Russia and perhaps the EU. Less importance should be assigned to the developing world. The Western powers, the United States and the EU are seen as important sources of technology, capital and investment, while Russia is considered above all a source of energy. In this context the US–China relations are considered a priority—the so-called 'America First Principle.' However, the views of this group are not homogeneous in the sense that some do not underestimate the strategic role of Russia—beyond its role in energy resources—and consequently they tend to be more suspicious and cautious about further opening up to the West. Others are surprised about the political instability within the EU. Others believe it would be impossible to maintain priority relations with all three blocs: the United States, Russia the EU. However, at the same time, they disagree with the policy of giving priority exclusively to the United States. In addition, some are skeptical about contributing to existing structures of global governance and are in favor of keeping a low profile, and not disclosing China's objectives. They follow the teachings of Deng Xiaoping who believed in avoiding conflicts, finding a common ground so as not to waste time following a strategy with few apparent benefits. This group tries to avoid increasing China's global involvement, even if China must not refuse participation in the United Nations peacekeeping operations: in fact, China participates in 11 of the 19 UN's current peacekeeping operations. To be sure, China's contributions to UN peacekeeping missions also take place due to tactical reasons and follow the logic of realists rather than institutional liberalists.

Institutional liberalists are in a Chinese context also referred to as 'globalists' since they believe that to deal with the problems of global governance is part of China's global responsibilities as a country with growing political and economic influence. The supporters of this school of thought endorse Western liberal institutionalism aimed at transforming international relations from a 'jungle' of chaotic political powers into a 'zoo' of regular peaceful relations with the creation of international organizations, first and foremost the UN. The attention focuses more on the less traditional aspects of security—its economic and human aspects, anti-terrorism, public health, organized crime, piracy, etc.—and in general connected to 'soft power' especially within the Security Council and in the activities of the United Nations, where they are expected to take on an active role. An influential representative of the liberal-institutional school is Wang Jisi, Head of the School of International Studies at Peking University. He argues that China's behavior has become increasingly assertive, as it was demonstrated by its strong reactions to a chain of events in 2010: Washington's decision to sell arms to Taiwan, the US–South Korean military training exercises in the Yellow Sea and the Japanese coast guard's seizing of a Chinese fishing trawler in the East China Sea. As a result of these episodes the international community needs to have a better understanding of Chinese strategic thought (Jisi 2011). According to Wang Jisi, China's strategy to simultaneously protect and defend its sovereignty, security and advance its economic development makes it difficult to formulate a coherent foreign policy, because it is unrealistic to build a strategy with the United States as China's rival or indeed enemy. Indeed, it is in China's interest, he argues, to continue applying an updated version of Deng's 'low-profile' foreign policy. China must continue to fight terrorism and piracy with other countries and must make contributions to the stability of the global economic and financial systems. According to this view, even if the United States and Japan are geopolitical competitors, they are still China's two major economic partners. Relations with the great powers, Wang concludes, are still vital: trilateral interactions between China, Japan and the US must remain stable and constructive.

In sum, we have the so-called 'liberal optimists' in one corner and the 'realist pessimists' in the other. The first group believes that, despite the instability in global politics and security, the current international order benefits China's economic growth and development. There is no need for China to seek to fundamentally change the existing world order. The pessimist realists on the other hand predict intense competition and conflict. China's growing strength will make the country pursue its interests in a more assertive way and conflict with the US will be inevitable. In this context, the concept of 'exceptionalism' of a country becomes important. US exceptionalism, due to a number of reasons—the absence of feudalism, Puritan roots, the heritage of a great continent with abundant natural resources, the ethnic US 'melting-pot', individualism, and its great sense of trust and responsibility—is different from Chinese 'exceptionalism.' Indeed, Chinese 'exceptionalism' is a relatively new phenomenon, even if China is aware and indeed proud of it ancient culture more than any other country in the world. Many of the recent writings on Chinese 'exceptionalism' cite the Chinese model of economic development perceived as a unique, 'exceptional' experience of world (economic) history.

Following the global financial crisis of 2008/2009 China was confident to have acquired the necessary means and resources to see its position as a 'superpower' recognized. However, contrary to the hopes of Beijing, the US do not seem ready to grant China the status of a privileged partner, which is what Chinese policymakers want in order to increase Chinese prestige and regional power. Evidence of that is Washington's preparedness to confirm its geopolitical involvement in the Asian area ("The United States are a power in the Pacific", as outgoing US President Obama stated) with the support of the group of regional powers, as demonstrated by increased US military cooperation with Vietnam, India, Indonesia and Australia.

8 The US Approach

The United States' policy towards the PRC has evolved since the end of the Second World War in three (20-year long) phases. The first phase covers the period from 1949 to 1969 and is characterized by the American policy of 'containment' towards China. It was a policy based entirely on ideological and military competition as we can see from the Korean War (1950–1953), without any element of cooperation. Despite the economic and social upheaval of China's 'Great Leap Forward' (1958–1961), the process of industrialization and the Chinese atomic bomb (1964) modified US policies towards China. In the second phase, from 1969 to 1989, Washington recognizes China diplomatically and bilateral trade and political relations resume. China becomes a member of the United Nations and obtains a permanent seat at the UN Security Council. Nixon and Kissinger's realist policy favored the improvement of relations with China: a policy of engagement, which aimed at involving China international politics.

The tragic events on Tiananmen Square in June 1989 once again shift the pendulum of United States' strategy. On the one hand, they further develop diplomatic and economic relations with Chinese membership of the WTO in 2001 and, on the other they restart a security policy which aims to protect the military supremacy of the Pacific. This strategy, which is defined as 'congagement', a neologism which combines two opposite terms: 'containment' and 'engagement', engaging China while at the same time keeping China's geopolitical ambitions in check (through e.g. 'hedging'). Within this framework, the position of many American analysts is very diverse and is not easy to classify into homogeneous groups. In any case, the schools in the United States which take an interest in international relations in Asia, and in particular the relations between the PRC and the United States, are usually defined as schools of *strategic* competition, *peaceful growth, pragmatic* or *competitive* competition.

For the supporters of *strategic competition*, Asia is playing a zero-sum power game along the lines of Tucidide's observations of the war in Peloponneso: Athen's growth in power and the fear which inspired Sparta meant war was inevitable (Mearsheimer 2003). If we transpose China to Athens and the United States to Sparta, we arrive at Mearsheimer's doctrine of 'offensive realism' and the 'tragic politics of the great powers'. If China continues its extraordinary economic growth, over the next decades, Mearsheimer argues, this will result in increasingly intense US–Sino security competition, which in turn will result in war. The school of 'strategic competition' is characterized by a position of rigid realism which assumes that Europe before 1945 probably reflects the future of Asia. The growth of China in Asia in the 21st century is the same as the growth of Imperial Germany in Europe in the 19th century, with Beijing which emerges as Washington's inevitable competitor.

Henry Kissinger is more optimistic. He believes that China wants to integrate itself into the international system and does not agree with the idea that Beijing aims at upsetting the international system and existing order. A more realistic hypothesis is that China, because of its rapid growth, will try to play a major role within the international system, both from a political and economic point of view. Against this background, the United States have to make sure, at least in the near future, to use military force as the main instrument of its foreign policy. Kissinger does not see why China, surrounded by great countries with a strong military force, should challenge the United States at a time when it is achieving extraordinary results from an economic point of view. He also adds that relations between China and the United States should not become zero-sum type of relationship. The right definition for the Sino–American relations is 'co-existence' rather than partnership. Coevolution means that both countries follow their national priorities, they cooperate when it is possible and regulate their relations in such a way as to reduce conflicts to a minimum. Each of the two countries is too big to be dominated by the other. Neither of them, therefore, could define the terms of victory if there were to be a conflict or a new 'Cold War' (Kissinger 2011).

John Ikenberry believes that China and the other great emerging powers do not want to contest the basic rules and principles of the global world order but instead want to be able to contribute to that order more actively. China is deeply involved in the world trade system—its exports make up 40% of its GDP, 25% goes to the United States—and if it wants the yuan to become a global currency, it will have to give up control of its currency and strengthen internal financial rules and institutions. As Barry Eichengreen and other economic historians have observed, the United States' dollar took on its international role after the Second World War not only because the American economy was big, but also because it had highly developed financial markets and internal economic and political institutions which were stable, open and based on the rule of law. China will have to establish the same institutional preconditions if it wants its currency to become global (Eichengreen 2008). An alternative, illiberal order—a 'Beijing model' so to speak—would probably be organized in terms of exclusive blocs, influential spheres and trade networks. It would be less open and less based on rules, and it would likely be dominated by a network of bilateral relations between countries. Ikenberry also believes that a stronger China makes the neighboring states potentially less safe, especially if China behaves in an aggressive way and if it manifests revisionist ambitions, as manifested in Beijing's assertive policies in the South China Sea. In the present liberal world order, the strategy of the United States and China should intensify forms of internationalism which not only include economic and security aspects, but also cooperation in the fields of clean energy, protection of the environment, non-proliferation and global economic governance (Ikenberry 2014).

Brzezinski believes that the United States should have a dual role in Asia: a balancer and mediator. The United States can and should be the central figure to help Asia avoid a battle for regional dominion and should mediate conflicts and smooth the imbalances in power among potential rivals. In order to do this, the US should respect China's special historical and geopolitical role and maintain the stability in the extreme eastern Rimland. If Washington re-engaged in serious talks with China regarding Asian regional security, this would not only help reduce the possibility of US–Chinese conflicts, but it would also reduce the risk of misperceptions and conflicts between China and Japan, China and India (and to a certain extent between China and Russia on energy resources and the status of the Central Asian States). In other words, stable balance of power structures in Asia are in China's interest. At the same time the United States must recognize that stability in Asia can no longer be imposed by a non-Asian power and even less so (especially after the useless Korean war, the failed Vietnamese war, the unprovoked attack in Iraq in 2003 and the prolonged conflict in Afghanistan) by the direct military intervention of the United States. In fact, the efforts of the United States to increase Asian stability could turn out to be self-destructive—leading the United States into a costly repetition of its most recent wars—and also a repetition of what happened in Europe in the 20th century. If America were to become active in forming an anti-Chinese alliance with India (and perhaps with some other continental states) or in promoting an anti-Chinese militarization of Japan, it could generate a dangerous reciprocal resentment. The geopolitical balance of the 21st century in Asia must be based on an approach, which should be regionally self-standing and constructive in its relations between states and less so in regionally divided military alliances with non-Asian powers (Brzezinski 2012).

Christensen (2015) argues that the US 'hedging strategy' towards China combines two elements which are usually disconnected: a very strong military presence in East Asia together with an invitation towards China to participate in forms of regional and global governance. Without a reassuring diplomatic presence, Beijing will interpret increasing US military presence in Asia as containment while on the other hand the lack military presence might be interpreted as a form of weakness. Consequently, US political and diplomatic exchanges with China must make sure to avoid imposing a 'zero-sum game' onto Beijing.

9 Conclusions

Since 1949 until today, cooperation and competition have been alternating in US–Sino relations. In recent years, Washington and Beijing seemed to have settled for what is referred to as 'competitive coexistence.' This is a state of relations also referred to as the 'new normal' of bilateral relations. China's leader Xi Jinping seems to have the upper hand in the context of US–Sino strategic competition: the Chinese militarization of disputed islets in the South China Sea is a clear indication that Beijing is aiming at increasing its power projection capabilities in the Asia–Pacific. The inclusion of the Yuan in turn into the 'Special Drawing Rights' basket is an essential step on the path towards the internationalization of China's currency. Moreover, The 'Silk Road' project and the functionally connected above-mentioned AIIB further support the objectives of Chinese foreign policy. The likely US withdrawal from the above-mentioned TPP could further facilitate the rise of China as the regional hegemon. Indeed, it is no coincidence that Chinese policy makers are accelerating their project of an extended 'Asian free trade area' supported by the AIIB and the New Development Bank (NDB), an institution with strong support from the BRICS countries (Brazil, Russia, India, China, South Africa). In the absence of a regional security architecture the geopolitical framework of this area is bound to evolve and to depend directly, more than ever before, on the state of US–China relations, to such extent that China and the United States are similar to a couple of 'tangled titans' confronting each other within a unsolvable twine made up of competition, conflict and cooperation. However, conflict is not necessarily inevitable. David Shambaugh argues that: "However complicated and fraught, this is a marriage in which divorce is not an option. Divorce = war" (Shambaugh 2016). This view is similar to the views held by Henry Kissinger, who argues that 'co-existence' between Washington and Beijing is the most desirable solution, even if it requires patience, tolerance and pragmatism by all involved parties.

References

Bader JA (2016) How Xi Jinping sees the world … and why. Order from Chaos, Asia Working Group, Paper 2, February 2016-Brooking

Brzezinski Z (1998) The grand chessboard: American primacy and its geostrategic imperatives. Basic Books, New York

Brzezinski Z (2012) Strategic vision. America and the crisis of global power. Basic Book, New York

Christensen TJ (2015) China challenge. Shaping the choices of a rising power. W.W. Norton and Co., New York

Clinton H (2011) America's Pacific century. Foreign policy, 11 Oct

Cordesman AH, Colley S (2015) Chinese strategy and military modernization in 2015: a comparative analysis. CSIS (Centre for Strategic & International Studies), Washington DC

Eichengreen B (2008) Globalizing capital: a history of the international monetary system. Princeton University Press

Ferguson N, Schularick M (2009) The end of chimerica. Harvard Businness School working paper 10-037

Guidetti A (2015) The silk road, sand castles and the US–China Rivalry. GCSP (Geneva Centre for Security Policy), Geneva, July n.7

Holmes O, Phillips T (2016) https://www.theguardian.com/news/2016/jul/12/south-china-sea-dispute-what-you-need-to-know-about-the-hague-court-ruling

Ikenberry GJ (ed) (2014) Power, order, and change in world politics. Cambridge Univ. Press

Information Office of the State Council of the People's Republic of China (2002) China's National Defense, Bejing, www.china.org.cn/e-white/20021209/

Jisi W (2011) China's search for a grand strategy. A rising great power finds its way. Foreign policy, Mar/Apr 2011

Kissinger H (2011) On China. Penguin Press, New York

Lang Q, Wang X (2002) Unrestricted warfare: China's master plan to destroy America. Pan American Publishing Company, Los Angeles

Li C (2016) Chinese politics in the Xi Jinping era. Reassessing Collective Leadership. Brookings Institution Press, Washington DC

Liu M (2015) The China dream: Great power thinking and strategic posture in the Post-American era. CN Times Books Inc., New York

Mearsheimer JJ (2003) The tragedy of great power politics. W.W. Norton & Company, New York-London

Nau HR, Ollapally DM (eds) (2012) Worldviews of aspiring powers: domestic foreign policy debates in China, India, Iran, Japan, and Russia. Oxford University Press

Saunders PC (2010) Will China's dream turn into America's nightmare? China brief Vol. 10, Issue 7. https://jamestown.org/program/will-chinas-dream-turn-into-americas-nightmare/ (1 Apr)

Shambaugh D (2014) China goes global. The partial power. Oxford University Press, Oxford, p 2014

Shambaugh D (2016) China's future. Polity Press, Cambridge, p 155

The White House—Office of the Press Secretary (2011) Remarks by President Obama to the Australian Parliament, briefing roomspeeches and remarks. https://www.whitehouse.gov/the-press-office/2011/11/17/remarks-president-obama-australian-parliament

Coping with the Rising Dragon: Italy–China Relations Beyond Business

Filippo Fasulo

Abstract The relations between Italy and China have gone through several stages, characterized by altering highs and lows. The geographical distance between Italy and China makes sure that the economic dimension of bilateral relations is more important than cooperation in politics and security. However, the kind of foreign policies adopted by Chinese leader Xi Jinping calls on Italy to seek to expand cooperation in the areas of politics and security. Since China is expanding its interests abroad, Italy is advised to seek to interact with Beijing on issues such as the fight against terrorism or the development of African countries from where the majority of migrants seek to reach the southernmost shores of the European Union. Such political cooperation can take place in parallel with economic cooperation, moving away from seeking to compete with China's manufacturing industry but instead seeking to exploit China's emerging high quality niches within its domestic market. In order to achieve this goal, it will be crucial to convince Beijing and Chinese authorities to forego protectionist trade policies aimed at protecting what in China is referred to as 'strategic sectors.'

1 Introduction

When talking about relations between Italy and China, the focus is usually on economic ties and interactions. In light of the rapid growth of the bilateral trade value and, more recently, the surge of Chinese FDI in Italy[1], an overwhelmingly importance is assigned to economic rather than political relations (Hanemann and Huotari 2016). Furthermore, the geographical distance between both countries and

[1]The leading example of this trend is the ChemChina's EUR 7 billion acquisition of Italian tire producer Pirelli, the biggest Chinese takeover in the EU to date.

F. Fasulo (✉)
Istituto per gli Studi di Politica Internazionale (ISPI)
and Academic Secretary, Class of Far Eastern Studies,
Accademia Ambrosiana, Milan, Italy
e-mail: filippo.fasulo@gmail.com

S. Beretta et al. (eds.), *Understanding China Today*, Understanding China,
DOI 10.1007/978-3-319-29625-8_7

different interests in different parts of the world made sure that there were few conflicts of geopolitical nature. However, since Xi Jinping inaugurated a new approach to China's international relations, new areas of cooperation are gaining momentum. Through the 'One Belt One Road' initiative, China is expanding its reach also to the Western shores of the Eurasian continent which is intertwined with China's long time engagement with and presence in Africa, the main source of migration flows to Italy. Moreover, increasing Chinese contributions to promoting security and political stability in Africa could in the medium term increase the possibilities for joint Italian-Chinese policies in countries and areas of common interest.

2 Italy–China Relations in the Past and the Start of a New Phase

From the first Sino–Italian relations through Marco Polo and the Jesuits' travels to the concession in Tianjin, there are many historical contacts that shaped the mutual understanding between Italy and China. Contemporary bilateral relations date back to the early 1970s, when Italy officially recognized the People's Republic of China (PRC). Since then, relations have changed profoundly and have been affected by developments in both Chinese and Italian domestic politics. Contemporary Sino-Italian relations have evolved through six stages (1) from the foundation of the People's Republic of China in 1949 to the establishment of official diplomatic relations in 1970 (2) from the opening of an Italian Embassy in Beijing in 1970 to the launch of economic reforms in China in 1978 (3) from the economic reforms launched by Deng Xiaoping in 1978[2] to the end of the First Republic in Italy in 1992 (4) from the start of the Italian Second Republic to the signing of the strategic partnership in 2014 (5) from the strategic partnership to the coming to power of Xi Jinping in 2012 and finally (6) from 2012 onwards and the adoption of foreign policies under Chinese leader Xi Jinping with an impact on relations with Italy.

The first and the second stages were characterized by a kind of pioneering approach. China, especially after the Communist takeover[3], was an 'unknown object', and the process of discovering China was not without difficulties. The opening of a diplomatic mission in Beijing was the result of a complex balancing act and negotiations between China and the US, who were secretly negotiating the normalisation of their bilateral relationship (Pini 2011; Romano 2010). What the first Italian diplomats experienced arriving in China in the 1970s was still the country of Mao Zedong and his Cultural Revolution in its final stage. At that time

[2]Deng Xiaoping's economic reforms in 1978 opened up the country to foreign investment.

[3]The foundation of the People's Republic of China dates back to October 1st of 1949, when Mao Zedong announced the establishment of the People's Republic of China (PRC) after the victory over Chiang Kai-shek and his Nationalist Party (Guomindang).

an important role was played by some frontrunners, such as Senator Vittorino Colombo who founded the *Istituto Italo Cinese* (Italian Chinese Institute) in 1971. The shift to the third phase took place in the late 1970s after Mao's death, when Deng Xiaoping was about to start the 'Open Door' policy that would change the future path of China's economic development (Naughton 2007). This stage benefitted from personal links and connections between Italian and Chinese politicians established during the previous phase. An increasingly open China was interested in cultivating its relationship with other communist parties in the world, including the Italian Communist Party, the biggest communist party in the West. Close ties between Chinese and Italian communists led to a number of visits, among them a two-week long summer holiday in China of the Italian communist leader Enrico Berlinguer with his family in 1983. In 1984, the Secretary-General of China's CCP Zhao Ziyang's attended Berlinguer's state funeral. Indeed, in the 1980s and early 1990s the entire Italian ruling class was very much interested in China, regardless of party affiliations. Against the background of the pioneering role of Christian Democrat Vittorino Colombo and relations between the communist parties in China and Italy, the Italian Socialist Party too began to establish relations with China's political leadership. Indeed, in 1990, a few months after the crackdown on student demonstrations on Tiananmen Square, the then Minister of Foreign Affairs Gianni De Michelis promoted closer ties with China. The timing was particularly significant because the Italian government was holding the rotating presidency of the European Union (Taggart 2014). In 1992, the Italian government announced to make an economic contribution to the development of the Pudong area in Shanghai. The investment in Pudong was consistent with the main characteristic of the third phase: moving closer to China was no longer just a matter of deepening mutual knowledge. It was time to talk about business and the expansion of bilateral trade and business ties. Economic relations, therefore, became the central issue of Sino-Italian talks and led to mutually beneficial results. In the mid-1980s Italy became China's second-largest trading partner within the EU, following West Germany (Coralluzzo 2008). Events and crisis in Italian domestic politics in the early 1990s had a negative impact on bilateral business and trade relations. In 1992, the eruption of a major corruption scandal, which decimated an entire class of Italian politicians, led to the establishment of Italy so-called 'Second Republic' and to the fourth phase of the Sino–Italian relations. The political uncertainties within Italy gave rise to a new generation of politicians without personal connections with China. This in turn had a negative impact on the expansion of ties with China. The slowdown of the expansion of Sino–Italian relations was so bad that Francesco Sisci described the rupture caused by the Italian corruption scandal as the event through which 'Italy lost China' (Sisci 2005). The Pudong affair, the symbol of the high point of Sino–Italian relationship turned sour when the Italian government was no longer able to fulfil its commitments and was forced to abandon previously envisioned investments. As the former Italian Prime Minister and President of the European Commission Romano Prodi stated, those were years of continuously shifting relations. A period of close relations was followed by a period of mutual suspicion and misunderstanding. The memory of the tragic events on Tiananmen

Square in June 1989 which interrupted relations with Italy's post-communist parties, together with competition from Chinese firms using cheap and non regulated labour contributed to generating a widespread feeling of Sinophobia among the Italian population (Andornino 2012, 2014; Coralluzzo 2008). This transitional phase was eventually overcome in 2004 when Italy and China established a comprehensive strategic partnership. The agreement was the result of the recognition that it is in Italy's interest to pursue stable relations with China 10 years after the establishment of the 'Second Republic.' As a result, the fifth phase of Italy–China relations became one with fully institutionalized ties in the framework of the above-mentioned strategic partnership. It became a relationship that was no longer supported by personal relationships between respective political leaders as it was the case during the Italian First Republic. What is more, it was no longer affected by volatilities within Italy's political system. A positive role was also played by the reform of the Minister of Foreign Affairs performed since the early 2000s (Andornino 2014). The most important challenge of the fifth phase was the state of bilateral economic relations after China became a member of the World Trade Organization (WTO) in 2001. The global economic and financial crisis in the late 2000s added another challenge to bilateral trade and investment ties. After five phases of relations with an almost exclusive focus on economic ties, Italy and China are today also adding cooperation in international politics and security to the bilateral agenda, thanks to new scope and quality of China's foreign policies introduced by China's leader Xi Jinping since 2012. Through trade and investment ties, China's global interests have increased enormously, obliging Beijing to pursue a foreign political strategy aimed at protecting its economic interests outside of China. As it will be explained below, many issues could be at stake. Among others, like China's presence in the Mediterranean Region and Africa, Italy's role in Europe might change after the British electorate has voted in favour of 'Brexit' with a referendum in June 2016. While Italy used to play a minor role compared to the one assumed by the UK, France and Germany in Europe, Rome's influence in Europe could increase in the years ahead. China today is targeting southern Europe to counterbalance the influence of northern countries and Italy could become the focus of such a Chinese economic approach towards southern Europe. Against this background, the sixth phase of Sino-Italian ties should embrace the intensification of bilateral political relations.

3 Economic Relations, Opportunities for Cooperation and Competing Fields

China's rapid and ongoing economic growth facilitated the steady expansion of Sino-Italian economic ties. In just a few decades, China was able to transform itself from a poor developing country into the world's second biggest economy. Such a rise was fuelled by a massive amount of Chinese public investment while its rapid economic growth and development relied on low-skilled labour. Cheap labour in the manufacturing sector in particular was responsible for the fact that China was perceived as a threat to Italy's manufacturing industry. The concerns of unfair competition by Chinese companies spread also in the domestic market, when Chinese companies operating in Italy were accused of not respecting domestic environment and labour safety regulations (Casarini and Sanfilippo 2015). The shift in the Chinese economic paradigm that Beijing is promoting against the background of what is referred to as the 'new normal' of the Chinese economy[4] could change the scenario. Indeed, since 2013 China's authorities acknowledged that an export driven economy alone cannot continue to sustain Chinese GDP growth, also against the background of rising labour costs in China and the kind of competition China's cheap labour industry is confronted with from South-East Asian countries. For this reason, China is today promoting a new development model based on domestic consumption and quality rather than quantity. The investments of Italian companies in China are no more, or not only, aimed at producing cheap components to be exported back to Italy or other advanced economies' markets. Instead, the new focus is on producing high-end and high-tech products for the Chinese domestic market. As a consequence, there is relatively less need to protect the Italian market from Chinese production, but instead a need to increase efforts to facilitate the entrance of Italy's high-quality industry into the Chinese market. Italian goods and services in sectors such as healthcare, food safety, aerospace and others are highly appreciated by Chinese consumers. This strategy is also highlighted by the plan developed by the Italian Ambassador in Beijing S.E. Ettore Sequi, under the label 'Road to 50.' In the ambassador's words, this initiative demonstrates that "Italy is ready to accompany China along its transition towards the so-called 'new normal'" especially taking opportunities coming from China's 13th Five-year-plan. 'Road to 50' refers to the 50th anniversary of the establishment of diplomatic relations between Italy and China that will be celebrated in 2020.

An example of a new path of cooperation is the agreement signed by the Italian Health Minister Beatrice Lorenzin and her Chinese counterpart Li Bin in January 2016 (Ministero della Salute 2016). The agreement is among others aimed at strengthening cooperation in the health, pharmaceutical, food safety and professional training sectors. It also opened the 'The Year of Italian Health Care in China under the slogan 'v-ITALY-ty'. In fact, the comparison between the top 10 sectors of Chinese export to Italy and of Italy's exports to China shows that nine out of ten sectors are the same (Rossi and Fasulo 2016). Italy and China are exporting to each other the same kind of products, and therefore Italy will suffer more in the future

---

[4]In 2013, the Chinese government declared that it was time to recognize 'the new normal' of the Chinese economy. Economic growth rates beyond 10% were no longer sustainable and achievable and the focus should move to an economic model with lower but qualitatively higher economic growth. China's 'new normal can be summarized as follows: (1) lower economic growth rates (2) less exports of low quality products (3) focus on domestic consumption (4) less public investments (5) a rising share of the service sector (6) innovation to improve the quality of production.

from China's competition, particularly if Beijing will become more competitive not only in terms of costs but also in terms of quality thanks to programs such as 'Made in China 2025'.[5] As a consequence, boosting innovation and exploiting niches is more than ever a necessity for Italy's business community. Furthermore, the competition between Italian and Chinese goods is evident also with reference to the dispute on the 'Market Economy Status' ('MES'), which China wants to be granted by the European Union. Italy can be placed among the 'hawks', which—at least for now and under the current circumstances—opposes the recognition of China as a market economy. Other EU member states too fear that granting China MES would weaken Europe's ability to file anti-dumping procedures against China. Being acknowledged as a market economy is a pressing issue for Beijing, as China's industry is confronted with the issue of massive overcapacity in many sectors, especially those connected to the construction sector. Chinese overcapacities in the steel sectors can be found on top of the list of European concerns. To be sure, among EU member countries there are different positions on this issue. In fact, those countries that are confronted with strong Chinese competition are against the recognition, while those countries whose companies compete less with China firms view positively an agreement with the aim of attracting more Chinese FDIs (Ewert and Pöter 2016; EPRS 2015; Stratfor 2016). Therefore, Italy needs to carefully deal with China both through bilateral agreements and within the European institutions in order to secure the opportunity to enter into the Chinese market. Indeed, an accusation often raised is that while Beijing asks for an easier access of Chinese goods into the European markets, Beijing continues to prevent foreign competition in sectors, which it refers as 'strategic' (and hence subject to protection by the state). The discrepancy between outward and inward behaviour in the field of market openness will probably become a central issue on the Sino–Italian bilateral economic and business agendas. Nevertheless, this issue will develop in parallel with the emergence of China as power of global reach. Therefore it should not be seen only as a matter of economic interests.

4 A Provider of Global Public Goods

If in the past Italy and China had very few common political interests, mainly due to China's international isolationism and Italy's political regional outlook, the scenario has changed in the 21st century. This is not because Italy has expanded its foreign policy profile but rather because China did. Since the 1950s China promoted a foreign policy based on the so-called 'five principles of peaceful coexistence.' This strategy was developed during the movement of the non-aligned countries, which

[5]The programme 'Made in China 2025' is an initiative promoted by the Chinese government with the goal to promote innovation in high-value industries and sectors such as healthcare, environment, aerospace, new materials and others.

gathered in Bandung (Indonesia) in 1955. For decades, China stuck to these principles, adding in the 1980s Deng Xiaoping's suggestion 'to keep a low profile' in international politics. Such a foreign policy approach—also adopted as a sort of antidote to US foreign policy which China criticized as 'interventionist'—was the right approach to foreign relations at the time, as China had relatively little interests abroad. Today, however, things have changed fundamentally as regards China's involvement in international politics and security. In fact, the more China invests abroad, the more it needs to protect those business interests abroad. This phenomenon led many scholars to express concern over China as a revisionist State and of a potential 'China Threat'. China scholar David Shambaugh, who expressed his doubts on the existence of such a threat, has contributed to the discussion about China's rise. Indeed, he questioned China's ability to become a global leader in the medium term because—he stated—it is only a partial superpower when compared to the US in terms of economy, soft power and military power (Shambaugh 2013). This assessment is useful because it counters a tendency to overestimate China's capabilities. However, even if China might not be ready to assume a global leadership role and China's authorities actually do agree since they set the 'China Dream' of achieving full modernization by 2049—Beijing can indeed start playing a relevant role within regional contexts. This evolution emerges from China's expanding interests abroad, mainly due to the need to secure economic growth and stability, energy supplies, trade routes and investments.

Relations between Italy and China entered into their sixth phase. As it happened for the other stages, this was possible after significant changes of either Italy's or China's domestic conditions. China's economic miracle started in the early 1980s and was fuelled by exports of low-quality products and huge public investments that were vital also for China's domestic infrastructure. After the global financial crisis of the late 2000s, China was affected by the reduced global demand and had to spur its growth through a massive economic stimulus plan worth 4 trillion of yuan ($586 billion). The plan was successful in reducing the impact of a slowing global demand, but it caused a severe overcapacity problem in the long term due to the misallocation of funds provided for by the Chinese government. In 2013, the Chinese government declared that it was the time to recognize the above-mentioned 'new normal' of the Chinese economy to be able to transform the Chinese model of economic growth and development and improve environmental standards. The China economic stimulus program also fuelled China's debt while the financial sector is widely recognized as being in need of reforms since many years, even before the 2015 stock exchange crash. The most relevant issue on Xi Jinping's economic policy agenda is the need for fundamental economic reforms, especially in the sectors dominated by China's State-Owned Enterprises (SOEs) burdened by debt and overcapacity. However, since the task of reforming the SOEs is facing domestic obstacles, the combination of debt and overcapacity is forcing the Chinese government to find new sources of growth abroad. Even if the economy's 'new normal' will reduce China's dependency on exports in the long term, in the short and medium term Beijing will continue to have to rely on them in order to be able to avoid an economic so-called 'hard landing' characterized by rapid and drastic decline of economic growth rates. For this reason, China needs to continue to increase its involvement in global trade. This explains China's agenda for the G20 and the launch of a project like the 'Belt and Road Initiative' aimed at expanding trade ties across Eurasia and Africa. 'The One Belt One Road' is the first initiative promoted by China in the 21st century. Indeed China is at a crucial crossroads: it can persist in acting as a free rider of the international community—confirming Shambaugh's evaluation of China as a 'partial superpower'—or it can start to build a network of partnerships that will help Beijing to enhance its new role as one of the leaders of the international community. In order to increase its global influence and convince countries to align themselves with China and not the US, China has turned to providing public goods in a significant and stable fashion.

As the global community is confronted with issues and crisis such as the migration crisis, Russia's annexation of Crimea and the existence of the so-called Islamic State (IS), disorder and lack of political coordination are currently its main features. Today's world can be described as undergoing a transition from a global unipolar to a multipolar order. However, this transition is still ongoing, and current global institutions are not able to adapt yet to the emerging balance of power. China is well aware of this kind of difficulties and is trying to step-up whenever it perceives that the traditional leaders of the international community could oppose its policies and actions. This can e.g. be the case of its behaviour in the South China Sea or the foundation of new economic institutions like the New Development Bank or the Asian Infrastructure Investment Bank (AIIB).[6] But the definitive way through which China can assume a role as global leader is the provision of global public goods. Among the most relevant public goods that China can provide are: (a) fighting against terrorism, (b) harmonizing global policy toward refugees' crisis management, (c) promoting stable and balanced economic growth of the world economy and (d) promoting the stabilization of the international financial system. While the latter two need contributions from multilateral institutions, the former two can be addressed through bilateral efforts. Such an opportunity might lead Italy to reconsider its approach towards China. As Kerry Brown and Sam Beatson suggest with reference to the European Union (Brown and Beatson 2016), Italy too should embrace the intensification of political (and security) relations with China. This new type of relationship should further engage China in international politics and security against the background of China's long-term objective to become a global leader. According to Brown and Beatson, if granting China 'Market Economy Status' is a political rather than an economic issue, then such a decision should be linked to asking Beijing to become a more active player in international

[6]In 2014 China and the other BRICS countries (Brazil, Russia, India and South Africa) established a new bank named New Development Bank based in Shanghai. The following year China also promoted the establishment of a regional Bank with the aim to finance Asian infrastructure needs. The AIIB is based in Beijing and among its founding members are major world economies, minus the US and Japan. The AIIB is at times referred to as a competitor to the Asian Development Bank (AIB) or even the World Bank and is currently in the process of finding ways to cooperate with other regional and global financial institutions.

politics and security. As indicated above, this is now possible because China has more interests abroad than before and can no longer continue to be a free rider of global stability provided for by the US. The first field of possible cooperation between China and Italy is the Mediterranean region and the Middle East. Since late 2013 China surpassed the US as the main oil importing country from the Middle East (Plumer 2014). This implies that the cost for China's economy of eventual regional instability is growing and that Beijing will have to become more prepared to cooperate in stabilising the MENA Region. However, China's new approach will still be based on the keywords of 'win-win cooperation' and 'non-interference into domestic affairs'. This might be an obstacle in some scenarios, whereas it might fit with the local conditions somewhere else. For example China is reported to be changing its policy of non-intervention with regard to the conflict in Syria due to a rising interest in promoting stability. As of September 2016, China's involvement is limited to the provision of training to the Syrian armed forces. To be sure, this is enough Chinese involvement for a foreign scholar to talk about 'China's new era of diplomacy' (Rudolf 2016). Among the issues at stake in Syria, there is the fight against international terrorism. After a series of attacks in China in 2013 and 2014, Beijing decided to re-visit and speed up the adoption of its laws on counterterrorism (Zhou 2016). Along with prescriptions about how to deal with domestic threats, China's new anti-terrorism legislation law provided a legal framework for sending Chinese troops abroad to fight terrorism outside of Chinese borders. A connected policy is China's strategy towards Afghanistan, where China has almost replaced the US in terms of involvement and influence. In Afghanistan China needs stability in light of its investments in the neighbouring Pakistan.

Last but certainly not least, China is already playing a very significant role in Africa, even if the reality and scope of its investments in Africa do not match the myth of China allegedly 'colonizing' the African continent (Chen et al. 2015). However, China has become the biggest trading partner of many African countries and its economic interests and involvement continues to grow steadily. In Africa, China is already displaying a new way of conducting foreign policy: through the deployment of UN Blue Helmets. The history of China's troop contributions to UN Peacekeeping operations dates back to 1982 (Fung 2016). However, while Beijing used to send only hard-to-source enabler troops, comprehensive security forces were dispatched to Mali in 2013 and a battalion of combat troops was sent to South Sudan in 2014. What is important to stress, especially in the latter case, is that in South Sudan there are significant Chinese investments in the country's oil sector and that the role of Chinese peacekeepers includes the protection of these investments. In addition, China has also become an important contributor of development aid and technical assistance in Africa. Indeed on the side-lines of the FOCA Meeting which was held in Zimbabwe in 2015, Xi Jinping announced China's pledge to fund development projects with up to 60 billion US dollars in a three year plan that is aimed at partly erasing the debt and promoting the modernization of agriculture (Brock and Mapenzauswa 2015).

The above-mentioned changing Chinese foreign and foreign economic policies indicate that Beijing is no longer a passive 'free-rider' of international politics and security. Instead, Beijing is prepared to contribute to political stability in various regional scenarios, some of which are of great interest to Italy too. China and Italy e.g. are both interested in containing the terrorist threat emerging from Syria and Iraq. Both Rome and Beijing are confronted with the phenomenon of so-called 'foreign fighters' returning to both Italy and China to conduct terrorist attacks. Secondly, it is worth trying to connect China's African strategy with that of Italy, which is currently monopolised by the migration crisis. In spring 2016, Italy presented a plan to contain the number of migrants coming from Africa. According to this plan, named 'Migration Compact', the European Union should offer investments and cooperation to the African countries in return for a better management of migration and refugee flows (Italian Government 2016). However, this plan, based on the idea of putting a stop to the movements in the countries of origin, did not receive enough substantial support from the other EU member states to be adopted as an EU-wide policy dealing with the flow of migration. However, it is still possible for Italy to cooperate with China in that area against the background of its above-mentioned investments in Africa. China, it seems, is open to that kind of cooperation with others as Chinese Prime Minister Li Keqiang announced at the 71st Session of the UN General Assembly on September 19, 2016 (The State Council—PRC 2016). The Chinese premier, attending the Summit for Refugees and Migrants stressed that the "Refugee and migrant problem concerns global peace and development and affects regional stability, so the global society needs to cope with it proactively. The issue is a humanitarian crisis and a question of moral conscience, so the global community must lend a hand to the refugees, promote humanitarianism and safeguard the moral bottom line." He then added that the "Resolution of such problems required global cooperation and the UN should fully exert their/exerts its coordinative functions, work out and implement comprehensive solutions to jointly crack down on stowaways, human trafficking and terrorism". If Li's words are taken at face value, they possibly offer opportunities for others to engage with China on the migration crisis in Africa (and the Middle East too). Italy and China could therefore consider cooperating on the migration crisis in Africa even if they cannot count always on the full support and involvement of the European Union. China for is part could use such kind of cooperation to improve its global image, providing evidence that its international model based on multilateralism and peaceful resolution of controversies, through the promotion of economic development, can be effective.

In Italy, the possibility of talking about political cooperation in the MENA region was raised by Ambassador Sequi in an interview with the Hong Kong daily newspaper South China Morning Post, titled *Italy seeks more Chinese help in security and humanitarian crises in Mediterranean and North Africa* (Liu 2016). Ambassador Sequi stated that "We [Italy] expect a growing Chinese presence in the Mediterranean region in the years to come" and that "greater flows of trade and investment will bring more Chinese nationals to the region, and with them the exposure of China to the risks that the region has for centuries presented to outside powers that settled there". During the interview, the Ambassador also noted that "Development is crucial to maintain stability" and that Chinese investment in development, similar to what it was giving to sub-Saharan Africa, would help maintain stability and manage migration. Italian and Chinese foreign political dossiers seem therefore increasingly compatible and Italy should take the opportunity to restore and upgrade its relations with China. Such a strategy would be useful not only to strengthen political relations with the final aim of improving the economic dimension, but also as a long term foreign policy strategy that considers China as a future global leader to engage with. If such a plan were to be successful, China would be able to lay the first stone towards becoming an active player of the international community.

5 Conclusions

The relationship between Italy and China stands on the shoulders of two millennia of exchanges, therefore the current links are the last product of multiple phases developed since the foundation of PRC in 1949. After almost thirty years dedicated to improving mutual understanding and knowledge on each other, in the 1980s economic cooperation boomed thanks to closer relations among the two countries' political elites. When Italian domestic politics were affected by corruption scandals in the 1990s political relations with China were severely affected by government instability. The establishment of a comprehensive strategic partnership eventually inaugurated the phase of fully institutionalized relations.

In conclusion, the shift from one phase of relations to another was caused by changes in the political landscape in both Italy and China. Since Xi Jinping took over power in China in 2012, Beijing has been adopting a more assertive foreign policy, largely driven by the need to invest abroad to sustain the country's economic development in times of the above-mentioned 'new normal.' Increasing Chinese economic interests in foreign countries is affecting the traditional isolationist policy in favour of a more active role accompanied by Chinese efforts to preserve stability in countries such as South Sudan or Afghanistan. China and Italy share interests in regions such as Africa and the Mediterranean. That should encourage Italy to engage with China not only through economic exchanges, but also in the political domain, given Beijing's obligation to protect its interests abroad. As elaborated above, the provision of public goods is becoming an important instrument for Beijing on its path to becoming a global leader in the medium and long term. Finally, Italy's political engagement with China should also be paired with the promotion of Italian economic interests. In line with the path of China's transition towards a development model with a focus on quality rather than quantity, an important task for Italian institutions is to discourage China from economic protectionism while opening the Italian market to Chinese goods and products.

References

Andornino GB (2012) The political economy of Italy's relations with China. Int Spect 47(2): 87–101

Andornino G B (2014) Strategic ambitions in times of transition: key patterns in contemporary Italy–China relations. In: Marinelli M, Andornino G (eds) Italy's encounters with modern China. Imperial dreams, strategic ambitions. Palgrave Macmillan, New York

Brock J, Mapenzauswa S (2015) China's Xi cheers African leaders with pledge of $60 billion for development, Reuters. http://www.reuters.com/article/us-china-africa-idUSKBN0TN0MD20151204 (4 Dec)

Brown K, Beatson S (2016) The European Union and China: The need for a more politicised relationship, Asia and the Pacific policy studies, vol 3, pp 412–419. http://onlinelibrary.wiley.com/doi/10.1002/app5.152/full

Casarini N, Sanfilippo M (2015) Italy and China: investing in each other. In: Huotari M et al (eds) Mapping Europe China relations. A bottom-up approach. European Think-tank Network on China (ETCN). https://www.ifri.org/sites/default/files/atoms/files/etnc_web_final_1-1.pdf

Chen W et al (2015) China's direct investment in Africa: reality versus myth. Brookings Institution. https://www.brookings.edu/blog/africa-in-focus/2015/09/03/chinas-direct-investment-in-africa-reality-versus-myth/ (3 Sept)

Coralluzzo V (2008) Italy's foreign policy toward China: missed opportunities and new chances. J Mod Italian Stud 13(1):6–24

European Parliamentary Research Service (2015) Granting market economy status to China, European Parliament. http://www.europarl.europa.eu/RegData/etudes/IDAN/2015/571325/EPRS_IDA(2015)571325_EN.pdf (Nov)

Ewert I, Pöter JP (2016) Market economy status for China: the views from Brussels and Beijing. The diplomat. http://thediplomat.com/2016/07/market-economy-status-for-china-the-views-from-brussels-and-beijing/ (25 Jul)

Fung CJ (2016) China's troop contributions to UN peacekeeping. United States Institute for Peace, Peace Brief 212. http://www.usip.org/sites/default/files/PB212-China-s-Troop-Contributions-to-UN-Peacekeeping.pdf (Jul)

Hanemann T, Huotari M (2016) A new record year for Chinese outbound investment in Europe. MERICS and Rhodium Group. http://rhg.com/wp-content/uploads/2016/02/A_New_Record_Year_for_Chinese_Outbound_Investment_in_Europe.pdf (Feb)

Italian Government (2016) Migration compact. Contribution to an EU strategy for external action on migration. http://www.governo.it/sites/governo.it/files/immigrazione_0.pdf (21 Apr)

Liu Z (2016) Italy seeks more Chinese help in security and humanitarian crises in Mediterranean and North Africa, South China Morning Post. http://www.scmp.com/news/china/diplomacy-defence/article/1899657/italy-seeks-more-chinese-help-security-and-humanitarian (10 Jan)

Ministero della Salute (2016) Collaborazione sanitaria Italia–Cina, il Ministro Lorenzin sigla Piano triennale, Febbraio 1, http://www.salute.gov.it/portale/news/p3_2_1_1_1.jsp?lingua=italiano&menu=notizie&p=dalministero&id=2430

Naughton B (2007) Chines economy. Transitions and Growth. The MIT Press, Cambridge (Massachussetts) and London (UK)

Pini MF (2011) Italia e Cina, 60 anni tra passato e futuro. L'asino d'oro, Roma

Plumer B (2014) China now gets more oil from the Middle East than the US does, Vox. http://www.vox.com/2014/9/3/6101885/middle-east-now-sells-more-oil-to-china-than-to-the-us (3 Sept)

Romano S (2010) Italia e Cina, la lunga marcia del riconoscimento. Aspenia, La Cina post-americana, n. 50, ottobre

Rossi A, Fasulo F (2016) La Cina nel 2016. Fondazione Italia Cina, Milano

Rudolf M (2016) China's new era of diplomacy: Engaging in Syria. The Diplomat. http://thediplomat.com/2016/01/chinas-new-era-of-diplomacy-engaging-in-syria/ (25 January)

Shambaugh D (2013) China goes global: the partial power. Oxford University Press

Sisci F (2005) Come abbiamo perso la Cina. Limes, n. 6

Stratfor (2016) Europe considers a new trading status for China. https://www.stratfor.com/analysis/europe-considers-new-trading-status-china (8 Feb)

Taggart S (2014) Italian relations with China 1978–1992: the long carnival decade—burgeoning trade and diplomatic Kudos. Cahiers de la Méditerranée 88, https://cdlm.revues.org/7512

The State Council—PRC (2016) Premier Li addresses UN General Assembly. http://english.gov.cn/premier/news/2016/09/20/content_281475446293659.htm (20 Sept)

Zhou Z (2016) China's comprehensive counter-terrorism law. The diplomat. http://thediplomat.com/2016/01/chinas-comprehensive-counter-terrorism-law/ (23 Jan)

China in Africa: Challenges and Opportunities

Barbara Onnis

Abstract China's current economic presence in Africa dates back to the early 1990s, and has increased exponentially since the start of the new century, becoming one of the most debated chapters on PRC's foreign policy agenda. While the mainstream trends to point at the asymmetric nature of the bilateral China-Africa relationship and considers China's activities in the continent the emblem of a new neo-colonial attitude, the Chinese presence in Africa presents both risks and challenges for China and opportunities for Africa. On the one hand, the growing instability that characterizes most of the countries where Chinese economic interests are concentrated represents a crucial challenge for Beijing, which requires a rethinking of some of the key pillars of its foreign policy. On the other hand, Africa's inclusion in the maritime branch of China's *New Silk Road Initiative*, named the *21st Century Maritime Silk Road*, can become an opportunity for African economic growth and development.

1 Introduction

Chinese current economic presence in Africa is a relatively recent phenomenon that begins in the course of the 1990s and increases dramatically with the beginning of the new century, becoming one of the most debated chapters on Beijing's foreign policy agenda. Its co-occurrence with the emergence of what French scholar Bergère (2000) has called the People's Republic of China (PRC)'s *glorious decade* that has seen the country re-emerge as a great power—not only in economic, but also in political and diplomatic terms—contributing to feed the notorious 'China threat' theory (*Zhongguo weixie lun*), is useful to explain the doubts raised within the international community over the nature of China's engagement in Africa. In fact, since the onset, China's interests in Africa seem to be entirely conditioned by

B. Onnis (✉)
Department of Social Sciences and Institutions,
University of Cagliari, Cagliari, Italy
e-mail: bonnis@unica.it

S. Beretta et al. (eds.), *Understanding China Today*, Understanding China,
DOI 10.1007/978-3-319-29625-8_8

the country's pressing need for crude oil and raw materials—a type of engagement free from any political or moral conditioning. Indeed, China's economic presence in Africa is often described with a strong negative connotation, since it is seen as emblematic of its selfish quest for natural resources, and considered responsible for the failures of the fragile efforts made by the continent to improve its governance and build a sustainable future. Unsurprisingly, one of the most controversially discussed aspects continues to be the asymmetric nature of the bilateral relationship. China is described as a 'hungry giant', a devourer of raw materials, and painted as a new colonizing power, putting its own interests at the centre of its policies. To be sure, such behaviour should not be so surprising, since a nation's foreign policy always serves its national interests, and China is no exception. According to Luo and Zhang (2014), both eminent experts of China–Africa relations, Beijing has never denied that its African policy has its own strategic interests, but argue that "One of the most outstanding features of the PRC's African policy from the very beginning is its aspiration to promote the South–South cooperation and achieve the renaissance of Asia and Africa". While admitting that there exist some problems in the bilateral cooperation—trade imbalances, the lack of corporate social responsibility of some Chinese enterprises—the two authors argue that China's engagement in Africa provides the continent with new development opportunities and helps Africa's integration into the global economic and trade system. It is no coincidence that, while African perceptions of China include a mix of both approval and disdain, African citizens and governments hold overall positive views of Beijing's engagement in the continent (Hanauer and Lyle 2014, p. xii). Being aware of the criticism by both specific segments of African society (such as labour unions and civil society groups) and the majority of Western governments, China has tried to adjust its approach to the continent by promoting sustainable economic development through what Beijing refers to as 'win-win' commercial deals, that are able to generate tangible, long-term economic benefits for African nations in the form of jobs, training, and technology. At the same time, it has increasingly worked to shape broader Sino–African relations through people-to-people ties, cultural and educational exchanges, Mandarin language training, and a robust public diplomacy campaign (Ibid.). To cope with the increasing accusations of neo-colonialism, Beijing has initiated a major strategy of diversification of its investments in Africa, concentrating less on the extractive sector and supporting more investments in the large infrastructure sectors, which contribute to promoting intra-African and regional development, as well as in social projects for the local population in sectors ranging from manufacturing to information technology, health aid, rural development, education and culture in general (Ibid., Chapter "Russia and China: Partners or Competitors? Views from Russia"). Hence, while it is undeniable that China's interests in Africa are many and varied, going far beyond the obvious economic or political sphere, and extending to ideological and safety-related considerations, it should be acknowledged that China's engagement also creates opportunities for Africa.

However, the Chinese economic presence in Africa is not without risks and challenges for Beijing. The most important of such risks is related to the necessity to protect the country's economic interests and safeguard the security of its Chinese citizens, considering that the countries where China operates in Africa are in most cases very unstable, upset by bloody civil wars, and prone to terrorist attacks. Equally pressing is the need to revise the PRC's non-interfering posture that appears to be increasingly inappropriate for a rising power with growing global interests.

The first three sections of this chapter will analyse the Sino–African relations since the early 1950, which is necessary to better understand the factors that initially led to the consolidation of Sino–African ties during the Maoist era. This is followed by an analysis of bilateral relations in the aftermath of the launch of the reformist policy by Deng Xiaoping, and an analysis of relations as one of important pillars of Beijing's post-1989 foreign policy. After that, the analysis will focus on two specific related aspects. Firstly, an analysis of the opportunities for both China and Africa by Africa's inclusion in Beijing's 'New Silk Road' initiative (*yi dao, yi lu*), the so called *21st Century Maritime Silk Road* (*21 shiji haishang sichou zhilu*). Secondly, the challenges for Beijing created by the growing instability in areas with Chinese investment and the presence of Chinese citizens are examined. It will be concluded that the challenges in particular require a profound rethinking of the PRC's low-profile and so-called *non-interference* policy. It is a crucial issue that has been animating an academic/intellectual/political debate over the last decade between those who would like a more assertive China, with a bigger say in the international affairs, and those who prefer a more secluded China focused on the solving of its internal problems first (Onnis 2013).

2 The Historical Roots of Chinese Presence in Africa

To better understand the nature and extent of the PRC's current involvement in Africa, it is useful to go back to the origins of Sino–African relations. In fact, while the current Chinese presence in Africa has its roots in relatively recent times, we must recall that the first contacts between China and the African continent date back to the times of the first Silk Road (between the second century BC and the second century AD), even if it was Admiral Zheng He, at the beginning of the 15th century, during his seven epic exploratory journeys across the globe, to inaugurate the beginning of the Sino–African relations, landing on African soil. These first contacts, however, were followed by an enormous hiatus that would last until the mid-twentieth century. Apart from the geographical distance and difficulties related to language and communication, it was mainly the colonial or pseudo-colonial events experienced by both China and Africa, during the 19th century, to determine this state of affairs (Kwaa Prah 2006). On the one hand, the signing of the *Treaty of Nanking* on 29 August 1842, which marked the end of the first Opium War (1839–1942) between the United Kingdom of Great Britain and Ireland and the Qing dynasty of China inaugurated the notorious *Unequal Treaties* (*bu pingdeng de tiaoyue*) era that would mark the beginning of the erosion of the Chinese empire's independence, followed by China becoming an exceptional experimental field of colonial policy, hosting in its territory a form of imperialism in modern history (even if China was never colonized in a strict sense) (Osterhammel 1992, pp. 590–3). Africa on the other hand was sliced-up at the table between the distant European powers at the Berlin Conference (1884), later becoming the theatre of confrontation between direct French colonial and indirect British rule. Interestingly, despite all the differences, it would be precisely their common experience of colonial rule to lay the basis for the relationship that the newly formed People's Republic of China and the 'new' Africa would start from the middle of the 20th century. In fact, those that would restart a dialogue after centuries of interruption were two completely different realities: on the one side, a new statehood emerged victorious from the civil war that had pitted the communists headed by Mao Zedong and the nationalists of Chiang Kai-shek. This put not only an end to the experience of the Republic of China, born in 1912 from the ashes of the two-thousand-year-old Chinese empire but also with it the long period of subjection of China to foreign domination.[1] On the other side, there was a very intricate reality represented by Africa at the beginning of its decolonization process, which had just started with the withdrawal of the French and the British from Libya in 1951, and would find its climax in 1960—dubbed *the year of Africa* with the access to independence by 17 countries—even if it would have to wait a long time before it could be considered concluded (Wilson 1994).

The relations between the two sides were further cemented during the Bandung Conference, a meeting of most newly independent 29 Asian and African states, which took place in April 1955 in Indonesia, with the stated aims to promote Afro-Asian economic and cultural cooperation and to oppose colonialism or neo-colonialism by any nation. In this sense, the conference was an important step toward the founding of the *Non-Aligned Movement*. With the skilful diplomatic leadership of Zhou Enlai, China intended to take over the direction of that historical process, introducing its own experience of a country that had freed itself from the domination of foreign powers. After the Bandung Conference, relations between China and African countries grew ever stronger, and the exchange of visits between Chinese and African leaders became more and more frequent. However only five years later, Sino–African relations suffered the repercussions of the Sino–Soviet rivalry, which, after a decade of a 'forced' alliance, met its breaking point in 1960. Since then, Moscow and Beijing become competitors in the underdeveloped countries of the Third World, and primarily in Africa, by providing economic and military aid in return for support of their respective ideologies. Consequently, while until then Beijing's goal had been to create a diplomatic space disconnected to some extent from its Soviet ally, with the breaking of relations with Moscow, those spaces became crucial to avoid total international isolation when the global bipolar structures entailed an ever greater

[1]The notorious *bainian chiru* ('century of shame and humiliation') began in 1842 with the signing of the *Treaty of Nanking*, and officially ended in 1949. The *Unequal treaties* had already been formally abrogated in 1943.

engagement on the part of the two superpowers towards developing countries in general and during those years toward Africa in particular.

Under those circumstances, Maoist China performed countless efforts and achieved promising results, mainly thanks to the capable diplomat Zhou Enlai, who travelled throughout the continent, establishing the principles that were supposed to regulate relations between China and Africa, starting with the *Five principles guiding China's relations with the Arab and African countries* and the *Eight principles for China's aid to foreign countries*.[2] These principles both stood for the concrete application of the *Five Principles of Peaceful Co-Existenc*e (*heping gongchu wuxiang yuanze*),[3] and the development of the Bandung spirit.

The radicalization of the revolutionary ideology in the years of the *Cultural Revolution* (1966–1976) had inevitable repercussions for the PRC's foreign posture. In the wake of the ideological thrust of those years, in fact, China would provide a massive quantity of aid to Africa, despite its own economic difficulties: one of the most outstanding examples was the construction—between 1970 and 1976—of the famous Tanzania-Zambia Railway (*Tanzan Tielu*), funded by a Chinese interest-free loan of 988 million yuan—which remains one of the largest foreign aid projects to date provided by China to Africa (Yun 2014, p. 4).

The combination of aid and ideology would prove successful in the long run, (after a phase of retreat of the Chinese influence in the continent in the late 1960s). In fact, the years of the *Cultural Revolution* coincided with the establishment of diplomatic relations with nineteen African countries, greatly contributing to the most important diplomatic success obtained by the PRC since its foundation. In 1971, Beijing finally obtained a seat at the United Nations Security Council at the expense of the seat of Republic of China (ROC), through the United Nations General Assembly Resolution 2758 (*Restoration of the lawful rights of the People's Republic of China in the United Nations*). That resolution was passed also thanks also to the votes of several African countries. 26 of the 76 total votes in favour were expressed by African UN members, which led Mao Zedong to declare that "It is our African brothers who have carried us into the UN" (Qi 2012).

3 The Policies of Reform and Opening and the Reshaping of China–Africa Ties

Deng Xiaoping's choice to give the highest priority to the economy in relation to the modernization of the country had inevitable implications for the conduct of Beijing's foreign policy too.

[2]http://www.fmprc.gov.cn/mfa_eng/ziliao_665539/3602_665543/3604_665547/t18001.shtml.

[3]"Mutual respect for each other's territorial integrity and sovereignty; mutual non-aggression; non-interference in each other's internal affairs; equality and mutual benefit; and peaceful coexistence".

Foreign policy became totally subservient to the objective of economic development and modernization. While China's economic relations with African countries had previously been accompanied by a strong ideological connotation and primarily guided by the provision of aid in order to facilitate the obtainment of political results, Deng's de-Maoization process led to the adoption of more pragmatic policies towards Africa under China's new leadership. Aiming at achieving concrete results was at the core of that new policy approach, within the context of Sino–African relations. In practice, this resulted in a reduction of the aid provided by China to more sustainable levels in favour of the adoption of new economic relations based on equality and mutual benefits, stressing practical results, diversity in quality; and common progress, as stated by then Chinese Premier Zhao Ziyang during a press conference in Dar es Salaam, in December of 1982, where he was paying an official visit, as part of a much wider African tour, which lasted four weeks and involved 11 countries (Brautigam 2010, pp. 53–4).

To be sure, China did not loose sight of its political interests in Africa. In 1981, the PRC was the only major power to support the African and *Third World* candidate for the post of UN Secretary General (namely, Salim Salim of Tanzania). And in 1982–3 Zhao Ziyang's tour to Africa was launched with the declaration that China was a socialist country and part of the *Third World* (Snow 1994, p. 310) even if China had by then become a country that had begun to base part of its legitimacy on economic performance- a development that would lead China's political leaders on several occasions to sacrifice ideology for the achievement of specific economic results in China's relations with China.

Under these circumstances, trade relations with Africa were gradually marginalized and Chinese aid to the continent was scaled back significantly. The downgrading of Africa's significance for Beijing also emerged from the significant reduction of high-profile visits to the continent in the mid-1980s. This was in stark contrast to the early years of the decade (Lin 1989, pp 87–88). However, it is also by the attitude of Chinese leaders towards Africa, sheltered but unusually critical, which pushed them to admonish their African counterparts for the way they uncritically embraced socialism as a development model. While talking with the Vice-President of Tanzania, during a visit to China in April 1985, Deng Xiaoping declared that "Socialism [did] not mean poverty", and went on to say that "without developing the productive forces and improving people's living standards you cannot say you are building socialism" (Quoted in Taylor 2001, p. 93). Furthermore, the reasons for the Chinese disengagement were closely related to the contemporary transformations of the international scenario, which saw Beijing and Moscow in a historical moment of improving their relations. From a geopolitical point of view, this implied that Africa became less important as it was no longer the theatre of clashes between the two socialist giants.

4 Africa on China's Post-1989 Foreign Policy Agenda

China's relations with Africa experienced a drastic reversal in the aftermath of the events of June 4, 1989, after which Beijing embarked on a major process of revaluation of its foreign policy towards Africa, giving rise to a new era in relations with the continent. For the first time since the death of Mao China had become a target of strong criticism from the West because of its human rights abuses. In that particular context, where Beijing entrenched itself in strong defence of the 'principle of non-interference', China received support from the African continent and, from that moment, the developing countries were re-elevated to a level of what Beijing referred to as 'fundamental pillar' of the Chinese post-1989 foreign policy.

Understandably, reactions in the face of the repression of the Tiananmen protests were much more contained in Africa-in essence, no protests and no accusations. On the contrary, in some cases there were even words of praise for the Chinese government's conduct. Many African leaders in fact shared with China the suspicions that Western criticism constituted an attempt to destabilize the country, rather than being motivated by the violation of human rights (Taylor 1988, p. 448). The decision to support Beijing was therefore a fairly spontaneous choice motivated not only by the spirit of the *Third World* solidarity, but also by resentment towards what in Beijing was described as the continuous 'neo-imperialist interference' by the Western world. The fact that most of the African elites were subjected to the same Western accusations further strengthened African support for the Chinese leadership at the time. At the same time, Africa's support was also influenced by pragmatic considerations. African leaders feared that open criticism of Beijing could mean the end of the development aid from the PRC—from 1956 to 1987 Africa had been the recipient of more than 60% of the total value of Chinese aid and assistance programs abroad (Ibid., p. 449).

The first-ever visits by foreign dignitaries in China after the Tiananmen events had as protagonists the foreign minister of Sao Tome and Principe and the President of Burkina Faso, Blaise Compaoré, who were also a constant target of criticism for human rights abuses on the part of the Western world. They both wanted to show the whole world the African continent's wavering friendship with China in its most difficult times, and Beijing's response was one of great gratitude, as shown by the resumption of lavish state visits of China's top leadership to Africa, starting with the one by then Foreign Minister Qian Qichen, who travelled to eight countries between August and September 1989 (Qian 2006, pp 201–2). Qian's visit was followed by visits by Chinese president Yang Shangkun's visit to Egypt, in December 1989 (Liu 2011, p. 83). From 1991 onwards, it seemed to become a routine practice for the Chinese foreign minister to visit Africa at the beginning of every year, thereby contributing to the creation of the foundation for the intense diplomatic Chinese–African partnerships that continue today (Qian 2006, p. 202).

In that critical juncture, Africa was useful for Beijing in the context of the construction of a new post-Cold War multipolar world order, which both countries envisioned as being more equitable and respectful of political and ideological differences. At the same time, Africa could be a useful instrument through which China could project its prestige and its international reputation, and strengthen its credentials as a 'responsible great power' (*fuzeren daguo*), through e.g. a growing participation in peace missions under the aegis of the UN[4] and a skilful exercise of soft power.

Chinese foreign policy in the post-1989 era assigned new importance to the African continent, leading Beijing to expand economic and business relations with a number of African countries. During a visit of President Jiang Zemin in 1996 at the headquarters of the Organization of African Unity in Addis Ababa, he referred to the Chinese will to strive for more political and economic cooperation on the African continent (Chen 2008). The announcement to increase Chinese economic engagement in Africa was part of what would then become part of China's so-called *Going Out Strategy* (*zou chuqu*), which was formally adopted by the Political Bureau in 2000 as a *national strategy* intended to encourage Chinese companies, and the country's State Owned Enterprises (SOEs) in particular, to invest overseas. That strategy was aimed at of putting Chinese companies into the position to compete with foreign and Western counterparts and consolidate China's international prestige and global economic influence. The government's call to invest abroad was met with enthusiasm by Chinese companies and Africa became the strategy's main target for a number of reasons, related to both the presence of rich natural resources and the friendship and brotherhood ties cultivated over previous decades (Wang 2013). Since the launch of the *Going Out Strategy*, Chinese overseas investments have increased significantly especially those of *SOEs*. Statistics indicate that Chinese Foreign Direct Investments (FDI) rose from US$ 3 billion in 1991 to US$ 35 billion in 2003 ('UN report: China becoming major investor abroad' 2004). In 2007, Chinese FDI reached US$ 92 billion ('China's direct investments abroad top $92b by 2007' 2007), even if China's FDI to Africa remained marginal in terms of China's total outward FDI flows (0.2% in 1991, 3.2% in 2005, with a peak of 9.28% in 2000) (Kaplinsky and Mike 2009, p. 554).[5] Nonetheless, the simultaneous creation of an institutional platform for Sino-African dialogue, the so-called *Forum for China–Africa Cooperation, FOCAC* (*Zhongfei*

[4]China started in the early 1990s, after a period of non-involvement in the United Nations, to become one of the major contributors to UN peacekeeping operations. As of September 2015, the PRC was the ninth largest contributor to the UN, and by far the biggest contributor of peacekeeping forces among five permanent members of the U.N. Security Council, with a total of 3084 troops deployed to ten UN missions, seven of which are in Africa ('UN Mission's Summary detailed by Country' 2015).

[5]While China continues to generate controversy with its rapidly growing investments in Africa, new research reveals that some of the West's biggest concerns over Chinese investment—its true size, its focus on natural resources, and its disregard for good governance—are not always well-grounded. Remaining on the scale of China's direct investment in Africa, Chinese statistics on what they refer to as *overseas direct investment* (*ODI*) show a stock of $26 billion in Africa as of the end of 2013. This number would amount to about 3% of total foreign direct investment (FDI) on the continent (Chen et al. 2015). The same can be said for Sino-African trade, which constitutes only 5% of China's overall global trade (Yun 2014, p. 14).

hezuo luntan) started a new period as regards the definition of common policy objectives and mutual development aspirations, discussed on a bilateral basis. China's economic involvement in Africa it was announced, were based on mutual benefits, and the so-called principle of 'non-interference.' *FOCAC* summit meetings —six of them held to date, with the most recent having taken place in Johannesburg in December 2015—have always been an important occasion to sign agreements worth billions of dollars, grant aid and loans, erase debts, and to launch important messages on the importance China assigned to its economic ties with African countries. Indeed, *FOCAC* summits have always provided China with an important platform to pay respect to African leaders on the world stage. "It is Beijing's way of giving face to African governments" and the African leaders in turn appreciate the respect and lavish treatment granted by their Chinese counterparts (Hanauer and Lyle 2014, p. 20).

As a result of the renewed importance attached to the African continent in China's post-1989 foreign policy, in January 2006—on the occasion of the 50th anniversary of the establishment of the first official diplomatic relations between the PRC and an African country (Gamal Abdel Nasser's Egypt) Beijing published a policy paper outlining the Chinese strategy towards Africa.[6] The most important points of the document, entitled *China's African Policy* (*Zhongguo dui Feizhou zhengce wenjian*), underlined the importance of Beijing treating its African partner countries on the basis of equality. The document states that China wants equal relationships for mutual benefits, relations based on friendship and respect promoting development and world peace. It mentions the intention to continue economic cooperation for a common goal, which is to the benefit of both parties. Finally, the document stresses the absence of constraints, both economically and politically, except for the acceptance of the *One-China Principle* ('*Yige Zhongguo*' *yuanze*). Abiding by the *One-China Principle* is not problematic for the vast majority of African countries as African countries with few exceptions maintain diplomatic ties with the PRC and not the ROC. Currently, there are 21 countries worldwide that recognize Taiwan, only two of which are in Africa (Burkina Faso and Swaziland, which until 1997 recognized the PRC). Interestingly, the break in relations of the Gambian government with Taipei, in November 2012 was not followed by the establishment of relations with Mainland China. This was in compliance with the so-called *diplomatic truce* agreed between Beijing and Taipei in 2008 (Drun 2014). However, things changed following the crushing victory of the Democratic Progressive Party's candidate in the presidential election in March 2016. In fact, China and Gambia renewed diplomatic ties in the aftermath of Tsai Ing-wen's election, in a clear message to the ROC's new president not to reverse the predecessor's shift towards warmer relations with the Mainland (Wong 2016).

[6]To date the PRC has published four policy papers (excluding their updated versions) dedicated to its foreign partners. Besides the one dedicated to Africa, the others are: *China's EU Policy Paper* (*Zhongguo dui Ouzhou zhengce wenjian*); *China's Policy Paper on Latin America and the Caribbean States* (*Zhongguo dui Lading Meizhou he Jialebi zhengce wenjian*); and *China's Arab Policy Paper* (*Zhongguo dui Alabo guojia zhengce wenjian*).

5 The *New Silk Road* Initiative—Opportunities for Africa

There is no doubt that the PRC's economic development benefits from China–Africa economic and trade cooperation. According to statistics, bilateral trade skyrocketed from US$10.6 billion in 2000 to US$220 billion at the end of 2014,[7] surpassing both the United States and the European Union (which totaled US $73 billion and US$177 billion respectively). The prospects for further growth of bilateral trade are good (Castagnoli 2016), especially in view of the fact that Sub-Saharan Africa has the fastest growing population in the world (+30 million per year) while the workforce is gradually reduced elsewhere ('Africa's growth potential—and its 'Next 10' biggest cities' 2014).

Beyond the statistical data, it is also interesting to focus the attention on the opportunities deriving for Africa from its inclusion in the *New Silk Road* initiative, in particular in its maritime branch, named the *21st Century Maritime Silk Road*, as unveiled for the first time by Chinese President Xi Jinping during a speech to the Indonesian Parliament in October 2013. The *New Silk Road* strategy is an essential part of a policy vision and concept Xi named the *Chinese Dream* (*Zhongguo meng*). Policies embedded in the *Chinese Dream* are aimed at turning China into a global geopolitical powerhouse by 2049, the year the PRC will celebrate its 100th birthday.

Xi first propagated the idea of the *New Silk Road* during two state visits to Kazakhstan and Indonesia in September and October 2013 respectively. Back then, Xi explained that the project included not one but two roads, a concept that became the '*One Belt, One Road*', i.e. a land route between China and Europe—the *Silk Road Economic Belt*, and a maritime trade route linking Chinese ports with the African coast and Europe's Mediterranean nations, called *Maritime Silk Road* or 21st *Century Maritime Silk Road* (Swaine 2015). This is an enormously huge project and "The most significant and far-reaching initiative that China has ever put forward" according to the former president of China's Foreign Affairs University (which is affiliated with the Ministry of Foreign Affairs) (Wu 2015). The project and the trade routes encompass more than 60 emerging markets and developing countries in Asia, Africa, the Middle East and Europe, with a total population of over 4 billion and an economic aggregate of about US$21 trillion, accounting for about 65 and 30% of the global total of land-based and maritime-based economic production values respectively (Swaine 2015). For its realization, Beijing has established a $40 billion so-called *Silk Road Infrastructure Fund* (Ren and Ng 2015), and furthermore set-up the *Asian Infrastructure Investment Bank* (*AIIB*), which was officially inaugurated on January 16, 2016. The AIIB's objective is to provide finance for infrastructure *Silk Road*-related projects with a special focus on strengthening links across Asia, the Middle East, and Europe (Zhang 2016). By building much-needed infrastructure across the *Silk Road* routes (from roads and

[7]As mentioned above, while in absolute terms China's investment and trade with Africa has grown significantly, its share of the total remains negligible.

rail links to ports and resource pipelines), China hopes to build a "Community of common interest, destiny, and responsibility" (Lin 2016). To demonstrate how China intended to materialize the project, Xi Jinping proposed the so-called *three togethers*: 1. concerned parties identifying projects of cooperation for mutual benefit 2. working together to realize the projects on the basis of common interest and 3. jointly enjoying the benefits deriving from joint project. In other words, China is, as Beijing argues, not looking for unilateral gains, but is working instead for common prosperity, since China's development is inseparable from the world and the world's stability and prosperity are inseparable from China (Wu 2015). Scott Kennedy, director of the Project on Chinese Business and Political Economy at the Center for Strategic and International Studies in Washington agrees that the envisioned infrastructure projects bring benefits: "By improving infrastructure, China could help lift growth in poor nations—and the entire global economy, since The construction projects will potentially create business for engineering and other companies from the West too" (Schuman 2015).

Arguably no country appears to be better suited than China to lead the way forward on infrastructure. In fact, the PRC is not a newcomer to so-called *infrastructure diplomacy* initiatives, even if the one China is building around the *New Silk Road* is geographically very vast. The African case is emblematic in this sense. During a meeting held on the side lines of the 24th African Union (AU) Summit in Addis Ababa (23–31 January 2015) between the Chinese Foreign Minister Wang Yi and the AU Commission's President, Nkosazana Dlamini-Zuma, Wang announced a Chinese investment plan of US$3.8 billion for the construction of logistics links between the port city of Mombasa and the Kenyan capital Nairobi (Kenya's capital is the only African port on the new route of the *Maritime Silk Road*, but is over four hundred kilometres away from the coast). Additionally, China signed a *Memorandum of Intent* for the construction of infrastructure across the continent. According to Zuma—who had often declared that her own dream was to connect African capitals with high-speed trains—it was a project with no precedent in the history of the AU. Deputy Chinese Foreign Minister Zhang Ming too defined it the *deal of the century* (Le Belzic 2015).

Beijing has a long experience in so-called *cement diplomacy* in Africa, having already participated in the construction of more than two thousand kilometres of railway in Ethiopia, Kenya, Angola, and especially Nigeria—where the opening of the railway lines along the coast became instrumental for the realization of major Chinese infrastructural works. Furthermore, Beijing has funded 5,000 km of roads in Africa and has also provided funding for numerous so-called *vanity projects*, which include soccer stadiums, parliament buildings, presidential palaces, and airports (Yomi 2013). Against this background Wang Yi promised the beginning of a 'new phase in Sino–African relations' (Coltrane 2015). Currently, the projects in the pipelines are numerous, beginning with the construction of seven new ports in Djibouti, Tanzania, Mozambique, Gabon, Ghana, Senegal, and Tunisia (Léautier et al. 2015). Let us take the case of the Bagamoyo Port in Tanzania, as an example. At the end of 2015, the Tanzania Ports Authority announced its approval for a US $10 billion project to develop a port at Bagamoyo, located about 60 km north of

Dar es Salaam. This was to be financed by both China and Oman. Once completed, the port is expected to become the biggest in Africa, handling 20 times more cargo than the Dar es Salaam port. According to the original plan, the project will link Bagamoyo port to the central corridor railway and the TAZARA Railway through an extended link. A parallel highway linking Bagamoyo to the Uhuru Highway going to Zambia will also be built. An integral part of the Bagamoyo project will be a so-called *Export Development Zone* (EDZ), which will include the construction of an industrial city as well as upgrades to road and railway infrastructure. Bagamoyo will therefore become a strategic pillar and connect the *Maritime Silk Road* with other East African countries, including Mozambique, Malawi, Zambia, the Democratic Republic of Congo, Burundi, Rwanda, Uganda, Kenya, South Sudan, Comoros, Madagascar, and Seychelles (Ibid.).

Politicians and experts have agreed that 2015 was the year when China–Africa relations reached new highs. As mentioned above, the year started with the AU and the PRC signing a *Memorandum of Understanding* on the improvement of Africa's transport system and the enhancement of industrialization infrastructure, and finished with Chinese President Xi opening the 6th *FOCAC* summit in South Africa by telling African political leaders that together they would "Open a new era of China–Africa win-win cooperation and common development" (Rotberg 2016).

It must be pointed out that within the *FOCAC* framework China has completed numerous projects in Africa, which contributed directly or indirectly to its economic development (Shelton 2015). In this sense, the Chinese government promises to follow-up on an earlier trends of Chinese involvement in Africa. During the VI *FOCAC* summit, Xi Jinping unveiled a US$60 billion aid package for Africa—exactly three times the figure promised at the 2012 *FOCAC*—for the following three years. The funds are aimed at helping Africa to industrialize and modernize its agricultural production, boost the skills of its workers, build infrastructure, and improve its health care systems (Kuo 2015). In particular, China took specific commitments for specific problems. To battle poverty, one of the most compelling African needs, Xi promised to launch 200 so-called *Happy Life* projects focusing on the improvement of the lives of women and children. In order to reduce budget constraints that would hinder growth in the poorest of the African countries, he proposed to cancel the outstanding debt Africa's poorest countries owed to China. China also offered US$60 million to the African Union to support the operation of the new African Standby Force (in training in 2015), and pledged to continue to participate in UN peacekeeping missions on the African continent, where it already constitutes a significance presence, especially in South Sudan (Rotberg 2016). Once again *FOCAC* offered a unique diplomatic mechanism to promote dialogue between China and Africa, while at the same time facilitating a common political and economic process, which advances constructive South-South co-operation. Against this background it is highly plausible that the *21st Century Maritime Silk Road*' will herald prosperity and renewal in Sub-Saharian Africa. At the same time, while fuelling industrialization on the African continent, it will also spur socio-economic benefits for the whole African population ('Kenyan scholar says China's Silk Road to power Africa's industrial progress' 2015a).

6 Interfering or Non-Interference: Beijing's Growing Dilemma

In the aftermath of the killing of a Chinese hostage, Fan Jinghui, by ISIS militants in Syria and the bloody terrorist attack at the Radisson Blue Hotel in Bamako, in Mali, during which three managers of the China Overseas Engineering Group were killed, numerous articles appeared in the Chinese media that reopened the debate on the safety of Chinese citizens and Chinese investments in highly unstable areas (Gong 2015; Zhou 2015). The debate had begun in 2011 during the 'epic' evacuation of 36,000 Chinese nationals from Libya, jointly carried out by the Chinese army, some governmental departments, and Chinese companies operating on African territory. China's official media referred to that event as 'the largest and most complicated overseas evacuation ever conducted by the Chinese government since 1949' (Wang 2011).

Indeed, this is part of a wider debate that has emerged in China in recent years over the continued importance of the strong defence of the principle of *non-interference*, and more in general of Deng Xiaoping's main dictum of China *keeping a low profile* (Onnis 2014, pp 48–51) in light of the growing challenges that are facing Chinese economic interests abroad, as well as the growing component of Chinese citizens traveling and living abroad (about 130 million). Africa is hosting more than one million Chinese citizens, constituting an almost 'second Chinese mainland', according to the American journalist French (2014). Currently, the expansion of China's foreign investment, starting from the supply of natural resources from Africa, has increased the possibility that international crisis might affect the safety of Chinese citizens and Chinese economic interests. A major cause for alarmism are recurring 'hostage crises' which in recent years affected a growing number of Chinese workers residing abroad. Although the number of Chinese citizens kidnapped abroad is not significant—it is nonetheless a worrying trend (Zhou 2015), and an unprecedented challenge to the Beijing government,[8] which is undeniably connected to both the growing number of Chinese people going abroad to work and to the *modus operandi* of the Chinese government, which, in most cases, develops relations only with the ruling parties, while neglecting to foster ties with the opposition forces or rebel groups and, more generally with the civil society as a whole (Zenn 2012). Another relevant factor pertains to the relatively low levels of security, which increases the possibility for Chinese workers to become an easy target for ransom and thus an alluring target for kidnappers. In fact, in order to limit costs, Chinese SOEs usually require workers to live in special encampments where their security staff is often inexperienced and underequipped (Ibid.).

[8]Terrorism is not new to either the Chinese people or the Chinese government, insomuch as the majority of the terrorist attacks within the country in recent history were carried out by the East Turkistan Islamic Movement (ETIM) (Gong 2015).

Confronted with these circumstances, the doctrine of *non-interference* is perceived as a growing dilemma by the Chinese leadership, given the lack of consensus on how to balance the respect for this traditional dogma with the growing Chinese overseas interests and the growing international responsibilities they entail. On the one hand, there is the concern about how the above-mentioned Chinese interests can be protected in the event of political and economic instability (Arduino 2015). On the other hand the Chinese leadership is facing a lot of pressure to re-evaluate the *principle of non-interference* because it does not appear to be an appropriate policy for a global power with growing international responsibilities. In this sense, many scholars and analysts believe that non-interference is becoming a growing burden that can damage China's national interests, since, in order to satisfy Chinese economic needs, the Beijing government is forced to deal with the countries, regardless of their political nature and/or level of stability.

We must acknowledge that Xi Jinping's administration became the protagonist of substantive changes as regards the priorities of Chinese foreign policies in general and Chinese strategies towards Africa in particular. This clearly emerges from an analysis of the PRC's conduct on the African continent in the first three years of Xi's government. The most significant change is related to Beijing's progressive involvement in African security issues, which attests to a growing sense of Chinese responsibility in the management of international crises ('Spotlight: China's peacekeeping contribution to UN missions in Africa shows growing sense of responsibility' 2015b). In June 2013, in an unprecedented move, China publicly committed combat troops (or 'security forces' according to Beijing) to a UN peacekeeping mission (the MINURSO in Mali), marking a major shift in the PRC's foreign policy (Hille 2013). A move that is all the more significant given the limited presence in the region of Chinese direct economic interests, unlike other contexts where China is present with its own peacekeepers (Lanteigne 2014). Even more important was the decision approved by China's *Central Military Commission* to deploy China's first infantry battalion to South Sudan, China's first infantry unit to participate in a United Nations peacekeeping mission. Previous Chinese peacekeepers were mainly conducting engineering, transportation, medical service, and security guard corps activities. The 700-strong infantry battalion consisted of 121 officers and 579 soldiers (including a squad composed of 13 females), equipped with drones, armoured infantry carriers, anti-tank missiles, mortars, light self-defence weapons, bulletproof uniforms and helmets. Weapons, Commander Wang Zhen declared, would serve "exclusively for self-defence purposes", ('China sends first infantry battalion for UN peacekeeping' 2014). Some analysts pointed out that the importance of South Sudan's oil reserves, exploited also by the *China National Petroleum Corp* (Ngor and Gridneff 2014) influenced China's decision to deploy troops to South Sudan. This is also to be understood in the context of unprecedented move by the Chinese government to openly intervene in the conflict in South Sudan through a direct work of mediation carried out in 2013 by the Ambassador Zhong Jianhua, special envoy of the Chinese government on the continent (Jorgic 2014), and a rare public intervention of the Foreign Minister Wang Yi, in January 2014, who called for an immediate cessation of hostilities in the country (Raghavan 2014). Equally significant has been the decision to set up China's first overseas military base in Djibouti, in the Horn of Africa, the confirmation of which came in late November 2015, in the aftermath of the two abovementioned dramatic episodes which occurred in Syria and in Mali, and following the terrorist attacks in Paris at the beginning of November 2015. According to Wu Qian, spokesperson for the Chinese Defence Ministry, the Djibouti base[9] will "Provide better logistics and safeguard Chinese peacekeeping forces in the Gulf of Aden, offshore Somalia and other humanitarian assistance tasks of the UN" (Wang 2015c). At the same time, Wu added "helping China to better perform its international obligations and maintain international and regional peace and stability".[10] When necessary, Djibouti might act as a springboard to allow China to play a more active role in combating terrorism, given the fact that Beijing has already demonstrated its willingness to support a more robust approach against the so-called *Islamic State*, (or *Daesh*) by voting in favour of the United Nations Security Council Resolution 2249, which was unanimously adopted on 20 November, 2015 (Ghiselli 2016, p. 9). Not to mention the fact that, according to China's 2015 defence white paper, the *People's Liberation Army's* (*PLA*) strategic tasks include safeguarding China's overseas interests, world peace, and counterterrorism (China's Military Strategy 2015, Sect. 2). That said, it is not easy to predict how an increased military presence abroad can effectively improve the safety of overseas Chinese. According to Wang (2015a), China has a duty to protect its citizens and its national interests from dangers and threats overseas, but the foothold of no military interference will nonetheless not be easily abandoned.

Either way, there are other factors that make re-visiting the principle of non-interference problematic as it has over decades been a fundamental the pillar Chinese foreign policy. *Non-interference* has been a important tool to build good relationships with African countries and other developing countries since the Cold War era and would go on to become one of the most appreciated pillars of the so-called Beijing Consensus (*Beijing gongshi*). Nor should we neglect the concerns related to a possible re-emergence of the notorious 'China threat' theory.

---

[9]The PRC has been very careful to avoid describing its facility in Djibouti as a 'military' or 'naval' base, preferring the use of more neutral terms, such as 'support facilities' or 'logistical facilities', or even 'protective facility' (*baozhang sheshi*), as defined by the People's Daily in an article published on 26 November, 2015 (*Renmin Ribao* 2015).

[10]Another demonstration in this sense was last spring, when China evacuated hundreds of Chinese and foreign nationals from the troubled cost of Yemen (Wang 2015b).

7 Conclusions

This chapter has examined the implications of the Chinese presence in Africa, both in terms of challenges and opportunities. Generally speaking, Chinese activities in Africa are often described with a strong negative connotation and China is depicted as a new colonizer and exploiter of African row materials. But the reality is more complex than that. While it cannot be denied that the PRC's interests in Africa are many and varied—pertaining not only to the economic or political sphere, but also to ideological and safety-related considerations—it should also be acknowledged that the opportunities have also turned out to be numerous for the African continent. Politicians and experts agree to point to 2015 as the year in which bilateral ties further improved significantly. 2015 started in fact with the African Union and PRC signing a *Memorandum of Understanding* on the improvement of Africa's transport system and the enhancement of industrialization infrastructure (whose deficiencies have always been considered one of the major factors of underdevelopment of the African continent), and ended with the Chinese paramount leader opening the 6th *FOCAC* summit in South Africa by unveiling a very generous aid package (exactly three times the figure promised at the previous FOCAC) for the following three years, aimed to help Africa to industrialize, modernize its agricultural production, boost the skills of its workers, build infrastructure, and improve its health care system. Currently, Xi Jinping's promises follow a well-established trend: within the *FOCAC* framework, China has completed numerous projects in Africa that contributed directly or indirectly to its economic development. Beijing has a long experience in what is referred to as *cement diplomacy* or *infrastructure diplomacy* on the African continent, having contributed to the construction of several thousand kilometers of railways, thousands of roads, not to mention Chinese contribution to the so-called *vanity projects*, which include soccer stadiums, parliament buildings, presidential palaces, and airports. The inclusion of Africa in the maritime branch of China *New Silk Road* can become another crucial opportunity for the continent's economic growth and development. It is plausible that, while fueling industrialization in the African continent, it will also spur socio-economic benefits for the entire African population.

At the same time, however, it is important to underline that the Chinese presence in Africa is not without challenges for Beijing, the most crucial one being related to the compelling necessity to protect its economic interests and safeguard the security of its compatriots, in consideration of the fact that the countries where China invests and operates are in most cases upset by bloody civil wars, that the recent wave of terrorist attacks only contributed to exacerbate. Equally pressing is the need to revise the PRC's *non-interference* posture that appears to be increasingly inadequate for a rising power with growing global interests. These arguments are part of an ongoing controversial debate in China for the last decade between those who press for a more assertive China and those who prefer a more secluded China focused on the solution of its impelling internal problems. Apparently, Xi Jinping's administration became the protagonist of a real change in the priorities and in the

Chinese strategies as well. The most significant change is related to Beijing's progressive involvement in African security-related issues, which attests a growing sense of the Chinese responsibility in the management of international crises.

Equally important has been the decision to set up the PRC's first overseas military base in Djibouti, in the Horn of Africa, aimed at providing better logistics, safeguarding Chinese peacekeepers forces present in the area, and helping China to better perform its international obligations and maintaining international and regional peace and stability. However, it is not easy to predict how an increased military presence abroad can effectively improve the safety of overseas Chinese. It is likely that the foothold of no military interference will not be easily abandoned. We should not forget that the above-mentioned *non-interference* doctrine has always been one of the pillars of the PRC's foreign policy. In particular, for China *non-interference* has been an important tool to build good relations with all the developing countries during the Cold War, and more recently one of the most appreciated aspects of the so-called *Beijing Consensus*.

References

Arduino A (2015) Security privatization with Chinese characteristics. The role of Chinese private security corporations in protecting Chinese outbound investments and citizens. *RSIS Policy Reports*. https://www.rsis.edu.sg/wp-content/uploads/2015/07/PR150630_Security-Privatisation.pdf (June)

Bergère MC (2000) La Repubblica popolare cinese (1949–1999). Bologna, il Mulino

Brautigam D (2010) The dragon's gift: the real story of China in Africa. Oxford University Press, Oxford

Castagnoli A (2016) Pechino scommette sull'Africa, Il Sole24ore (online ed.) (30 Jan). http://www.ilsole24ore.com/art/commenti-e-idee/2016–01-30/-pechino-scommette-sull-africa–101324.shtml?uuid=ACginVKC, Accessed 1 Feb 2016

Chen Y (2008) The creation of Jiang Zemin's 'going out' strategy and its importance (Jiang Zemin 'zou chuqu' zhanlue de xingcheng jiqi zhongyao yiyi). Renminwang (10 Nov). http://finance.people.com.cn/GB/70392/8313311.html. Accessed 12 Oct 2015

Chen W et al. (2015) China's direct investment in Africa: reality versus myth. Brookings Institution (3 Sept). http://www.brookings.edu/blogs/africa-in-focus/posts/2015/09/03-china-africa-investment-trade-myth-chen-dollar-tang. Accessed 12 Oct 2015

Coltrane M (2015) Sino–African relations to be strengthened by 'one belt, one road'. *Yibada* (Jan 31). http://en.yibada.com/articles/11390/20150131/sino-african-relations-to-be-strengthened-by-one-belt-one-road.htm. Accessed 2 Feb 2016

Drun J (2014) China–Taiwan diplomatic truce holds despite Gambia. The diplomat (29 Mar). http://thediplomat.com/2014/03/china-taiwan-diplomatic-truce-holds-despite-gambia/. Accessed 15 Sept 2015

French HW (2014) China's second continent. How a million migrants are building a new empire in Africa. Knopf, New York

Ghiselli A (2016) China's first overseas base in Djibouti, an enabler of its middle east policy. China Brief 16(2):6–9. http://www.jamestown.org/uploads/media/CB_16_2__3_01.pdf (25 Jan)

Gong H (2015) How to protect Chinese nationals overseas. Chinadaily (26 Nov). http://www.chinadaily.com.cn/opinion/2015–11/26/content_22519504.htm. Accessed 27 Nov 2015

Hanauer L, Lyle JM (2014) Chinese engagement in Africa. Drivers, reactions, and implications for U.S. policy. National Security Research Division, Rand Corporation
Hille K (2013) China commits combat troops to Mali. *The Financial Times* (27 June). http://www.ft.com/cms/s/0/e46f3e42-defe-11e2–881f-00144feab7de.html#ixzz3vhOh9sIY. Accessed 15 Sept 2015
http://www.chinausfocus.com/foreign-policy/trapped-in-the-bipolar-trap/. Accessed 15 Sept 2015
Jorgic D (2014) China takes more assertive line in South Sudan diplomacy. Reuters (4 June). http://www.reuters.com/article/us-china-southsudan-oil-idUSBRE88E03920120915. Accessed 15 Sept 2015
Kaplinsky R, Mike M (2009) Chinese FDI in Sub-Saharan Africa: engaging with large dragons. Eur J Dev Res 21(4):551–569
Kuo L (2015) China's Xi Jinping pledges $60 billion to help Africa solve its problems its own way. *Quartz Africa* (4 Dec). http://qz.com/565819/chinas-xi-jinping-pledges-60-billion-to-help-africa-solve-its-problems-its-own-way/. Accessed 10 Dec 2015
Kwaa Prah K (2006) Africa and China: then and now. Pambazuka 282 (14 Dec). http://www.pambazuka.net/en/category.php/comment/38854
Lanteigne M (2014) China's peacekeeping policies in Mali: new security thinking or balancing Europe? *NFG Working Paper* 11. http://www.diss.fu-berlin.de/docs/servlets/MCRFileNodeServlet/FUDOCS_derivate_000000004251/wp1114-china-peacekeeping-policies-mali.pdf
Le Belzic S (2015) La Chine et la 'diplomatie des transports' en Afrique. Le Monde (2 Feb). http://www.lemonde.fr/afrique/article/2015/02/02/la-chine-et-la-diplomatie-des-transports-en-afrique_4567960_3212.html. Accessed 2 Dec 2015
Léautier FA et al. (2015) The port of Bagamoyo: a test for China's new maritime silk road in Africa. The diplomat (1 Dec). http://thediplomat.com/2015/12/the-port-of-bagamoyo-a-test-for-chinas-new-maritime-silk-road-in-africa/. Accessed 2 Dec 2015
Lin Y (1989) Peking's African policy in the 1980s. Iss Stud 25(4):76–96
Lin YJ (2016) China's silk road vision. Project syndicate (21 Jan). https://www.project-syndicate.org/commentary/china-maritime-silk-road-economic-belt-by-justin-yifu-lin-2016–01?barrier=true. Accessed 2 Feb 2016
Liu H (2011) Sino–African relations through three decades: a window of China's progress in foreign relations. In: Yizhou Wang (ed) Transformation of foreign affairs and international relations in China, 1978–2008. Brill, Leiden, pp 73–103
Luo J, Zhang X (2014) China in Africa: devil or angel? Pambazuka News 666 (19 Feb). http://www.pambazuka.net/en/category.php/features/90638
Ministry of National Defense, The People's Republic of China (2015) China's military strategy (26 May). http://eng.mod.gov.cn/Press/2015–05/26/content_4586805.htm. Accessed 10 Feb 2016
Ngor M, Gridneff I (2014) China to deploy troops to protect South Sudan oil facilities. Bloomberg Business (10 Sept). http://www.bloomberg.com/news/articles/2014–09-10/china-to-deploy-troops-to-protect-south-sudan-oil-installations. Accessed 11 Sept 2014
Onnis B (2013) Has China plans for world domination? Comp Civiliz Rev 68:55–73
Onnis B (2014) The new 'selective diplomacy' of the People's Republic of China: towards a 'partial' interference in global affairs? In: Mierzejewski D (ed) The quandaries of China's domestic and foreign development. Łódź University Press, Łódź, pp 43–57
Osterhammel J (1992) Storia della Cina moderna (secoli XVIII–XX). Einaudi, Torino
People's Daily Online (2004) UN report: China becoming major investor abroad (7 Jan). http://en.people.cn/200401/07/eng20040107_132003.shtml. Accessed 15 Dec 2015
Qi L (2012) The 'secrets' behind the success of China–Africa relations. China Daily (20 Jul). http://www.chinadaily.com.cn/opinion/2012–07/20/content_15603361.htm. Accessed 10 Sept 2015
Qian Q (2006) Ten episodes in China's diplomacy. HarperCollins, New York
Raghavan S (2014) With oil at stake, South Sudan's crisis matters to its customers. The Washington Post (20 Jan). https://www.washingtonpost.com/world/africa/with-oil-at-stake-the-

war-in-south-sudan-matters-to-its-customers/2014/01/20/dcca9432–7d25-11e3-97d3-b9925ce2c57b_story.html. Accessed 11 Sept 2014
Ren D, Ng T (2015) China's silk road dream falls into place with US$40 b fund. South China Morning Post (17 Feb). http://www.scmp.com/news/china/article/1715764/chinas-silk-road-dream-falls-place-us40-billion-fund. Accessed 18 Feb 2015
Renminwang (2015) China will build protective facilities in Gjibouti (Zhongguo jiang zai Jibuti jianshe houqin baozhang sheshi) (26 Nov). http://world.people.com.cn/n/2015/1126/c157278–27860707.html. Accessed 27 Nov 2015
Rotberg IR (2016) China's new promises to Africa. ChinaUsFocus (6 Jan). http://www.chinausfocus.com/foreign-policy/chinas-new-promises-to-africa/. Accessed 7 Jan 2016
Schuman M (2015) China's new silk road dream. Bloomberg Business (25 Nov). http://www.bloomberg.com/news/articles/2015–11-25/china-s-new-silk-road-dream. Accessed 10 Dec 2015
Shelton G (2015) Forum opens door to the silk road. Sunday Independent (6 Dec). http://www.iol.co.za/sundayindependent/forum-opens-door-to-the-silk-road-1955910. Accessed 7 Dec 2015
Snow P (1994) China and Africa: consensus and camouflages. In: Robinson TW, Shambaugh D (eds) Chinese foreign policy: theory and practice. Clarendon Press, Oxford, pp 283–321
SouthAfrica.info (2014) Africa's growth potential—and its 'next 10' biggest cities (Aug 29). http://www.southafrica.info/africa/cities-180814.htm#.VthrqPnhBD8. Accessed 15 Jan 2016
Swaine MD (2015) Chinese views and commentary on the 'one belt, one road' initiative. Chinese Leadership Monitor 47. http://www.hoover.org/sites/default/files/research/docs/clm47ms.pdf
Taylor I (1988) China's foreign policy towards Africa in the 1990s. J Mod Afr Stud 36(3):443–460
Taylor I (2001) China's relations with Sub-Saharan Africa in the post-maoist era, 1978–1999. In: Columbus FH (ed) Politics and economics of Africa, vol 1. Nova Science Publishers Inc., Huntington New York, pp 83–106
UN Mission's Summary detailed by Country (2015) Month of report (30 Sept). http://www.un.org/en/peacekeeping/contributors/2015/sep15_3.pdf
Wang G (2011) 35,860 Chinese evacuated from unrest-torn Libya. Xinhuanet (3 Ma). http://news.xinhuanet.com/english2010/china/2011–03/03/c_13759456.htm. Accessed 20 Nov 2015
Wang T (2013) Africa is the top choice for China's 'going out' strategy (Feizhou shi Zhongguo 'zou chuqu' de shouxuan). Huanqiu shibao (26 Mar). http://news.xinhuanet.com/world/2013-03/26/c_124504930.htm. Accessed 15 Sept 2015
Wang H (2015a) China walks careful line on anti-terrorism. Global Times (19 Nov). http://www.globaltimes.cn/content/953707.shtml. Accessed 20 Nov 2015
Wang K (2015b) Yemen evacuation a strategic step forward for China. The diplomat (10 Apr). http://thediplomat.com/2015/04/yemen-evacuation-a-strategic-step-forward-for-china/. Accessed 11 Apr 2015
Wang X (2015c) Beijing confirms military support facilities in Djibouti. Chinadaily (27 Nov). http://www.chinadaily.com.cn/world/2015-11/27/content_22522423.htm. Accessed 28 Nov 2015
Wong CH (2016) Beijing esumes formal ties with Gambia, in signal to Taipei. Wall St J (17 Ma). https://www.wsj.com/articles/beijing-resumes-formal-ties-with-gambia-in-signal-to-taipei-1458233742. Accessed 1 Apr 2017
Wilson HS (1994) African decolonization. Edward Arnold Publishers, London
Wu J (2015) 'One belt and one road', far-reaching initiative. ChinaUs Focus (26 Mar)
Xinhua News (2007) China's direct investments abroad top $92 b by 2007 (17 Apr). http://www.chinadaily.com.cn/bizchina/2008-04/17/content_6624488.htm. Accessed 12 Oct 2015
Xinhuanet (2014) China sends first infantry battalion for UN peacekeeping (22 Dec). http://news.xinhuanet.com/english/china/2014-12/22/c_133871006.htm. Accessed 1 Dec 2015
Xinhuanet (2015) Kenyan scholar says China's silk road to power Africa's industrial progress (15 Nov). http://news.xinhuanet.com/english/2015-11/15/c_134818901.htm. Accessed 16 Nov 2015
Xinhuanet (2015) Spotlight: China's peacekeeping contribution to UN missions in Africa shows growing sense of responsibility (27 Mar). http://news.xinhuanet.com/english/2015-03/27/c_134104184.htm. Accessed 30 Mar 2015

Yomi K (2013) China's 'stadium diplomacy' in Africa and its top beneficiaries. Venturesafrica (29 Mar). http://venturesafrica.com/chinas-stadium-diplomacy-in-africa-and-its-top-beneficiaries/. Accessed 2 Dec 2015

Yun S (2014) Africa in China's foreign policy. John L. Thornton China Center and Africa growth initiative. Brookings Institution. http://www.brookings.edu/~/media/research/files/papers/2014/04/africa-china-policy-sun/africa-in-china-web_cmg7.pdf

Zenn J (2012) Chinese, overseas, and insecure. Asia Times online (6 Sept). http://www.atimes.com/atimes/China/NI06Ad02.html. Accessed 15 Sep 2015

Zhang M (2016) Significance of establishing the AIIB. China.org (22 Feb). http://china.org.cn/opinion/2016-02/22/content_37840678_2.htm. Accessed 23 Feb 2016

Zhou B (2015) PLA obliged to protect overseas interests. Chinadaily (30 Dec). http://www.chinadaily.com.cn/opinion/2015-12/30/content_22863019.htm. Accessed 7 Jan 2016

Enemies, Friends and Comrades-in-Arms. The Awkward Relations Between the GDR and China in the 1980s

Axel Berkofsky

Abstract East Berlin and Beijing lived an 'eventful' decade in the 1980s, to say the very least. While Beijing decided to interrupt the process of implementing Deng Xiaoping's economic reforms by shooting on unarmed and peacefully demonstrating on Tiananmen Square in June 1989, The German Democratic Republic (GDR) collapsed altogether without a single shot fired in the same year. What the GDR and China said to and did with each other before Beijing crushed what it ludicrously referred to as 'counter-revolution' on Tiananmen Square in 1989 with violence and the GDR landed on the dustbin of history, is analyzed in this chapter.

1 Introduction

When Erich Honecker, Secretary-General of the GDR's Socialist Unity Party of Germany (SED) visited Beijing in October 1986, the Soviet Union and China had—due to the so-called 'Sino-Soviet split' of the late 1950s/early 1960s no political relations to speak of and would only re-establish high-level political relations in the early 1990s (Lüthi 2008). Consequently, Honecker's visit to China was always going to be observed with great scepticism and indeed suspicion by Honecker's political and ideological masters in Moscow. When the GDR 'congratulated' Beijing's political leaders for having ended peaceful demonstrations on Tiananmen Square in June 1989 with military force on the other hand, Moscow under Mikhail Gorbachev had very little left to be suspicious about and knew—unlike Honecker and the yes men among the GDR's political leadership around him—that the GDR was about to collapse irreversibly. East Berlin's unconditional support and endorsement of Beijing's violent response to peaceful demonstrations on Tiananmen Square in June 1989 at the time stood in stark contrast to Moscow's

A. Berkofsky (✉)
Department of Political and Social Sciences, University of Pavia, Pavia, Italy
e-mail: Axel.Berkofsky@unipv.it

A. Berkofsky
Istituto per gli Studi di Politica Internazionale (ISPI), Milan, Italy

S. Beretta et al. (eds.), *Understanding China Today*, Understanding China,
DOI 10.1007/978-3-319-29625-8_9

reaction to Beijing shooting on unarmed students. Moscow—like all the other countries from the socialist bloc of countries in Eastern Europe—condemned Beijing's decision to end peaceful demonstrations with military violence. In fact, East Berlin 'congratulating' Beijing made the GDR the 'odd man out' out of touch with political realities in Eastern Europe and the Soviet Union in the camp of socialist countries at the time.

Indeed, East Berlin's cynical support for Beijing opting for violence to end what it claimed was a Western-inspired and sponsored 'conspiracy' to overthrow the Chinese government was the ultimate expression of the GDR's political helplessness and a desperate attempt to replace the Soviet Union with China as East Berlin's 'best friend' when Moscow adopted political and economic reforms, which were perceived as 'regime-threatening' in East Berlin. However, as it turned out, East Berlin's decision to stand by Beijing's political leadership on a come-what-may basis came much too late as the GDR would collapse only a few months later. The signs that domestic and foreign policies of the Soviet Union run by Mikhail Gorbachev in the mid-1980s were about to change fundamentally were there and for all to see—except for Honecker and his new best friends in Beijing as it seemed. On the occasion of the XXVII Party Congress of the Communist Party of the Soviet Union (CPSU) in February 1986 Gorbachev announced that he was planning to profoundly re-visit the Soviet Union's foreign policy and renounced central elements of Marxist-Leninist ideology as a basis for Moscow's international relations and policies. Honecker and the GDR's political leadership, however, continued—at least so it seemed on the official record—to believe that Gorbachev was 'only' planning to modernize socialism as opposed to dismantling it completely. Indeed, little did Honecker in 1986 know that only three years later in 1989 he would be toppled from power by his close one-time political ally Erich Krenz. Honecker's stubborn and categorical refusal to adopt economic and political reforms in the GDR and his inability to understand that Gorbachev wanted to end the Cold War with the West made sure that the GDR and its 'real existing socialism' would land on the dustbin of history when East German protestors and activists started to march for democracy and against the regime in Leipzig and Dresden in late 1989.

The archive material used for this chapter provides scholars and historians with very valuable sources and accounts of how East Berlin viewed its present and foresaw its future relations Beijing, allowing for a comprehensive analysis of East Berlin's official policies towards and relations with Beijing. The larger part of archive material in German language cited in this chapter comes from the GDR's former Institut für Geschichte der Arbeiterbewegung, Zentrales Parteiarchiv, ZPA[1])—the archive of the GDR's ruling Sozialistische Einheitspartei Deutschland (SED).[2] That archive material was made available in January 1992 when the German Bundestag adopted a law, which suspended the usual 30-year retention period for documents published by GDR authorities and party organizations. Since 1993, that

[1]To be translated as 'Institute for the History of the Workers' Movement, Central Party Archive'.
[2]Socialist Unity Party of Germany.

archive material belongs to Germany's Bundesarchiv (Federal Archive) and is called 'Stiftung Archiv der Parteien und Massenorganisation der DDR im Bundesarchiv[3]' (cited in this chapter as 'SAPMO-BARch, ZPA').

2 China-GDR Ties in the Early 1980s

In 1980, East German university professors began to return to Chinese universities while at the same time official party relations between the SED and China's CCP were resumed. Furthermore, East Berlin decided in 1981 to terminate the so-called 'solidarity week' for Vietnam and ordered an East German publishing house to stop the publication and circulation of publications critical of China.[4] In February 1981 during the 10th SED party convention Honecker announced that the GDR is—under certain conditions—prepared to normalize relations with Beijing: "As far as the GDR is concerned, it is remains prepared to normalize relations with the People's Republic of China based on the principles of equality, respect for sovereignty, territorial integrity and non-interference. We are convinced that peaceful and normal relations are also of interest to the Chinese people" (Parteitag der Sozialistischen Einheitspartei Deutschlands 1981).

That sounded somehow conciliatory, but it was only the very last paragraph of Honecker's speech on relations with China that struck a more conciliatory tone. The previous paragraphs of that speech stroke an indeed very different tone and focussed on the alleged disadvantages of China establishing relations with the 'imperialist' United States. "For the fight against imperialism it would crucially important if such a big country as China made its contribution. However, it turned out that the opposite was the case. Chinese cooperation with the U.S. helps the policies of confrontation among the most reactionary forces of global imperialism. That in particular is true for Beijing anti-Soviet attitude and its hostile toward the community of Socialist countries", Honecker maintained.

Only a few weeks later after Honecker's 'semi-reconciliatory' China speech an official East German delegation travelled to Beijing—a delegation from the department of international relations of the SED's Central Committee headed by Bruno Mahlow met a group of officials from China's Ministry of Foreign Affairs and the Institute for International Relations.[5] This visit was in July 1981 followed by a visit of two officials from the Chinese Communist Party's Central Committee to East Berlin, the first official Chinese visit to East Berlin since the mid-1960. When the two Chinese officials from the committee's department of international relations with the Soviet Union and East European countries met two counterparts

[3]Roughly to be translated as 'Foundation Archive of GDR Party and Mass Organizations in the German Federal Archive.'

[4]Publications critical of China already in circulation were taken out of circulation.

[5]Most probably an institute directly affiliated with China's Ministry of Foreign Affairs.

from the SED's Central Committee, the protocol of the visit stresses twice that the Chinese visitors did not talk about relations between China's Communist Party and East Germany's SED.[6] The protocol, however, does not provide any information on what they actually talked about during the visit from July 16 to August 23, 1981 either. The lack of information in the protocol on the issues discussed between Chinese and East German party officials during a visit that lasted five weeks is indeed remarkable. While it remains—due to the lack of verifiable information—speculation why the protocol does not provide any information on the contents of the talks, it can indeed be taken for granted that Chinese and East German officials did during the 5-week official visit also talk about bilateral relations—in fact it is hard to imagine that they did not. Put differently: 5 weeks is a very long time trying to avoid talking about bilateral relations. However, the GDR's decision not to publish any information on what was discussed in East Berlin could have been related to concerns about what Moscow thought about a long and official GDR-Chinese encounter when Moscow and Beijing were not on speaking terms (SAPMO-BArch, ZPA JIV 2/20/139).

To be sure, Moscow was apprehensive, if indeed not very suspicious, about the Chinese-East German encounters at the time. Indeed, a secret note most probably written by an official from Central Committee of the Communist Party of the Soviet Union (CPSU) in June 1982 indicates that the Central Committee was clearly worried about possible Chinese attempts to improve relations with East Berlin at the expense of relations between Moscow and East Berlin and joint and coordinated policies towards Beijing (SAPMO-BArch, ZPA IV 2/2.035/64).[7] "Typical for Beijing's tactics are urgent requests towards the GDR to intensify bilateral relations with Beijing while at the same attempting to harm relations between the GDR and Soviet Union." As alleged evidence that Beijing was trying to drive a wedge between Moscow and East Berlin, the official cites Beijing's proposal to resume the exchange of university students and professors, journalists and writers. Furthermore, the officials mentions that the Chinese ambassador to East Berlin proposed at the end of 1981 to resume and increase bilateral trade and scientific relations. The list of evidence allegedly pointing to Chinese tactics to improve relations with East Berlin at the expense of the GDR's relations with Moscow looked rather implausible and indeed irrelevant when the official e.g. cited the fact that Beijing invited an East German historian to a conference in Tianjin and East Berlin invited a Chinese scholar to a conference in Dresden. Finally, the official sounded concerned about the fact that bilateral East German-Chinese trade for the

[6]The protocol limited itself to e.g. pointing out that the Chinese visitors showed themselves interested in the economic development of the GDR. Interestingly or indeed tellingly, the protocol furthermore mentioned that the Chinese Embassy in East Berlin covered all costs for the Chinese visitors in Berlin, probably to make it clear that the visit was not an 'official' invitation important enough for the GDR to cover the costs for the visiting delegation.

[7]The source cannot be verified with complete accuracy, but based on the available information and the contents of that note, it is very likely that it was indeed written by an official from the Central Committee.

year 1982 would increase by seven percent and that the years 1981 and 1982 saw increased exchanges between the Communist Party in China and the Socialist Party in East Germany respectively. The official concluded by saying that what he refers to as 'Chinese propaganda' voiced during encounters with GDR officials suggested that the Soviet Union-led Council for Mutual Economic Assistance (CMEA) Comecon, founded in 1949 and dissolved in 1989)—the equivalent of the U.S. Marshall Plan for Eastern European economic reconstruction—would have 'undesired consequences' for the East German economy.

3 'Neutralizing' Beijing, East Berlin Says (to Moscow)

East Berlin of course, staunchly denied having been used and indeed exploited by Beijing as interlocutor acting against the interests of the Soviet Union. In fact, East Berlin claimed that the very opposite was the case, offering its very own explanation of what the expansion of bilateral ties with Beijing stands for: it was aimed at 'neutralizing' China in order to be able to later and again include China again in what is dramatically referred to as the global 'anti-imperialist fight.' The SED Central Committee wrote to the Central Committee of the Communist Party of the Soviet Union that all instruments—trade and economic ties, scientific ties, cultural ties, sports ties—will be used to that end. Ties and cooperation, which would strengthen China's military capabilities, the document emphasised, would be excluded. The SED's Central Committee gave itself very concerned that China's rapprochement with the U.S. could impose what is referred to as 'two-front war' onto the Warsaw Pact—an anti-socialist coalition consisting of the U.S. China, Western Europe and Japan (SAPMO-BArch, ZPA JIV 2/2/1960). Reality, of course, was very different and the fear of a 'two-front war' with China fighting on the side of the U.S. was indeed completely unrealistic and a product of East Berlin's hysterical obsession with an alleged threat posed by Western 'imperialism.'

East Berlin's argument that the expansion of the above-mentioned trade, scientific and cultural ties would serve to 'neutralize' Beijing and keep it from intensifying relations with the 'imperialist' West sounded very odd indeed and must have been perceived as such in Moscow at the time. Indeed, the entire above-mentioned letter from the SED's Central Committee to their comrades in the Soviet Union has a surreal touch to it and somehow indicates that East Berlin's political elites were at the time already out of touch with political realities in China. Indeed, China's economic opening-up and Deng Xiaoping's economic reforms made sure that trade relations with and technology imports from the West in general and the U.S. and Japan in particular[8] became far important than imports from the

[8]Obviously, while Japan does geographically not belong to the 'West', economically, ideologically and politically the country was referred to as belonging to the Western camp during the Cold War.

GDR. After the phase of 'neutralizing' China, the letter reads, the country would be included in "Dealing the final blow to the imperialist enemy."[9] That does indeed sound dramatic but sounded credible to GDR policymakers who through their policies towards Beijing aimed at "Freeing China from a complot" with the U.S. as the letter reads. China, the letter continues, should be treated like any other "imperialist trading partner." In retrospect, such language and terms used in official documents sound rather theatrical if not completely void of any sense. Confirming in the same letter that the GDR has successfully kept Beijing from supporting alleged Western Germany revanchism towards the GDR falls into that same category. In reality, Western German policies towards the GDR were in the early 1980s instead reconciliatory while Bonn used the fact that the GDR depended on Western Germany for economic and financial aid undoubtedly for its own purposes. The Soviet Union was obviously aware of the fact that Bonn's financial aid towards East Berlin in particular was instrumental in keeping the regime from economically collapsing and rhetoric speaking of 'revanchist policies' towards the GDR must have sounded hollow to Moscow's ears in the early 1980s. In sum, the letter's tenor, terms and nuances are arguably those of an underage son telling his father what he wants to hear in dramatic language as a confirmation of unconditional loyalty and devotion (to what was left of the socialist cause).

4 Getting Even Closer

The expansion of relations between East Berlin and Beijing in the course of 1982–1984 further confirmed the impression that the above-mentioned term 'neutralize' did not describe what the GDR was pursuing with China at the time. In 1983, East Berlin and Beijing adopted their first bilateral agreement in the sector of telecommunications and in April 1984 a newly established joint committee covering economic, trade and scientific cooperation started meeting on a regular basis. Among others it was agreed that the GDR would contribute to the construction and development phases of more than 40 industrial projects in China. This resumed economic and industrial cooperation was accompanied by the resumption of bilateral visits in 1984, 1985 and 1986.[10]

[9]'Hauptstoβ' is the term that was used in German: a very belligerent and dramatic term describing what China would in the view of the GDR be part of in the future.

[10]By several GDR politicians and policymakers such as Margot Honecker, Erich Honecker's wife and Minister of Education and Gerhard Schürer, chairman of the State Planning Commission, Minister of the and members of the Politbüro (Günther Kleiber and Horst Sindermann). Margot Honecker was what was referred to as 'Minister of People's Education' from 1963 until the collapse of the GDR in 1989. Margot Honecker is above all if not exclusive remembered for her hard-line Stalinist policies and her (successful) attempts to militarize the GDR's education system. She exploited her relationship with Erich Honecker to make her Stalinist fantasies come true and in 1965 introduced the so-called 'Uniform Socialist Education System' ('Sozialistisches Einheitserziehungssystem'), which foresaw military training in schools and a focus on

Between the summer of 1982 and 1985 relations between the GDR and China intensified up to a level that cannot by any account be described as part of the above-mentioned 'neutralization' process. In fact, the quality and quantity of exchanges between East Berlin and Beijing rather suggested that East Berlin was looking to charm an old new friend in case it needed one in the years ahead. At the time East German and Chinese universities intensified contacts and in the summer of 1982 East German athletes took part in an athletics competition in Beijing. GDR media increased their coverage on China without criticizing the country in any way. Kurt Vogel, a high-ranking official of the GDR journalists' union[11] returned from a visit to Berlin and wrote in the news magazine 'Horizont' that his visit was "An emotional reunion with former comrades and comrade-in-arms from the 1950, who have never lost faith in the correctness and superiority of the socialist Weltanschauung"[12] (Meiβner 1995, 349). What followed in terms of visits and official high-level exchanges in 1984 and 1985 did indeed look nothing like a policy of 'neutralizing' but instead like one engaging China. East Germany's Vice-Minister of Foreign Affairs Herbert Krolikowski travelled to Beijing in May 1984 after which the SED's Central Committee developed an entire catalogue of how to intensify relations and exchanges with Beijing in the years ahead. This catalogue included the continuation of bilateral political dialogue and the preparation of a bilateral meeting between the East German and Chinese foreign ministers, the resumption of official relations between East Berlin's 'Chamber of the People' ('Volkskammer', East Berlin's parliament) and China's National People's Congress (NPC) and various other agreements in the areas of health, non-commercial payment transactions, scientific and technology cooperation and trade and commerce (SAPMO-BArch, ZPA JIV 2/3/3671).

Krolikowski's visit to Beijing was followed by a visit of China's Politburo member Li Peng[13] to East Berlin in the summer of 1985, without a doubt a high-level enough

(Footnote 10 continued)

indoctrination. Arguably comparable to what the Nazis in Germany referred to as 'Gleichschaltung' (literally: 'render everything equal') in schools, universities and public life from 1933 to 1945. Furthermore, M. Honecker was also responsible for the forced adoption of children of jailed dissidents and activists. She is also referred to as the 'most hated person' in East Germany next to Erich Mielke, notorious Minister of East Germany's Ministerium für Staatsicherheit (Stasi) (Ministry for State Security). After the collapse of the GDR in 1989 M. Honecker fled to Chile to escape criminal prosecution (where she was joined by husband Erich who was convicted in Germany but was allowed to emigrate to Chile in 1992 due to his poor health). M. Honecker remained a convinced socialist until the very end and her death in Chile in May 2016 and never regretted any of her crimes and brutality disguised as 'socialist education.'

[11]General-Secretary of the Central Committee of the 'DDR-Journalistenverband.'

[12]The German term 'Weltanschauung' (also used in English) is used here as the English term 'ideology' does not accurately describe what the above-mentioned Kurt Vogel meant.

[13]Who was to have a key role in Beijing's decision to end peaceful student demonstrations on Tiananmen Square in June 1989 with violent means. Indeed, it was Li Peng, who urged Deng Xiaoping to declare martial law in Beijing at the time.

visit[14] to make Honecker and his colleagues believe that East Berlin really mattered to Beijing as a partner with whom to trade goods and coordinate political views.

However, what really mattered to Beijing were its trade and investment ties with West Germany. Bilateral trade volume between Beijing and Bonn were at the time more than ten times bigger than the respective volume between Beijing and East Berlin and Bonn was a central source for badly needed technology and know-how in China. As regards China's relations with West Germany, it is probably accurate to conclude that what Li Peng said on China's relations with West Germany to Honecker and others in East Berlin is not necessarily what East Berlin wanted to hear. Li Peng promised that China would not interfere in bilateral relations between East Berlin and Bonn and told East German officials that Zhao Ziyang, high-ranking CCP official (and later CCP Secretary-General) would convey the same message during a visit to Bonn roughly at the same time. China, most probably due to its trade and commercial relations West Germany, which included the export of German know-how and technology crucial for China's economic reforms, chose not to explicitly support East Berlin hard-line policies towards the ideological enemy in the West beyond Li Peng saying that he favours student exchanges with East and not West German as the GDR is equipped with the 'right ideology' as he put it. SAPMO-BArch, ZPA JIV 2/2A/2758; SAPMO-BArch, ZPA IIV 2/20/22). East Berlin, it must be assumed, expected something very different such as unconditional Chinese support for East Berlin's policies countering alleged West German 'revanchism.'

And the mid-1980s saw more official East German-Chinese encounters, e.g. the meeting between Gerhard Schürer, chairman of the GDR's State Planning Commission and Hu Yaobang, then CCP Secretary-General in Beijing in July 1985 (SAPMO-BArch, ZPA JIV 2/20/22). Hu said that China supported the concept of 'peaceful co-existence' of the two German states while he warned Bonn during his encounters with West German leaders not to 'swallow' the GDR. To be sure, West Berlin never had the intention to do so and Hu himself did not have that impression either. Based on his own experience and impressions, Hu said 'revanchist forces' in West Germany do not seem to have great influence. On a conciliatory note, Hu again confirmed that China would in his relations with West Germany not do anything that would jeopardize relations with the GDR. However, Hu who de facto denied the existence of what East Berlin claimed are 'revanchist forces' in West Germany made it unambiguously clear that Beijing valued economic and trade relations with West Germany higher than political and ideological relations with a country that very little, or indeed next to nothing, to offer in terms badly-needed technology and know-how. Hu furthermore concluded that socialist countries cannot go on fighting capitalist countries indefinitely and that China would pursue policies towards those countries on the basis of the principle of 'peaceful co-existence.' No high-ranking politician or party member in the GDR said anything like that in public at the time and it can be concluded with certainty that East Berlin's attempts—through the

[14]Roughly at the same time when high-ranking CCP official Zhao Ziyang visited West Germany.

above-mentioned numerous bilateral encounters—to secure China as a new ally against alleged Western German 'revanchism' and probably more importantly to secure China as a counterbalance against what was increasingly feared were Soviet Union reform policies directly threatening the survival of the GDR.

Indeed, the GDR leadership must towards the second half of the 1980s have realized that the Soviet Union under Gorbachev was—put bluntly—no longer the Soviet Union they used to know and that looking for new friends and allies was probably advisable from East Berlin's perspective. From a Chinese perspective, the intensification of bilateral exchanges in the mid-1980s on the other hand also needs to be understood against the background of the intensification of Beijing's relations with West Germany: Beijing, Werner Meiβner argues, was de facto obliged to expand exchanges and relations with East Berlin in order not to give the impression to favor ties with Bonn over East Berlin.

5 Honecker's Beijing Visit in 1986—Comrades-in-Arms, Up to a Point

In 1985, Honecker gave himself concerned that the absence of good relations or indeed hostilities between Moscow and Beijing would continue to bring with it geo-strategic disadvantages for the Warsaw Pact. However, such a dramatic assumption lacked any real credibility as the 'Sino-Soviet Split' occurred 25 years earlier and the alleged 'disadvantages' for the Warsaw Pact would have materialized a long time ago and not only in 1985. Honecker, however, was seemingly convinced of the accuracy of his geopolitical vision and urged Moscow to coordinate respective policies towards Beijing, also in the hope of assuming a role as mediator between Moscow and Beijing (Scholtyseck 2003, 42–44).

That is when Honecker decided to make use of his 'mediation skills' and visit Beijing in October 1986. Indeed, during his visit to Beijing in 1986 Honecker sought to present himself as mediator between China and the Soviet Union, albeit with very limited success as it eventually turned out. Honecker, of course, would interpret the quality and output of his visit with differently and was received with all possible honours in Beijing and his Chinese hosts seemed indeed prepared to exchange views with the man, whose eyes according to the Chinese magazine Liaowang display 'wisdom' and 'self-confidence' (Der Spiegel 1986). Honecker returned the compliment and praised the 'diligent Chinese people' and the 'beautiful country' and the General-Secretary of China's Communist Party Hu Yaobang called Honeckers's visit a 'big event.' Honecker's visit to China was according to Honecker's own account not coordinated with Moscow and was—at least as far as Honecker was concerned—an expression of the GDR's foreign policy independence and the ability to act as mediator or 'honest broker' between Moscow and Beijing. To be sure, that was the way Honecker and Honecker only saw it—his decade-long control over the GDR made him completely blind to reality and his deteriorating health in the second half of the 1980s did not help him to understand that his days on top of the GDR's leadership were numbered.

Honecker's China visit to Beijing in 1986, it is at times argued in the literature, was evidence that the GDR was able to conduct its own and independent foreign policy, free from pressure and influence from the Soviet Union. However, in retrospect and against the background what would happen in the GDR in the late 1980s, one could instead be tempted to argue that his visit to China was also borne out of desperation and the need to look for a new ally and a new 'best friend', who would like Honecker be and remain opposed to any kind of 'regime-threatening' political and/or social reforms Gorbachev would in the 1980s in a very determined fashion adopt in the Soviet Union.

To be sure, from Honecker's perspective the visit was something completely different: the result of his year-long—and in his view successful—efforts to overcome the above-mentioned 'Sino-Soviet Split' of the early 1960s and pave the way for the normalization between the Soviet Union and China. Indeed, in 1989 Honecker praised himself as the 'forerunner of normalization' ('Wegbereiter der Normalisierung'). While Honecker clearly overvalued the positive impact of its trip to Beijing and the consequences for the GDR's relations with China, it did—at least according to Günter Schabowski,[15] member of the Sozialistische Einheitspartei Deutschlands (SED) Politburo—help to encourage other socialist countries to seek to improve relations with Beijing at the time (Schabowski 1991, 210). That, however, was suggested as Honecker was without much doubt driven by a compulsion to ignore reality and instead overstate his personal influence on global politics as leader of a country, which in 1986 had not much to offer to China other than high-sounding rhetoric on 'brotherhood between socialist countries' and the joint 'struggle against the imperialist West.' Indeed, there is no empirical evidence that other socialist countries took Honecker's visit to Beijing in 1986 to seek to improve or indeed resume relations with Beijing.

Finally, Honecker claimed that his talks in China gave another impetus to intensify bilateral trade and business relations. However, that is simply not accurate as Beijing shortly after the visit e.g. announced that it would reduce the export of Chinese commercial vehicles from yearly 10,000 to 6,000 in the years ahead and in turn East Berlin turned down the Chinese request to establish a joint-venture to build a carbo-chemical industrial complex in the Chinese city of Wuhai.

[15]Günter Schabowski was a former high-ranking GDR official and member of the Politbüro-hence, he was on top of a system, which he has (in more than one book authored by himself) strongly criticized. The credibility of former officials of authoritarian states writing and commenting on the authoritarian system they were very much part of is—at least in this author's view—very limited. In other words: former East German party officials, who enjoyed the privileges at the top of a totalitarian system they helped to keep alive for 40 years are consequently not always to be taken seriously as reliable and credible sources of information.

6 And the Chinese?

Honecker's Chinese interlocutors in Beijing put on a brave face and promised that Beijing would maintain relations with both parts of Germany based on the principle of 'peaceful co-existence.' Beijing maintaining that West Berlin should never be allowed to re-unify West and East Germany with force might have sounded re-assuring to Honecker's ears, but that was probably nothing more than something the Chinese leadership said to please East Berlin, not least because West Berlin or the West in general never had any intention to re-unify the two German states with force. The same was true for Beijing's re-assurance that its relations with West Germany's Social-Democratic Party (Sozialdemokratische Partei Deutschlands, SPD) would not have a negative impact on the relations between the CCP and SED.

Honecker and Chinese leader Deng Xiaoping agreed during a bilateral meeting that the visit was not about resuming but instead continuing relations as Beijing—even in times of the Sino-Soviet border conflict—did not close its embassy in East Berlin. However, Honecker's (timid) initiative to advertise Gorbachev's idea to seek to improve Sino-Soviet relations as suggested during the Reykjavik Summit in October 1986 was censored and not reported by the Chinese media. Instead, Beijing suggested to not rely too much on the two superpowers and instead conduct policies more independent from the Soviet Union—an option for Honecker and the GDR suggested against the background of what was taking place in terms of reforms in the Soviet Union at the time.

What was remarkable is that Beijing during the visit spoke about the 'nation of the GDR', which led the West German Ambassador in Beijing Per Fischer to call China's Ministry of Foreign Affairs in protest, maintaining that there is only one 'German nation', i.e. the people who both live in East and West Germany. While the East German delegation on the other hand was delighted about Beijing talking about the 'nation of the GDR', Beijing chose to play down the alleged political significance of the term 'nation of the GDR' and declared it to be an 'idiomatic' concept rather than a declaration that they were two German nations. More importantly, however, Beijing sought to use the visit for its own purposes in the context of what the scholar Joachim Krüger calls 'Policy of Differentiation' (also 'Policy of Diversification'), i.e. Beijing's attempt to improve relations with the GDR at the expense of relations between the GDR and the Soviet Union (Krüger 1994). In other words, Beijing attempting to drive a wedge between East Berlin and Moscow and, as Eberhard Sandschneider argues, not a Chinese opening to the possibility of repairing relations with the Soviet Union (Sandschneider 1987). Whether or whether not this is exactly what Beijing at the time had in mind when hosting Honecker is difficult if not possible to verify today.

The meeting between Honecker's and Hu Yaobang, then Secretary-General of China's Communist Party in turn suggested that Beijing was not interested in offering to improve relations with East Berlin at the expense of East Berlin's relations with Moscow. In fact, Hu said that China would never do anything to undermine relations between the socialist countries and the Soviet Union. "We fully respect the particular good relations, which have over decades developed between the socialist countries and the Soviet Union. We will not declare or do anything, which negatively influence the relations between Eastern European socialist countries and the Soviet Union" (Meißner 1995, 350). In a second conversation with Hu Honecker expressed his interest in seeing improved relations between Beijing and Moscow and saw himself as a mediator and Moscow's 'messenger.' Hu told Honecker that Deng Xiaoping would be willing to consider the possibility of visiting the Soviet Union if Vietnam withdrew its troops from Cambodia. Hu, however, complained in the same conversation with Honecker (in Nanjing) that Moscow had seemingly no intention whatsoever to meet that Chinese request. In a speech in Vladivostok in July 1986, Hu argued, Gorbachev did not address the Cambodia issue and during a bilateral meeting between the Chinese and Soviet Union's Vice-Foreign Ministers in October of the same year, there were according to Hu no indications that the Soviet Union would address Chinese concerns about Moscow's support for Vietnam (SAPMO-BArch, ZPA JIV 2/2/2191). Honecker, who clearly took the opportunity of presenting himself as a 'mediator-in-chief', sought to assure that Gorbachev is not only to be fully trusted but also one who is prepared to meet the Chinese leadership any time. "Make no mistake, comrade Hu Yaobang, I know comrade Gorbachev as a man whose word can be trusted and who has a sincere interest in improving relations between the communist parties in China and the Soviet Union. We, I told Gorbachev, are interested to see improved relations between the Soviet Union and the People's Republic of China and the best way to do that is to talk to our Vietnamese comrades. I know that comrade Gorbachev is at your disposal to meet anytime. We would be very happy to see outstanding problems resolved and I am saying this as a Communist." Hu Yaobang during his first meeting with Honecker on the other hand told him that China would no longer speak of 'US imperialism', 'Japanese militarism' and 'Western German revanchism.' The message was clear: Deng Xiaoping's economic pragmatism accompanied by policies to attract as Western foreign direct investment as possible from the West had priority over an ideological confrontation with the West in general and the U.S. in particular.

7 The Disappointing Aftermath

When Mikhail Gorbachev became Secretary-General of the Communist Party of the Soviet Union (CPSU) in 1985 Honecker and like-minded followers in the GDR realized and indeed feared that the kind of political reforms Gorbachev announced and indeed adopted in the second half of the 1980s would become a threat to the entire socialist system the way they knew it. Indeed, anxiety about Gorbachev's 'system-threatening' reforms shaped Honecker and the GDR's domestic and foreign policy thinking from the mid to the end-1980s leaving very little or indeed no room for a GDR mediating role. Already in November 1986 Gorbachev decided to completely abandon the so-called 'Brezhnev Doctrine', through which the Soviet

Union since 1968 had authorized itself to intervene in popular protests and demonstrations against the Socialist regimes in Warsaw Pact nations (and the Soviet Union's Eastern European satellite states).[16]

The end of the 'Brezhnev Doctrine' must have set off the alarm bells in East Berlin, which also feared that the doctrine's termination would further result in and lead to the continuation of Moscow's strategy to pursue a course of rapprochement towards West Germany driven by economic and financial need and necessity. At the time, however, East Berlin pretended not to notice that Gorbachev pursued very fundamental political and economic reforms and indeed pretended to be strong and independent enough to dismiss Moscow's plan to fundamentally renew the contents and goals of the decade-old Moscow's version of Socialism as irrelevant and not a threat to the GDR's regime survival. As it turned out, he could not have been more wrong about that and Honecker's defiant attitude towards Gorbachev's Moscow and his refusal to follow Gorbachev's advice to consider economic and social reforms in turn confirmed Gorbachev that Honecker could not be counted on as reformed-minded partner. Indeed, when GDR citizens started to leave the country over the course of 1989 and when it became increasingly clear that East Berlin could not do anything much to stop the crowds from leaving, Gorbachev didn't do anything to intervene and stop the GDR citizens from seeking refuge in West Germany.

According to the Chinese scholar Chen Feng Beijing was fully aware that the majority of policymakers in East Berlin wanted improved relations with Beijing in order to strengthen East Berlin's position in the context of its bilateral relations with Moscow and enable Honecker to conduct a more independent foreign policy (Chen 1987).

However, Chinese policymakers must also have been aware that East Berlin in 1986 was in a state of permanent economic crisis and near-collapse and that the GDR had very little (if anything) to offer what Beijing wanted in terms of know-how and technology. China's economic policies in the mid-1980s needed to display economic pragmatism and such kind of pragmatism called for the intensification of relations with West and not East Germany. Furthermore, if Beijing had really decided to—put bluntly—exploit the Honecker visit to Beijing for its own purposes Beijing's top policymakers would probably have decided to visit East Berlin as a follow-up of the Honecker visit in 1986. However, from a Chinese perspective the GDR was most probably and simply not and no longer important enough to be worth being used as 'ally' against the Soviet Union (that would change—albeit briefly—after June 1989, for details see below).

[16]The doctrine was also adopted to retroactively justify the Soviet Union's invasion of Czechoslovakia in 1968 during the 'The Spring of Prague', i.e. the Soviet military intervention in Prague's pro-democracy and anti-regime protests. More generally, the 'Brezhnev Doctrine' was aimed at terminating and sustainably suppressing resistance against oppressive Socialist regimes dependent on and controlled by Moscow.

All of that, however, did not seem to matter at all to Honecker who enjoyed a 'field day' presenting and actively offering himself as the mediator between China and the Soviet Union and it was no surprise that Honecker—also in view of his habit to glorify his own achievements—called his visit to China and his mission an 'extraordinary success' upon his return to East Berlin. Reality, however, turned out to be different, for a number of reasons. Firstly, an invitation for a bilateral meeting between Beijing and was declined and Honecker's Chinese interlocutors must have suspected that Moscow encouraged and indeed instructed Honecker to promote a bilateral encounter between Moscow and Beijing. Therefore, they probably had little choice but to tell Honecker that a bilateral meeting was not in the cards, at least not now. Beijing was undoubtedly aware that Honecker's GDR did not have the authority and the kind of independent foreign policy to suggest Beijing to meet resume bilateral relations with Moscow without having been instructed by Moscow to do so during the visit to Beijing. Against this background, it can therefore be concluded that Honecker's visit to Beijing was at least a partial failure as Beijing did almost categorically refused to meet Moscow bilaterally. Secondly, if Honecker's visit to China really had been the kind of success Honecker portrayed the visit to be, then Deng Xiaoping, Chinese President Li Xiannian, and Hu Yaobang would probably not have declined Honecker's invitation to the GDR. Indeed, in retrospect the assessment of the above-cited scholar Sandschneider is probably accurate: Beijing exploited Honecker's Beijing visit for its own purposes and the visit never was an eye-to-eye meeting between fellow Communist leaders.

In retrospect and due to the lack of reliable information from Chinese sources it remains difficult to assess the 'real' quality of the meeting and the 'real' intentions China had when receiving Honecker at the time, not least as the meeting was accompanied by high-sounding political rhetoric and mutual declarations of friendship, solidarity and confirmations to jointly fight for 'socialist cause.' Hence, the actual and officially reported conversations between Honecker and various Chinese political leaders are not necessarily an indication or indeed evidence on the actual quality of bilateral talks and indeed overall bilateral relations. Consequently, one is inevitably obliged to judge the quality of the bilateral talks by the actual outcome and results of the bilateral encounter weeks and months after that meeting.

In sum, while Honecker presented his visit to Beijing as a stunning success to the public, reality of what that visit resulted in was very different indeed. His visit was not followed-up by further high-level bilateral visits and Honecker's GDR has not—despite him declaring otherwise—become a mediator between China and the Soviet Union. Indeed, the visit's follow-up was disappointing from East Berlin's point of view: Deng Xiaoping declined an invitation to the GDR, as did Chinese President Li Xiannian and Hu Yaobang. The months and first two 2 years after the Honecker visit to Beijing confirmed that the bilateral encounter—put bluntly—did not turn not out to be the 'big bang' of GDR-Chinese relations of the mid-1980s. After 1986 the GDR was gradually but indeed surely on its way to the dustbin of history, had nothing to offer in terms of know-how, technology and products that China could not get elsewhere (above all from East Berlin's arch-enemy Bonn). Already in 1987,

Beijing e.g. announced that it felt no longer bound by the agreement of the 1980s to buy 10,000 GDR-made commercial vehicles and by 1990s and instead agreed to buy only 2000. Beijing clearly put commercial interests over ideology and opted for technology and equipment from West Germany instead.

8 June 1989: Cheering the Violence on Tiananmen Square

The GDR's final policy mistake was undoubtedly Honecker's decision to support the Chinese leadership for its orders to open fire on unarmed students on Tiananmen Square in June 1989. The GDR's political leadership did in June 1989 repeate in parrot-style what the Chinese called the demonstrations on Tiananmen Square: a 'counter-revolutionary disturbance by a small group of people determined to topple the country's political leadership' (Der Spiegel 1989a). To be sure, that assessment could not have been any further away from the truth: what Beijing and East Berlin agreed was a 'small group of misguided counter-revolutionaries' were in reality up to 100 million Chinese people all over China, who in 1989 protested for what the government promised in the 1980s and did not deliver: political and social reforms in China (Lim 2014).

In complete denial of reality of what happened in Beijing in May and June 1989, East Berlin's Allgemeiner Deutscher Nachrichtendienst (ADN) (General German News Service) declared on June 5, 1989 that China's People's Liberation Army had suppressed a 'counter-revolutionary upheaval', thereby adopting Beijing's terminology as to who the students on Tiananmen Square were and what they did in May and June 1989. On June 8, 1989 East Berlin's parliament adopted a declaration in which it declared its unconditional solidarity with the Chinese leadership and its decision to end peaceful demonstrations with military force on June 4, 1989 (SAPMO-Arch, ZPA JIV 2/2/2231). That declaration was made when the large majority of Eastern European countries and most importantly the Soviet Union did not express any of that support. The declaration concluded that Beijing had been "Obliged to re-establish order and security through force. Unfortunately this led to number of casualties and deaths." While such declaration made it unambiguously clear how far East Berlin's leadership was detached from reality, it also can be understood as a desperate attempt by the GDR leadership to align itself with China in the wake Moscow's political reforms which were perceived as threatening the existence of the respective authoritarian and dictatorial regimes in East Berlin and Beijing. The literature even speaks of a short-lived 'East Berlin—Beijing axis' aimed at counterbalancing Soviet Union liberalism. The result of that 'axis' in turn was East Berlin's cynical support for Beijing's decision to shoot into the crowds on Tiananmen Square in June 1989. Indeed, the SED leadership did not lose any time and did not spare efforts to justify what Chinese armed forces were allegedly 'obliged' to do on Tiananmen Square in June 1989. A report by the SED Central

Committee on June 23, 1989 claimed that the Western media have produced 'horror news' on what happened on June 4 on Tiananmen Square and has therefore through the declarations and reports published by China's Communist Party informed itself on what 'really' happened during that night. Based on that information the SED—obviously like the CCP in China—concluded that 'counter-revolutionaries forces' turned a peaceful demonstration into an event to topple the Chinese government. Again like its comrades in Beijing, the SED maintained that what happened in Beijing in June 1989 is strictly an internal affair and not for outsiders to interfere in (Neues Deutschland 1989a). What is remarkable is the fact that the SED thought it would be credible and plausible to cite what China's Communist Party—as opposed to sources outside the CCP—said had happened why on Tiananmen Square in June.

The outside sources the SED cited in other instances to 'explain' what happened during that night in Beijing came to the very same conclusions, but the SED first and foremost referred to official Chinese sources—the same sources, which authorized to open fire on unarmed students on the square—at a time when the public in the GDR protested against the SED and was no longer willing to take government propaganda and lies at face value. The GDR's ill-fated and cynical solidarity with Beijing was interpreted as a warning that people in the GDR would be presented with what was referred to as 'Chinese solution' as a reaction to what happened in Beijing in May and June 1989 in case of similar demonstrations in the GDR. Beijing for its part showed itself incredibly grateful for East Berlin's solidarity and dispatched its Minister for Foreign Affairs Qian Qichen to East Berlin[17] roughly one week after the Tiananmen massacre. Tellingly, the violent events on Tiananmen Square did not even make it onto the agenda of his visit to East Berlin. Instead, East Berlin and Beijing spoke about further expanding relations and confirmed their solidarity against alleged Western attempts and policies to drive a wedge between the communities of socialist countries (Neues Deutschland 1989b). It must have been a surreal encounter between two countries, which were about to be internationally isolated (in the case of China, subject to economic and political sanctions imposed by the West) and as in the case of the GDR on the verge of complete collapse. Honeckers' tenure was to last another 3 months until he was toppled by Egon Krenz in October 1989 at a time when East German citizens left the country en masse to reach the West via Hungary and the former Czechoslovakia.

9 Public Protests

East Germany's public on the other hand reacted very differently to the violent ending of protests in Beijing. Two weeks after the violence on Tiananmen Square the protestant church in Saxony published a protest note protesting against the

[17]He was on his way back from Cuba to Beijing and stopped over in East Berlin.

violence against the peaceful protesters during after the events of June 4, 1989. "With great consternation have we heard and later seen how a non-violent movement was crushed with violence and followed by the persecution of involved people" (Rein 1990, 180). In July 1989 the protestant church published another—and even more outspoken—report protesting against the state's response to attempts to deliver a protest letter to the Chinese Embassy in East Berlin. Those who attempted to deliver that protest note to the embassy were arrested along the way while attempting to deliver the note, shortly detained and again released. Another attempt to deliver that letter two weeks later (that time by roughly 50 protesters) again ended in beatings and arrests. The protestant church, however, did not give up but instead continued to organize events protesting against Beijing's brutal response in June 1989. The protestant church organized services, during which it protested against the violence on Tiananmen Square. One church service in the Samariter Church in East Berlin was attended by 1500 people and churchgoers were joined by civil and human rights activists in East Berlin. That was July 1989 when the SED and the GDR's leadership were irreversibly weakened or indeed on the verge of collapse and the SED's existential crisis made such an outspoken and by GDR standards very courageous letter possible. "The SED's cynical justification of the Chinese armed forces' violent response to China's democracy movement, the morbid solidarity with the Chinese leadership, with which we are presented in the mass media every day, have only increased the anger and mourning of critical young people. Never was the discrepancy between the official SED opinion and the how common citizens viewed reality so immense. The SED's message to the GDR's population is clear: that is the way how we will treat counter-revolutionaries. For those who think that is an exaggeration, I would like to refer to a neo-Stalinist sentence voiced by Minister Margot Honecker during the recently completed Pedagogical Congress. Margot Honecker, wife of the SED's secretary-general urged the country's youth on June 13 to look for 'enemies', 'traitors' and 'counter-revolutionaries.'"

The GDR leadership of course ignored all of the protests and continued to pretend that it was still in control. A few days after the shootings on Tiananmen Square Egon Krenz who as a member of the Politburo was in charge of the GDR's internal security told the German politician Oskar Lafontaine[18] during a symposium in the Western Germany city of Saarbrücken that China's political leadership has merely taken the necessary steps to restore order in Beijing and China. Krenz dismissed the Western German television coverage of the Tiananmen massacred as vicious 'propaganda' of Western German television.

[18]Then member of the Social-Democratic Party (SPD) and today member of the political party Die Linke, the SED's successor party.

10 Egon Krenz—China Apologist

That was the same Egon Krenz, who in September 1989 was dispatched to Beijing to 'congratulate' his Chinese comrades on their successful policy of having crushed 'counter-revolutionary elements' among the peacefully demonstrating students on Tiananmen Square. Krenz's mission in Beijing was to express East Berlin's solidarity with the Chinese leadership and both East Berlin and Beijing agreed on who was to blame for the violence on Tiananmen Square in June 1989: the U.S. and the West in general together with 'reactionary forces' in Taiwan, Hong Kong and Macao, all intent to topple socialism in China, concluded Egon Krenz and Qiao Shi, then member of China's Politburo's Standing Committee (PSC) (SAPMO-BArch, ZPA JIA 2/2A/3247). Qiao maintained that any Western-sponsored attempts to introduce capitalism in China are bound to fail, to which Krenz replied with a platitude about how it is impossible to challenge what he referred to as the 'power of the people' (what he really meant of course was the oppressive power of the ruling SED). Indeed, the entire conversation between Krenz and Qiao had a surreal touch to it: a conversation between two politicians who were in complete denial of the political realities in both the GDR and China engaged in a conversation void of any substance addressing the causes of what happened in Beijing in May and June 1989.

Anything else but expressing blind and cynical solidarity while blaming the West for what happened in June 1989 in Beijing would obviously have been a surprise during that visit, but it is suggested in the literature that both Krenz and his Chinese interlocutors in China really and sincerely believed that how they interpreted the causes and assessed the result of the events on Tiananmen Square was accurate. In retrospect, such a conclusion, however, is not necessarily plausible as it must have been very difficult for politicians like Krenz and Shi, both at the top of their respective political systems, not to have understood what really caused the student protests. Indeed, the demonstrations in Beijing and other parts in China (like in Chengu in the province of Sichuan) were not a result of a Western 'conspiracy' aimed at toppling the Chinese state but instead was a movement in which 100 million people all over China took part in. Instead, Krenz, Qiao and all the other high-level Chinese officials Krenz met in Beijing in 1989 were without a doubt aware of the fact that the Chinese people turned against the authorities and the state to demonstrate against Beijing's refusal and inability to address the numerous social, economic and political problems Deng Xiaoping's fundamental economic and structural reforms had been accompanied by. Krenz's report on his conversation with Qiao Shi in particular reads like—to put it bluntly—like a description of a meeting between two countries on the right side of history discussing international politics as if both China and the GDR at the time were influential countries able to shape events and developments.

When they discussed the internal problems China was at the time confronted with, they seemed to have been in perfect agreement that the 'imperialist' West and its campaign to topple the Chinese state were to blame. Qiao confirmed to Krenz that China would not change policies and positions and that Western economic and political sanctions would not be able to exert pressure onto the country. Krenz's encounter with then newly-appointed CCP Secretary-General Jiang Zemin struck the same tone and what was said during that meeting was so completely out of touch with reality that it can be assumed that Krenz and his Chinese interlocutors did nonetheless realize that their description of events and trends in international politics at the time must have—to say the very least—sounded awkward to anybody outside of East German and Chinese policymaking circles. When Jiang Zemin thanked Krenz for the GDR's solidarity after the events in Beijing in June 1989, Krenz went out of his way to flatter Jiang Zemin saying that East Berlin's support for Beijing's was a 'matter of honour and duty' for fellow socialist countries (SAPMO-BArch, ZPA JIV 2/2A/3247).

Krenz was determined to shower Jiang Zemin with praise for all the alleged Chinese achievements in promoting global socialism for the 'benefit of global societal progress.' Krenz's characterization and praise of a country's leadership which had only a few months earlier shot possibly thousands of its own citizens during (largely) peaceful demonstrations was as repulsive as it gets. That became even more true when Krenz after the fall of the Berlin Wall and the collapse of the GDR (falsely) maintained that it was thanks to him and his orders not to shoot on peacefully demonstrating East German citizens during and after the summer of 1989 that no violence broke out in East Berlin, Leipzig, Dresden and other East German cities at the time. While that turned out to be a lie, his conversations with his Chinese counterparts did indeed suggest that he not only endorsed what Beijing did in June 1989 but also would consider acting in the same way if the people in the GDR demonstrated against the state. The counter-revolutionary forces claimed to want freedom and democracy, while their real objective was to topple the Communist Party and the State (SAPMO-BArch, ZPA JIV 2/2A/3247). Ironically, Egon Krenz had a point although from the students' point of view the connection between freedom and democracy and the Communist Party was distinctively different: the Communist Party and the oppressive state stood in the way of the kind of freedom and democracy the students were demonstrating for.

Krenz's visit to Beijing and the hapless expression of solidarity with the Chinese political leadership was a display of enormous cynicism as it was probably also an expression of complete political helplessness and inability to tell right from (completely) wrong. Krenz said on various occasions during his talks with his Chinese interlocutors that it must not be allowed to 'play with the power of the people' when he elaborated on why China's armed forces were allegedly obliged to end the demonstrations on Tiananmen Square with violence. Such a statement is void of any sense—good or common—and what Krenz really meant was that the people (he spoke of the Chinese people but he obviously also had the East German people in mind), must not be allowed to challenge the monopoly of the Communist Party[19] SAPMO BArch, ZPA JIV 2/2A/3247).

[19]Krenz said that on at least on two occasions during his visit to China. Ironically, the same people Krenz wanted to control and keep from challenging the state monopoly of power marched through the streets of East Berlin and Leipzig on October 7 and October 9, 1989 respectively chanting "We are the people" ("Wir sind das Volk").

Indeed, demonstrators taking part in demonstrations against the regime in East Berlin and Leipzig in October and November 1989 were in constant fear that Egon Krenz (who by then had toppled Erich Honecker at the top of the SED) would opt what was referred to the 'Chinese solution': ending peaceful demonstrations with military means and violence.

Upon his return to East Berlin, Krenz reported to his fellow Politburo members that the esteem China already held for the GDR further increased when East Berlin expressed its unconditional support for Beijing's decision to end the 'counter-revolutionary activities' in Beijing in June 1989. Beijing returned the favour of on paper solidarity with the GDR when in October 1989—at the time East German people took the GDR's looming collapse as an opportunity to leave the country en masse—Beijing offered to send Chinese workers to the GDR to make up for a possible shortage of workers in the GDR. To be sure, that was a very obscure response to the collapse of the GDR, made at a time when GDR was quite clearly heading for certain collapse and when the Soviet Union made it all but very clear that it would not intervene in the demonstrations in the GDR, i.e. would not keep the GDR regime from loosing control.

While the Chinese leadership thanked Krenz for his solidarity during his visit to Beijing in October dissidents in the GDR understood Krenz's visit as something else, the German weekly magazine Der Spiegel reported in October 1989: the visit to Beijing was meant as a warning to the people of the GDR not to do what the students in Beijing have done unless they want to be treated like the students on Tiananmen Square on June 4, 1989 (Der Spiegel 1989b). To be sure, Krenz has always consistently denied to have ever planned to respond to demonstrations with military force. Instead, he later portrayed himself as the one who took the decision not to end demonstrations violently. As it turned out, that was a lie and there is no evidence whatsoever to support Krenz's claims that he was the one who decided not to respond with violence to demonstrations in the GDR.

11 Agreeing on a Scapegoat

An inner-SED report on what happened in May and June 1989 in Beijing and a report about the political situation in general went beyond praising the Chinese leadership for having crushed the demonstrations with violence and sought to analyse—at least in parts and until a certain extent—the causes for the student protests in Beijing (SAPMO-BArch, ZPA IV2/2.035/33). Naturally, according to that report Washington together with other 'foreign conspirators' were responsible for the escalation on Tiananmen Square and hence Beijing had according to that inner-SED report every right to respond with violence to end the students' alleged 'counter-revolution.' Furthermore, the GDR leadership joined their comrades in Beijing, assigning the responsibility to then CCP Secretary-General Zhao Ziyang. Beijing needed a scapegoat and the CCP Secretary-General, who went onto Tiananmen Square during the protests urging the demonstrating students to interrupt their hunger-strike and go home was that scapegoat. Zhao talked to the students and therefore displayed a division and disagreements among Beijing's policymakers on how to deal with the demonstrating students. "Responsible for the uncontrolled and snowballing escalation of anti-socialist forces is the former General-Secretary of the Central Committee of the Communist Party Zhao Ziyang and other party officials, supported by parts of the mass media and other institutions", the report concludes. However, the report also concluded that the violence escalated on Tiananmen Square on June 4 because of the Chinese leadership's misjudgement of the significance of the demonstrations, its reluctance to act earlier and because China's armed forces were ill-prepared for what the leadership was asking them to do on that tragic and violent night in Beijing. Furthermore, the report pointed out that the leadership was divided on how to respond to the protests and concluded (correctly) that during the night of June 4 1989 due to divisions within the army's leadership there was a possibility of armed clashes between different army units. To be sure, such concerns were never, neither in Beijing nor in East Berlin, discussed openly, but the inner-SED report is evidence that the East German authorities were aware of the fact that June 4 1989 on Tiananmen Square could have turned out to be very differently when Beijing's political leadership could not—at least temporarily during the night of June 4, 1989—always and unconditionally count on the armed forces' undivided loyalty.

12 All Under Control, Beijing Says

Against the background of Egon Krenz assuring the Chinese leadership in September 1989 that the GDR was in full control of the state and its people, the GDR's collapse only very months later reportedly took many Chinese policymakers and party officials by complete surprise. However, those in China's policymaking circles who were surprised about the fact that peacefully demonstrating East German people brought down a brutal dictatorship must have chosen to ignore reality at the time when the Chinese Embassy in East Berlin must have reported to Beijing that the regime in East was on the verge of collapse. Chinese policymakers must have chosen to take Erich Honecker's assurances in early October 1989—during the celebrations of the 40th anniversary of the GDR—at face value that the GDR will hang to socialism come what may and not collapse. When thousands of GDR citizens sought refuge in the West German embassies in East Berlin, Budapest and Prague, Beijing chose not to report any of this to the Chinese citizens.

The strategy of the Chinese government to spread completely false information on the situation in the GDR arguably reached its climax when the newspaper The People's Daily on November 11 portrayed the opening of the inner-German border as a sovereign decision taken by East Berlin's political leadership (Renmin Ribao 1989a). The paper must not have understood—or rather was under political pressure from above obliged not to understand—the historical importance of the opening of the inner-German border. Instead of reporting on the historical dimension of what was taking place in the GDR, it instead warned that East German refugees would become competitors to West German citizens on the jobs and housing market. In terms of reporting and journalism this is probably as distorted as it gets and possible problems on West Germany's house and job markets was probably the last thing on the minds of East and West German people when the Berlin Wall fell and the GDR collapsed.

But investigative journalism Chinese-style didn't stop there. Another Chinese newspaper report from the same People's Daily reported on November 5, 1989 that two East German citizens who decided to move to West Germany in September 1989 did not find the conditions they hoped they would and decided to move back to the GDR only a few months later. The People's Daily cited an interview the two German citizens conducted with the GDR newspaper 'Junge Welt' ('Young World'), in which they said that they were not able to find well-paid employment, were confronted with high living costs and were unable to afford decent accommodation. According to that newspaper interview they then concluded that life in West Germany was 'chaotic' and decided to return when it turned out that the GDR authorities allowed them to return 'home' in the GDR (Renmin Ribao 5 November 1989b).

Finally, when the Chinese leadership realized and acknowledged that the GDR was history, a newspaper article in the Guangming Ribao argued—obviously on behalf of the leadership in Beijing—that the end of the GDR does not stand for the end of socialism. Socialism, the newspaper insisted, is still superior to capitalism. Oddly—against the background of the fact that the GDR was at the time about to collapse—the article concluded that an analysis of the history and development of both German states over the decades have revealed "The contradictions within the capitalist system have in West Germany become evident and stronger while the socialist system (in the GDR) has over the course of the years solved problems efficiently." Such a conclusion—together with many other odd assumptions in that article about the alleged superiority of the socialist system when reporting on a socialist country on the verge of complete collapse—is nonsensical and quite simply ridiculous and does not in any way correspond with reality (Guangming Ribao 1989).

13 Conclusions

If Beijing and East Berlin had known what Gorbachev had in mind in terms of fundamental political and economic reforms in the Soviet Union in the second part of the 1980s, Beijing and East Berlin would possibly have found more common ground during their bilateral encounters in the 1980s, i.e. could have expressed joint opposition against the reforms and changes Gorbachev was about to unleash in the Soviet Union. However, it is probably accurate to conclude that neither Honecker nor the Chinese political leadership could have imagined the scope and quality kind of Gorbachev's fundamental reforms at the time. While China's political leaders maintained next to no contact with their political counterparts in the Soviet Union, Honecker's ability to imagine to kind of changes that were about to take place in the Soviet Union was arguably very limited at the time: just like other dictators before and after him, Honecker refused to understand and interpret the reality outside his own sphere of influence and refused to officially acknowledge that the political and more importantly economic foundations of the GDR were collapsing in the mid-1980s. Indeed, already in the early 1980s East Germany was obliged to ask West Germany for two big loans in order to avoid default. In 1983, the GDR was granted one billion deutschmarks by Bonn and the deal was brokered between the (very) controversial[20] East German politician and head of the department 'Kommerzielle Koordinierung' ('Commercial Coordination') in East Germany's Ministry of Trade Alexander Schalck-Golodkowski and the equally controversial Bavarian politician and former West German Minister of Defence Franz-Josef Strauβ.

Honecker and his allies in East Berlin were in the mid-1980s clearly on the wrong side of history, but like many dictators before and after he did not realize or chose to ignore that. Ever since Honecker had Walter Ulbricht replaced in a coup d'état in the GDR 1971, his power was close to absolute in the GDR and it seemed inconceivable to him that what he did to Ulbricht could in 1989 happen to him too.

If East Berlin had not been on 'its way out' heading for collapse in 1989, its cynical support for Beijing's massacre to end (largely) peaceful demonstrations on Tiananmen Square and in many other parts of China with brute military force in June 1989 could maybe have been the basis of a closer relationship between East Berlin and Beijing at a time when the West (and Japan) imposed economic sanctions onto Beijing. However, that was not to be as peacefully marching East German citizens made it very clear through the course of 1989 that they were no longer willing to be locked-up and terrorized by a weak and out-dated dictatorship, which had just 'celebrated' 40 years of disastrous governance, oppression, state terror and violence against its own people.

The last chapter of the GDR's undignified and shameful reaction to the Tiananmen massacre in June 1989 was a late apology published by the DDR's Volkskammer in June 1990 (Volkskammer 1990).

The parliament apologized for the outrageous declaration on the events on Tiananmen Square it made in June 1989 and announced to mourn for the victims who lost their lives on Tiananmen Square in the night of June 4, 1989. That apology came precisely one year too late and many of those parliamentarians who apologized in 1990 were the same parliaments who endorsed the above-mentioned Volkskammer statement of June 1989, in which it congratulated Beijing on its violent response to the demonstrations on Tiananmen Square. Consequently, the credibility and relevance of the Volkskammer's (1990) apology is arguably as low

[20]Controversial as well as under suspicion of having misused ministry funds, which made him flee East Berlin in December 1989. He settled in Bavaria where he died in June 2015.

as the above-mentioned Chinese newspaper claiming that the opening of the inner-German frontier was a sovereign and voluntary decision taken by the GDR authorities at the time.

In sum, far too little and far too late for to be taken seriously as anything resembling a dignified apology.

References

Chen F (1987) Die Beziehungen zwischen der DDR und der VR China. In: Deutschlandarchiv, Heft 9

Krüger J (1994) Zu Gast in Peking. Die DDR und die VR China in der 80er Jahren, Conference Paper 'Deutsch-Chinesische Beziehungen in Geschichte und Gegenwart', Ostasiatische Seminar Free University of Berlin, July

Lim L (2014) The People's Republic of Amnesia-Tiananmen revisited. Oxford University Press, New York

Lüthi L (2008) The Sino-Soviet split. Princeton University Press, Princeton, New Jersey

Meißner W (1995) Die DDR und China 1949–1990: Politik, Wirtschaft, Kultur: Eine Quellensammlung. Akademie Verlag, Berlin

Rein G (1990) Die Protestantische revolution 1987–1990. Wichern-Verlag, Berlin, Ein Deutsches Lesebuch, p 1990

Sandschneider E (1987) Die DDR und die VR China. Bilaterale Beziehungen im Schatten Moskaus. In: Deutschland Archiv (Hrsg): Das Profil der DDR in der sozialistischen Staatengemeinschaft. Zwanzigste Tagung zum Stand der DDR-Forschung in der Bundesrepublik Deutschland, 9–12.Juni, Köln

Schabowski G (1991) Der Absturz. Rowohlt Verlag, Berlin

Scholtyseck J (2003) Die Aussenpolitik der DDR. Enzyklopädie Deutscher Geschichte Band 69, R. Oldenbourg Verlag, München

Newspaper Sources and Other Sources

Außenpolitische Kommission des Politbüros des ZK der SED 15.6. 1989

Der Spiegel (1986) Blick nach Oben, 27 Oktober, http://www.spiegel.de/spiegel/print/d-13521735.html

Der Spiegel (1989a) Am Leben Bleiben, 12 Juni, pp 27/28, http://www.spiegel.de/spiegel/print/d-13493717.html

Der Spiegel (1989b) Erich Krenz—Ein Reformer?, 23 Oktober, pp 16–23, http://www.spiegel.de/spiegel/print/d-13498709.html

Guangming Ribao (1989) Liangee Deguo de bijiao neng shuoming shehuizhuyi shibaima?, 6 November

Neues Deutschland (1989a) Aus dem Bericht des Politbüros an die 8. Tagung des Zentralkomitees der SED, June 23

Neues Deutschland (1989b) Oskar Fischer Empfing Qian Qichen/Hoher Stand der Brüderlichen Beziehungen, 13 June

Protokoll der Verhandlungen des X. Parteitages der Sozialistischen Einheitspartei Deutschland im Palast der Republik 11 bis 16 April 1981, Band 1, 1–3. Beratungstag, Dietz Verlag, Berlin 1981

Renmin Ribao (People's Daily) (1989a) Minzhu Deguo xuanbu kaifang bianjie, 11 November

Renmin Ribao (People's Daily) (1989b) Minde liang gongmin tan zai Xide de zaoyou/meiyou ziji zhusuo/meiyiu guding gongzuo/shenghuo meiyou baozhang, 5 November
Tagung der Volkskammer der DDR am 7 Juni 1990, Volkskammer der DDR

Archive Sources[21]

Bericht für das Politbüro über die Lage in der VR China. SAPMO-BArch, ZPA IV2/2.035/33
Bericht über den Zwischenaufenthalt einer Delegation der Abteilung Internationale Verbindungen des ZK der SED an der Botschaft der DDR in der VR China. SAPMO-BArch, ZPA JIV 2/20/139
Bericht über den Aufenthalt der Partei-und Staatsdelegation der DDR unter Leitung des Mitglieds des Politbüros und Sekretärs des ZK der SED, Genossen Egon Krenz, Stellvertreter des Vorsitzenden des Staatsrats der DDR, vom 25. September bis 2. Oktober 1989 in der VR China. SAPMO-BArch, ZPA JIA 2/2A/3247
Information-Vertraulich. SAPMO-BArch, ZPA IV 2/2.035/64
Information über die Beratungen mit dem Stellvertreter des Ministerpräsidenten des Staatsrates der Volksrepublik China, Genossen Li Peng 25.5. 1985. SAPMO-BArch, ZPA JIV 2/2A/2758
Niederschrift über das Gespräch des Genossen Erich Honecker, Generalsekretär des ZK der SED, mit Genossen Hu Yaobang, Generalsekretär des ZK der KP Chinas, am 22.10.1986. SAPMO-BArch, ZPA JIV 2/2/2191
Niederschrift über das Gespräch des Generalsekretärs des ZK der KP Chinas, Genossen Hu Yaobang, mit Genossen Gerhard Schürer am 10.7.1985 im Sitz der Partei-und Staatsführung der VR China, Zhongnanhai. SAPMO-BArch, ZPA JIV 2/20/22
Tagung der Volkskammer der DDR am 8. Juni 1989. SAPMO-Arch, ZPA JIV 2/2/2231
Schreiben des ZK der SED an das ZK der KPdSU 27.7. 1982. SAPMO-BArch, ZPA JIV 2/2/1960
Schlussfolgerungen des Sekretariats des ZK der SED 6. Juni 1984. SAPMO-BArch, ZPA JIV 2/3/3671
Vermerk über ein Gespräch des Generalsekretärs des ZK der SED und Vorsitzenden des Staatsrats der DDR, Genossen Erich Honecker, mit dem stellvertrenden Vorsitzenden des Ministerrats der Volksrepublik China, Genossen Li Peng, am 20.5.1985. SAPMO-BArch, ZPA IIV 2/20/22
Vermerk über das Gespräch des Mitglieds des Politbüros und Sekretärs des ZK der SED, Genossen Egon Krenz, Stellvertreter des Vorsitzenden des Staatsrats der DDR, mit Genossen Qiao Shi, Mitglied des Ständigen Ausschusses des Politbüros und des Sekretariats des ZK der KP Chinas, Sekretär des Disziplinkontrollkommission beim ZK der KP Chinas, am 25. September 1989 im Gebäude des Nationalen Volkskongresses. SAPMO-BArch, ZPA JIV 2/2A/3247
Vermerk über das Gespräch des Mitglieds des Politbüros und Sekretärs des ZK der SED, Genossen Egon Krenz, Stellvertreter des Vorsitzenden des Staatsrats der DDR, mit Genossen Wan Li, Mitglied des Politbüros des ZK der KP China, Vorsitzender des Ständigen Ausschusses des Nationalen Volkskongresses der Volksrepublik China, am 26. September 1989 im Gebäude des Nationalen Volkskongresses. SAPMO BArch, ZPA JIV 2/2A/3247
Vermerk über das Gespräch des Generalsekretärs des ZK der KP China, Genossen Jiang Zemin, mit Genossen Egon Krenz am 26. September 1989 in Peking. SAPMO-BArch, ZPA JIV 2/2A/3247

[21]Sources from this archive: 'Stiftung Archiv der Parteien und Massenorganisation der DDR im Bundesarchiv', cited in this chapter as 'SAPMO-BArch, ZPA'; for an explanation see also the introduction of this chapter.

China's Foreign Policy and Ideational Narratives: Key Trends and Major Challenges

Silvia Menegazzi

Abstract When Xi Jinping was designated as the head of the People's Republic of China (PRC) in 2012, many analysts and observers argued that China's foreign policy entered a new phase. In less than one term in power, as the 'core leader' of the second world largest economy Xi Jinping has managed to reshape China's image and behaviour at home and abroad. He has reinterpreted the relation with the superpower United States through what he called a 'New Model of Major-Country Relations'. He promoted the so-called 'China Dream', a concept calling for the 'rejuvenation' of the Chinese nation. Xi Jinping, through the complex bureaucratic machine of China's state apparatus, was able to unify political elites and party officials, together with some major public intellectuals and academics to marry and support the project expected to return China to the kind glory and grandeur the country enjoyed since the Roman Empire: the 'New Silk Road', better known as the 'One Belt One Road' (OBOR) initiative. However, even though support of Chinese ideational narratives has grown vis-à-vis the more significant role China plays at the international level, serious gaps persist as regards to how the People's Republic of China (PRC) practically conducts its foreign policy in terms of international rules and standards already set by other countries. In fact, with regards to specific issues and areas such as climate change, nuclear deterrence or cyber-security, leaders in Beijing are still struggling to reach a comprehensive understanding in line with the ideas and policies supported by the majority of countries in the West. As a consequence, this chapter concludes that only combing Chinese ideational narratives of world order with a practical understanding of how such policies are discussed at the international level, will allow China to play a growing role in the realm of global governance.

S. Menegazzi (✉)
Department of Political Science, LUISS Guido Carli University, Rome, Italy
e-mail: smenegazzi@luiss.it

S. Beretta et al. (eds.), *Understanding China Today*, Understanding China,
DOI 10.1007/978-3-319-29625-8_10

1 Introduction

Since Xi Jinping took office in October 2012, the world witnessed some gradual but essential changes of Chinese foreign policy. China's involvement in today's international politics is today much more evident than it was during Jiang Zemin or Hu Jintao's mandates. Furthermore, the role of expertise in the complex decision-making process has changed, with many think tanks, non-governmental organizations, academics and public intellectuals involved in and taking part in Chinese political decision-making processes. At the same time, showing some continuity with the past, Chinese foreign policy maintains certain characteristics—characteristics necessary to understand and analyze policies in an in-depth fashion by applying familiar categories and patterns used to analyze Chinese foreign policies. To be sure, in the case of Chinese politics the role and influence of individual leaders remain central—'key figures' of policymaking. Xi Jinping e.g. is expected to have the last word on everything related to China's political affairs and at present, he functions as the world's most 'multi-tasking' leader. Indeed, Xi is the head of the ruling Communist Party of China (CCP) (as the CCP's secretary-general), the head of state (as president of the PRC) and the chairman of China's Central Military Commission (CMC). Chinese foreign policy today therefore allows for two conclusions. With regards to China's participation and involvement in global governance and international politics, China not only operates today in a more responsible and integrated manner as it did in the past, but it is now able to push forward a new concept of world order based on its own initiatives, e.g. the Asian Infrastructure Investment Bank (AIIB), the 'One Belt One Road' initiative, and its own ideas, e.g. the above-mentioned 'China Dream' and 'New Type of Great Power Relations.' At the same time, tighter centralization, ideological supervision and domestic anti-corruption campaigns have had an impact on the perception of China's foreign policy and some of its core policy areas. Indeed, the fact that Xi Jinping was designated as the 'core leader' of the Chinese Communist Party (CCP) in November 2016 made it very clear that the position Xi holds in China is that of a strong leader, able to obtain both in China and abroad the recognition and respect China claims for itself. To be sure, such policies have made sure that China's image has over the last four years become that of an increasingly authoritarian country.

This chapter explores some practical and theoretical issues of China's foreign policy by examining several ideas and policy areas toward which the Xi Jinping's administration paid increasing attention since 2012. Section 2 examines China's growing engagement toward those which are considered today by leaders in Beijing key strategic ideational paradigms about China's foreign policy: a 'New Type of Major Power Relations', the 'China Dream' and the 'One Belt One Road Initiative' (OBOR). Section 3 addresses the current state of the debate of some key policy areas in which China is manifesting growing concerns to deal with at the international level, e.g. nuclear deterrence, cyber security and climate change. The chapter concludes in Sect. 3 by exploring the stakes of China's foreign policy at the international level and China's strategies to pursue its major interests, strategies and ideas.

2 China's Foreign Policy: Some of the Main Ideas and Concepts

2.1 Managing China-US Relations: A New Model of Major-Country Relations

In the international politics debates, one should not underestimate the role played by ideas. Models of ideas and ideologies help political actors reinforce political discourses and references at the international level and enable them to promote and justify their policy actions and policies (Marchetti and Fabbrini 2016). According to William H. Callahan, ideas in Chinese foreign policy are as essential as material interests. Indeed, although some key ideas conceptualized within Chinese official slogans are commonly addressed as propaganda (*tifa*) they are indeed crucial in order to understand how Chinese policies are developed and implemented (Callahan 2016). Xi Jinping first announced the concept of 'a New Type of Great Gower Relations' in May 2012 during the fourth China-US Strategic and Economic Dialogue.

> First, we should treat each other's strategic intentions objectively and rationally, persist in being partners and not opponents, and properly handle contradictions and differences through dialogue and cooperation rather than confrontation. Second, we should respect each other's social system and development path, each other's core interests and major concerns, seeking common ground while reserving differences, embracing each other's experiences, and making common progress. Third, we should abandon the zero-sum thinking, in the pursuit of our own interests while taking into account the interests of each other in seeking our own development to promote common development, deepening the pattern of blending interests (Beijing News 2013).

Although some scholars believe the concept should be applied to China's overall foreign policy, to many others it addresses exclusively China's relations with the United States (Qi 2015). To some extent, the idea also became the example of the narrative of two major developments regarding China's international identity. The first one is China distancing itself from the *tao guang yang hui* policy, i.e. the policy of keeping a low profile at the international level. The second is China's choice and strategy to contest international norms and the U.S.-led world order (Zeng and Breslin 2016). Both developments highlight China's willingness to play a more proactive role in international affairs in pursuit of its interests.

The recent triumph (or shock) of Donald Trump's victory in the U.S. presidential elections led to concerns of how U.S. policies towards Asia in general and China in particular could change. Trump e.g. announced on the campaign trail to impose tariffs amounting to 45% on Chinese goods and products. According to Chinese official newspapers however, the reality of Sino-U.S. relations will be far less dramatic than this and very few commentators in China believe Trump's election victory will have a significant impact on China's role at the international level. Indeed, 'The leadership of the U.S. is irreplaceable, meanwhile, China's further rise is inevitable', the Global Times argued (Global Times 2016). In Beijing there is a growing tendency to believe that the time has come for China to be confident enough in world affairs to be able to change the global structure of power changes that should increase China's influence on international affairs. The compilation of Xi Jinping's political theories, 'The Governance of China' published in 2015 mentioned a 'New Model of Major-Country Relations', a concept defining relations with the U.S., Russia and Europe (Swaine 2013). Although China supports a G2 scenario in the future, it still pursues the idea of a multipolar rather than a bipolar world order.

2.2 *The China Dream*

In 2014, while delivering its official speech at the UNESCO headquarters in Paris, Xi Jinping affirmed:

> The Chinese Dream is about prosperity of the country, rejuvenation of the nation, and happiness of the people. It reflects both the ideal of the Chinese people today and our time-honored tradition to seek constant progress … The Chinese Dream will be realized through balanced development and mutual reinforcement of material and cultural progress … without the continuation and development of civilization, or the promotion of prosperity and culture, the Chinese dream will not come true (Ministry of Foreign Affairs 2014).

The concept of the 'China Dream' (中国梦 *Zhongguo meng*) seems, at glance, mostly oriented toward China's domestic political audience. It serves as a narrative aimed at stressing both the party and the regime's legitimacy while opposing Western values such as individualism and democracy (Ferdinand 2016). In fact, the idea of the 'China Dream' has met with criticism in the West, especially among journalists but also scholars and policy analysts. The concept, the Economist e.g. argues, has further encouraged Chinese nationalism, exacerbated historical victimhood among the population, and assigned additional power to the Communist Party under Xi's rule (The Economist 2013). At the same time, the 'Chinese Dream' exemplifies important directives of Chinese foreign policy. First and foremost, as the concept of the above-mentioned 'New Type of Major Power Relations' demonstrates, the 'China Dream' is an indication that Deng Xiaoping's *tao guang yang hui* approach to international politics has been replaced with very assertive regional policies, which cause anxiety in China's neighborhood (Berkofsky 2016). Secondly, it is a narrative employed by Chinese leaders in order to ensure China's peaceful development strategy abroad (Sorensen 2015). Finally, the idea of the 'China Dream' is part of a narrative constructed by the Xi Jinping administration in order to build China's image at the international level as a 'normative power' whose foreign policy initiatives and interests are driven by the intent to build a Sino-centric world order and Chinese rules for global governance (Callahan 2016). At a time when Chinese assertiveness in world politics is under scrutiny, to many the 'China Dream' is designed to sustain China's international strategy. The 'rejuvenation of the Chinese nation' as part of the 'China Dream', it is argued, is just another slogan employed by leaders in Beijing to reinforce and promote nationalism, and legitimize China's one-party system. Yet, other scholars argue that China's foreign policy under Xi Jinping stands for continuity with the past and the perception of China's new assertiveness is problematic on two grounds. Firstly, there is no clear definition of what is meant with the concept of Chinese new foreign policy 'assertiveness.' Secondly, there is no clear evidence that Chinese foreign policy under Xi Jinping is more assertive or indeed more aggressive than China's foreign under the country's previous leaders. (Johnston 2013).

2.3 *The 'One Belt One Road'*

The 'One Belt One Road' (OBOR) initiative is one of the major ideational narratives discussed by leaders in Beijing since it first announced in 2013. As for the 'China Dream' and the 'New Type of Major Power Relations' discussed in previous paragraphs, the 'OBOR' initiative too has been at the core of diplomatic activities carried out Beijing's leaders over the last three years. Yet to those in power the 'OBOR' is not just an 'idea' put forward by Xi and its administration- it is a real project. When first announced by Xi Jinping in 2013 during his trip to Kazakhstan, the 'OBOR' was discussed within an official framework with the intent to improve economic cooperation among China and Central Asian countries on various levels: policy communication, road connectivity, trade facilitation, monetary circulation and people-to-people exchanges (Ministry of Foreign Affairs 2013). Initially at least the narrative of this project was meant as a follow-up and 'spill-over effect' of already existing security and military cooperation between China, Russia and Central Asian countries taking place in the framework of the Shanghai Cooperation Organization (SCO). However, today the 'OBOR' project has been transformed into an all-encompassing initiative spanning from Southeast Asia to Africa and Northern Europe. Not surprisingly, the new initiative has over the last three years been the subject of numerous official meetings between Chinese leaders and their counterparts in the world as well as among scholars, experts and China watchers in general. The CNKI (China National Knowledge Infrastructure) database for academic articles is listing hundreds of articles when searching for the words *yidai yi lu* (i.e. the Chinese translation for the One Belt one Road). Xinhua, the official news agency of the Chinese Communist Party, has launched a special section on its website entirely dedicated to the initiative.[1] The People's Daily Online too has a section on the 'OBOR' although it is not as detailed as the one offered by Xinhua. The European Union (EU) too has shown great interest in the 'OBOR' and for Beijing it is also meant as an initiative to further intensify EU-China relations. However, there are concerns in Europe that the 'OBOR' could increase the gap

[1]See for instance: http://www.xinhuanet.com/silkroad/english/index.htm.

between how China deals with the EU on the one hand and the EU member states on the other.

While the 'OBOR' is meant to improve China's political and economic relations with countries along the Silk Road, the initiative is a central part of China's global geopolitical and economic strategy. Indeed, there is a consensus that Chinese leaders will in the years ahead continue to make the 'OBOR' a central element of the country's domestic and foreign policy agenda (Zhao 2016). Projects related to the 'OBOR' will among others funded by the 'Silk Road Fund.'[2] Bilateral memoranda of understanding (MoU) have been signed, such as the one China signed with Hungary. In October 2016, China and Belgium "The Belt and Road China and Belgium Cooperation Forum" was held in Brussels. It remains yet to be seen whether China will prioritize a bilateral or multilateral (through the EU institutions) approach when cooperating with Europe in the 'OBOR' framework.

3 China's Foreign Policy: Some Key Policy Areas

3.1 Nuclear Policy

Nuclear policy rests a key policy area on the Chinese foreign policy agenda. The regional dimension of its nuclear policy, however, takes priority over the global dimension. When on July 14, 2015, the P5+1 (China, France, Germany, Russia, the United Kingdom, and the United States), the European Union (EU), and Iran adopted the Joint Comprehensive Plan of Action (JCPOA) China was criticized for not supporting the agreement the same way the involved Western countries do. China's behavior has been defined as 'multilateralism with Chinese characteristics'. Such definition does not simply denote a different approach led by China's ideational narrative over Iran's nuclear policy, but is rather meant to express frustration with China's lack of efforts to combat global nuclear proliferation (The Diplomat 2016). China is subject to the same criticism as regards the North Korean nuclear development program. Beijing has been accused of maintaining an ambiguous stance that is not in line with the position sustained by the international community. Too many observers that is the case because China—as it is the case for the Iran's nuclear issue—chooses to combine diplomatic international efforts with economic interests. Although Chinese leaders are concerned about maintaining security and stability in North East Asia, China's economic interests in North Korea are significant and have an impact on China's overall policies towards Pyongyang. Consequently, as stated in a recent editorial in the *Global Times*, the international community should not expect China to adopt tougher sanctions against Pyongyang

[2]The Silk Road Fund is an investment fund with a total amount of US$40 billion financed respectively by Export-Import Bank of China (15%), China Development Bank (5%), China Investment Corporation (15%), and State Administration of Foreign Exchange (65%).

in the near future. China has already suspended the transport to North Korea of auxiliary materials necessary for the production of nuclear weapons, but is unlikely to ban overland transportation (marine trade) to North Korea (as indeed the UN Resolution R2270 requires). Moreover, from a Chinese perspective, the Korean unification process remains a domestic issue between the two Koreas. Both North and South Korea should, therefore, follow the objective of 'matching methods and goals' (目表与手段匹配 *mubiao yu shouduan pipei*), which would entail reaching a high level of cooperation vis-à-vis the goal of integration (Wang 2016). According to that approach, North and South Korea should first and foremost establish long-term objectives on the nature of unification. Secondly, methods to deal with the unification process should be based on the principle of flexibility, should lead to a common strategy regarding the terms of political, military and economic objectives (which in turn guarantees that the interests of both parties are safeguarded). Thirdly, North and South Korea will have to be willing to adopt pragmatic policies while sharing the same strategic interests in Northeast Asia (Wang 2016).

3.2 Cyber Security

Often treated as a policy area of secondary importance in Chinese foreign policy, cyber security has become an increasingly hot topic in Beijing since Xi Jinping took office in 2012. On November 7, 2016, China passed its first law dealing with cyber security, which is expected to come into effect in July 2017. In the West the law was immediately demonized as a further attempt by Xi Jinping's administration to further restrict individual rights and tighten virtual control over China's Internet users. Similar to when a new law on foreign Non-Governmental Organizations (NGOs) was adopted in 2016, civil rights activists feared that China's new cyber security law will allow the Chinese Communist Party to further improve its already very sophisticated censorship system. In the West, the new law has been therefore perceived as another sign of Chinese leaders' will to restrict individual rights, as well as domestic and foreign organizations and firms. In China though, reactions were based on a different explanation, that is, concentrated on cyber security threats and the right China has to react responsibly in the ways countries are requested to when facing new challenges. As such, for Chinese authorities and the media, cyber security is intended to guarantee 'technological safety and political stability'. More specifically, "The Chinese side emphasizes information content and safety, and they state that cyberspace should not develop into a realm of political struggle" (Dong 2014). The basic definition Chinese leaders offer is the following: "Cyber security means technological safety and political stability". In other words, "the Chinese side emphasizes information content and safety, and they state that cyberspace should not develop into a realm for political struggle" (Dong 2014).

3.3 Environment and Climate Change

When China ratified the Paris climate change agreement ahead of the G20 in September 2016, Beijing sought to create an image of itself as responsible power committed to fighting climate change and environmental pollution. Through the COP21 negotiations leaders in Beijing manifested an attempt to behave like other major powers, which translates into being 'responsibly worried' about the fact that 'low politics issues' (such as climate change) could develop into major threats to the international community. Thus, one year earlier, during the Paris Conference held in November 2015, China's Foreign Minister Wang Yi declared: "Paris is not Copenhagen, and China has now a new, more proactive role to play in international affairs" (Qi and Tong 2015). Wang Yi words and more generally, China's attitude towards climate change is another example of how China plans to show its growing commitment towards alternative development to tackle global environmental degradation. Estimates warn that China—the world's biggest consumer and producer of coal—will have to modernize its coal plants and cut emissions by 60% and significantly cut its fossil fuels emissions by 2020 (COP21 2016). However, China will continue to remain among the countries supporting the principle of 'Common But Differentiated Responsibilities' (CBDR). At the same time, despite China's potential in tackling climate change, the lack of compliance with environmental standards by Chinese private companies and state-owned enterprises investing abroad (especially in developing countries) remains a major concern of the international community. It is therefore not a coincidence that the major projects recently launched by China through e.g. the Asian Infrastructure and Investment Bank (AIIB) are subject to concerns about whether and to what extent in the countries China is investing and constructing it will respect and comply with environmental standards (Qin 2016). Although there are growing expectations as regards China's preparedness to act responsibly at the international level, doubts and concerns remains as to what extent China will be able to maintain its promises.

4 Conclusions

The most recent G20 Summit was held in the city of Hangzhou, in the province of Zhejiang on 4–5 September, 2016. Xi Jinping, during the opening ceremony announced five proposals in order to meet the current challenges of the global economy: (1) strengthen macroeconomic policy coordination, (2) generate a new growth momentum, (3) improve global economic governance, (4) promote the facilitation of free trade and investment and (5) implement the 2030 Agenda for Sustainable Development promoting inclusive development. On 3 September 2016 during the B20 Summit—a parallel multilateral forum devoted to the business community dealing with global economic governance—President Xi affirmed China's commitment to continue to be an important contributor to global economic governance in the 21st century:

> We will continue to be fully involved in economic globalization and support the multilateral trading regime. We will expand access for foreign investment, facilitate such investment to promote fair and open competition and create a sound business environment. We will also accelerate negotiation on FTAs and investment treaties with relevant countries and the development of high-standard pilot free trade zones in China. While carrying out market-based reform of the RMB exchange rate in an orderly manner and phasing in the opening of domestic capital market, we will continue efforts to make the RMB an international currency and further internationalize China's financial sector (G 20 China 2016).

Whereas China in the past above all accepted and pursued those global economic rules favourable to its own economy, it has now also acknowledged the necessity to share the burden of global governance responsibilities shared by G7 members and the Bretton Woods institutions. While the above-mentioned AIIB has in the past been criticized as a Chinese-led initiative exclusively serving Chinese interests, its first projects were in fact launched in cooperation with Western-led institutions such as the World Bank and the European Bank for Reconstruction and Development. As long as leaders in Beijing continue to commit themselves to further collaborate with the international community, China is expected to play a crucial role in climate change, cyber security, nuclear security and global economic governance (Li and Zhang 2016). As elaborated above, China, however, is not only intentioned to contribute to the shaping of global governance. China's 'core leader' Xi Jinping and the country's political elites have also started to debate on the type of global world order China possibly foresees and is planning shape in the years ahead. Indeed, time has come for China to manifest a clear commitment to global governance in line the one expected from a responsible power. Understandably from a Chinese perspective, China above all sought to advance its own ideas and concepts of an international order—ideas and concepts, which often sounded like propaganda to Western ears. The ideational narratives of China's foreign policy previously discussed are a fundamental part of how China today approaches and interacts with other countries in world affairs. Examples of such interaction are China's infrastructure development projects in Central Asia through the above-mentioned 'OBOR'. There there is a broad consensus among scholars and analysts that the way leaders in Beijing approach certain policies and practices at the international level such as cyber security or nuclear policy, are above all to be understood as inner-Chinese discourses, which are rarely properly understood or endorsed by the international community. This will have consequences and China, its policies and its approaches to global governance will in Western countries continue not to receive the kind of positive assessments and feedback it receives in non-Western countries in general and African countries in particular. While this chapter underlined the importance of taking into account Chinese ideas as a mean to understand the motivations and basis for Chinese foreign policies, the chapter also pointed out some specific policy areas where Chinese ideas and ideal models pose limits to China's role in and influence on global governance. It remains yet to be whether and when China will take the opportunity to become what is referred as 'rule-shaping' actor.

References

Almond RG (2016) China and the Iran NUCLEAR Deal. The Diplomat March, August. http://thediplomat.com/2016/03/china-and-the-iran-nuclear-deal/

Beijing News (2013) 习近平概括中美新型大国关系: 不冲突、不对抗,相互尊重,合作共赢 (Xi Jinping summed up the new Sino-US relations: no conflict, no confrontation, mutual respect, win-win cooperation), 10 June. http://news.xinhuanet.com/politics/2013-06/10/c_116107914.htm

Berkofsky A (2016) "The Chinese Dream" and Chinese foreign and security policies—Rosy rhetoric versus harsh realities. Asia-Pac Rev 23(2):109–128

Callahan WH (2016) China's "Asia Dream": the belt and road initiative and the new regional order. Asian J Comp. Polit 1–18

Chinese Ministry of Foreign Affairs (2013) President Xi Jinping delivers important speech and propose to build a Silk Road Economic Belt wit Central Asian Countries. 7 Sept http://www.fmprc.gov.cn/mfa_eng/topics_665678/xjpfwzysiesgjtfhshzzfh_665686/t1076334.shtml

Chinese Ministry of Foreign Affairs (2014) Speech by H.E. Xi Jinping President at the People's Republic of China at UNESCO Headquarters. 28 Mar. http://www.fmprc.gov.cn/mfa_eng/wjdt_665385/zyjh_665391/t1142560.shtml

COP21 (2016) China has promised to cut its emission from its coal power plants by 60% by 2020. http://www.cop21.gouv.fr/en/china-has-promised-to-cut-emissions-from-its-coal-power-plants-by-60-by-2020/

Dong Q (2014) Confidence building for cyber security between China and the United States. China Institute of International Studies (CIIS), 23 Sept. http://www.ciis.org.cn/english/2014-09/23/content_7254470.htm

Ferdinand P (2016) Westward ho—the China Dream and 'one belt one road': Chinese foreign policy under Xi Jinping. Int Affairs 92(4):941–957

G20 China (2016) Keynote speech by H.E. Xi Jinping, president of the People's Republic of China at the opening ceremony of the B20 summit. http://www.g20chn.org/English/Dynamic/201609/t20160909_3414.html

Global Times (2016) What would Trump bring on China?, 21 Nov. http://www.globaltimes.cn/content/981390.shtml

Johnston AI (2013) How new and assertive is China's new assertiveness? Int Secur 37(4):7–48

Li C, Zhang N (2016) China plays increasing role in global governance. Brookings Institution, 1 Apr. https://www.brookings.edu/on-the-record/china-plays-increasing-role-in-global-governance/

Marchetti R, Fabbrini S (2016) Still a Western world? Continuity and change in world politics. New Routdlege, New York

Qi H (2015) China debates the 'New Type of Great Power Relations'. Chinese J Int Polit 8 (4):349–370

Qin L (2016) Pressures mont on AIIB for greater clarity on green landing. China Dialogue, 27 Jan. https://www.chinadialogue.net/article/show/single/en/8554-Pressure-mounts-on-AIIB-for-greater-clarity-on-green-lending

Qi Y, Tong W (2015) China's "yes" to new role in climate battle December 4. Brookings Institution. https://www.brookings.edu/articles/chinas-yes-to-new-role-in-climate-battle/

Sorensen CTN (2015) The significance of Xi Jinping's "Chinese Dream" for Chinese Foreign Policy: from "Tao Guang Yang Hui" to "Fen Fa You Wei". J China Int Relat. file:///Users/a/Downloads/1146-3704-1-PB%20(1).pdf

Swaine M (2013) Xi Jinping on Chinese foreign relations: The Governance of China and Chinese commentary. China Leadership Monitor. http://www.hoover.org/sites/default/files/research/docs/clm48ms.pdf

The Economist (2013) Xi Jinping and the Chinese dream, 4 May. http://www.economist.com/news/leaders/21577070-vision-chinas-new-president-should-serve-his-people-not-nationalist-state-xi-jinping

Wang X (2016) 朝鲜半岛统一的症结, 变与不变 (The crux, changes and unchanges of the Korean peninsula's reunification), 东疆学刊 (Dongjiang J) 33(3):47–53

Zeng J, Breslin S (2016) China's new type of great power relations: a G2 with Chinese characteristics? Int Affairs 92(4):773–794

Zhao Y (2016) China not expected to ban land transport to North Korea: analysts. The Global Times, 22 Sept. http://www.globaltimes.cn/content/1007607.shtml

Part II
China in the International Economy

National Egoism or Cooperation in Providing Global Public Goods? China's Foreign Economic Strategy Under Review

Giuseppe Iannini and Silvio Beretta

Abstract The remarkable success of the Chinese economy is not unprecedented and was preceded by other Asian economies' development according to what is referred to as the so-called 'Asian development model.' In particular, the Japanese economy shows a development path that, apart from some significant dissimilarity, proves to be forerunner of the Chinese one. This is relevant when we analyse the ambiguous behaviour of Chinese policymakers in providing and safeguarding the economic global public goods in cooperation with other countries (The concept of global public goods [GPG] has become an integral part on the agendas of bodies and institutions like the United Nations, The International Monetary Fund [IMF], the World Bank and non-governmental organizations. Education and knowledge, a clean environment, health services, intellectual property rights, peace and security are among others defined as global public goods.). Like for Japan in the past, China's mercantilist practices today are a central cause for its problematic trade and investment relations with its major economic and trading partners (the United States and the European Union). China's political elites and policymakers do not seem to be sufficiently convinced that the provision of 'global public goods' is eventually beneficial for China's economic development. Moreover, the debate on Chinese contributions to 'global public goods' takes place at the time when the country is seeking to develop and present a viable alternative to existing (Western) geopolitical and geo-economic models. Consequently, the level and frequency of China providing 'global public goods' will also depend on the country's ability to adopt economic and structural reforms (as the instrumental basis for the provision of such goods) in the years ahead. To be sure, cooperation between Washington and Beijing could become even more difficult under the US administration led by Donald Trump.

G. Iannini · S. Beretta (✉)
Department of Political and Social Sciences, University of Pavia, Pavia, Italy
e-mail: silvio.beretta@unipv.it

G. Iannini
e-mail: giuseppe.iannini@unipv.it

S. Beretta et al. (eds.), *Understanding China Today*, Understanding China,
DOI 10.1007/978-3-319-29625-8_11

1 Introduction

China's self-perception and the perception of its global role is fundamentally different from how the rest of the world perceives and interprets China. It is worth recalling how, some years ago, a Chinese author concludes an essay on Chinese economic system. That essay describes the main aspects of the Chinese society: the political system, culture, history, the legal system, science, the country's international relations etc. (Wu et al. 2010, 159–160). The author concludes that: "... China has become an engine of the world economic growth. China's economy will never collapse, as its modernization mission has not been accomplished. China has a lot of work to do and is progressing on the road to a prosperous, democratic and harmonious country. It is China's goal to 'promote friendship and partnership with the neighbouring countries and coexist in harmony with all the nations in the world'. China poses no threat to anyone. On the contrary, it will become an important and indispensable force to maintain peace, development and stability in the world". This text expresses some very clear views: China should be guiding a universalistic 'millenarism',[1] and promote global 'harmony', which should characterize the system of international relations. However there is no—neither inside nor outside of China—consensus on the issue of China's international positioning and its strategic goals. Evidence thereof is the recurring debate on the 'mercantilist' tendencies of China's global economic policies and on the country's willingness to cooperate with the international community.

One driving force behind China's economic performance, starting from the 'four modernizations' policy launched by Deng Xiaoping in the late 1970s, lies undoubtedly in the internationalization of its economy. Since its admission to the WTO in 2001, China has become the world's second biggest economy (having overtaken Japan in 2009). The impressive figures of Chinese economic growth and its position as the world's biggest exporter are revealing to what extent the world's geo-economic framework has been profoundly changed by China's economic growth and development over the last three decades. Throughout the period from 2001 to 2015 China's GDP (in terms of PPP) grew 4.8 times (from 8 to 17.5% of world GDP) and GDP per capita more than quadrupled.[2] Furthermore, at the end of

[1]In Wu Li (156–158) it is further stated: "... Through its own transformation China is changing the world and gaining the attention of the world community ... While China's economy cannot develop in isolation from the rest of the world, neither can the world economy develop without China" and then: "... its achievements in improving the people's living standards have attracted worldwide attention". This optimistic view of China's position in the world is also mentioned by Henry Kissinger in the conclusions of his book *On China* (Kissinger 2011).

[2]China's share of global GDP has increased over the last 15 years, and is on the path of reaching the share of global GDP it had in the past. According to Maddison, in fact, in 1500 the Chinese share represented even 25% of total world production, climbing to 29.2% in 1600, dropping to 22.3% in 1700 and climbing up again to 32.9% in 1820. The following decades have witnessed a continuing and relevant decrease: down to 17.2% in 1870, 8.9% in 1913, 4.5% in 1950, 4.6% in 1973, and a trend reversal in 1998. At the same time the Western Europe's share of global GDP

2014 China ranked first in the world among exporting countries (13.2% of total world exports) ahead of the United States (8.4%) and the European Union (7.9%) (wits.worldbank 2016). Moreover, the development model on which the Chinese economic success is grounded, challenges some fundamental certainties of economic theory and has over the last two decades stimulated analysts and economists to look into the mix of its contrasting characteristics: statism versus market, state versus private ownership and protectionism versus trade openness (Global Studies Association 2006).

In fact, the essence of the Chinese model can be found in a multi-faceted set of elements: more or less orthodox versions of mercantilism (e.g. neo-mercantilism[3]), command accumulation and financial repression. In other words a model that, although artificially attributed to the 'socialist market economies', de facto aims at achieving above all domestic economic development as well as the above-mentioned 'four modernizations' (Beretta and Iannini 2014). At the same time the Chinese economic development model seeks to avoid, or at least to minimize, the disequilibria that could compromise or delay such goals. This strategy is not unprecedented since it replicates the one adopted, albeit differently, by some South East Asian countries (the former 'Asian Tigers' economies) and Japan. However, what makes the Chinese experience exceptional are both its long-term time perspective and the kind of problematic economic relations China has with the rest of the world. In particular it is accurate to argue that China, compared to the other 'virtuous' Asian economies, is behaving in a self-protectionist and opportunistic way, adopting a mercantilist economic approach adjusted to the actual global contest. On this subject the inherent questions are the following: is China really willing to cooperate for the purpose of guaranteeing global stability, balanced economic development and sufficient supply of 'global

(Footnote 2 continued)

increased from 17.9% in 1500 to 19.9% in 1600 and from 22.5% in 1700 to 23.6% in 1820, peaking in 1870 (33.6%) and in 1913 (33.5%) and dropping to 26.3% in 1950, 25.7% in 1973 and 20.6% in 1998. From a trivial position until early 1800s, the United States bounced from 1.8% of the world production to 8.9% in 1870, 19.1% in 1913, 23.3% in 1950, dropping to 22.0 and 21.9% in 1998 (Maddison 2006, p. 263). The 'great divergence' phenomenon is also analysed by K. Pomeranz in his *The Great Divergence. China, Europe and the making of the modern world economy* (Pomeranz 2000).

[3]For a brief description of the differences within the mercantilist approach—from the 'classic' mercantilism to the actual one—see Fand (1989), in particular (p. 8): "The current neo-mercantilism emphasizes the promotion of economic growth utilizing advanced technology and reaching for more pervasive and more subtle techniques of intervention in international trade which utilize the vast power of the government in the national economy", and also (p. 13) "Traditional protectionism focused almost exclusively on policies to expand or restrict trade, such as a tariff or an export subsidy. In contrast, modern mercantilism utilizes the full panoply of government intervention to tailor international trade according to some plan. Moreover, all government activity—including defence and foreign policy—is considered for its potential impact on international economic activity, although trade measures are emphasized". Taking into account this distinction, we use in our analysis the term 'mercantilism' according to its actual meaning, which is more suitable when describing the practices in contemporary China.

public goods' to the world economy? Could its mercantilist approach, never explicitly repudiated, clash with its self-characterization of being a 'benign' country willing to help others to develop economically? The answer to the above-posed questions is not a clear-cut one, not least due to at times ambiguous and inscrutable behaviour of Chinese policymakers.

2 China and Japan in the International Economy: A Comparative View

The recent economic history of Japan and South East Asian countries suggests that a mercantilist approach does not categorically exclude or restrain international cooperation. Taking into account all differences, Japan is the case most comparable to China, not least for its relevance within the group of the most industrialized economies. Japan, after its defeat in the Second World War, entered the protecting sphere of the United States and aligned itself with the so-called 'free world' and the 'West' until the end of the Cold War and the collapse of the Berlin Wall. Japan's international positioning acted as a formidable deterrent against rival moves in international economic relations and favoured an open attitude towards institutional cooperation as well. China, conversely, during a long post-war period, positioned itself among the 'enemies' of the United States and only 20 years before the collapse of the Soviet Union started a process of rapprochement with the U.S, even if Beijing never became Washington's 'friend' or 'ally.' When Deng Xiaoping took over power in Beijing, China adopted the South East Asian economic model of development (Boltho and Weber 2009, pp. 267–286). In particular, exports contributed in both China and Japan a significant share to economic growth and the policies are focused on creating a micro and macroeconomic framework consistent with that goal. China and Japan have adopted and executed mercantilist practices, which regularly have created tensions with both countries' economic and trading partners. These practices can be connected to:

- Policies aimed at safeguarding the domestic market, in particular those sectors (e.g. manufacturing) in which Asian countries' global market share has increased. Although not similar in their model of specialization Japan and China both, like other South East Asian countries, aimed at strengthening the domestic industry and use FDI to absorb and assimilate foreign technology.
- Difficulties as regards compliance with the rules of international trade and the protection of intellectual property rights (especially in China)
- Pursuit of macroeconomic policies—including monetary policy and the control of exchange rate—frequently poorly coordinated at the international level, aimed foremost at ensuring economic growth within a framework of domestic macroeconomic stability.

However, some of the widely criticized Chinese economic policies are consistent with the Asian model of development. To be sure, China suggesting and adopting what it refers to as 'alternative' policies aimed at establishing an alternative international economic system remain controversial. While following the peculiarities of the Asian model of development, Japan—like China later—has prioritized and adopted policies aimed at speeding up economic growth, which positioned it at the top position among the other industrial and exporting powers. Taking advantage of its manufacturing capacities as well of the scarcity of raw materials, Japan prioritized economic relations with resource-rich developing countries, while at the same time privileging the markets of developed countries (especially the United States) for its exports. The 1990–96 period was characterized instead by the intensification of Japan's trade and investment relations within Asia, a period during which Japanese overall trade within Asia rose from 25% (in the mid-1980s) to over 36.0% in the mid-1990s (Katada 2001). Such mercantilist economic policies which are a distinctive aspect of the economic policy of that period (the cornerstone of Japan's so-called 'Yoshida Doctrine'), aimed at maximizing Japan's economic growth development while at the same strengthening close relations with resource-rich countries. Japan became the main supporter of Asia's developing economies, while Tokyo saw itself confronted with accusations of conducting mercantilist policies. Indeed, at the end of the 1990s Japan became the biggest donor of Official Development Assistance (ODA),[4] while at the same time Washington accused Tokyo of being a 'free-rider' of international trade relations and indeed a 'hegemonic threat' to international finance (Cooper 2014). However, as regards monetary policy and finance management China and Japan differ fundamentally. The stability of the yen-dollar parity became a priority since the beginning of the 1970s, when the Bretton Woods architecture collapsed. Deprived of the fixed exchange rate system's umbrella Japan acted in a more cooperative way than China today when it accepted the flexible rate-exchange mechanism and, in accordance with the 'Plaza Agreement' of 1985, cooperated in keeping the dollar depreciated. Nevertheless, the monetary compliance did not result in Japanese preparedness to reduce international financial imbalances, which in the 1980s progressively increased. In fact, back then Japan reached the highest levels of trade surplus with the United States and, at the same time, became Washington's top creditor when the US economy began to tackle its so-called 'twin deficits' (federal and external deficits). Japanese policies anticipated therefore those events, which in the 2000s would cause the financial crisis. Further significant differences should be mentioned. Apart from practicing a less mercantilist exchange rate policy, Japan—after the financial liberalization carried out in the first half of the 1980s—became one of the top global financial actors and investors, accompanied by acquisitions of companies and real estate abroad. This was further followed by the relocation of manufacturing to developing countries (thereby taking advantage of cheap labour).

China's strategy was different and the country only recently emerged as a leading foreign investor. Although so far the stock of Chinese FDI remains modest

[4]While Japan ranked number one as donor of ODA until 1998, it was only the fifth largest donor by 2014 (OECD 2015).

when compared to the relative size of the country's economy,[5] since the early 2000s the growth of its FDI has nonetheless been remarkable. In 2015, China ranked third in terms of foreign direct investment worldwide ($116 US billion) for the third year running within the group of non-financial investor countries. Furthermore, the geographic diversification of Chinese FDI was significant too (6.128 overseas companies across 156 countries) (Global Markets 2015). China's 'Go Global' policy in 2014 led to outbound exceeding inbound investments. The growth of Chinese FDI abroad went along with increased Chinese willingness to comply with rules of international trade and increase its contributions in terms of global public goods. Such a Chinese approach as international investor pursued by Chinese policymakers has suggested a more responsible behaviour accepting both the international rules and the criteria of international agreements.[6] As regards Chinese financial investments, despite their recent impressive growth, severe impediments remain in force[7]: it is worth recalling that only since 1984 China replaced the Soviet Union-style 'monobank' system with a real central bank (People Bank of China) and created 'commercial banks' in place of previous specialized institutions operating as branches of the 'monobank.' To be sure, administrative controls over

[5]In 2015 Chinese FDI represented 4% of the world total compared to 24% of those of the United States and 6.2% of the United Kingdom, a country whose GDP is significantly smaller than the Chinese one (Unctad 2016).

[6]As early as the mid-1959s China became increasingly involved in foreign markets in order to secure the supply of raw materials and agriculture products and achieve more diversified economic growth. In order to acquire technological and managerial know-how and satisfy a domestic consumption, against the background of a new 'consumer oriented' model, China later adopted the so-called 'go global' strategy. The changed sectoral mix of its outbound FDI (healthcare, entertainment and high-tech sectors) helped China to increase its FDI by 50 from the 2011 to 2014. Geographical diversification (which privileges Europe and the United States) has furthermore increased China's profile as international investor (KPMG Global China Practice 2016). It is foreseeable that this unprecedented activism can affect the behaviour of China as international investor around many negotiating tables. M&A deals targeting 'host country' firms and the massive presence of Chinese multinational companies connected to the State (through State-Owned Enterprises, SOEs) are emblematic of an approach still conditioned by mercantilist and 'command' practices. On this issues see also Sauvant and Nolan (2015), 1–42.

[7]As early as the mid-1980s the Chinese experience demonstrates that, provided that the capital movements are controlled, it is possible to reconcile a more or less fixed exchange rate with discretionary adjustable domestic interest rates: on this point see also McKinnon and Schnabl (2009, 1–32). One can agree with Polansky when he argues: "The Chinese monetary policy has been … a hybrid one … Its annual targets refer formally to inflation (set by the government) and the growth of the money supply (the pace of the two declining this decade). Both capital and exchange rate liberalizations have been implemented very gradually; in fact until now the presence of administrative controls is noticeable. Portfolio flows are still highly restricted in China and the exchange rate is fixed, although since the mid-2000s it is subject to a peg (crawl-like) mechanism vis-à-vis a trade weighted basket of currencies with a trading band (which in March 2014 expanded from +/−1% to +/−2%). These cautious policies paid off: the country has not experienced any currency crisis while its inflation rates reached lower single digit levels, and its long-term economic growth achievements are well-known" (Polanski 2016 in Hölscher, H. Tomann [eds], 101–102); on the same subject see Ma and McCauley (2007) and also Reade and Volz (2010).

interest rates and credit allocation continued to remain in place. Furthermore, unlike Japan, which in the past adopted policies to protect the domestic markets from foreign competition, China in the early 1980s created 'Special Economic Zones' ('SEZ') in China to attract FDI from abroad. As a consequence China's manufacturing sector experienced a historic boom. Deng Xiaoping pronounced in 1987, seven years after the launch of China's fundamental economic reforms: "All sorts of small enterprises boomed in the countryside, as if a strange army appeared suddenly from nowhere…was not something I had thought about. Nor had the other comrades. This surprised us".[8]

As regards China's preparedness to cooperate with the other partners, China and Japan display some interesting similarities. Firstly, the priority assigned to domestic economic development pursued by means of systematic mercantilist practices. Secondly, both Tokyo and Beijing aimed at securing a large trade surplus with their main trading partners while compensating enormous international financial imbalances through foreign reserves accumulation (China) or a monetary-financial mix (Japan). Both China and Japan have been accused of having so-called 'saving glut', which gave rise to an (intentional) accumulation of huge precautionary 'war chests' (The Federal Reserve Board 2005). China, following the Japanese experience, is accused of 'free-riding' on Washington's accommodating policies. Furthermore—like Japan in the past—China is criticized for not encouraging and facilitating increased domestic consumption and for its high level of savings. As regards China's aid strategies and policies towards developing countries, it is argued that Chinese policies (again like Japanese policies of the past) combine both economic and political/security interests. On the subject of Sino-Japanese comparative propensity to the international cooperation, we have to acknowledge that China is a too big, both as market and as industrial powerhouse, and too 'special' in terms of its economic development model to be considered a genuinely reliable partner for cooperation on a sustainable basis. We turn to examining in detail some aspects of economic international relations, concluding with an interpretation of the reason behind the controversies.

3 China Between Controversies and the 'Westphalian Dilemma'

International trade, patents and intellectual property rights are at the core part of the controversy between China and the United States, the member states of the European Union and the EU institutions. The list of litigations is long and features

[8]Recalling these words Sukanya (2016) in Hölscher, Tomann (eds), cit., p. 346, argues: "These start-up firms drove China's reform momentum; they were arguably the single main source of China's growth".

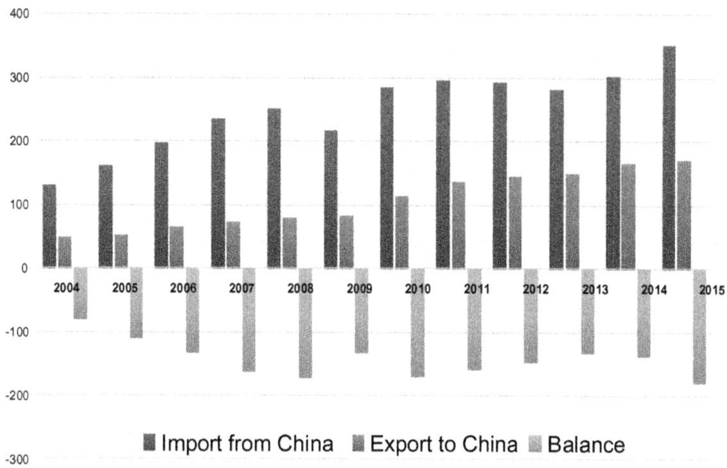

Source: http://ec.europa.eu/trade/policy/countries-andregions/countries/china

Fig. 1 EU-China merchandise trade, flows and balance 2005–2015 bln.Euro

on the agenda of official and unofficial meetings with trading partners absorbing the biggest share of Chinese exports (see Figs. 1 and 2).

Japan too has been entangled in numerous trade disputes, which as mentioned above go hand in hand with its traditional aversion to capital inflows. Moreover, like in China, the rapid growth of Japanese manufacturing was driven by exports, in particular towards the United States, although Japanese exports to the US significantly decreased during Japan's so-called 'Lost Decade' (1995-2007) and particularly in 2000s when strong demand from Asia (above all China), worked as a 'trade diversion' factor of its exports. The competition coming from some Japanese industrial sectors (automotive, steel, consumer electronic equipment, semiconductors) has been always a source of tension with the United States, despite the very close political and military ties between Tokyo and Washington.[9]

However, eventually, US-China trade disputes ended up marginalizing Washington's disputes with Japan. US-Chinese trade disputes are not necessarily the result of geopolitical rivalry or competition but rather a consequence of endogenous constraints of the Chinese development model. The Chinese model aims at modernizing China's resource-scarce economy and accelerate economic growth against the background of instability caused by adverse fluctuations of the balance of payments. To provide a better framework we can refer to the so-called

[9]Although trade disputes with Japan have long been dealt with some issues remain unresolved on the bilateral US-Japan trade and investment agenda. Examples are: meat imports from the US, imports of Japanese cars and car parts, the favourable regulatory treatment for Japan Post in the market of insurance services. For an analysis of bilateral and multilateral free trade initiative and deals, among them the Transpacific Partnership Agreement (TPP) see Cooper (1914).

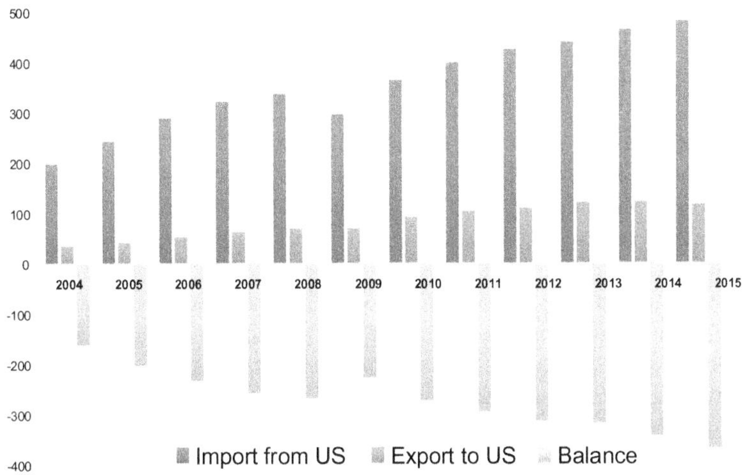

Source: https://www.census.gov/foreign-trade/balance/c5700.html

Fig. 2 US-China merchandise trade, flows and balance 2005–2015 bln. US dollar

'late comer' paradigm introduced by Gerschenkron (Gerschenkron 1962). According to this view, China's reasons for sticking with mercantilist economic policies are the following:

- A problematic legacy of industrial backwardness, among other a result of failed collectivisation experiments (during the so-called 'Great Leap Forward' in China from 1958–1961), pushed China to promote and safeguard 'national champions' by expanding the presence of China's State-Owned Enterprises (SOEs) in raw materials and energy/resource sectors. China's big SOEs prevail in those sectors, which Beijing refers to as 'strategic.'[10]
- Like Japan, a 'first-comer', Chinese industry-driven growth resorted massively to international raw and natural resources markets as well as on international agricultural resources in an attempt to compete with the developed economies. Hence having to compete with the incumbent highly industrialized countries, China, using its SOEs, invested heavily in some African and Latin America markets to secure the supply for natural resources necessary for its economic

[10]Such categories reflect roughly the guidelines issued by China's 'State-owned Assets Supervision and Administration Commission of the State Council' ('SASAC'). The guidelines define the following sectors as 'strategic': defence, electric generation and connected distribution, petroleum and petrochemicals, telecommunication, coal, civil aviation and waterway transport. A strong state presence in other relevant 'pillars' sectors is also recommended: machinery, automotive, information technology, chemicals, construction, steel, base metals. In the absence of reliable statistics, the weight of these sectors within the Chinese economy may be indirectly estimated on the basis of sales volume data. For an attempt to assess the real weight of these sectors see e.g. Szamosszegi et al. (2011).

growth and development. China in fact was not in the condition to profit the historical 'dividend', which allowed the European ex-colonial powers to expand their trade beyond their domestic boundaries: consequently, its growing 'political' focus on resource-rich countries is not comparable to European hegemonic influence in Africa and elsewhere in the past.

- Furthermore, it is worth recalling that many Chinese manufacturing sectors incorporate a significant share of 'non-domestic' production. This is the outcome either of successful policy aimed at attracting direct investments from abroad, in particular after its accession to WTO, and of manufacturing restructuring based on global production chain links and encouraged by market globalization and IT innovations. Such export trade processing is practiced not only by Chinese companies but also or indeed above all by Japanese, Korean, American and European multinational companies. According to calculation of 2007 (the last time year the share of 'foreign' value added has been calculated for China) 'foreign' value added of exported Chinese merchandise ranged from 27.0 to 40.3%: obviously, the highest figures concerned foreign owned firms and joint ventures.[11]

Against the background of the nature of the global production chain, calling China a 'free rider' of global trade is inaccurate or indeed unfair. However, in 2014, China was the top target of antidumping investigations (Fig. 3) and, at the same time, the bigger supplier of assembled cheap merchandise to those countries, for their part, *user* of hostile investigations (above all the United States and the European Union): we are facing a very unusual defendant since, if from one hand it proves poorly cooperating in safeguarding the public good 'fair trade', on the other it is considered extremely helpful in guaranteeing low prices for big international manufacturers, in particular those operating in consumer electronics and IT (OECD 2012).

In short, the accusations brought against China concern:

- The policies aimed at protecting industrial sectors and parts of the domestic market where Chinese SOEs dominate;
- The discriminating procedures activated to protect those markets where Chinese firms dominate;
- The poor protection of intellectual property;
- The ambiguous results in implementing binding commitments of WTO agreements;
- The foreign exchange control and the pervasive interventions in financial markets.

[11]In particular, wholly foreign-owned enterprises, which generate 38.1% of China's total exports, generated a 'local' value added amounting to 44.1% of their total exports, out of which the incorporated 'processing' value (i.e. intermediate goods) represented 83.0%. Greater contributions to local value added came from joint ventures enterprises (17.0% of national exports, China's SOEs (exporting roughly 19% of China's total exports) generated a value added amounting to 72.0% and a processing share of 25.8%. For private enterprises, the figures were 21.3, 80.8 and 9.6% respectively (Koopman et al. 2008).

	Main countries targets of anti-dumping measures in 2014	Anti-dumping distribution of measures: by exporter 01/01/1995 - 30/06/2016
China	63	840
South Korea	18	229
India	15	119
China Taipei	13	187
USA	11	175
Malaysia	10	82
Thailand	9	139
EU	8	82
Turkey	8	40
Japan	7	140

Source:http://www.antidumpingpublishing.com/statistics/;
https://www.wto.org/english/tratop_e/adp_e/AD_Sectoral_MeasuresByExpCty.pdf

Fig. 3 Main targets of antidumping activity

The number of litigations between China and its main trading partners (US and EU) is evidence that the level of cooperation is still low.[12] Indeed, against this trend we must recognize that, despite the volume of litigations, an acceptable ground of cooperation has been achieved by subtracting the controversy's management from the bilateral arrangements and resorting to WTO arbitrage. Furthermore, throughout the last decade an increase of institutional initiatives and fora for dialogue testify the efforts to manage disputes and conflicts.[13] The growing commitment for dialogue

[12]Since China's accession to the WTO, the United States has brought 17 WTO cases against China, more than twice as many WTO cases as any other WTO member has brought against China. In doing so, the United States has placed a strong emphasis on the need for China to adhere to WTO rules, holding China fully accountable as a mature participant in the WTO's global trading system (United States Trade Representative 2015). At the end 2015 much of the 'great power' litigation takes place with the US (12 disputes) and the EU (7 disputes). For China, these two sets constitute 19 out of its 23 disputes, the remaining ones being against Japan (2 disputes), Canada, and Mexico (Vidigal 2015).

[13]Since 2006 China and the United States, on the initiative of then US President George W. Bush and then Chinese President Hu Jintao, established the US-China 'SED' ('Strategic and Economic Dialogue'). In 2009, the dialogue was renamed as S&ED (US-China 'Strategic and Economic Dialogue'). That 'dialogue' is based on two tracks: the 'Strategic Track' and 'Economic Track' which take place once a year and is supplemented by an annual meeting of the US-China 'Joint Commission on Commerce and Trade' ('JCCT'), established in 1983, which focuses primarily on bilateral trade and investment issues. The 'JCCT' has 16 working groups which meet throughout the year and cover issues such as intellectual property rights, information technology, pharmaceutical and medical devices, statistics, commercial law, agriculture, trade and investment. The China-EU trade and investment agenda too is prone to conflict due to the EU's inability to harmonise fragmented national interests when dealing with China. In 2013, the EU adopted the EU-China Strategic 2020 Agenda (http:/eeas.europa.eu, accessed May 2016). Furthermore,

(or better 'dialogues'), however, has left unsolved many issues, which mostly concern governments and public opinion of the involved countries and are successfully negotiable only on a foundation of shared values and principles. It is emblematic that the Report to Congress on China's WTO Compliance issued in 2015 by the United States Trade Representative recalls: "... It was at this time that USTR began reporting on Chinese government policies and practices that demonstrated a stronger embrace of state capitalism, a trend that continued into 2012, the last full year under the Chinese leaders who had taken over in 2003. USTR also reported that some of these policies and practices suggested that China had not yet fully embraced key WTO principles, such as market access, non-discrimination and transparency ..." (United States Trade Representative, cit.).

The current debate on the issue of granting China market economy status (MES) shows the reluctance of many European countries to revise defensive policies towards a country, which hesitates to implement fundamental economic reforms (Puccio 2015).

The narrative that opposes a 'defaulting' China to virtuous counterparts monitoring compliance with international rules fails to capture the underlying reasons standing in the way of China cooperating more. Beneath the surface of the controversy lurks an 'ideological' rejection of the Chinese reluctance to revise a model which, despite its contradictions and problems, was the basis of China's rapid and decade-long economic growth and development. In particular, China is blamed for its trade practices as well as for financial and monetary policies and criticised for its economic governance referred to as 'state capitalism' protecting the Chinese market and China's SOEs from foreign competition. Furthermore, problematic issues are those concerning intellectual property rights and counterfeiting, which are blamed not only for illegally altering market prices but also enabling Chinese companies to get cheap (and illegal) access to technology and know-how.

Far from being successful is also the action (predominantly undertaken by the United States) against the Chinese non tariff-barriers, which helps to protect the domestic services sector in which the Chinese economy shows evident backwardness. Equally urgent are policies aimed at fostering cooperation in cyber security, an extremely sensitive area, which touches upon economic and military interests.[14] However, the areas in which cooperation must urgently be strengthened

(Footnote 13 continued)

Brussels and Beijing discuss trade and investment issues in the framework of the so-called 'High-Level Economic and Trade Dialogue.'

[14]In order to overcome frictions concerning the barriers to foreign investments, Washington and Beijing in 2012 established the US-China 'Bilateral Investment Treaty' ('BIT'). For a detailed overview of the issues and problems on the US-China trade and investment agenda see Morrison (2015). The issues and problems on the EU-China trade and investment agenda are similar to the ones controversially discussed between Washington and Beijing. On the most relevant issues on the EU-China economic agenda see European Commission, Directorate-General for Trade, Annual activity Report (2014).

are related to monetary issues and financial stability- both central 'global public goods'.[15]

A lack of cooperation and opportunistic behaviour are the main charges brought to China by the United States as regards Beijing's exchange rate policy. Criticism comes from US companies and trade unions as well as from academia. Companies and trade unions identify trade with China as the source both of macroeconomic disequilibria and of demand shortage of some American manufacturing sectors. The trade deficit with China therefore is in Washington's view the consequence of non-market and non-competition China is practicing. Indeed, the charge of commercial dominance supported by currency dumping and by unfair competition continues to be subject to controversial debates in scholarly and policymaking circles.[16] Within the academic field, the positions are rather vague and tend to distinguish the exchange rate issue from that concerning the effects of the Chinese competition on the domestic job market.[17] Neither criticism in academia nor the one (more assertive) prevailing among American politicians and trade unionists seem to have altered the positions of Chinese rulers who continue to reject both arguments, and indeed blame the United States for having put global financial and monetary stability at risk through its low interest rates policy and quantitative easing (QE).

The delayed liberalization of capital movements, a measure that goes hand in hand with the liberalization of the exchange rate, would furthermore be a setback of the adaptation process of the Chinese financial market to the 'holy grail' of the financial liberalization, namely the free circulation of capital. This position has been firmly reiterated in June 2015,[18] at the *US-China Strategic and Economic Dialogue—Economic Track.* To be sure, such reforms are likely to have consequences for Chinese economy's stability. However, we have to acknowledge that sustainable

[15]The nature of global public goods can be multi-faceted: they can be 'pure', frequently contested', underprovided'. On this subject see also Ersoy (2011) (accessed in May 2016).

[16]The pegged Renminbi (RMB)-US dollar exchange rate, according to US trade unionists and US policymakers, is among other responsible for the US trade deficit (together with job losses) with China. The magnitude of these consequences tends however to be overestimated in the US. Since China's accession to the WTO in 2001 and until 2010, 2,400,000 jobs were lost in US manufacturing sector according to the Alliance for American Manufacturing (the Alliance uses data provided by Scott (2010)). Those job losses were—by trade unions and the US administration likewise—cited as justification to resort to retaliatory measures against Chinese manufacturers. Such position has been emphasized throughout the first term of the Obama presidency, thereby responding to trade unions' requests. To be sure, such retaliatory measures will most probably gain further prominence under the Trump presidency.

[17]Cline and Williamson (2010) present a critical review of 18 studies on exchange rate movements; they note that only one among them confirms the hypothesis of overvaluation. Irrespective of the results, this review demonstrates that the divergences depend on the definition of the concept of the term 'equilibrium.' For a critical analysis see also Eichengreen (2004).

[18]In the chapter 'Creating a More Open, Resilient Chinese Financial System' the conditions for achieving such goals are explained: (a) Opening Up China's Capital Markets, (b) Expanding Opportunities for US Financial Services Providers, c) Strengthening Bilateral Cooperation to Safeguard Financial Stability (US Department of Treasury 2015).

cooperative initiatives are highly problematic,[19] not least because a cooperative solution of each of these issues involves the concomitant solution of the other connected issues. Specifically, liberalization of capital movement must be consistent with the exchange rate policy as well as take place in coordination with the adjustment of domestic interest rates: interventions must not be disconnected from the reforms of the domestic financial market. In essence, it is futile to argue that the optimal solution capable to guarantee the public good 'international financial stability' corresponds with the allegedly 'neutral' solution featuring in the documents of international organizations.[20]

4 Can China Become a Provider of 'Global Public Goods'?

The issue regarding the controversially debated Chinese conduct as regards the provision of 'global public goods' can be analysed, against the background of the 'Westphalian dilemma'. According to this view and unlike the agreements on 'ordinary' public goods which can efficiently be tackled at the local level (nation, region, village), for global public goods neither a 'workable market' nor some sort of 'governmental mechanism' appropriate for resolving the worldwide problems exist. As pointed out by Nordhaus: "… under international law as it has evolved in the West and then the world, there is no legal mechanism by which disinterested majorities, or supermajorities short of unanimities, can coerce reluctant free-riding countries into mechanisms that provide for global public goods …" "… Particularly where there are strong asymmetries in the costs and benefits (as is the case for nuclear non-proliferation or global warming), the requirement of reaching unanimity means that it is extremely difficult to reach universal and binding international agreements …" (Nordhaus 2005). Such an inherent systemic constraint entails a real difficulty in identifying those who are responsible for the shortcoming

[19]C. Wyplotz has no doubts about defining financial stability as 'global public good'. In fact, for him financial instability is a 'public bad' that can represent a negative externality for other countries (Wyplotz 1999).

[20]This issue has been debated since the 'Bretton Woods Agreement'. Paradoxically, financial stability as public good is repeatedly reaffirmed in a context of flexible exchange rates which, unlike the 'Bretton Woods Agreement' ceased to exist in August 1971, made less attainable the stability and more precarious the path leading to it. According to the $n - 1$ model the fixed exchange rate system allows for at least a couple of solutions, cooperative and non-cooperative, the stability of both depending on countries' preparedness to cooperate (cooperative solution) and on the $(n - 1)$ common approval of the monetary policy conducted by the leading member (non-cooperative solution). In a world of flexible exchange rates, such an agreement is unrealistic. In absence of a monetary 'anchor' any attempt to set a governance of the international monetary system is indeed unrealistic. According to the 'public choice' approach Nordhaus asserts that any tools or path that will be adopted (additive technologies, best-shot technologies, weakest-link technologies, efficient provision) produce different and potentially underperforming results (Nordhaus 2005).

and failures of cooperation.[21] A more realistic view suggests to consider the parties involved not as stylized subjects but rather dissimilar 'regimes' which confront each other while at the same time protecting their national interests. In fact, China likes to call itself a 'market economy with Chinese characteristics'[22] whereas the United States and the European Union declare themselves 'market economies' *tout-court*. To these two economic models correspond different political regimes—single-party and authoritative government in the former case, a multi-party system and democratic governance in the latter—which in the global economic scenario pursue strategies resulting from non-comparable domestic processes. If we take into account that China aims at becoming a 'great power' (and not only in economic terms), it becomes understandable how reciprocal economic cooperation becomes a complex game, which only becomes an instrument of mutually beneficial results with great difficulties. This in turn requires deep economic and structural reforms of the Chinese economic system, including above all changes to what China refers to as 'socialist market economy' model.[23] It is therefore useful to briefly recall some meaningful cases. Whenever critics complain about little commitment in implementing the 'investment' agenda (BIT), aimed at enlarging the domestic services market to foreign operators (the most coming from the United States), or at allowing foreign firms to access the government procurement sector in foreign countries (for China it is assumed totalling over $200 billion) it is useful to bear in mind that some sectors characterised by the dominant presence of Chinese State Owned Enterprises (SOEs) could be seriously compromised. Moreover, some manufacturing sectors, in particular the audio-visual and media, are by Chinese authorities referred to as 'strategic' and are hence to be protected to be able to secure political and social stability in China. The discretionary and lengthy approval of foreign investment projects and the discriminating enforcement of the Chinese Antimonopoly Law are placed on top of the US-China agenda dealing with investment liberalization. This policy acts as a strategic asset to promote indigenous new sectors' growth (the so-called 'infant industry argumentum') and above all protect monopolies (and quasi-monopolies) in which the Communist Party

[21]Obviously, the concept of the 'Westphalian dilemma' is not the only one explaining the difficulties of providing global public goods. In fact, political scientists and economists offer different interpretations and explanations such as the 'prisoner dilemma', the 'common-pool' theory, the 'focal-point' theory. All of these approaches have their limits as they either consider states as mere bargaining subjects or as actors which underestimate the external projection of their domestic policies (Martin 1999).

[22]"… now completely different from the previous socialist economic system before 1978 which was characterized by singular public ownership and a planned economy" (Wu et al., cit. p. 64).

[23]In the Chinese literature we can find several oxymora, which express such difficulties. Quoting a public speech by Zhou Xiaochuan, Governor of the People's Bank of China, Wu Li et al. (cit.) on page 149, recall a passage where he stresses, among others, the ultimate task at which China must aim at: "… improve the objectivity, consistency and effectiveness of international financial regulatory standards *based on sovereignty in regulation* [our italic]".

maintains a strong stake. Also the monetary policy and the reforms of the financial sector, two domains to which Chinese policy makers have widely resorted for countering the recent global financial crisis, do not seem to move away from the 'command economy' approach. However, even though some significant improvements have been achieved in reducing the role of the state in liberalizing the interest rates and enhancing bank competition, the Chinese state reacted to market volatility by heavily intervening in the stock and capital markets. Moreover, immediate but not unexpected was the intervention to depreciate the exchange rate on two occasions (first in August 2015 and early 2016) causing a breakdown of the automatic adjustment of the Renminbi under the procedure based on the currency basket operating from 2005.[24] A World Bank report from 2012 elaborates on the necessary policies China will have to adopt to be able to reach 'high income status, increase international cooperation and provide global public goods in accordance with its economic weight (The World Bank 2012). However, the report does not explain which transformation China's political system ought to undergo in order to be able to adopt necessary economic reforms. The report recommends: "... Public consultations and policy debate ensure that all points of view are considered before government reforms are introduced ..." (The World Bank, cit., p. 20) in order to foster consensus 'from below' and go down the right track leading to *Building a Modern, Harmonious, and Creative High-Income Society*. However, this recipe sounds somewhat unrealistic when we take into account the structure of the political governance in China and the geopolitical ambitions of its leaders. Against this background it is questionable whether China will be equipped with the instruments and eager enough to embark on this 'virtuous' track, which on the one hand could lay the groundwork for international cooperation, while obliging Beijing to adopt structural change of its economic model and political governance, from which the current model draws its strength and legitimacy. There is a near-consensus among observers and China scholars that Xi Jinping's economic reform plans and policies do not fully match current and actual economic policies. Despite some partial successes, the recent financial crisis and instability have made the Chinese

[24]The controversial centralist intervention on exchange rates that took place in the summer of 2015 resulted in the crashing of the Shanghai stock market (it lost 30% of its value, the trading of 1,400 company shares was temporarily suspended, and roughly three trillion Chinese Yuan of capital was wiped out). This episode revealed to the outside world one of the strongest contradictions of the Chinese model, namely the conflict between two opposite pressures: on one hand the will to maintain the State control of the markets, on the other hand to use audaciously free market practices (Chiecon wordpress.com, accessed in May 2016, and Deer 2015). On the ineffective regulations of the Chinese stock market and the role of the state-owned banks see also Hsu (2015).

leadership more hesitant to fully accomplish economic and financial reforms[25] and persuaded it to adopt a macroeconomic course by resorting to domestic consumption rather than to embark in an challenging and comprehensive program of reforms.[26] While in China's 'Third Plenum Programme' the emphasis is placed on the importance of adopting economic reforms in general, it remains vague on what concrete monetary and financial reforms the country should adopt in order to achieve increased and meaningful monetary integration with the rest of the world.

5 Conclusions

We conclude by addressing a question. If the adaptation of Chinese economic model to the 'Western' model, widely considered a condition for a stable international cooperation, is not what Chinese policymakers are aiming for, then does that mean that they are working on developing and presenting a new geopolitical and geo-economic model? If that is the case, then to what extent is this model a viable and realistic alternative to the one which defined global economic and political structures after the Second World War? Without getting into a detailed debate on 'unilateralism' versus 'multilateralism', it is undeniable that China is moving on the international stage as key player in its attempt to set up institutions and organizations competing with those promoted by the United States and their allies. Three initiatives support this hypothesis:

(1) In March 2015, China inaugurated the (Beijing-based) Asian Infrastructure Investment Bank (AIIB). It is considered by some observers a real alternative to the World Bank and, as such, regarded with mistrust by the United States. Currently, it consists of 57 members, including the most industrialized European countries and Russia.
(2) In February 2016, the 11th round of negotiations of the Regional Comprehensive Economic Partnership (RCEP) gathering the ten nations of the Association of Southeast Asian Nations (ASEAN) plus China, Japan, South

[25]The economic program of Xi Jinping presented at the 'Third Party Plenum' (November 2013), targeted at making Chinese economic growth more sustainable, facilitating the increase of private consumption, reducing domestic investment and the country's trade balance. Despite some progress, the crisis raised doubts whether Beijing was committed to adopting further reforms. Such reforms would be aimed at enhancing the private economy, implementing the restructuring of Chinese SOEs and opening up the country to foreign competition, including in protected sectors. The Chinese leadership, however, remains very cautious as regards the liberalization of capital movements and the exchange rate. Basically, Chinese policymakers remain committed to reforms initiated by China's previous political leadership while seeking to make sure that economic reforms and the policies of opening up work towards achieving what the official narrative refers to as a 'harmonious society.' In 2012, China's leader Xi Jinping also introduced the concept of the so-called 'China Dream' (*Zhongguo meng*); for a critical analysis on the state of China's economic reforms see also Salidjanova and Koch-Weser (2013).

[26]On the decision and reasons to postpone exchange rate liberalization see also Godement (2015).

Korea, Australia, New Zealand, India was held. This initiative raises relevant questions about its co-existence with the 'Trans-Pacific Partnership' ('TPP') signed on October 2015 by 12 Asia-Pacific countries, strongly supported by outgoing US President Obama.[27] China is not a member of the TPP and makes no secret of its lack of enthusiasm for an inter-regional free trade agreement it is not—at least not yet—a member of (BBC News Asia 2015).

(3) Since 2013 China is active in the 'Chiang Mai Initiative Multilateralization' ('CMIM'), a multilateral currency swap arrangement, which includes the ten ASEAN nations plus China (Hong Kong included), and Japan and Korea (ASEAN+3). Originally conceived as a network of bilateral swap arrangements aimed at coping with liquidity shortage of its members after the Asian financial crisis of 1997, the regional monetary cooperation gave rise later (2010) to a functional reserve regional fund based on a single bilateral agreement. Also in this case some critical comments detected in this agreement an alternative (and not complementary) initiative albeit at a regional scale, to the International Monetary Fund.

The ambitions of the Chinese leadership to expand its economic ties and influence in Eurasia finds an instrument in Beijing's 'One Belt One Road' ('OBOR') project. The 'OBOR'—a revival of the ancient 'Silk Road'—aspires—through massive infrastructure programmes—to connect China with a number of Central Asian and European countries. The goal of this Chinese strategy is among others to expand the Chinese economic and energy ties with natural resources-rich Central Asian countries and to create fast land and maritime routes connecting China with Russia and Europe.[28] Less evident and long-term oriented is instead the objective of uniting Russia and Europe in an economic and political block to counter the so-called 'Asian belt', in which the United States play a leading role. To be sure analysts point out that these ambitious projects do not necessarily lead to a decrease of the international cooperation and the setting up of opposing 'blocks'. The Chinese initiatives conversely can—at least for now—be understood as 'complementary' to those dominated by the United States and, in any case, they do not exclude a 'double membership' and do not necessarily lead to economic rivalry and conflict. (Meltzer 2015). In fact, the United States, Japan and the European Union keep their position as privileged trade partners of China, despite the fact that emerging and other Asian countries (Japan excluded) have significantly increased

[27]US-China policies under US President Trump could have an impact on Beijing's willingness to adopt further economic, monetary and financial reforms that Washington (and others) urge Beijing to adopt (Sevastopulo 2016).

[28]Indeed, China has big ambitions as regards the re-vitalization of the ancient 'Silk Road' connecting China and Europe. Announced by Chinese President Xi at the end of 2013, the 'One Belt One Road' ('OBOR') project aims not only at enhancing economic integration among countries along the former 'Silk Road' but also at creating a "... community with shared interests, destiny and responsibilities ...". Furthermore, aware of geopolitical limitations along the land route, the 'OBOR'also foresees a maritime link ('The 21st Century Maritime Silk Road') connecting China with Europe (Shuaihua 2015, accessed in May 2016).

their share of global GDP and trade.[29] Furthermore, a competing economic block, void of a strong monetary anchor, would lack the technical instruments and capabilities essential for meaningful financial integration and trade stability. In fact, although the Chinese currency has been performing successfully, serious constraints still prevent it to reach an international status and to be acknowledged as a fully accepted currency in the international exchanges.[30]

China becoming a leading provider of common global goods is still unlikely, not least Beijing has yet to define and adopt ways of cooperating efficiently with other major actors and institutions internationally. As mentioned above, while China has made some progress reforming its macroeconomic model, it has yet to adopt further systemic reforms as the basis for more result-oriented cooperation on an international level. Chinese concerns about safeguarding national interests will continue to make sure that cooperation will continue to be expanded slowly and prone to obstacles. However, it is necessary to examine more analytically the Chinese-style concept of global common goods seeking to understand how Beijing defines a 'virtuous' market economy model.

References

Beretta S, Iannini G (2014) China: a case of 'Mercantilism' in a backward Country? Eur Sci J (ESJ), Special Edition. vol. 1, June. http://eujournal.org/index.php/esj/issue/view/134. Accessed May 2016

Boltho A, Weber M (2009) Did China follow the East Asian development model? Eur J Comp Econ 6(2):267–286

[29]In 2014, contributions to global GDP (in current US dollar) was geographically distributed as follows: advanced economies: 60.7%; emerging and development economies: 39.9%; European Union: 23.7%; United States: 22.4%; China: 13.3% (http://www.economywatch.com, accessed May 2016), whereas in 2015 China's top trading partners, sorted by their descending respective share of total Chinese export (in current US dollar), were: United States: 18.0%; European Union: 5.6%; Hong Kong: 14.6%; ASEAN: 12.2%; Japan: 5.9; South Korea: 4.4% (http://www.statista.com, accessed May 2016).

[30]Although in 2015 trade settlements in RMB amounted to about $1.7 trillion, roughly one quarter of China's annual trade, and outstanding stock of RMB-denominated bonds was worth nearly $400 billion (there are other 15 offshore RMB clearing centres, such as Frankfurt, Paris, and London) the RMB is the fifth most important payment currency but still accounts for less than three percent of worldwide payments for cross-border trade and financial transactions and for less than two percent of turnover in global foreign exchange markets (Prasad 2016). Recently, across the range of economic indicators the internationalisation of the Renminbi has slowed and slipped into reverse. In fact, investors are offloading Renminbi assets and exploiting the loopholes in capital control regulations to move funds into the opposite direction. Meanwhile, against this backdrop, China's recent initiatives to tighten approvals for foreign acquisitions by Chinese companies, as well as other transactions that require selling of Renminbi for foreign currency, cast further doubts on Beijing's commitment to currency internationalisation (Wildau and Mitchell 2016).

China cautiously welcomes Trans-Pacific free trade deal (2015) BBC News Asia, 6 Oct. http://www.bbc.com/news/world-asia-34451326. Accessed May 2016

Chinese government gaming itself in the markets (2016) Published 17th February. https://chiecon.wordpress.com/2016/02/17/chinese-government-gaming-itself-in-the-markets/. Accessed May 2016

Cline WR, Williamson J (2010) Estimates of the equilibrium exchange rate of the Renminbi: is there a consensus and if not, why not? Peterson Institute for International Economics Policy Brief. https://piie.com/publications/chapters_preview/4150/04iie4150.pdf. Accessed May 2016

Cooper WH (2014) US-Japan economic relations: significance, prospects, and policy options. Congressional Research Service, 18 Feb

Deer L (2015) China's stock market crash reveals financial policy tensions. Institute for Economic Thinking, July 24. https://ineteconomics.org/ideas-papers/blog/chinas-stock-market-crash-reveals-financial-policy-tensions. Accessed May 2016

Eichengreen B (2004) Chinese currency controversies. CEPR Discussion Paper Series, 4375

Ersoy BA (2011) Globalization and global public goods. http://www.intechopen.com/books/new-knowledge-in-a-new-era-of-globalization/globalization-and-global-public-goods. Accessed May 2016

European Commission, Directorate-General for Trade (2014) Annual activity report. http://trade.ec.europa.eu/doclib/docs/2015/September/tradoc_153811.pdf. Accessed May 2016

Fand DI (1989) Classical mercantilism, neomercantilism and contemporary rent seeking. J Publ Finan Publ Choice 3–16

Gerschenkron A (1962) Economic backwardness in historical perspective: a book of essays. Belknap Press of Harvard University Press, Cambridge, MA

Global Markets-EY Knowledge (2015) Riding the silk road: China sees outbound investment boom – Outlook for China's outward foreign direct investment, March. http://www.ey.com/Publication/vwLUAssets/ey-china-outbound-investment-report-en/%24FILE/ey-china-outbound-investment-report-en.pdf

Global Studies Association DePaul University (2006) China: market socialism or capitalism? 13 May. http://www.luc.edu/faculty/dschwei/ChinaCap.GSA.pdf

Godement F (2015) China's economic downturn: the facts behind the myth. European Council on Foreign Relations (ecfr.eu). http://www.ecfr.eu/publications/summary/chinas_economic_downturn_the_facts_behind_the_myth_4079

Hsu S (2015) China's volatile stock market and its implications, China Policy Institute Policy Paper: No 7. https://www.nottingham.ac.uk/cpi/documents/policy-papers/cpi-policy-paper-2015-no-7-hsu.pdf. Accessed May 2016

http://ec.europa.eu/trade/policy/countries-and-regions/countries/china/. Accessed May 2016

http://wits.worldbank.org/. Accessed May 2016

http://www.antidumpingpublishing.com/statistics/. Accessed May 2016

http:/eeas.europa.eu. Accessed May 2016

http://www.ecfr.eu/publications/summary/chinas_economic_downturn_the_facts_behind_the_myth_4079. Accessed May 2016

http://www.economywatch.com/economic-statistics/. Accessed May 2016

http://www.federalreserve.gov/boarddocs/speeches/2005/200503102/default.htm. Accessed May 2016

http://www.statista.com/statistics/270326/main-export-partners-for-china/. Accessed May 2016

Katada SN (2001) Banking on stability. Japan and the cross-pacific dynamics of international financial crisis management. The University of Michigan Press

Kissinger H (2011) On China. Penguin Press, New York

Koopman RB, Zhi W, Shang JW (2008) How much of Chinese exports is really made in China? Assessing domestic value-added when processing trade is pervasive, NBER Working Paper, 14109

KPMG Global China Practice (2016) China outlook 2016. https://home.kpmg.com/content/dam/kpmg/pdf/2016/03/china-outlook-2016-synopsis-2.pdf

Ma G, McCauley RN (2007) Do China's capital controls still bind? Implications for monetary autonomy and capital liberalization. Basel, BIS Working Papers, WP/233

Maddison A (2006) The world economy. OECD Publishing, Development Centre Studies

Martin LL (1999) The political economy of international cooperation. In: Kaul I, Grunberg I, Stern M A (eds) Global public goods, international cooperation in the 21st century. Published for The United Nations Development Programme (UNDP). Oxford University Press, New York-Oxford

McKinnon R, Schnabl G (2009) The case for stabilizing China's exchange rate: setting the stage for fiscal expansion. China World Econ 17(1)

Meltzer PJ (2015) Why China should join the trans-pacific partnership. http://www.brookings.edu/blogs/order-from-chaos/posts/2015/09/21-us-china-economic-integration-tpp-meltzer. Accessed May 2016

Morrison WM (2015) China-U.S. Trade Issues. Congressional Research Service, December 15

Nordhaus D (2005) Paul Samuelson and global public goods, 5 May. www.econ.yale.edu/~nordhaus/…/PASandGPG.pdf. Accessed May 2016

OECD (2012) Mapping global value chains. The OECD Conference Centre. Paris, 4–5 Dec

OECD (2015) Development Co-operation Report 2015 Making Partnerships Effective Coalitions for Action. http://www.compareyourcountry.org/oda?cr=oecd&lg=en. Accessed May 2015

Polański K (2016) Monetary stabilization. In: Hölscher J, Tomann H (eds) Palgrave dictionary of emerging markets and transition economics. Insights from archival research, Palgrave Macmillan

Pomeranz K (2000) The great divergence. China, Europe and the making of the modern world economy. Princeton University Press, Princeton, N.J.

Prasad ES (2016) China's efforts to expand the international use of the Renminbi. Report prepared for the US-China Economic and Security Review Commission, 4 Feb. http://www.brookings.edu/research/reports/2016/02/04-china-efforts-international-use-renminbi-prasad. Accessed May 2016

Puccio L (2015) Granting market economy status to China, an analysis of WTO law and of selected WTO members' policy. European Parliamentary Research Service, November-PE 571.325.

Reade JJ, Volz U (2010) Chinese monetary policy and the dollar peg. School of Business and Economics Discussion Paper: Economics, No. 35. Free University Berlin

Salidjanova N, Koch-Weser I (2013) Third plenum economic reform proposals: a scorecard. US-China Economic and Security Review Commission Staff Research Backgrounder, 19 Nov 2013. http://origin.www.uscc.gov/sites/default/files/Research/Backgrounder_Third%20Plenum%20Economic%20Reform%20Proposals–A%20Scorecard%20(2).pdf. Accessed May 2016

Sauvant KP, Nolan D (2015) China's outward foreign direct investment and international investment law. J Int Econ Law 18(4)

Scott RE (2010) Unfair China trade costs local jobs. Economic Policy Institute [EPI], 23 Mar. http://www.epi.org/publications/entry/bp260/. Accessed May 2016

Sevastopulo D (2016) Trump vows to renounce Pacific trade deal on first day in office. Financial Times, 22 Nov

Shuaihua WC (2015) China's new silk road: implications for the US, Yale Global on line. http://yaleglobal.yale.edu/content/china%E2%80%99s-new-silk-road-implications-us. Accessed May 2016

Sukanya A (2016). In: Hölscher J, Tomann H (eds), cit

Szamosszegi A, Kyle C (2011) An analysis of state—owned enterprises and state capitalism in China, US-China. Economic and Security Review Commission. Washington DC, 26 Oct.

The World Bank (2012) China 2030, building a modern, harmonious, and creative high-income society. Washington, DC

Unctad (2016) World Investment Report

United States Trade Representative (2015) 2015 Report to Congress on China's WTO compliance, December. https://ustr.gov/sites/default/files/2015-Report-to-Congress-China-WTO-Compliance.pdf. Accessed May 2016

US Department of Treasury (2015) US-China strategic and economic dialogue US fact sheet—economic track. https://www.treasury.gov/press-center/press-releases/Pages/jl0094.aspx. Accessed May 2016

Vidigal G (2015) WTO: the first 500 disputes and the last 100 disputes, EIJL:Talk!, 11 Nov. http://www.ejiltalk.org/wto-the-first-500-disputes-and-the-last-100-disputes/. Accessed May 2016

Wildau G, Mitchell T (2016) China: Renminbi stalls on road to being a global currency. Financial Times, 11 Dec

Wu L, Sui F, Zheng L (2010) China's economy. China Intercontinental Press

Wyplotz C (1999) International Financial Instability. In: Kaul I, Grunberg I, Stern MA (eds) Global public goods, international cooperation in the 21st century. Published for The United Nations Development Programme (UNDP), Oxford University Press, New York-Oxford

Chinese Population Policies: Towards a Free Choice

Patrizia Farina

Abstract Demographic policies carried out in China over the past 50 years have dictated the speed and timing of demographic transition in this country. The population's health conditions have improved bringing the life expectancy at birth to a very high level compared with other developing countries while China's *One-Child Policy* has led to the reduction of fertility. It also created a relatively long period of demographic bonus, providing long-term economic development with manpower. However, in 2015 the aging of population and gender bias let the Chinese government abandon the country's *One-Child Policy* in favor of the *Two-Child Policy*. We will know only in the future if this option will have a positive impact on the demographic balance or whether it is coming too late for Chinese couples.

1 Introduction

From a historical point of view, the relationship between population and territory—a crucial theme in the development of Chinese culture—is an institutionalized one, as it proceeds from the emperor's role in his capacity of intermediary between man and nature and guarantor of the balance between people and their land. The current demographic landscape is a reflection of China's political system, which allowed the development of a population mostly gathered in naturally fertile areas or areas that became fertile thanks to human intervention (Bielenstein 1987).

Like any other society, the imperial one was equally concerned with taking a census of the population for fiscal, military and labor reasons, and it could do so due to the nationwide presence of the bureaucracy. Population estimates along the timeline of different ages are abundant: they can be found in dynastic history as well as in purpose-drawn registers for the sake of census. It was only in the last two decades that the new methodologies and the more proactive attitudes towards

P. Farina (✉)
Department of Sociology and Social Research,
University of Milano-Bicocca, Milan, Italy
e-mail: patrizia.farina@unimib.it

S. Beretta et al. (eds.), *Understanding China Today*, Understanding China,
DOI 10.1007/978-3-319-29625-8_12

population studies have amplified the circulation of widely converging data about the demographic trends of the past centuries, mainly linear when cleansed from the effects of the dynastic cycle of formation, ascendance, and decline (Zhao and Xia 1988).

The Great Leap Forward of population was undertaken during the last dynasty: by the mid-19th century and with a territorial area being almost the same, the Qing Empire—whose population was about 90 million in 1644—more than quadrupled which meant figures six to eight times higher than those ensuring stability in the past. Foods and crafts commercialization, along with the consolidation of monetary economics and the update of the fiscal system were the basis of both Chinese economic development and food supply in those centuries. Implanting new varieties of precocious and stable rice along with the introduction of recently imported farming, allowed cultivation growth over marginal areas (Gernet 1978). From the second half of the 18th century onward, demographic pressure emerging from the past two centuries led to the country's political and economical crisis—a crisis, which migration to other Asian countries and the U.S. could barely relieve (Ho 1959).

Up to the founding of People's Republic of China (PRC) in 1949 and in particular between the end of the 19th and the first decades of the 20th century, the population was essentially sized up from a qualitative point of view rather than from a Malthusian perspective (Peng 1991). Nonetheless, since the foundation of People's Republic in 1949, population policies became central in at least three spheres of action controlled by many different actors:

(a) Control on internal migrations, aimed at both containing migrant flows to cities and settling sparsely populated areas; (b) control on population growth, at first by increasing the age at marriage and intervals between births, subsequently with the *One-Child Population policy*; (c) quality control of population especially addressed to mothers and children (Poston et al. 2006). Throughout the last decades, the party issued guidelines reflecting party ideology, which in turn were adopted through plans, rules and reinforcements. Keeping in mind the actual achievements of demographic-oriented actions, it is possible to identify several phases linking policies to Chinese political leaders: Mao, Deng, Jiang, Hu and now Xi are the leaders of different demographic policies.

2 Population Policies

The arrival of the communist leadership in 1949 met with the first stage of demographic transition in China. The first baby boom was the most tangible outcome of that transition: between 1950 and 1957, the Chinese population had increased by almost 86 million people (an increase of 16%) due to a fertility estimated in no less than six children per woman and a fast decreasing mortality rate (Coale 1984). In 1950, the Chinese population lived in an extremely poor state of health; research carried out throughout the 1930s and 1940s show a death rate around 40‰ while infant mortality was about 200 per 1000 live births. It is a small wonder that any improvement in people's health took priority in the new government (Banister 1987). The issue was a crucial one, so much that several national conferences were held between 1950 and 1952 to analyze diseases prevention and health care. They ended up highlighting four key topics: (a) meeting the needs of workers, farmers and soldiers; (b) supporting prevention of diseases; (c) strengthening of the link between Eastern and Western medicine and (d) acting with the support of the mass movement.

Prevention materialized through mass mobilization and the establishment of health facilities. In particular, the *Patriotic Health Movement* was founded to prevent diseases, train people in hygiene and treat the most widespread endemic and professional pathologies. Pre-existing health organizations were maintained and many others were established to deal with epidemic monitoring and prevention, along with medical centers for children and women care. Health campaigns and training programs aiming at food storage, handle and use of organic fertilizers, along with techniques to overcome parasites and other noxious organisms, improved the environment. However, in order to eradicate infectious diseases a state intervention was needed, specifically for plague, typhus, leprosy and smallpox. Later on the action was extended to tuberculosis, above all in the area of child care. The improved state of health of the Chinese population—an objective to be regarded as a form of active population policies—was also due to the recovery of those who suffered from opium addiction and prostitution-carried venereal diseases, all of which were considered the results of the decline of the empire (Greenhalgh and Winckler 2005). While the conditions for the first baby boom were about to materialize, the communist government gave up on birth control and planned parenthood policies, just as any other poor country. The title of an article issued by the People's Daily in January 1952, *Birth control may bust China up*, emphasized that China too was concerned about the many calls for demographic control by rich countries, since they were regarded as an updated version of imperialism. An insight favored by the political isolation of the country. These ideological orientations and positions led to restrictive guidelines as far as induced abortion was concerned, allowed as an exception only. Sterilization and the import of contraceptive devices were also prohibited.

It was only in the mid-1950s that the first influential voices began to endorse birth control: the launch of campaigns to support use of contraceptives date back to that time. The debate revolved around the relationship between population and resources. The leader of such a trend was Ma Yinchu, author of the *New Population Theory* (Ma 2002). By confuting Marxist theory, he emphasized that further population growth would be detrimental to China's demographic development. He also proposed to raise legal age at marriage and decided to increase taxes in direct ratio to the increasing number of children, beginning with the third. Despite the backing of influential representatives within both party and government, Ma Yinchu's proposals were not realized—on the contrary his group was isolated and prosecuted as 'Malthus of China' during the reaction to the *Hundred Flowers Campaign*. Or better still, thenceforth and up to the beginning of the 1960s the main position about the issue was pronatalist, with a climax in 1960 when the beginning of the *Great Leap Forward* encouraged the idea that China was short of population rather than overpopulated.

Such opposing views changed only after the economic and demographic crisis that hit the country between 1959 and 1961, as a consequence of the policies of the *Great Leap Forward.* During that period China experienced a famine on a massive scale with extremely negative effects on the population. Different authors converge on estimates between 26 and 30 million excess deaths during those years. Nearly half of those excess dead were children, whose death rate reached the peak during the first year of the crisis. Not to mention the profoundly negative effects of famine on fertility: in the light of the subsequent drops and recoveries occurred during the period, between 1958 and 1963 the deficit in expected cohort fertility was about 10%. This three-year demographic and human smash-up was only ended when some important measures were taken, among them sending millions of farm-workers back to the countryside. The set of measures passed by the Chinese government in 1963 aiming at birth control, seem to be paradoxical after such a demographic collapse, which had drastically reduced the population. Yet it is understandable taking into account that that they were carried out in the midst of a baby boom as result of post-famine recovery. In particular, abortion was allowed up until the fifth month of pregnancy and actions in support of population containment were intensified, also through the establishment of political organizations devoted to direction and control, along with the mobilization of healthcare workers to promote the use of contraceptive (Sharping 2003).

The Cultural Revolution moved the demographic policies back to the beginning of the 1950s. Health organizations were dismantled and workers persecuted, yet the override of the efforts made until then was rather limited and much more imaginary than real. Since June 1967, for example, during a conference on family planning in Shanghai, it was determined to authorize large large-scale production of those chemicals required in the making of birth-control pills. Moreover, several articles in the leading press pointed to early marriage and 'blind' procreation as relics of the feudal system and—as such—a legacy to fight against.

From these feeble signs the situation soon evolved into a formal recognition of the necessity for a nationwide birth-control policy. By the end of the 1960s, China's *State Council* devoted itself to establish public health units. Later on, the distribution of instruments and knowledge to achieve an effective birth control policy both in the countryside and urban areas took place. That is how the third birth control campaign came into being, made official at the beginning of the 1970s and also proved by the Chinese position at the of *Bucarest Third International Conference on Population*. The meeting didn't take a stand on the establishment of a family planning of any sort, yet China's spokesman stated the importance of a population program to go in accordance with China's five-year economic plans. National debate revived thanks to keywords such as *Planning* (two children per couple), *Rules* (marriageable age limit, for example), *Support* (incentives and benefits). The success of the so-called *wan xi shao* campaign turned out to be significant due to the conjunction with several factors. First, it met an unsatisfied need for contraception mostly designed to reduce childbirth in urban areas and some parts of the countryside. A second reason for their outcome—which indeed testifies the fast decline of fertility in the country—relates to the profound changes motivated by planning: from an individual level (offspring decrease in behalf of women's emancipation and to safeguard both mother and children's health) to a political and community-based one (slowdown in population's growth aiming at development). Mao never acknowledged China's overpopulation and thus any need for control; nonetheless he laid the foundations for compulsoriness, by addressing the issue as follows: family planning is a rational and scientific political action, thus basically socialist and for this reason it must be pursued. That is why he defined family planning as *you jihua shengyu*, which can be translated as 'planned childbirth'. Anchoring birth control to the full achievement of socialism gave demographic matters an ideological mark; doing that, procreation attitudes came to be judged from a political point of view and therefore opposition against family planning became a political crime.

The demographic policies of the 1970s primarily aimed at fertility reduction: the intervention plans in the field of procreation were meant to be similar to the economic ones. The fundamentals of such policies encompassed three basic rules: marry late, plan for births at long intervals, and have few children. The second and third rules could be met by using contraceptives aiming at limiting one's offspring. Postponing marriage has also the effect of limiting the offspring through shortening the reproductive life since only marriage let people to have children (Sharping 2003). The campaign got under way in the country's biggest cities and was indissolubly tied to health. Furthermore, from the 1970s onwards it was associated with territorial goals chiefly related to population growth. The system had planned a sort of birth distribution on a local basis, thus favoring childless couples, then those with an only child and finally the ones with more than one child already. The adhesion to such a system, backed-up of the *One-Child Policy*, was solicited throughout the entire decade, until it became compulsory in the mid-1970s. The results were remarkable: between 1970 and 1980 fertility collapsed to two and a half children per woman, equal to 88% on the scale towards replacement level. Despite these extraordinary performances, at the end of the decade the decline of the population growth rate became even more pressing, due to the approaching of reproductive age of generations born during previous baby-boom periods. Preventive birth control turned out to be a central issue within the debate on development and was thus transformed into even more determinant action when the *One-Child Policy* was established.

After several decades, demography had been restored to good repute. The demographic intervention policy was given ground by a cogent argument: since population is a body of producers, its growth rate should be consistent with both the means of production and the existing development standard in such a society. Hence there emerged the need to put things under control, to plan the population's growth according to clear goals and present the achievements of such goals in conjunction with the economic ones.

Both propaganda and demographic mobilization throughout the 1980s were designed to achieve the following goal: the population's decrease to 1.2 billion within 2000, meant as the halfway mark towards the optimum of 650–700 million to be reached by the end of the 21st century. The framework of birth control policies was to go in accordance with economic planning, local administrative structures, province-based goals, procedures by local authorities and annual balance sheets. Mobilization and propaganda were drawn up alongside within the party organizations and many family-planning cells popped up all over the country. The outcome of the *One-Child Policy* depended on how the system was able to impose its goals onto the population at all levels. Being successful meant that all the couples with more than one child accepted not have more children, while the childless couples agreed to give birth to only child (Farina 2005).

Furthermore, it was established that parents of children who were not first-born ones became liable to sanctions, while benefits and rewards were provided for those who applied for the one-child certificate. The coercive nature of the campaign—much more inadmissible as national politics were taking a turn towards a capitalist economy—brought about two violent clashes between 1980 and 1995, with mainly women being the victim (Greenhalgh 2008).

As far as the number of children was concerned, the expected demand was certainly higher than the one imposed by the *One-Child Policy*; what is more, it was gender-sensitive, which means that while most of the Chinese couples desired to have a boy, only almost half of them could benefit from such an 'advantage'. To bring a girl into the world was regarded as a sacrifice, being not only a sort of break-up in the all along male-mastered ancestral line, but also a profound change in old parents' support, a task which had always been assigned to the son (Attané and Guilmoto 2007). The practice of sex-selective abortion dates back exactly to that time; indeed, it's still widespread and causes the so-called phenomenon of the so-called 'missing girls'. It was only in the mid-1990s that the Chinese government —in order to fight sex-selective abortion—relaxed the *One-Child Policy* and allowed two children if the first child was a girl.

3 Toward Free Choice

The aggressive demographic policies of the 1980s resulted—when compared with the one twenty years earlier—to a completely different demographic situation when Jiang Zemin took over power in China in 1989. Demographic transition was basically over and China's population reached 1.3 billion. While continuing to emphasize the virtuous circle of development, accompanied by the creation of wealth and prosperity, Jiang's rule introduced small changes to China's very rigid demographic policies. A process of pacification thus began, also due to the fact that the majority of the population abided by the rules of the *One-Child Policy* (even if gender selection was still practiced).

It was time for the cautious implementation of the *Cairo Guidelines* adopted in January 2002, the first set of new guidelines after twenty years of rigid Chinese birth control. It places the responsibility for birth control upon local boards and made some basic principles clear; among other, it ratifies the right of repealing the law. Moreover, it reasserts the citizens' right to procreation and their responsibility of birth control. The 2002 guidelines also underline the prize-based nature of the system, which rewards the couples with single children and explicitly forbids the use of sex-checking instruments aimed at sex-selective abortion. It was established that any couple in the reproductive age must consciously use contraceptives and conform to the guidelines and principles of birth control (Pen 1999). Control and guidance on such issues were still strong during the 1990s, yet a change to a biopolitics-based society became evident. In fact, by 1998 the demographic plan was dispelled: quotas were abolished and coordination introduced. Control was indirectly exercised through law and no longer by institutions, while terms like 'coordinated action' and 'sustainable development' entered the Chinese political vocabulary (Jia 2009).

The Chinese authorities introduced terms such as 'quality care' and 'quality services'. Chinese President Hu Jintao stayed on the path of family planning reform, embedded in a legal framework. The most important contribution depended on the changeover in formerly control-oriented demographic policies, and then switched to population. Doing that, issues like aging and the variation in sex ratio at birth were revisited. Public health, reduced poverty and social security were the new catch-phrases of Hu Jintao's social policy. The debate on demographic issues was still heated: many scholars insisted on a nationwide *Two-Child Policy*, some advocated it only in some areas and others warned that abandoning the *One-Child Policy* would be a serious mistake. However, exceptions to the one-child rule became progressively very common until the *One-Child Policy* was formally abandoned in favour of the *Two-Child Policy*. The Chinese government come to this decision progressively. While throughout the year 2014 many signals indicated the arrival of the *Two-Child Policy,* it took the government some time to adopt the policy (Xinhuanet 2016).[1]

Some researchers focused on the consequences of a new wave of births for the country's socioeconomic development. At the present stage, about 90 million couples are eligible for a second child. After the introduction of the new policy, the infant population will increase in the years ahead, expected to reach over 20 million at its peak. Others emphasized that only parts of the eligible couples will apply for permission to give birth to a second child. This position was supported by results in the provinces where the *Two-Child Policy* was adopted earlier: couples asking for permission to have a second child were fewer than expected.

The end the *One-Child Policy* was announced through the Communique of the Fifth Plenary Session of the Communist Party's 18th Central Committee (Xinhuanet 2015). It clearly stated that "China will end its decades-long one child policy, and all married couples will be allowed to have two children." A final plan, however, cementing the policy change will be ratified by the annual session of China's top legislature in March 2015. At that time, the national *Population and*

[1]The policy was adopted in 2015.

Family Planning Policy may be revised to incorporate the new policy as well as the population and family planning regulations promulgated in the last ten years by several provinces. The following month Wang Pei'an, vice minister of *National Health and Family Plan Commission* (*NHFPC*) explained the new *Two-Child Policy* through several questions and answers (NHFPC 2015). She confirmed that China will fully introduce the policy of *one couple, two-children* policy controlling the growth of the total population and optimize the overall national demographic structure. The procedures of having a second child will be simplified and the new *Two-Child Policy* will be applied to all couples. Couples who want a second child should register with the authorities of either the husband or the wife's registered address. A couple eligible to have a second child will still need to follow registration procedures. Spouses who voluntarily choose to have only one child will not be issued with the *One-Child Certificate* and will no longer be eligible for the benefits. Those couples, which already have the certificate will continue to be entitled to all benefits where the regulations apply (NHFPC 2015).

On January of 2016, Chinese Premier Li Keqiang said the *Two-Child Policy* is "a good deed that benefits people's livelihoods and the future" (Xinhuanet). He also asked the authorities to improve policies concerning education, employment, housing and social security to meet the challenges of the new *Two-Child Policy*.

4 Conclusions

Several reasons drive the change of population policy in China nowadays. The past 40 years have seen remarkable achievements with the family planning policy. The demographic transition from high to low mortality and fertility rates is remarkable. In the first phase of transition, between 1950 and 1980, China's population increased by 433 million and from 1980 to the present 300 million more have been added. Population is now about ten times its figure of the 18th century and even the most conservative estimates point to an increase, which will take it to the goal of 1.45 billion in 2030, which will be later followed by a slow decline. The population policies and particularly the *One-Child Policy* created a relatively long period of demographic bonus, providing manpower to long-term economic development. However, the structural population problem is becoming noticeable. The working-age population is dropping while the aging population is climbing. The number of Chinese citizens over sixty years in today's China has reached 132 million and will be 400 million in 2040, 5% of whom will be over 80 years old. By the mid-21st century China will have one of the oldest populations on the planet with a very high old-age-dependency ratio. These figures provide unambiguous evidence of the consequences of China's decade-long '*One-Child Policy*' and explain why a national commission has for some time been active with regard to ageing, working on plans and strategies of social and economical inclusion taking into account the themes of aging and the elderly. The effects of such a change in the population's profile will become more and more evident in the countryside, where a system of public social protection is underdeveloped—once guaranteed by cross generational migration flows. With the population getting older and older, the numerical ratio among generations has been completely twisted.

The only adult son has to take care of both his parents (and at times also of his grandfather) as well as of his wife's parents. What is more, the deep alteration in sex ratio at birth has muddled up the marriage market: between 1980 and 2001 about 25 million boys were born, who won't be able to find a wife in their adulthood. Consequently, they will not be able to find a spouse for a traditional couple, while taking care of their respective parents and grandparents. Another and even serious phenomenon—partly due to coercive demographic policies—is the increase of sex-selective abortion in order to have an only male child. Such a phenomenon is not uncommon in other countries—for example India, South Korea, Taiwan—all of which share (a) a decreasing demand for children, (b) can identify the baby's sex during pregnancy, (c) live in a discriminatory cultural background. The first phenomenon is a result of by the *One-Child Policy*, the second a consequence of modernization and the third a result of culture, customs and traditions.

From the 1980s onwards, birth control strategies in China were taken away from women and handed over the country. Women were then considered responsible for the outcome of the campaign and were defined and described according to the reproductive life cycle they find themselves in. Major abuses of birth control policies continued in rural areas. No longer the protagonists of the Maoist revolution, peasants turned into obstacles to development and a symbol of underdevelopment in China. They found themselves on the lowest step of the country's social pyramid, while women in the countryside would be obliged to become protagonists of what was referred to as *reproductive modernization*. It has been this very approach, which not only dehumanized any demographic policies in the country, but also legitimized the use of force on the eve of the incoming baby booms of the 1980s and 1990s. Girls' mortality rate turned out to be much higher than previously expected, even higher than boys' mortality rate. However, grown-ups girls' health was decisively better than their mothers' had been.

The government, however, reacted: from 2000 onwards, it adopted a program, which would provide economic benefits to parents with an only daughter. In 2006, that programme was extended to all of China with the aim of significantly reducing sex ratio at birth within fifteen years. From 2008 positive results of this policy became visible. The most recent statistics released by the *National Bureau of Statistics* at the beginning of 2016 show a decline of sex ratio at birth to 113.51 males for every 100 females (Women of China 2016). To be sure, many people obtained benefits from the pressing and coercive demographic policies of the past: the planet witnessed a crucial slowdown in its demographic growth. Chinese people in general and the urban population in particular were to benefit from Chinese decade-long economic growth and development: the only child's opportunities are far better than they were in previous generations and also the city-daughters' opportunities are becoming more and more similar to their male coevals' one (NHFPC 2016).

Not everyone got the same share of benefits and indeed, some got none at all. By means of the '*One-Child Policy*', Chinese post-Maoist governments produced two kinds of children: a *good* one—that is, a planned one—and a *bad* one. i.e. the second child. This created two separate worlds for childhood: one world in which an only child may have access to high quality education and facilities. This is the world of boys and girls who are nurturing the popular idea that a generation of *modern* children was brought up. The other world is one that is more harsher and of much lower quality as regards the access to education and other services provided by the state—a world full of mostly women and girls, often moving to towns as illegal aliens or girls who are left behind. These socially invisible people are called *black children* first and, once grown-up, are referred to as *persons*.

In the middle of the 1980s, Boongarts and Greenhalgh (1985) have shown how the implementation of a strict two-child policy over the period of four years would enable China to successfully deal with its demographic transition not much later than the *One-Child Policy* had planned, with a better-balanced structure as for age and gender and a slightly bigger population. Thirty years later the Chinese government is taking the road towards a two-child policy. We will know only in the future if this option will be successful in demographic terms, and especially if it is coming too late for changing the desire of the Chinese people to have children.

References

Attané I, Guilmoto CZ (2007) Watering the neighbour's garden. Cicred and Ined, Paris

Banister J (1987) China's changing population. Stanford University Press, Stanford

Bielenstein H (1987) Chinese historical demography A.D. 2-1982. Bull Museum Far East Antiquities, Stockhol 59

Boongarts J, Greenhalgh S (1985) An alternative to the one-child policy. Popul Dev Rev 4:585–617

Coale AJ (1984) Rapid Population change in China, 1952–1982. National Academic Press, Washington D.C

Farina P (2005) Le politiche di controllo delle nascite. In: Scarpari M, Lippiello T (eds) Caro Maestro. Ca Foscarina, Venice, pp 505–518

Gernet J (1978) Il mondo cinese. Einaudi, Torino

Greenhalgh S, Winckler EA (2005) Governing China's population. From Leninist to Neoliberal biopolitics. Stanford University Press, Stanford

Greenhalgh S (2008) Just one child: science and policy in Deng's China. University of California Press, Oakland

Ho P (1959) Studies on the population of China, 1368–1953. Harward University Press, Harward. http://news.xinhuanet.com/english/2016-01/07/c_134988103.htm. Accessed 10 Feb 2016

http://news.xinhuanet.com/english/2016-01/07/c_134988103.htm. Accessed 10 Feb 2016

Jia Z (2009) 20 shijie 50 niandaihou woguo jumin shengyu yiyuan de bianhua. Renkou Yu Jingji 4:24–28

Ma Y (2002) Xinrenkou lun, Beijing: Zhongguo renkou chubanshe

NHFPC (National Health and Family Planning Commission) (2015) Q&A about the new two-child policy. http://en.nhfpc.gov.cn/2015-11/06/content_22390244.htm. Accessed 10 Feb 2016

NHFPC (National Health and Family Planning Commission) (2016) Success factors for women's and children's health, http://www.who.int/pmnch/knowledge/publications/china_country_report.pdf?ua=. Accessed 10 Feb 2016
Pen G (1999) Guanyu Zhongguo Jihua Shengyu lifa de taolun. Renkou yanjiu 3:25–37
Peng X (1991) Demographic transition in China. Clarendon Press, Oxford
People's Daily (1952) Birth control may bust China up, 24 January 1952
Poston DL et al. (eds) (2006) Fertility, family planning and population control in China. Routledge Studies in Asia's Transformations, Routledge, Oxford
Sharping T (2003) Birth control in China 1949–2000: population policy and demographic development. Routledge Publisher, New York
Women of China (2016) China sees drop in birth sex ratio for the 7th running. http://www.womenofchina.cn/womenofchina/html1/features/1601/1610-1.htm. Accessed 10 Feb 2016
Xinhuanet (2015) Zhongguo Gongchandang Di Shiba Jie Zhongyang Weiyuanhui Di Wu Ci Quanti Huiyi Gongbao, http://news.xinhuanet.com/politics/2015-10/29/c_1116983078.htm. Accessed 10 Feb 2016
Xinhuanet (2016) Li Keqiang urges sound implementation of two-child policy. http://news.xinhuanet.com/english/2016-01/07/c_134988103.htm
Zhao W, Xia S (1988) Zhongguo renkou shi. Renmin chubanshe, Beijing

The Chinese Banking and Financial System: A Fast-Paced Evolution Journey

Guido Masella

Abstract The author, former Financial Attaché at the Italian Embassy of the People's Republic of China (PRC) in Beijing, analyzes the structure and evolution of the Chinese banking and financial systems since the adoption of China's economic reforms in the late 1970s. Furthermore, the chapter examines the system's persistent 'command' approach, analyzes the quality and problems of the supervisory and regulatory frameworks and assesses the challenges ahead for financial stability. Moreover, the chapter provides a brief overview of the non-banking segments of the financial market and the more flexible non-bank financial operators. The chapter concludes with an assessment of the state and prospects of the internationalization of the Chinese currency.

1 Introduction. Structure and Recent History of the Chinese Banking System

The Chinese financial system underwent a major transformation in the last two decades, moving at a much higher pace than in other emerging economies (or even advanced economies, for that matter; Elliot and Yan 2013). Back in the 1980s, the banking system—for instance—was operated directly by the People's Bank of China (the central bank), whose branches across the countries were offering basic financial intermediation services to an equally basic real economy. A small number of large, state-owned banking groups were created in the 1990s with the idea of differentiating the services by target sector of the economy rather than to foster competition. By the turn of the millennium, those banks accumulated such a huge amount of defaulted loans that a massive re-haul of the system was needed: each of the four major banking groups was split in two halves, a performing and a non-performing one; the troubled assets were dislocated into 'asset management companies', bad banks supposed to dispose of the bad loans over a relatively long period of time.

G. Masella (✉)
Rome, Italy
e-mail: masellaguido@gmail.com

S. Beretta et al. (eds.), *Understanding China Today*, Understanding China,
DOI 10.1007/978-3-319-29625-8_13

It was in the second half of last decade that both the largest and the so-called 'second-tier' banks boosted their internal organisation and upgraded their business model to become fully-fledged 'universal banks' in the way we understand in the West. It was the time of strategic minority investments by major foreign groups and of the listing on domestic and international stock markets.

The number of banking institutions in the Chinese market exceeds 3,000 (People's Bank of China 2016), but that includes all sort of small banks operating in the vast countryside (rural commercial banks, rural credit cooperatives and village banks). Not considering these, there were less than 200 banks active at the end of 2015 (Table 1).

The five major credit institutions (Industrial and Commercial Bank of China, China Construction Bank, Bank of China, Agricultural Bank of China and Bank of Communications) are still largely state-owned corporations with wide retail presence across China, a growing foreign network and a universal bank business model. Their combined share of the banking market fell, over a couple of decades, from over 60% to the current (2015) 39%, a relatively moderate degree of concentration.

Behind these five, are a dozen so-called "second-tier" banks, which are mid-sized institutions with branches in every provincial capital and in most of the other important urban centers, but with limited or no overseas reach. Also in this case, ownership is mostly concentrated either in central government or in provincial governments, with some notable exceptions.

Local banks existed in most of the major cities, generally owned by the municipal government of the city they were headquartered in. These were called "city commercial banks", but this category[1] has become less standardized in the last decade or so, when many of these institutions underwent either a consolidation process or a transformation into joint-stock companies, opening up to private sector minority shareholders.

A fourth and very important category of banks is the one represented by the three so-called 'policy banks', large bodies not operating in retail banking but generally funding themselves on the bond market and contributing to the development of the real economy by financing specific compartments (China Development Bank is mostly active in infrastructure projects, China Export Import Bank in foreign trade and the Agricultural Development Bank of China in sustaining the modernization of the immense rural countryside). These institutions have an extremely important role in the Chinese financial sector and are usually chaired by pre-eminent figures of the political spectrum.[2] Two of the three banks recently (2015) received a capital injection in excess of 90 billion US dollars, directly from the foreign exchange reserves, in order to further strengthen their capability to deliver adequate support to key strategic projects.

With the exception of the policy banks, it was common to the three other segments the phenomenon of foreign strategic investment, which took place mostly

[1] 133 banks at the end of 2015 (source: People's Bank of China 2016).

[2] The three Chairmen have the title of Governor and are equivalent, in the ranking of Chinese officials, to the Governor of the central bank.

Table 1 Main categories of banks in the Chinese banking system

	Total asset 2015 (RMB bn)
Large Commercial Banks	98,839
Joint-Stock Commercial Banks	46,375
City Commercial Banks	38,662
Rural Credit Cooperatives	8,595
Foreign Financial Institutions	2,768
Other	3,917
System total	199,156

Source People's Bank of China (2016)

in the first decade of the new millennium. Interest from major international financial institutions was conveyed in a frenzy of minority stake acquisitions, targeting not only the big five banks but also the second-tier ones and selected minor entities operating in what were deemed to be promising local markets (major urban areas all across the country, eastern and southern coastal areas in general). Foreign ownership of a Chinese banking institution is limited to 25% of equity, but no single foreign investor can own more than 20% of the capital. In most cases, the investment was carried out by a single investor fulfilling the 20% quota, but for the three main institutions (ICBC, BOC, Bank of China) consortiums were formed amongst two or three different groups of different nationalities.

The sealing of a deal with foreign strategic investors shortly preceded the big step of "going public". Between 2005 and 2010 all the major banks got listed on either the Shanghai or the Hong Kong stock markets, in some cases on both. This process meant the start of a privatization process, albeit in all instances the state maintained control (i.e. the quota of shares issued on the market ranged from 20 to 30% of the total). Considerable amounts of new capital were raised to fund the ensuing growth and the banks came overnight under the spotlight of global investors, with positive effects in terms of transparency and organizational change. The reliability of listed banks' statements and of their accounting standards in general improved considerably, especially for banks listed on the Hong Kong stock exchange, whose reporting and transparency requirements have been in line with those of its Western peers for decades.[3] Boards' structure has also been enhanced with the inclusion of independent Members (Table 2).

The expansion of the banking industry in the following years was three-fold: traditional lending activity kept on growing at a very high pace, while banks also started developing new product to offer to their retail, corporate and—most of all—private customers. The major banks were finally engaged in a strong internationalization effort, having both size and resources to confront themselves with foreign markets.

[3]Nowadays, the Shanghai Stock Exchange also aligned its standards to the most common international practices by the way.

Table 2 Time and size of listings by the main Chinese banks

Bank	Shanghai		Hong Kong		Total raised
	Date	Raised (USD mn)	Date	Raised (USD mn)	
ICBC	27 Oct 2006	5,904	27 Oct 2006	16,049	21,953
Bank of China	5 Jul 2007	2,491	1 Jun 2006	11,115	13,606
China Construction Bank	19 Sep 2007	7,600	27 Oct 2005	9,177	16,777
Agricultural Bank of China	13 Aug 2010	10,000	13 Aug 2010	12,100	22,100
Bank of Communications	15 May 2007	3,277	23 Jun 2005	3,277	5,154
China Merchants Bank[a]			22 Sep 2006	2,412	2,412
CITIC Bank	27 Apr 2007	1,717	27 Apr 2007	1,717	5,387
Industrial Bank	5 Feb 2007	2,070			2,070

Source Bank Reports, official press releases
[a]China Merchants Bank was listed on the Shanghai Stock Exchange already in 2001

At the end of 2015, the Chinese banking sector's total asset reached the amount of 200 trillion renminbi (around 28 trillion euro at the 2015 average RMB/EUR exchange rate). Loans have kept growing at a two-digit rate for the last 10 years, reaching 100 trillion renminbi on an aggregate basis at the end of 2015, i.e. in excess of 150% of China's Gross Domestic Product for the same year. The banking channel is largely dominant in the financing of the real economy and, while capital markets funding sources are on the rise, bank loans still represented over 73% of new financing aggregates in 2015.

The growth of disposable income in the urban middle class allowed for the formation of a class of affluent customers, sparkling the creation of a more and more articulated offer of wealth management products. The main banks started opening overseas branches in the major currency areas of China's trade partners (United States, Europe, United Kingdom, Australia, Japan and Korea), while a few selected acquisitions took place in more peripheral, but still strategic, markets.[4]

Direct presence of foreign banks in the Chinese retail banking market is still very marginal and generally limited to a small number of global banking groups with a strong focus on Asia (HSBC, Standard Chartered, Citigroup) or to Asian players (headquartered in Hong Kong, Singapore, Japan or Korea).

[4]As an example, Industrial and Commercial Bank of China acquired significant minority shares in leading South African and Indonesian banks.

2 The Supervisory and Regulatory Framework and the Challenges Ahead for Financial Stability

The supervisory framework was extremely basic until the creation of the China Banking Regulatory Commission and its sister authorities for markets and insurance in 2003,[5] as a spin-off from the Central Bank (People's Bank of China), which remains the ultimate body responsible for setting guidelines and ensuring the overall financial stability. In a phase of fast economic growth, the initial focus of the authorities was mainly put on the volume of credit in the system. The main tool has traditionally been—and still is, to some extent—the mandatory reserve ratio, adjusted on a frequent basis and generally in small increments.[6] Rather than forcing banks to create a wide enough cushion able to protect them from credit risk in times of macroeconomic downturn, the reserve ratio was actually used as a monetary policy tool, out of concern that too rapid growth of available credit could overheat the economy.

The very idea of capital adequacy was almost non-existent until formal capital requirements were introduced in 2006. Since then, regulation has been brought in line, with a certain lag, with international standards, including the full implementation of the Basel III framework.[7] China is stably participating to the work of both the Financial Stability Board and the Basel Committee on Banking Supervision. Recent reviews of the domestic regulation have been focusing on leverage ratios and on liquidity management.

The liquidity position of the Chinese banking system is still being considered comfortable by the authorities, even if a trend has been observed of increasing the share of less stable and reliable sources of funding (especially interbank liabilities, particularly high in some of the smaller banks). Another area of concern is represented by the strong growth of off-balance sheet activities, which surpassed 40% of the on-balance sheet ones in 2015.[8]

Non-performing loans were hampering growth and profitability of Chinese banks at the turning of the millennium, when the Ministry of Finance and the People's Bank jointly created an agency, Central Huijin Investments, which acted in the following years to help banks solving the issue of poor credit quality. On one hand, Huijin proceeded to directly re-capitalize a significant number of banks while on the other it funded four special-purpose entities (called Asset Management Companies, AMC) which in turn acted as bad banks for the four major credit

---

[5]China Securities Regulatory Commission (CSRC) and China Insurance Regulatory Commission (CIRC).

[6]The RRR (Reserve Requirement Ratio) has been cut five times during 2015 for example, even if a single cut during the whole 2016, might be signaling a shift to a new paradigm, a combination of moral suasion and self-regulating market mechanisms.

[7]At the end of 2015, the capital position of Chinese banks was quite satisfactory: on an aggregate basis, the capital adequacy ratio was 13.45%, with the core tier-1 component touching almost 11%.

[8]A growth of almost 25% in that year.

institutions in the Country, buying the dubious credit and subsequently managing the recovery of residual assets.

By 2005, NPL ratios at most banks were brought down to a very comfortable level (around 1% of outstanding loans) and stayed under control for roughly a decade. Only very recently (since 2014 onwards) there have been signs of an increase in delinquency rates, which is kept under tight check by the supervision authority.[9] A mitigating factor is the high level of provisioning[10] the banks have been able to undertake in many years of sound profitability.

A general lack of risk management culture (especially credit risk) has been stemming by the perception that the state-owned nature of almost all banks might have implied an implicit guarantee by the government against any possible default. This assumption was reinforced by the absence of a formal deposit insurance system until May 2015, when a pilot scheme was introduced. Since then, all deposit-taking institutions have been required to pay premium to the deposit insurance regime, meaning that depositors' protection is now ensured by a mechanism driven by market participants rather than by expectation of State intervention.

A very peculiar feature of the Chinese banking system is the interest rates formation. The People's Bank normally imposes ranges within which banks are free to set active and passive rates actually applied to the customers for the different credit and deposit facilities. These ranges are what actually determine the market rates, rather than a mark-up on refinancing rates as it happens in western economies. Talks of a full liberalization of interest rates have been going on for a decade now, and the above-mentioned ranges widened considerably during the last few years, but the first concrete step was only taken in October 2015 with the outright removal of the upper limit on deposit rates. From the banks' point of view, strict control of interest rates (both active and passive) has translated in relatively subsided competition and in a pretty good stability of profits, since net interest margins still represent by far the largest component of banks' revenues (57% at the end of 2015 (J.P. Morgan Asset Management 2015)).

Looking at the Chinese banking system from a distance, an area of concern has always been the difficulty of recognizing the lending decisions as purely commercial ones or rather politically-inspired ones. This topic is quite tightly linked to the role of the Communist Party in the banks' management and the selection and appointment of key organizational figures. It is still perfectly visible that almost all the major institutions have a seat in the board reserved for a Party representative, and if that is not the case, Party-appointed figures sit in important committees. As for the top executives, it's difficult to imagine a scenario where appointments are made independently from—let alone against—the will or the appreciation of the Party. Two-way moves between Government positions and banks' Boards are far

[9]The NPL ratio at the end of 2015 was 1.94%, but the 'special-mention' loans (credit positions that are still "performing" but under various degree of stress) increate more dramatically, reaching 4.7% of the total loan book.

[10]Well in excess of 100%, while the Italian banking system—for example—is struggling to reach 50% on average.

from uncommon. On the other hand, increasing exposure of the Chinese major banks to the global financial markets ensured over the time that most of the senior managers were and are selected because of their proven results in the industry.

3 Brief Overview of the Non-banking Segments of the Financial Market

The Chinese bond market is still relatively small compared to the size of the economy (48 trillion renminbi of outstanding bonds at the end of 2015, roughly 70% of GDP), and is dominated by the government sector and (state-owned) banks, as corporate issues were traditionally marginal and enjoyed limited liquidity even in the secondary market. Until 2010, issue of corporate bonds was almost discouraged by a series of inter-locking regulations which made largely preferable, even for large companies, to resort to the banking channel for funding. Regulation has been streamlined since then and in the last few years issuing activity finally surged in this segment as well.

The stock market consists of two separate exchanges, in Shanghai and Shenzhen, with a characterization which is partly geographical (firms from the northern half of the country tend to be listed in Shanghai while the south-based ones ten to get listed in Shenzhen) and partly a specialization issue, with large conglomerates mostly listed in Shanghai while smaller and more innovative firms preferably listed in Shenzhen. Stocks experienced a spectacular growth in the 10 years between the Asian crisis of 1997 and the global financial crisis of 2007–2008. Since then, development has been more subsided, in line with other markets in the region. At the end of 2015, there were over 2,800 listed companies, for a total market capitalization of 53 trillion renminbi (i.e. just over a quarter of the banking system's total asset, or half of the outstanding bank loans[11]). The Chinese stock market has been traditionally exposed to a higher than average incidence of 'bump and bust' cycles, either in selected individual shares or in groups of shares, with the phenomenon originating both in a relative 'financial illiteracy' of the investors community as well as in the nature of the listed companies, mostly State-owned corporations with very unpredictable—at best—dividend policy. On one hand, the presence and size of institutional investors is limited compared to other markets and (sometimes emotional or purely speculative) decisions by groups of individual investors still play a very important role in determining share price dynamics. On the other hand, these individual investors are incapable, but largely not even in the position, of applying valuation criteria based on fundamental analysis elements such as dividend policies, for example. It is a fact that state-owned corporations are very resistant to distribute cash dividends, and the average dividend ratio of

[11]Also, the amount of new financing raised on the stock market in 2015 via initial public offerings or secondary offerings was just 7% of the amount of new bank loans in the same year.

Chinese listed companies is well below that of other markets.[12] Participation of foreign investors is strictly regulated via the Qualified Foreign Institutional Investor scheme (QFII), under which the applicants (they need to be primary financial institutions both in size and continuity of operation) are assigned a maximum investment quota. Since inception of the scheme back in 2002, over 200 foreign financial institutions applied, and their combined investment quota was standing at 80 billion US dollars at the end of 2015, around 1% of the stock market capitalization.[13]

The mutual fund industry has undergone an enormous development since the late 1990s albeit probably not to its full potential yet. Total asset under management at the end of 2015 were in the area of 8.4 trillion renminbi, a mere 12.5% of the GDP. The rate of expansion was spectacular during the 'golden age' of Chinese stock market (2003–2007) while in the 2008–2012 period a lacklustre performance of the exchanges, as well as the chronic lack of institutional investors, brought the growth to a halt. Some signs of renewed vigour have been observed in the last couple of years but the market remains a very speculative one, considering a still high quota of equity and hybrid instruments. The competition amongst the 101 fund management companies is particularly stiff, and there's probably room for some degree of industry consolidation in the years to come. Banks are the largely dominant distribution channel, to an extent that significantly compresses profitability margins at the fund manager level.

A segment of financial markets probably unique to the Chinese environment is the trust industry. Trusts are a special category of asset managers, who mainly invest assets of wealthy individuals or corporations in a range of different activities, normally implying a higher risk/reward profile when compared to ordinary mutual funds (i.e. real estate, infrastructure projects, local government bonds, bank loans portfolios). Their combined assets (16 trillion renminbi) were comparable, in size, with the fund management compartment, but growing at a much higher pace during the last few years.[14] The authorities are closely following developments in the sector, last but not least because of the implicit opacity existing between the trusts and the local governments they provide finance to, as a good number of the 68 trusts active at the end of 2015 are directly or indirectly controlled by municipal or provincial governments.

Finally, a feature of the Chinese financial system is the presence of a large enough volume of financial activity carried out by institutions, which do not belong to any of the licensed category of players. These are usually groups of people or wealthy families operating as fully-fledged banks within their local community and channeling funds (sometimes at competitive, sometimes at punitive conditions)

[12]While the S&P 500 average ratio has traditionally been in excess of 50%, the Shanghai Stock Exchange is struggling to maintain a 30% threshold amongst its listed companies.

[13]It is understood, of course, that foreign investors can freely acquire shares of those Chinese companies that are listed on the Hong Kong stock exchange or other overseas exchanges (i.e. NASDAQ), building up that way their exposure to China.

[14]The assets under management actually tripled during the last five years.

to small businesses, which wouldn't normally have easy access to official credit. The authorities' approach towards this grey area of the financial system has obviously been steered towards a crackdown of the phenomenon, even if it cannot be denied that these informal banks play at times a positive role from a distributional perspective.

4 The Internationalization of the Currency

The Chinese government has attached great importance to the process of internationalization of the domestic currency, the renminbi. And the process has certainly come a long way since the 2005 lifting of the peg with the US dollar. The use of the renminbi in the settlement of foreign trade has grown dramatically in recent years and the Chinese currency was the third-most used in this field at the end of 2015, consistently with the consolidation of China's position among the leading countries in international trade.[15] There is a strong incentive for importers of Chinese goods to settle their trades in renminbi, as this can improve considerably the pricing and other conditions.

Several partner countries were granted the status of offshore renminbi centers, allowing renminbi transactions to take place outside the Chinese territory and financial institutions based in those centers to channel investments on the Chinese domestic markets (so-called Renminbi Qualified Foreign Institutional Investors, RQFII).

Issues of renminbi-denominated bonds took place in a number of these offshore centers (Luxemburg is trying to develop an edge in this respect) and primary issuers, even sovereign, showed big interest.[16]

As of today, the renminbi is the fifth-most traded currency on the global foreign exchange market, with clearing and settlement provided by one of the main Chinese commercial banks, appointed by the People's Bank for every individual jurisdiction.

In this context, the decision of the International Monetary Fund to include the renminbi, alongside the other four main international currencies (US dollar, euro, yen and British pound). in the basket for the Special Drawing Rights at the November 2015 review was only logical.

[15]The 2015 increment alone in renminbi cross-border payments registered in China was 22% (SWIFT data).

[16]United Kingdom was the first country to issue sovereign bonds denominated in renminbi already in 2014.

References

Elliot D, Yan K (2013) The Chinese financial system: an introduction and overview. John L. Thornton China Center, Brookings Institution
J.P. Morgan Asset Management (2015) The Path to Interest Rate Liberalization, China
People's Bank of China (2016) Financial stability report 2016

Chinese Multinationals in Europe

Vito Amendolagine, Alessia Amighini and Roberta Rabellotti

Abstract Since 2013, China is the third largest foreign investor in the world and Europe is a major destination for Chinese investing firms, especially the largest European economies where the great majority of their investments are concentrated. In this chapter, we provide a comprehensive map of Chinese Foreign Direct Investments (FDI) in Europe, taking into account their distribution by country, sector, entry-mode and business activity. The empirical analysis relies on firm-level data compiled from diverse data sources on *greenfield* investments and Merger & Acquisitions (M&As). We show that Chinese FDI in Europe are very concentrated in a few host countries and in a few sectors, namely automotive, communications, electronics, machinery and engines.

1 Introduction

After being the largest recipient of foreign direct investments (FDI) among developing countries for more than two decades, China has become an important outbound investor, especially since the so-called *Go Global Strategy* was launched in 1999, as an effort by the Chinese government to promote investments abroad. The Government, together with the China Council for the Promotion of International Trade (CCPIT), introduced several schemes to assist domestic companies in

V. Amendolagine · R. Rabellotti (✉)
Department of Political and Social Sciences, University of Pavia, Pavia, Italy
e-mail: roberta.rabellotti@unipv.it

V. Amendolagine
e-mail: vito.amendolagine@unipv.it

A. Amighini
Department of Economics and Business Studies,
University of Piemonte Orientale, Novara, Italy
e-mail: alessia.amighini@uniupo.it

A. Amighini
Istituto per gli Studi di Politica Internazionale (ISPI), Milan, Italy

S. Beretta et al. (eds.), *Understanding China Today*, Understanding China,
DOI 10.1007/978-3-319-29625-8_14

developing a global strategy to exploit opportunities for expanding in international markets. Since then, Chinese companies, especially State Owned Enterprises (SOEs) and mostly large companies, but increasingly also medium-sized ones, have invested overseas to diversify their assets and location portfolios. In the following years, especially since 2006, China has accelerated its outward expansion through FDI, and in 2013 it has become the third largest foreign investor in the world, while remaining a top destination for global investments (the largest outside of the OECD) (UNCTAD 2015). In particular, in 2014 China's outstanding investment stock amounted to around 730 billion US$, which is around 3% of all outward FDI in the world (UNCTAD 2015). In terms of destinations, the largest share of Chinese FDI stock is located in Hong Kong (58%) and, overall, 84% of the entire stock is directed to other developing countries (in particular, South-East Asia, 5% and Sub-Saharan Africa, 3%). Among the destinations in advanced economies, the EU (6%) and the US (3%) are among the top ones; besides, it is worth adding that FDI stocks directed to Europe have increased by around 77 times from 2003 to 2012, an increase that is much higher if compared with the US, where Chinese FDI have increased by 47 times (UNCTAD 2014).

In this chapter, we rely on firm-level data on investment deals by Chinese firms, with the aim to provide an updated picture of Chinese outward FDI patterns in Europe. In Sect. 2, we introduce our data sources and in Sect. 3 we present a map of Chinese investments in Europe by sector, country and entry-mode. With a focus on greenfield investments, Sect. 4 offers a description of the distribution of Chinese FDI along the value chain of the recipient sectors. In Sect. 5, we shift our attention to acquisitions describing some notable cases. Section 6 concludes with some policy implications.

2 Data Sources

This chapter relies on data at the level of deals and firms for mapping the presence of Chinese investors in Europe by sector and country. This represents an advantage with respect to most of the existing studies based either on aggregate FDI data from the Balance of Payments or on official FDI data from the Chinese Ministry of Commerce (MOFCOM) (among others, see Buckley et al. 2007; Kolstad and Wiig 2012).[1] Our data come from different sources. Information on Chinese greenfield investments to EU-27—in the time-span 2003–2014—are from *FDI Markets* (Financial Times Group), which is a deal-based database reporting all cross-border investments resulting in a wholly-owned subsidiary covering all sectors and

[1]FDI data provided by MOFCOM are based on officially approved investments. Despite recent data improvements and the formal commitment by MOFCOM to comply with international standards, there are still some concerns about their reliability and within the research community there is broad consensus that there are problems of underestimation. For a detailed analysis of these methodological problems see Amighini et al. (2014).

countries worldwide. *FDI Markets* collects data through media sources and companies' websites. For each investment, it provides details about the name and the location of the investor, the year of the deal, the sector, the main business activity undertaken with the project and the location where the investment takes place (in terms of country, region and city).

Merger & Acquisitions (M&A) are obtained from two different sources. The first one is *Zephyr* (Bureau van Dijk's—BvD) and the second is *SDC Platinum* (Thomson Reuter).[2] On M&A, we do have various data and information (coming from different sources, such as press releases and companies' websites), among them the name and the location of the acquirer and the target company, the status of the deal (i.e. 'completed', 'rumor', 'pending'), the percentage of the ownership transferred from the target to the investor and the date of the project. In the current analysis, we have taken into account all the 'completed' deals by Chinese acquirers of European targets within the time-span 2003–2014.

For the period from 2003 to 2011, the data about greenfield and acquisitions have been matched and harmonized at the firm-level (both investors and target companies), including information about the ownership structure, the location of domestic and foreign subsidiaries, the sector of economic activity, the consolidated and unconsolidated balance indicators, some firm size variables, the names and types of shareholders, and the patenting activity. All these additional variables have been sourced by the database *Orbis*, published by Bureau van Dijk.

It is useful to add that our unit of analysis is the number of deals, which is more appropriate than the value of the investment when investigating the location strategies of multinationals because the choice of a specific country might be largely independent of the (initial) amount of capital invested. Moreover, the investment size varies widely across sectors, with resource-intensive industries showing higher average investment size than consumer goods sectors or services. This is the main reason why several empirical studies have chosen the number of deals (and not the investment size) as their unit of analysis (among others see Crescenzi et al. 2013; Amighini et al. 2013; Amighini and Franco 2013; Ramasamy et al. 2012).

3 An Overview of Chinese Greenfield FDI and M&A in the EU-27

Figure 1 shows the geographical distribution of Chinese FDI in the EU-27. Between 2003 and 2014, the countries receiving the largest number of investments are Germany, United Kingdom France, Netherlands Italy and Spain. These countries account for almost 76% of the total of Chinese investments in Europe. Other important destinations are Hungary, Ireland, Poland, Romania and Sweden.

[2]41% of the deals n EMENDATA is both in *Zephyr* and *SDC Platinum*, 28% are only reported in *Zephyr* and 31% are only in *SDC Platinum*.

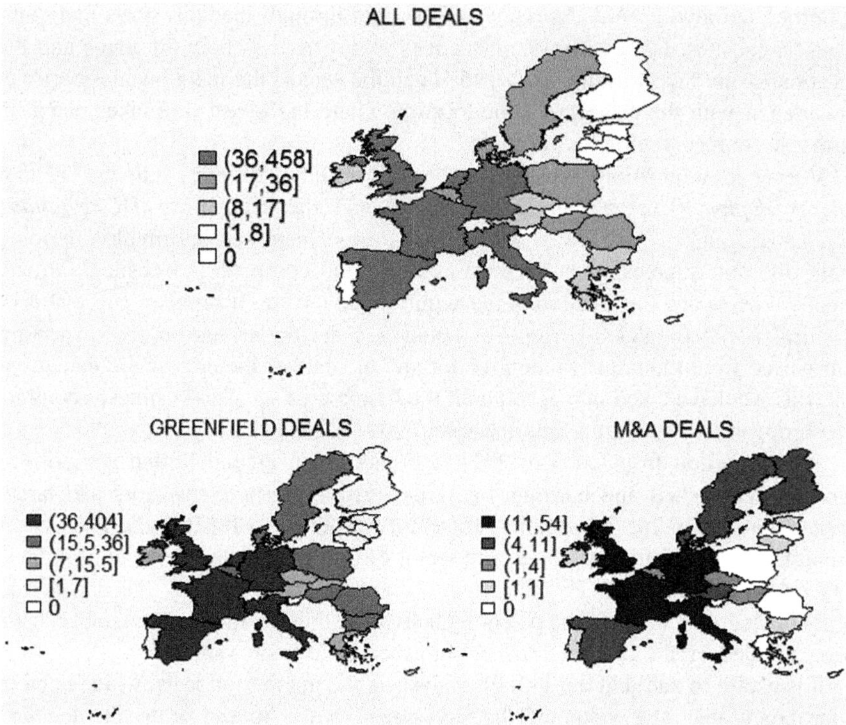

Fig. 1 The geography of Chinese investments in the EU-27 (2003–2014). *Data source* FDI markets and BvD Zephir

Interesting differences emerge when comparing the geography of investments according to their entry mode. Greenfield deals are more widespread across the EU27 countries, also locating besides the top six countries, in Central and Eastern Europe (mainly in Bulgaria, Hungary, Poland and Romania). Instead, M&A are much more concentrated in the EU 'core' as well as in some Northern European EU member states (i.e. Finland and Sweden).

Table 1 provides a snapshot of the top destination countries. Within the time period 2003–2014, Germany is by far the top destination of Chinese investments, receiving 37% of total investments (458 deals): 39% of greenfield projects (404 deals) and 26% of M&A (54 deals). The United Kingdom follows at a certain distance with less than half of the investments directed to Germany (202) but, at the same time, a number of M&A that is only slightly lower than Chinese M&A in Germany (41). The other European countries receiving a large number of investments form China are France (104), Netherlands (66), Italy (57) and Spain (49).

Table 1 Top destinations in the EU-27 (# of deals and %)

	M&A (%)	Greenfield (%)	Total (%)
Germany	54 (26.3)	404 (39.3)	458 (37.1)
United Kingdom	41 (20)	161 (15.6)	202 (16.3)
France	27 (13.2)	77 (7.5)	104 (8.4)
Netherlands	24 (11.7)	42 (4.1)	66 (5.3)
Italy	16 (7.8)	41 (4)	57 (4.6)
Spain	6 (2.9)	43 (4.2)	49 (4)
Total above	168 (82)	768 (74.6)	936 (75.8)
Total EU-27	205 (100)	1029 (100)	1234 (100)

Data source FDI markets and BvD Zephir

Fig. 2 Chinese FDI to the EU-27 (2003–2014). *Data source* FDI markets and BvD Zephir

In general, the *greenfield* entry mode is by far the most preferred, reaching 83% of the total investments (1029 out of 1234). However, as shown in Fig. 2 considering time trends, greenfield investments have been increasing up to 2011 and, then, started decreasing while Chinese M&A have been increasing throughout the considered period, although at a slower pace.

Table 2 Top destination sectors in the EU-27 (# deals and %) (2003–2011)

Sector	M&A (%)	Green (%)	Tot. (%)
Electronics	14 (8.3)	114 (16.9)	128 (15.2)
Machinery and engines	35 (20.8)	79 (11.7)	114 (13.6)
Communications	0 (0.0)	97 (14.4)	97 (11.5)
Automotive	13 (7.7)	49 (7.2)	62 (7.4)
All sectors	168 (100)	673 (100)	841 (100)

Data source Our elaborations on FDI markets and BvD Zephir

Table 3 Investments in top destination sectors within top destination countries (#deals and %) (2003–2011)

	France	Germany	Italy	Netherlands	Spain	UK	Total
Automotive	0 (0.0)	19 (12.7)	8 (29.6)	3 (21.4)	0 (0.0)	16 (34.8)	46 (16.7)
Communications	12 (48.0)	17 (11.4)	8 (29.6)	4 (28.6)	5 (35.7)	16 (34.8)	62 (22.6)
Electronics	4 (16.0)	45 (30.3)	9 (33.3)	4 (28.6)	9 (64.3)	5 (10.9)	76 (27.6)
Machinery and engines	9 (36.0)	68 (45.6)	2 (7.5)	3 (21.4)	0 (0.0)	9 (19.5)	91 (33.1)
Total	25 (100)	149 (100)	27 (100)	14 (100)	14 (100)	46 (100)	275 (100)

Data source Our elaborations on FDI Markets and BvD Zephir

Extending our descriptive analysis to sector- and investor-level details across the different entry modes, for the period 2003–2011, Table 2 shows that Chinese FDI in Europe are very concentrated not only in terms of destination countries (as seen in Table 1), but also of target sectors. In particular, almost half of the Chinese investments (47.7%) is directed to only four industrial sectors: electronics (128 deals), machinery and engines (114), communications (97) and automotive (62). Moreover, the machinery and engines sector hosts the largest number of M&A (35, i.e. 20.8%), while Electronics and Communications sectors receive the largest amounts of greenfield-type FDI (114 and 97, respectively).

Table 3 shows the distribution of Chinese FDI across the top destination sectors within the main EU destination countries, showing a very concentrated pattern. Machinery & Engines sector receives the largest shares of Chinese investments in Germany and the UK (45.6 and 33.1% of total investments, respectively); in Italy and Spain the most targeted sector is Electronics (33.3 and 64.3%, respectively); finally, Communications is the top destination sector in France (48%) and in the Netherlands (along with Electronics with 28.6%).

Turning to top investors, Table 4 list the six investing companies with more than 10 deals, which undertake around 16% of all Chinese FDI in the EU-27. Investors relying on complex entry mode strategies (i.e. both greenfield and M&A) belong to the capital and knowledge intensive manufacturing sectors, such as automotive (SAIC), chemicals (ChemChina, China National Chemical), and energy (Suntech Power Holdings). Besides, investors in the service sector (ICBC) and the electronics industry (Huawei and ZTE) only rely on the greenfield entry mode.

Table 4 Top investors (# deals and %) (2003–2011)

Company	M&A (%)	Green (%)	Total (%)
Huawei Technologies	0 (0.0)	52 (7.7)	52 (6.2)
ZTE	0 (0.0)	24 (3.5)	24 (2.8)
China National Chemical	9 (5.3)	13 (1.9)	22 (2.6)
Industrial and Commercial Bank of China (ICBC)	0 (0.0)	15 (2.2)	15 (1.8)
Shanghai Automotive Industry Corporation (SAIC)	3 (1.8)	8 (1.2)	11 (1.3)
Suntech Power Holdings	1 (0.6)	9 (1.3)	10 (1.2)
All investors	168 (100)	673 (100)	841 (100)

Data source Our elaborations on FDI markets and BvD Zephir

4 Greenfield Investments by Business Activity

As reported in Sect. 2, the *FDI Markets* database provides information about 18 specific business activities carried out by each deal. This information makes it possible to locate investments along the value chain and following Crescenzi et al. (2013), we have associated each business activity to one of the following value chain stages: Headquarters (HQ), Innovative Activities (INNOVATION), Commercial Activities (SALES), Logistic and Distribution Activities (LOG & DIST), and Manufacturing Activities (MANUFACTURING).

Figure 3 shows that the majority of Chinese greenfield investments in the EU-27 between 2003 and 2014 follows commercial purposes (47.7%) as long as they are

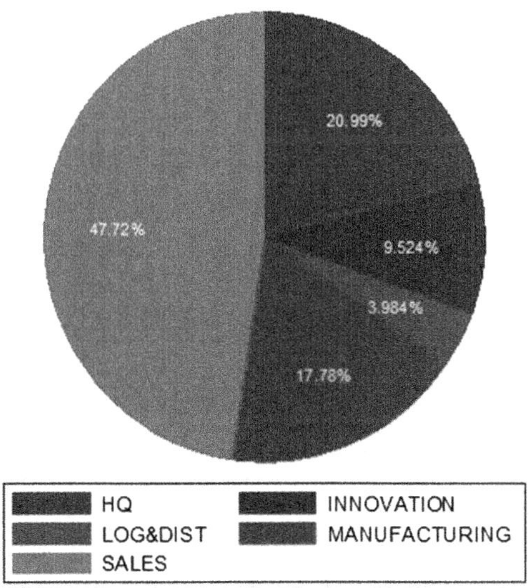

Fig. 3 Distribution of investments along the value chain (2003–2014). *Data source* FDI markets and BvD Zephir

connected to Sales, Marketing and Retail activities. Headquarters and Manufacturing activities are also important, as they represent respectively, 21 and 17.8% of all activities. Finally, innovative activities (i.e. R&D, Design, Development and Testing, Training), along with Logistic and Distribution activities currently represent a smaller share of Chinese investments (respectively, 9.5 and 4%).

Figure 4 presents the trend of the different business activities. Interestingly, commercial activities have been decreasing over the last years, while investments associated with higher value added activities, such as strategic and innovative activities, have been—albeit slowly—increasing. Furthermore, deals related to manufacturing activities also follow an upward trend.

Finally, the geography of Chinese investments in the EU-27 seems to differ according to the business activities undertaken (Fig. 5). In particular, while commercial activities are more homogeneously spread over European countries, higher value-added activities (HQ and INNOVATION are more concentrated in the EU 'core' destinations, such as France, Germany, Italy, Netherlands and UK). Interestingly, the map of greenfield-type investments associated with innovative activities is almost overlapping with that of M&A-type investments (Fig. 1) and this might suggest that the M&A entry mode is more likely to be chosen for asset-seeking purposes (Amendolagine et al. 2015). Finally, manufacturing

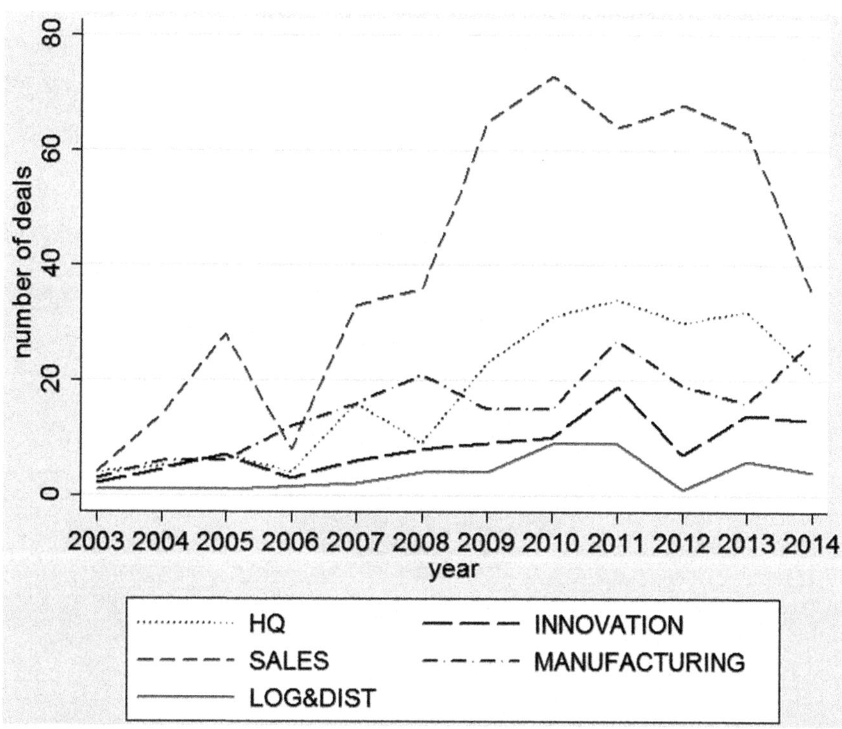

Fig. 4 Investments over time along the value chain. *Data source* FDI markets and BvD Zephir

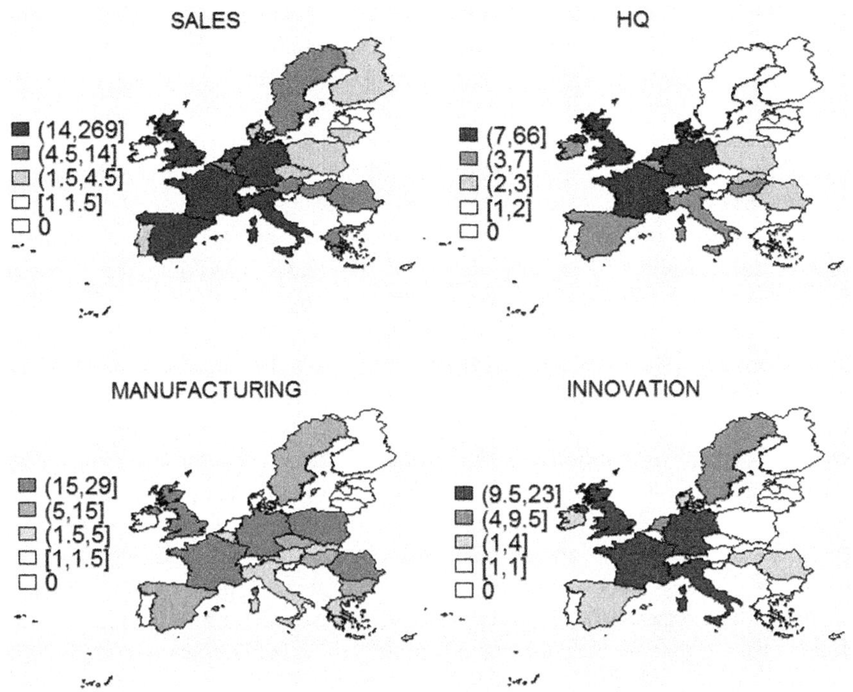

Fig. 5 Map of Chinese investments in EU27 by value chain stage (2003–2014). *Data source* FDI markets and BvD Zephir

activities are mostly associated to investments undertaken not only in some EU 'core' countries, such as France, Germany and UK, but also in some lower labor cost economies in the Eastern part of the EU (i.e. Poland and Romania), following closer the distribution of greenfield investments.

5 Some M&A Cases

As shown in Fig. 3, although most of Chinese FDI in the EU-27 are greenfield investments, the number of M&A deals has been almost constantly increasing since 2003. Indeed, acquisitions are crucial in terms of catch-up strategies as long as they can lead to rapidly developing new skills and competencies and, further, to organizational and technological learning (Vermeulen and Barkema 2001; Piscitello et al. 2014). There is significant empirical evidence pointing to a tendency by Chinese companies—particularly within high-tech industries—to acquire firms located in advanced countries with the main aim at accessing technologically advanced assets, which are a scarce resource at home (Amendolagine et al. 2015; Zhou et al. 2014).

However, in order to fully exploit the knowledge-relative assets embedded in the target companies, acquirers need to develop their own absorptive capacity (Buckley et al. 2014; Deng 2010; Wu et al. 2016; Zheng et al. 2016). A case in point is the acquisition of the French Thomson's TV business by the Chinese company TCL in 2004. This is a clear example of how complex and painful international acquisitions can be. In fact, in 2006, just two years after the deal, TCL reported a cumulative loss of US$680 million. The motives of such a failure were several: first, TCL lacked a proper financial and competitive plan at the moment of the acquisition; second, the acquirer was also deficient in terms capability to 'absorb' knowledge-relative assets from the target company, mostly because Chinese managers had poor international experience and expertise in global marketing; and finally, the cultural distance resulted to be a big issue to face as long as the Chinese management had to deal with local managers and workers accustomed to different rules and routines (Deng 2010). The takeover of the Italian motorbike producer Benelli by Qianjiang Group (QJ), one of the top Chinese state-owned enterprises and the largest Chinese motorcycles producer, is another interesting case dating back to 2005 and is analyzed by Spigarelli et al. (2012). With this acquisition, QJ was targeting the technology necessary to produce more energy saving and environmental friendly motorbikes, following the general plan of the Chinese Government to reduce CO_2 emissions. However, several issues hindered the integration process with the Italian company, among them communication problems in the technical area, big cultural differences in terms of laws and rules and, particularly, a business strategy focusing more on short-term goals (i.e. reducing costs) than on long-run objectives.

Another interesting case is the Delta Group, a Chinese supplier of biomass boiler and power plants, which acquired two world-leading biomass technology companies in Denmark between 2007 and 2009 (Hansen et al. 2014). It has also faced integration problems and difficulties in developing innovative capabilities, notwithstanding a strong political support, given that the development of a biomass energy sector was also aimed at increasing Chinese rural farmers' income by offering them the opportunity to supply agriculture biomass waste to power plants. The Delta Group has benefitted from its acquisitions in terms of product, process and functional upgrading, thanks to the knowledge transfer of processes and more advanced control procedures. However, the ability to manage the acquired knowledge resources resulted to be quite limited and, therefore, the technological catch-up has not yet been achieved.

The successful example of the Volvo takeover by Geely in 2010 shows that Chinese companies are learning from their previous mistakes and are taking advantage of the experience accumulated. Geely is among the top ten automobile producers in China and one of the top 500 Chinese companies (Fetscherin and Beuttenmuller 2012). After some experience in international cross-border acquisitions (in 2006 it acquired the British Manganese Bronze Holdings, London's leading taxi company and in 2009 the Australian auto parts maker Drivetrain Systems International), Geely undertook the largest Chinese acquisition of a foreign carmaker, by taking over 100% of Volvo from Ford Motor Company for

US$1.8 billion. After the acquisition, Geely has increased profits and sales volume and has been able to upgrade the quality of its cars in terms of safety, energy efficiency and environmental protection. Furthermore, it has filled about 1200 patents (30 of which have been granted out of China (Fetscherin and Beuttenmuller 2012).

It is still early to draw conclusions, but we expect that Chinese companies will be increasingly more careful in choosing their targets and will improve their acquisition strategies, relying on the so called light touch approach, therefore leaving a lot of autonomy to their acquired firms in the immediate post-acquisition phase (Liu and Woywode 2013; Zheng et al. 2016). Indeed, some of the last Chinese deals in Europe, such as the acquisition of the 143-year-old Italian company Pirelli, one of the largest tire makers worldwide, and that of Syngenta, a big Swiss maker of seeds and pesticides, both by ChemChina, show that Chinese multinationals are becoming more sophisticated and hands off with their acquisitions (The Economist 2016).[3]

6 Conclusions

In this chapter we have mapped the patterns of Chinese FDI in Europe with firm-level data. Our analysis shows that Chinese FDI in Europe are very concentrated on a few host countries (the largest European economies), which account for the majority of Chinese investments to the continent. Moreover, Chinese investments in Europe are concentrated in a few sectors, namely automotive, communications, electronics, machinery and engines. Interestingly, while the majority of investments has so far aimed at servicing European markets through sales by foreign subsidiaries, producing in Europe is an increasing relevant activity for Chinese multinationals. Central and Eastern Europe is an important destination for greenfield investment for manufacturing purposes, which suggest that intra-regional differences in the business environment and factor advantages are relevant elements driving the location choices of Chinese investors (Crescenzi et al. 2016).

An increasingly important motivation for Chinese investments is the acquisition of strategic assets, which is taking place through greenfield investments and increasingly through acquisitions. There is evidence showing that buying knowledge and technology are complex activities that require strong absorptive capacity and there are also signals that Chinese multinational are rapidly learning how to be successful in their asset seeking acquisitions.

Policy makers in advanced countries will need to come to grips with finding ways to ensure that these acquisitions are equally beneficial and asset-augmenting for the taken over firms and for the regions where they are located, especially when their technological assets are of strategic value for the countries they belong to. They should try to minimize the probability of predatory behaviors and attract investors

[3]Better than barbarians, The Economist, January 16th 2016.

interested in embedding in the local contexts where their acquired companies are located (Giuliani et al. 2014). Acquisitions and the arrival of new entrepreneurial forces from emerging countries may open up opportunities for advanced host country managers and entrepreneurs to learn from the new investors, which could be exploited to bridge the cultural and market distance with emerging economies.

References

Amighini A, Franco C (2013) A sector perspective on Chinese outward FDI: the automotive case. China Econ Rev 27:148–161

Amighini A et al (2013) Do Chinese state-owned and private enterprises differ in their internationalization strategies? China Econ Rev 27:312–325

Amighini A et al (2014) Chinese outward FDI: what can be done with firm-level data? China World Econ 22:44–63

Amendolagine V et al (2015) Chinese and Indian multinationals: a firm-level analysis of their investments in Europe. Glob Econ Rev 44:452–469

Buckley PJ et al (2007) The determinants of Chinese outward foreign direct investment. J Int Bus Stud 38:499–518

Buckley PJ et al (2014) Acquisitions by emerging market multinationals: implications for firm performance. J World Bus 49:611–632

Crescenzi R et al (2013) Innovation drivers, value chains and the geography of multinational corporations in Europe. J Econ Geogr 14:1053–1086

Crescenzi R et al (2016) Regional strategic assets and the location strategies of emerging countries' multinationals in Europe. Eur Plan Stud 24:645–667

Deng P (2010) What determines performance of cross-border M&A by Chinese companies? An absorptive capacity perspective. Thunderbird Int Bus Rev 52:509–524

Fetscherin M, Beuttenmuller P (2012) Geely's internationalization and Volvo's acquisition. In: Alon I et al (eds) Chinese international investments. Palgrave MacMillan, New York, pp 376–390

Giuliani E et al (2014) Emerging versus advanced country MNEs investing in Europe: a typology of subsidiary global–local connections. Int Bus Rev 23:680–691

Hansen U et al (2014) Upgrading to lead firm position via international acquisition: learning from the global biomass power plant industry. J Econ Geogr 1:1–23

Kolstad I, Wiig A (2012) What determines chinese outward FDI? J World Bus 47:26–34

Liu Y, Woywode M (2013) Light-touch integration of Chinese cross-border M&A: THE INflUENCES OF CULTURE AND ABSORPTIVE CAPACITY. Thunderbird Int Bus Rev 55:469–483

Piscitello L et al (2014) Chinese and Indian acquisitions in Europe: the relationship between motivation and entry mode choice. In: Risberg A et al (eds) The Routledge companion to merger and acquisition. Routledge, London, pp 114–129

Ramasamy B et al (2012) China's outward foreign direct investment: location choice and firm ownership. J World Bus 47:17–25

Spigarelli F et al (2012) Benelli and QJ compete in the international motorbike Arena. In: Alon I et al (eds) Chinese international investments. Palgrave MacMillan, New York, pp 355–375

UNCTAD (2014) Bilateral FDI statistics 2014. United Nations Conference on Trade and Development, Geneva

UNCTAD (2015) World investment report 2015: reforming international investment governance. United Nations Conference on Trade and Development, Geneva

Vermeulen F, Barkema HG (2001) Learning through acquisitions. Acad Manag J 44:457–476

Wu JS et al (2016) Internationalization and innovation performance of emerging market enterprises: the role of host-country institutional development. J World Bus 51:251–263

Zheng N et al (2016) In search of strategic assets through cross-border merger and acquisitions: evidence from Chinese multinational enterprises in developed economies. Int Bus Rev 25: 177–186

Zhou C et al (2014) The internationalization of Chinese industries: overseas acquisition activity in Chinese mining and manufacturing industries. Asian Bus Manag 13:89–116

Sustainability and Law-Assessing: The New 'Green Rules' for Foreign Companies Doing Business in China

Marina Timoteo

Abstract In recent years China has become a key protagonist in the discourse on sustainability, a discourse that goes well beyond environmental concerns. The growing stress on sustainability has had wide effects on the ongoing reforms of China's legal systems, leading to the drafting of new rules in several legal fields and the shaping or re-shaping of legal institutions affecting the implementation of these new rules. These developments have also led to several relevant transformations of the legal framework within which foreign businesses operate, such as the publication of a fundamental regulatory document establishing Chinese government priorities for foreign investment: the so-called Catalogue for the Guidance of Foreign Investment Industries. This chapter will analyse some of these transformations, focusing on the issue of legal incentives for foreign investors' sustainable investments.

1 Introduction

The concept of sustainable development, one of the key words of the discourse on growth and development[1] of the last few decades, reached China in the middle of significant economic and structural reforms, which continue to have an important

[1]The concept of sustainable development has been on the forefront since 1987, when the World Commission on the Environment and Development, commissioned by a General Assembly Resolution and chaired by Gro Harlem Brundtland, issued a report entitled 'Our Common Future' also known as the 'Brundtland Report'. This document defined sustainable development as a "Development that meets present needs without compromising the ability of future generations to meet their own needs." The concept was reaffirmed in the United Nations 1992 'Declaration on Environment and Development' and then inspired the 2002 World Summit on Sustainable Development in Johannesburg. In the more recent 'Rio + 20 Declaration' 'The Future we Want', issued at the end of the 2012 United Nations Conference on Sustainable Development, the commitment to sustainable development was renewed.

M. Timoteo (✉)
School of Law, Alma Mater Studiorum, University of Bologna, Bologna, Italy
e-mail: marina.timoteo@unibo.it

S. Beretta et al. (eds.), *Understanding China Today*, Understanding China,
DOI 10.1007/978-3-319-29625-8_15

impact on global economic dynamics. Using the technique of semantic loans[2] (Cao 2004, p. 94) the concept has been translated into Chinese with the expression kechixu fazhan (可持续发展) where the second part, made by the compound *fazhan* (发展) has the univocal meaning of 'development', while the first part, which means 'sustainable', composed of the three characters kechixu (可持续) literally meaning 'what can be continued'. In this way greater emphasis is given to the idea of ongoing development (Morgan 2011). The language expresses the intrinsic ambiguity of the concept that, since its introduction has been criticized for its vagueness and elusiveness (Pesqueux 2009, pp. 231–245). With particular reference to China, the concept embodies the typical developmental dilemma of a country where rapid economic growth has gone hand in hand with a very dramatic rise of pollution and environmental degradation. This dilemma, that also characterized the processes of economic development experienced in the past by other countries such as the United States, Japan, and the United Kingdom, has assumed exceptional dimensions in China against the background of unprecedented economic growth and rapidly increasing Chinese global influence on trade and manufacturing processes (Wang 2006, p 198).

Thus, China has over recent years become a central protagonist of the discourse on sustainability, a discourse that goes well beyond environmental concerns. Indeed, following the principles put forward in the aforementioned international documents, in recent years the discourse on sustainability has been connected with the more inclusive idea that "A truly sustainable society is one where wider questions of social needs and welfare, and economic opportunity are integrally connected to environmental concerns" (Agyeman et al. 2002, pp. 77–90).

The need to steer the Chinese economy into a new phase, towards more sustainable growth was clearly outlined in Beijing's 'Twelfth Five-Year Plan', covering 2011–2015, whose key themes were, in the perspective of a new stage of 'inclusive growth' and 'ecological civilization', rebalancing the economy, ameliorating the social inequality and protecting the environment (Hilton et al. 2011, pp. 5–12).

The growing emphasis on sustainability has had wide-ranging effects on China's currently ongoing legal reforms, leading to the drafting of new rules in several legal fields—first of all environmental protection, torts, corporate social responsibility—and the shaping or re-shaping of legal institutions affecting the implementation of these new rules, such as environmental public participation and environmental courts (Wang 2013, pp. 365–440).

These developments have also led to several important transformations in the legal framework in which foreign businesses operate, starting from the fundamental regulatory document establishing Chinese government priorities for foreign investment, i.e. the 'Catalogue for the Guidance of Foreign Investment Industries.'

---

[2]The technique of semantic loans is still widely used since it was introduced into the Chinese language, through the creation of neologisms, concepts and expressions deriving from foreign and international legal and political language.

This chapter will seek to analyse these transformations, focusing on legal incentives for foreign investors' sustainable.

2 The Catalogue for the Guidance of Foreign Investment Industries

One of the key expressions of China's economic development since the very beginning of the reforms was 'Foreign Direct Investments' (FDIs) which describes investment by foreign enterprises and economic organizations or individuals (including overseas Chinese residents of Hong Kong, Macao, and Taiwan, and Chinese enterprises registered overseas) through one of the available business vehicles: representative offices, solely foreign-funded enterprises (known as 'Wholly 'Foreign-Owned Enterprises' or 'WFOEs') (which are limited liability companies[3]), joint-ventures—either Sino-Foreign Equity Joint Ventures (EJVs), or Sino-Foreign Cooperative Joint Ventures (CJVs), which are almost always limited liability companies, projects to co-develop resources with any enterprises or economic organizations within Chinese territory in the form of spot exchange, real object, or technology (including re-investment of income from foreign investment) as well as the actions of any enterprises borrowing funds from overseas within the total amount of project investment approved by relevant government authorities (Lubman 2006).

Since the beginning of China's economic reforms in the late 1970s, attracting foreign capital has been a key source for funding fixed assets in China and an important way for the country to participate in economic globalization. Since the beginning of enacting China's economic reforms 35 years ago, however, the massive influx of FDI into China had a significant impact on the environment, which resulted in qualitative changes of incoming FDI. Four stages of FDIs fluxes into China can be listed in this context[4]: in the first stage, that was marked by the 1978 'Law of the People's Republic of China on Chinese Foreign Equity Joint Ventures', foreign investments were still on a small scale, with a limited impact on the environment. The following stage, covering the period from 1986 to 1995, was characterized by the acceleration of China's so-called 'Open Door Policy' and the rapid growth of foreign investments in manufacturing, chemical, and other pollution-intensive industries. In the following decade the average scale of foreign investment continued to expand. The industrial structure of foreign investment was further adjusted and foreign investment in high-tech, infrastructure, and other sectors increased substantially. The environmental impact of foreign investment

[3]This is the most common form of business vehicle used by foreign investors, particularly if no foreign-ownership restrictions apply to the relevant industry.

[4]For an analysis of these stages see the 2012 report of the China Council for International Cooperation on Environment and Development.

attracted more and more attention and led to a new FDI deal that was marked by a new Chinese development strategy, more attentive to the social costs of growth, in the name of building a 'harmonious society.' This new strategy started with the '11th Five-Year Plan for National Economic and Social Development' (2006–2010),[5] which introduced the issue of climate change, qihou bianhua (气候变化) and was further implemented by the '12th Five-Year Plan' (2011–2015), promulgated on 16, March 2011[6] (Hilton et al. 2011, p. 13 ff.).

This plan, where sustainability became a key focus of development, was based on the concept of 'inclusive growth', and identified seven so-called 'strategic emerging industries' (SEIs), to be promoted in the five years implementation period. Out of these seven strategic industries, three strictly belong to the sector of 'green industries' (new energy industry, new energy auto industry and energy saving and environmental protection industry), while the others (biology industry, high-end equipment manufacturing industry, new materials industry and new generation information technology) are closely connected with them (Wang 2006, 2013, pp. 365–440).

The guidelines of the plan were subsequently specified in China's '12th Five-year Development Plan for National Strategic Emerging Industries', No. 28, issued by China's State Council on July 9, 2012 and in 'The Catalogue for the Guidance of Foreign Investment Industries'[7] (Yao 2012). The catalogue, which reflects Chinese government priorities for foreign investment, classified industries into three broad categories, the industries in which foreign investment is either (a) 'encouraged (b) 'restricted' or (c) 'prohibited.'[8]

The previous 2007 review had already included as part of the investment projects encouraged those for the treatment of solid waste and those implying reduced emission rate, as well as projects related to the production of alternative energy sources, tools for measuring the quality of air, water, and facilities for the prevention and control of water pollution. With the revision of December 2011 the scope of the encouraged green investments section has been expanded, including: manufacturing of equipment for the production of renewable energy, production of

[5]'Zhonghua renmin goingheguo guomin jingji he shehui fazhan di shiyi ge wunianguihua gangyao' [People's Republic of China 11th Five-Year for National Economic and Social Development]. It is important to remember that since 2006, the official name of the 'Five Year Plan' was changed: from the former jihua 'plan', originally deriving from the Soviet Union planning model, to guihua, 'program', reflecting the transformation from a straightforward list of economic objectives to a more general guideline for both economic and social policy goals.

[6]'Zhonghua renmin goingheguo guomin jingji he shehui fazhan di shi'er ge wunianguihua gangyao' [People's Republic of China 12th Five-Year for National Economic and Social Development].

[7]Chinese/Pinyin: Waishang touzi chanye zhidao mulu.

[8]Projects not listed in the Catalogue are generally classified as permitted.

energy saving, environmental-friendly construction materials pollution control equipment, key components for the development of fuel-efficient vehicles and for the construction of stations battery charging, the production of instruments with high energy efficiency and reducing emissions in the textile industry, and the production technology for water purification.

On 10 March 2015, the 'Catalogue for the Guidance of Foreign Investment Industries' was again revised,[9] in order to accommodate the new national demand for foreign capital. While the scope of permissible foreign investments in the new catalogue was further, greatly, expanded,[10] the new catalogue aims also at encouraging more foreign business to get involved into the environment-protection and energy-saving industries[11] (Qin 2015).

The policy of attracting foreign investments flowing into green developments industries, was confirmed in China's '13th Five Years Plan for Economic and Social Development',[12] according to which innovation and sustainable development will still be among the key priorities for China in the next five years. The new plan's target and policies will continue to strengthen China's efforts to shift to a more sustainable model of growth, at least judging by the details that will be provided by the follow-on specific plans that are scheduled to be released in the near future.

---

[9]Waishang touzi chanye zhidao mulu (2015 nian xiuding) ('Catalogue for the Guidance of Foreign Investment Industries, Amended in 2015'), promulgated by the National Development and Reform Commission (NDRC) and the Ministry of Commerce, Decree No. 22, 10 March 2015. This new catalogue went into force on 10 April 2015. While in the 2011 catalogue, there was a list of 43 industries that could only be organized in the form of 'Sino-Foreign Joint-Ventures', such restrictions have been reduced to 15 industries in the new catalogue. It is plausible that this change promoted more foreign investments flowing into environment-friendly industries. For instance, in the previous catalogue, the manufacturing of large pumped-storage aggregates with the conventional power of 350 MW was limited to joint-ventures. Today, this restriction has been removed. It is plausible to assume that foreign capital would be incentivized to flow into this sector, and meanwhile, advanced environment-protection and energy-saving technologies might be introduced.

[10]According to statistics, 41 items under the former 'restricted category' industry were cancelled in the 2015 catalogue.

[11]Foreign investment, as pointed out by the spokesman of China's Commerce Ministry, shall be further incentivized in the environment-protection and energy-saving industries in order to help China to upgrade its economic structure promoting the establishment of an ecologically 'harmonious society'.

[12]The plan has been approved on 16 March 2016, following the Communist Party of China's draft suggestions, enacted last December, in which 'Promoting green manufacturing and lifestyle' has been emphasized as the basic idea and object in the process of next five-years development. See 'Zhonghua renmin gongheguo guomin jingji he shehui fazhan di shi san ge wunianguihua de jianyi' [Suggestions on China's 13th five-year national social and economic development], the state-owned Xinhua Net News Agency was authorized to promulgate this document.

3 The System of Tax Incentives to Encourage Green FDIs

The Chinese legislator has provided a general framework of promoting measures to encourage and support the environmental industries, starting from article 21 of the 'Environmental Protection Law' which states that the state adopts policies and measures in terms of fiscal assistance, taxation, prices and government procurement. Other specific environmental statutes stipulate analogous provisions. For example, the 'Energy Conservation Law' devotes an entire chapter (Chap. 5) to incentivize measures; particularly, the law specifies that the state adopts taxes or other policies in order to promote: energy conservation technologies and products listed in the popularization catalogue[13]; the paid use system of energy and mineral resources, and the conservation of energy resources;[14] the importing of advanced energy conservation technologies and equipment.[15] Moreover, Chap. 5 of the 'Circular Economy Promotion Law' recognises tax benefits for industrial activities promoting the development of circular economy,[16] and requires enterprises to opt for recycled products and energy-saving, water-saving, material-saving, environment-friendly products in the case of purchases sponsored with public funds.[17]

[13]Art. 61 of the Zhonghua renmin gongheguo jieyue nengyuan fa [Energy Conservation Law of the People's Republic of China]. Art. 58 stipulates that "The department in charge of energy conservation under the State Council shall, in conjunction with the relevant departments under the same, compile and publish a catalogue of energy-saving technologies and products for popularization, guide the energy consumers in adopting advanced energy-saving technologies and products". Promulgated by the 8th National People's Congress Standing Committee, 1 Nov 1997, and amended by the 28th Meeting of the Standing Committee of the 10th National People's Congress, 28 Oct 2007.

[14]Art. 62 of the Zhonghua renmin gongheguo jieyue nengyuan fa [Energy Conservation Law of the People's Republic of China]. Promulgated by the 8th National People's Congress Standing Committee, 1 Nov 1997, and amended by the 28th Meeting of the Standing Committee of the 10th National People's Congress, 28 Oct 2007.

[15]Art. 63 of the Zhonghua renmin gongheguo jieyue nengyuan fa [Energy Conservation Law of the People's Republic of China]. Promulgated by the 8th National People's Congress Standing Committee, 1 Nov 1997, and amended by the 28th Meeting of the Standing Committee of the 10th National People's Congress, 28 Oct 2007.

[16]Art. 44 of the Zhonghua renmin gongheguo xunhuan jingji cujin fa [Circular Economy Promotion Law of the People's Republic of China]. Promulgated by the 4th Session of the 11th National People's Congress, 29 Aug 2008.

[17]Art. 47 of the Zhonghua renmin gongheguo xunhuan jingji cujin fa [Circular Economy Promotion Law of the People's Republic of China]. Promulgated by the 4th Session of the 11th National People's Congress, 29 Aug 2008.

As for FDIs, in the range of the advantages that are related to the so-called 'encouraged investments' (including from expedited approvals and registrations[18]), tax relief measures, implemented at both national and local levels, have traditionally been the most relevant. The Chinese government in the tax reform of 2008, where it has, in principle, eliminated the system of preferential treatment for non-Chinese companies, provided a series of fiscal measures and subsidies for FDI projects that use green technologies. The 2008 'Enterprises Income Tax Law' and related regulations[19] have introduced the 'three-plus-three' formula for companies that adopt policies and use advanced technology to ensure energy saving and water saving conservation projects, and for companies that develop environmental projection projects and so-called 'Clean Development Mechanism' projects. The revenues earned by the aforementioned green projects[20] are eligible for a three-year exemption and three-year 50% reduction in corporate income taxes, beginning from the year in which the taxpayer earns his first amount of revenue from such projects (EIT Regulation, arts. 87 and 88). Also eligible for this tax incentive is investment in and operation of infrastructure projects which significant support of the state, including electric power and water conservancy projects.

The 'Enterprise Income Tax Law' and its implementing regulations provide other tax incentives to a number of areas in the green sector, including purchases of environmental protection, conservation equipment and comprehensive use of resources (EIT Law, 33 and EIT Regulations, art. 99): "Where an enterprise purchases and actually utilizes any of the special-purpose equipment related to environmental protection, energy and water conservation and work safety, 10% of the investment in the special-purpose equipment may be offset against its tax payable for the current year. Where the tax payable is insufficient for the credit, the excess may be carried forward for credit in the following five taxable years. Where an enterprise uses any of the materials listed in the Catalogue of Income Tax

[18]The incorporation of a 'Foreign Investment Enterprise' takes place on the issuance of a business license by the local Administration of Industry and Commerce. Prior to this, the applicant needs the approval from the Ministry of Commerce or its local counterpart, depending on, among other things, the amount of investment that is to be made in the company. Projects categorized as 'encouraged' face relatively less scrutiny while those categorized as 'restricted' are subject to stringent requirements and examination.

[19]Zhonghua renmin gongheguo qiye suodeshui fa [Enterprise Income Tax Law of the People's Republic of China], promulgated by the 5th Session of the 10th National People's Congress, 16 March 2007 (hereinafter referred to as 'EIT Law'); Zhonghua renmin gongheguo qiye suodeshui fa shishi tiaoli [Implementation Regulations of Enterprise Income Tax Law of the People's Republic of China] promulgated by Decree No. 512 of the State Council on December 6, 2007, effective January 1, 2008 (hereinafter referred to as 'EIT Regulations').

[20]The projects mentioned in the text could include technological innovations with respect to energy conservation and emission reduction, comprehensive exploitation and utilization of methane, as well as public sewage treatment, public garbage treatment and sea-water desalination.

Concessions for Enterprises Engaged in Comprehensive Resource Utilization as its major raw materials, the income it obtains shall be included in the total income at the reduced rate of 90%."[21]

Many enterprises engaging in activities in the green sector are considered high and new technology enterprises and receive several types of tax incentives, including: (a) a reduced tax rate of 15% (EIT Law, art. 28); (b) the exemption of income from transfer of technology (EIT Law, art. 27); (c) a 50% super deduction for research and development expenses (EIT Law, art. 30 and EIT Regulations, art. 95); (d) accelerated depreciation (EIT Law, art. 32 and EIT Regulation, art. 98). If a venture capital enterprise invests in a shareholdings of a private small or medium size new and high-tech enterprise by stock for two years or more, 70% of the amount of the investment is deductible against the taxable income. The deductions can be carried over to the following tax year (EIT Law, art. 31 and EIT Regulations, art. 97).

Reductions in corporate income tax can be linked to specific industries, such as the energy saving service industry: effective January 1, 2011, income earned by qualified energy-saving service companies engaging in energy management contracting projects is temporarily exempted from business tax. When an energy-saving service company transfers its taxable goods from qualified energy management contracting projects to energy consuming enterprises, the generated value-added will be temporarily exempted. Such companies are also eligible for the EIT three-year exemption plus three and a half years reduction scheme.[22]

Tax incentives also operate with respect to VAT exemption or reduction measures. Since December 2008, products and services making a so-called 'comprehensive utilization of resources' through the utilization of waste as production inputs or energy-efficient processing, such as green building materials, combined heat and power pollutions, and reclaimed waste-water have been eligible for VAT exclusion.[23]

4 The Introduction of Credit Incentives to Encourage 'Environmental-Friendly' Investments

Credit policy is an emerging instrument, used by the Chinese government to encourage foreign investment to invest into the environment-protection and energy-saving sectors. Such policy, commonly referred to as 'Green Credit Policy', requires the financial institutions to take enterprises' environmental behavior into account when extending loans. Enterprises which promote the protection of the environment, receive credit privileges, while those ones employing less

[21]See China Briefing (2011a).

[22]See the Circular Caishui 2010/10 in China Tax Regulation Update.

[23]See China Briefing (2011b).

environment-friendly production processes or even violating environment encounter difficulties in applying for credit.

In July 2007, the State Environment Protection Administration (SEPA),[24] the People's Bank of China (PBOC) and the China Banking Regulatory Commission (CBRC) jointly promulgated China's green credit regulation: 'Opinions on Implementing Environmental policies and Preventing Credit Risk.'[25] This regulation provided basic principles for financial institutions to implement the green credit policy, in which it is clearly stipulated that financial institutions are encouraged to grant credit to projects and enterprises which operate within the framework of the so-called 'encouraged industry' of the catalogue, while they shall not provide funds to the newly-initiated projects falling into the category of 'restricted' or 'prohibited industries' according to the national industry strategy.[26] Therefore, as regards foreign direct investment (FDI), those investments promoting environment protection or energy saving have easier access to credit from China's financial institutions.

In order to reinforce the implementation of the aforementioned 'opinions', the CBRC enacted a specific regulation, the 'Notice on Issuing Green Credit Guidelines', in 2012,[27] in which several important rules were stipulated: inter alia, the financial institutions are required to establish a so-called 'client list management system' on the basis of their clients' environmental behavior.[28] Article 11 of these guideline reads: "Banking institutions shall develop client environmental and social risk assessment criteria, dynamically assess and classify client environment risks, and consider the results as important basis for credit rating, access, management. Banking institutions shall prepare a list of clients currently faced with major environmental and social risks, and take risk mitigation actions."[29] Following this rule, many banks established their own client list according to the criteria of potential environmental risk. For example, the Industrial and Commercial Bank of China divided its clients into four groups in the green information based client list, namely the group of 'environment-friendly', 'qualified', 'under-observation and 'to-be-rectified' enterprises. Within each group, according to the score of environment assessment, enterprises would be further classified into three additional categories (Yin 2013, p. 7).

---

[24]The SEPA now has in 2008 been upgraded into the Ministry of Environmental Protection (MEP).

[25]Guanyu luoshi huanbao zhengce fagui fangfan xindai fengxian de yijian [Opinions on Implementing Environmental policies and Preventing Credit Risk], promulgated by the SEPA, PBOC and CBRC, Decree No. 108, 2007.

[26]Ibid

[27]Zhongguo yinjianhui guanyu yinfa lvse xindai zhiyin de tongzhi [Notice on Issuing Green Credit Guidelines], enacted by the China Banking Regulatory Commission, on 24 February 2012.

[28]Ibid.

[29]Zhongguo yinjianhui guanyu yinfa lvse xindai zhiyin de tongzhi [Notice on Issuing Green Credit Guidelines], Article 11.

Following these initiatives, several domestic and foreign-capital banks also actively promoted their own environmental-friendly credit policies, such as the Bank of East Asia which launched a 'Recruitment and Selection of Green Credit Program' to promote its green business model. Standard Chartered Bank issued a green credit policy system, which especially targets small and medium-size enterprises[30] (Marquis et al. 2011, p. 54). Moreover, many foreign banks, such as ABN Amro, Deutsche Bank, and HSBC, supported targets for a 'low carbon economy' and developed new financial products addressing climate change, thereby taking advantage of the carbon trading system.

5 Conclusions

The creation of a system of incentives to favour FDIs increasingly aiming towards a 'green approach' is a part of a set of legal reforms for the implementation of sustainable development objectives. This new legal framework in the making marks an overcoming of the command-and-control approach that China has traditionally followed to deal with environmental issues and which relied on a combination of regulations prescribing standards and limits to be complied with. In order to achieve the new goals of a more sustainable process of growth, China has started to introduce market-based instruments, including incentives and awards that not only help achieving the goals set forth in regulations but also encourage the adoption of green technologies on a voluntary basis and encourage companies to take part in a process of awareness about possible paths of development and environmental concerns (Orts 2003, 558 ff.). Therefore, today, an integrated regulatory approach is pursued in order to favour more sustainable development, an approach based on a combination of traditional command-and-control and new market-based instruments[31] (Faure 2012, pp. 8–12). Being at the beginning of this complex transition, a lot of work is still to be done and the legal framework to sustain a new model of development has yet to established. This can offer new business opportunities for foreign companies. In this regard another emerging sector that needs to be carefully followed is that of green insurance. In 2013, a new set of guidelines, the so-called 'Guidelines on Pilot Project of Compulsory Environmental Pollution Liability Insurance',[32] was jointly published by the Ministry of Environmental Protection and the China Insurance Regulatory Commission. These guidelines, for the first time, required compulsory purchase of environmental liability insurance by

[30]WWF (World Wild Fund for Nature) Report (China).

[31]Regarding the difference between the command-and-control and the market-based instruments; the author suggests that the combination of command-and-control approach and market-based instruments may be the most suitable solution to improve the environmental quality.

[32]Guan Yu Kai Zhan Huan Jing Qiang Zhi Ze Ren Bao Xian Shi Dian Gong Zuo De Zhi Dao Yi Jian (Guidelines on Pilot Project of Compulsory Environmental Pollution Liability Insurance), issued by the Ministry of Environmental Protection (MEP), 21 January 2013.

enterprises with high environmental risks. Moreover, they provide incentives and restrictive mechanisms to require and encourage enterprises to purchase environmental pollution liability insurance products. For example, special funds, such as an environmental protection special fund, are provided to enterprises that apply the compulsory environmental liability insurance, while those enterprises failing to apply for insurance will be subject to restrictions, many of them in connection with the aforementioned credit ratings in the banking system[33] (Zhan et al. 2013).

Those described in this first enquiry appear to be the first, just preliminary steps of a new 'long march, a march that will overcome Chinese borders, assuming a new geographical and historical global dimension, to design new patterns of production and consumption, where "human beings are at the centre of concerns for sustainable development."[34]

References

Agyeman J et al (2002) Exploring the nexus: bringing together sustainability, environmental justice and equity. Space Polity 6:77–90. doi:10.1080/13562570220137907

Cao D (2004) Chinese Law—a language perspective. Ashgate Publishing Limited, Aldershot

Catalogue for the Guidance of Foreign Investment Industries (2015) Promulgated by the National Development and Reform Commission (NDRC) and the Ministry of Commerce, Decree No. 22, 10 March 2015

China Banking Regulatory Commission (CBRC) (2012) Zhongguo yinjianhui guanyu yinfa lvse xindai zhiyin de tongzhi [Notice on Issuing Green Credit Guidelines], February 24. http://www.cbrc.gov.cn/chinese/home/docDOC_ReadView/127DE230BC31468B9329EFB01AF78BD4.html. Accessed 2 Feb 2016

China Council for International Cooperation on Environment and Development (CCICED) (2012) Going global, going green China investment, trade and environment. http://www.cciced.net/encciced/. Accessed 20 Jan 2016

Chinabriefing.com (2011a) Selected tax incentives in China's renewable energy sector. China Briefing. http://www.china-briefing.com/news/2011/06/15. Accessed 9 Aug 2015

Chinabriefing.com (2011b) Foreign investment in China green sector. China Briefing. http://www.china-briefing.com/news/2011/06/15. Accessed 10 Oct 2015

Chinatax.gov.cn. (2007a) Zhonghua renmin gongheguo qiye suodeshui fa [Enterprise Income Tax Law of the People's Republic of China]. www.chinatax.gov.cn. Accessed 2 March 2016

Chinatax.gov.cn. (2007b) Zhonghua renmin gongheguo qiye suodeshui fa shishi tiaoli [Implementation Regulations of Enterprise Income Tax Law of the People's Republic of China]. www.chinatax.gov.cn. Accessed 2 March 2016

China Tax Regulation Update (2010) Caishui [Circular]. http://www.cms-lawnow.com/ealerts/2015/01/26-jan-2015-china-tax-regulation-update?cc_lang=en. Accessed 9 Aug 2015

Faure GM (2012) Instruments for environmental governance: what works? In: Martin P et al (eds) Environmental governance and sustainability, vol 3. Elgar Publishing, Cheltenham, p 23

[33]Guidelines on Pilot Project of Compulsory Environmental Pollution Liability Insurance, (MEP) Part 6.

[34]Principle 1, Report of the United Nations Conference of Environment and Development (1992).

Gov.cn, Central People's Government of the People's Republic of China (2007) Zhonghua renmin gongheguo jieyue nengyuan fa [Energy Conservation Law of the People's Republic of China], 28 Oct. http://www.gov.cn/flfg/2007-10/28/content_788493.htm. Accessed 10 Feb 2016

Gov.cn, Central People's Government of the People's Republic of China (2006) Zhonghua renmin goingheguo guomin jingji he shehui fazhan di shiyi ge wunianguihua gangyao [People's Republic of China11th Five-Year for National Economic and Social Development], 14 March. http://www.gov.cn/2011lh/content_1825838.htm. Accessed 15 Feb 2016. http://www.gov.cn/gongbao/content/2006/content_268766.htm. Accessed 10 Feb 2016

Gov.cn, Central People's Government of the People's Republic of China (2008) Zhonghua renmin gongheguo xunhuan jingji cujin fa [Circular Economy Promotion Law of the People's republic of China], 29 Aug. http://www.gov.cn/flfg/2008-08/29/content_1084355.htm. Accessed 15 Jan 2016

Gov.cn, Central People's Government of the People's Republic of China (2011) Zhonghua renmin goingheguo guomin jingji he shehui fazhan di shi'er ge wunianguihua gangyao [People's Republic of China 12th Five-Year for National Economic and Social Development], 16 March. http://www.gov.cn/2011lh/content_1825838.htm. Accessed 15 Feb 2016

Hilton I et al (2011) China's green revolution. energy, environment and the 12th five-year plan. https://www.chinadialogue.net/UserFiles/File/PDF_ebook001.pdf. Accessed on 30 Oct 2015

Lubman S (2006) Looking for Law in China. Columbia J Asian Law 20:1. http://scholarship.law.berkeley.edu/cgi/viewcontent.cgi?article=1444&context=facpubs. Accessed 5 Dec 2015

Marquis C et al (2011) Regulatory uncertainty and corporate responses to environmental protection in China. Calif Manag Rev 54(1):39–63. doi:10.1525/cmr.2011.54.1.39

Ministry of Environmental Protection of the People's Republic of China (MEP) (2013) Guan yu kai zhan huan jing qiang zhi ze ren bao xian shi dian gong zuo de zhi dao yi jian [Guidelines on Pilot Project of Compulsory Environmental Pollution Liability Insurance]. http://english.mep.gov.cn/News_service/news_release/201302/t20130227_248567.htm. Accessed 3 March 2016

Morgan G (2011) A critique of development through the analysis of potable water projects in rural China. https://digital.lib.washington.edu/researchworks/handle/1773/16589. Accessed 30 Oct 2015

Orts WE (2003) Environmental Law with Chinese characteristics. William & Mary Bill of Rights J 11:545–567. http://opim.wharton.upenn.edu/risk/downloads/03-02-EO.pdf. Accessed 31 Oct 2015

Pesqueux Y (2009) Sustainable development: a vague and ambiguous 'theory'. Soc Bus Rev 4:231–245. doi:10.1108/17465680910994227

Qin L (2015) Shangwu bu jiedu <waishang touzi chanye zhidao mulu 2015>: Xianzhi dafu jianshao [Interpretation of the Ministry of Commerce 'Foreign Investment Industrial Guidance Catalogue 2015': Limits substantially reduced]. http://intl.ce.cn/specials/zxxx/201503/17/t20150317_4844820.shtml. Accessed 16 June 2015

SEPA (promulgated by) (2007) Guanyu luoshi huanbao zhengce fagui fangfan xindai fengxian de yijian [Opinions on Implementing Environmental policies and Preventing Credit Risk], PBOC and CBRC, Decree No. 108. http://www.zhb.gov.cn/info/gw/huanfa/200707/t20070718_106850.htm. Accessed 8 June 2015

UNGA, United Nations (2012) The future we want: resolution adopted by the general assembly on 27 July, A/RES/66/288. https://documents-dds-ny.un.org/doc/UNDOC/GEN/N11/476/10/PDF/N1147610.pdf?OpenElement. Accessed 12 Feb 2016

UNGA (2016) United Nations. Report of the United Nations Conference on Environment and Development, 3–14 June 1992. vol. I, Resolutions Adopted by the Conference (United Nations publication, Sales No. E.93.I.8 and corrigendum), resolution 1, annex I. Rio de Janeiro. https://sustainabledevelopment.un.org/content/documents/Agenda21.pdf. Accessed 1 March 2016

UNGA, United Nations (1987) Our common future: report of the world commission on environment and development, A/42/427, Chapter 2.IV.1. http://www.un-documents.net/a42-427.htm. Accessed 12 Feb 2016

Wang A (2006) The role of law in environmental protection in China: recent developments. 8 Vt. J. Envt. L. Berkeley Law Scholarship Repository. http://scholarship.law.berkeley.edu/cgi/viewcontent.cgi?article=2688&context=facpubs. Accessed 12 Feb 2016

Wang A (2013) The search for sustainable legitimacy: environmental law and bureaucracy in China. Harv J Environ Law 37:365–440

WWF Report (China) (2013) The sustainable performance of Chinese banking and international financial institutions comparative study. http://www.wwfchina.org/content/press/publication/2015/greenfinanceen.pdf. Accessed 30 May 2015

Xihuanet (2015) Zhonggong zhongyang guanyu zhiding guomin jingji he shehui fazhan di shisan ge wu nian guihua de jianyi [Suggestions on China's 13th five-year national social and economic development]. http://news.xinhuanet.com/fortune/2015-11/03/c_1117027676.htm. Accessed 5 March 2016

Yao L (2012) China releases 12th five-year plan for national strategic emerging industries. China Briefing. http://www.china-briefing.com/news/2012/07/25/. Accessed 9 Dec 2015

Yin H (2013) Zhongguo yinhangye lvse xindai biaozhun he yuanze—gongshang yinhang lvse xindai xiangguan shijian [Standards and principles of green credit in China's banking sector—the green credit practice of China Industrial and Commercial Bank]. http://www.bsr.org/pdfs/sic/s1-2-yin-hong.pdf. Accessed 30 May 2015

Zhan H et al (2013) Another kind of compulsory insurance?. Chinalawvision. http://www.chinalawvision.com/2013/03/articles/insurance-law-of-the-peoples-r/another-kind-of-compulsory-insurance/. Accessed 30 May 2015

Part III
Chinese Politics and Culture

The Issue of Political Reform and the Evolution of the So-Called 'Deng Xiaoping Model' in Hu Jintao and Xi Jinping's China

Marina Miranda

Abstract This chapter analyses the position of recent Chinese leaders on political reform: the similarities between Xi Jinping and Hu Jintao, and the different rhetoric and approach by Wen Jiabao. Moreover, it examines the concept of the so-called 'democracy with Chinese characteristics' and the concept's interpretation by Yu Keping, an innovative theorist of the Chinese Communist Party (CCP). The final part of the chapter deals with the special features of the model of reference pursued by Chinese leaders—the so-called 'Deng Xiaoping Model', which over the last decade underwent evolution and revision.

1 Introduction

Terms such as 'democracy' or 'political reform' are not often part of the political discourse of Xi Jinping's China. However, since he took power in 2012, the Secretary-General of China's Communist Party has been confronted with a rather complex Chinese reality and the main task of his administration seems to be the adoption of social and economic reforms. The quality of Xi Jinping's reformist approach can be assessed through an assessment of the social and economic measures introduced by the 3rd and the 5th Plenums of the 18th Central Committee, respectively in 2013 and 2015. Furthermore, the guidelines recently outlined in China's 13th Five-Year Program provide further indications on Xi's vision for the above-mentioned reforms (Tanner 2016; Naughton 2015).

Xi's reformist attitude was supported by increased political strength that he gained through his rapid rise to power since he took over the leadership in China in 2012 (Miranda 2016). Owing to such strong political position, a lot was expected from him, as has been confirmed by appels from intellectuals of liberal tendencies to Xi asking for reform. In fact, a veteran of the Party, Xin Ziling, Colonel of the PLA, in an article published by a Hong Kong magazine in 2013, urged Xi to make

M. Miranda (✉)
Faculty of Humanities and Philosophy, La Sapienza University of Rome, Rome, Italy
e-mail: marina.miranda@uniroma1.it

S. Beretta et al. (eds.), *Understanding China Today*, Understanding China,
DOI 10.1007/978-3-319-29625-8_16

tough choices and to follow in the footsteps of his father, Xi Zhongxun. The latter, in the course of his political career, showed great courage on several occasions, especially in 1987, when he dared to denounce the procedure—incorrect and in violation of the Party constitution in his opinion—which was followed by the ousting of then Secretary-General of the Communist Party Hu Yaobang (Xin 2013).

2 Recent Chinese Leaders and Political Reform

The above-mentioned inducements were made necessary because political debate was not intense on the eve of the 18th Congress of the Chinese Communist Party (CCP) in 2012. On the contrary, previous party congresses had witnessed a lively debate on political issues. In fact, on the eve of the 17th Party Congress even radical positions were discussed. Xie Tao, former deputy dean of Beijing People's University e.g. dared to propose the model of North European social democracy for the first time (Xie 2007; Hu 2007). This is evidence that the debate on democracy was developed extensively in the 1990s and the 2000s, but in a different way as compared to the 1980s, when the liberal wing in the Communist Party made the idea of achieving feasible political reform (Béjà 2004). This, however, was then completely neglected after the Tian'anmen crisis in 1989. In fact, Hu Jintao stated many times that the adoption of a multi-party system is an impasse and a dead end for China (*Renmin Ribao* 15.09.2004). A similar view was shared by Wu Bangguo, then chairman of the People's National Congress, who was against a system based on the tripartite division of powers (Kwok 2009).

In a similar way Xi Jinping rejected Western democracy and a multi-party system in many statements since the beginning of his tenure as the CCP's General-Secretary in 2012 (Huang 2014). Today, the CCP also rejects the concept of 'universal values' (*pushi jiazhi*), out of the fear that recognizing the universality of freedom of expression and religion, universal suffrage, rule of law and independence of the judiciary could mean accepting the superiority of the Western over the Socialist political system. In this scenario, the only exception was the position of former Prime Minister Wen Jiabao, who unexpectedly released some surprising statements dealing with the issue of political reform between the autumn 2010 and spring 2012. For the first time, in September 2010, on the 30th anniversary of the establishment of Shenzhen Special Economic Zone and in an interview with CNN, he spoke of the need of not only promoting economic but also political reforms (Wen 2010). The Chinese phrase that he used—*zhengzhi tizhi gaige* (*Reform of the political system*)—has a high symbolic and eminently metaphorical value: it played a key political significance almost twenty years before, at the time connected to Zhao Ziyang and the debate on political reforms in the late 1980s.

Wen made further similar statements in the following months, mainly during his visits to Malaysia in April–May 2011, Great Britain and Germany in June 2011, at the World Economic Forum in Dalian in September 2011, in Qatar in January 2012 and in Sweden in April 2012 (Chan 2011; Miranda 2013, 2014). However, Wen's words were not supplemented by any kind of specific details on policies aimed at or leading to political reforms, which made Wen's announcement a sort of mission statement. References to concrete steps to achieve democracy were generic and gave way to many ambiguities. In fact, in major magazines and on the web in China, Hong Kong and abroad, Wen's statements unleashed a heated debate, in which very different opinions and interpretations about his real intentions emerged (Miranda 2011).

According to some authors, the vagueness and lack of specifics were merely a way of formally broadening the agenda, a kind of "air exchange in the room" (Zhu 2010). Moreover, since the former Premier's position was unclear and somewhat ambiguous, many wondered whether Wen had any support from the Party Secretary-General Hu Jintao: on the one hand, he seemed to lack broad support within the Party, on the other hand, he had not been sanctioned, although he went far beyond what other leaders have previously said as regards the recognition of the universality of values related to democracy (Hu 2010). Moreover, since Wen's statements were all made abroad or in contexts where there was an opening to the international audience, a well-known Hong Kong magazine suggested that the rationale of Wen statements was to communicate outside of China the existence of a liberal faction within the CCP (Jiang 2010). Making evident a liberal opening by a senior member of the Party would help to enhance China's soft power: a potentially more democratic People's Republic would appear to be a more credible partner and would win over the international public opinion, making sure that Westerners would listen with greater attention to China's concerns on issues of international politics relevant for China.

In a similar way the dissident essayist Yu Jie suggested that Wen was not a true reformer (Yu 2010). Instead, he pretended to be a reformer, in order to be remembered as the most reformist leader of his generation. The declarations made by Wen over the last two years of his tenure suggest that perhaps he was preparing his own political legacy ahead of the end of his second term. Close to the end of his second mandate as Prime Minister, Yu Jie argues, Wen sought to shape a liberal image of himself, concerned primarily with what position he would occupy in the history books.

3 Democracy with 'Chinese Characteristics', Incremental Democracy and Good Governance

If on the one hand the case of Wen Jiabao was an isolated voice—with perhaps an instrumental purpose—in academic and intellectual circles on the other hand the debate on democracy developed mainly in a way that was controlled and channeled by the Communist Party. In fact, the official line of CCP leaders on democracy was embraced by the majority of Chinese scholars during the early 2000s.

According to some authors, Western democracy is not replicable in China for the uniqueness of the historical conditions under which it was accomplished in the West. Western democracy, the argument goes, was the result of a gradual process, as opposed to abrupt events and procedures (Song 2009). Among various scholars, Fang Ning, deputy director of the Institute of Political Science of Chinese Academy of Social Sciences (CASS), in his writings repeatedly stressed the need for China to follow its own path, emphasizing the relativity and not the universality of democratic values (Fang 2009). According to his explanations, Western elections are controlled by capitalists, especially in the United States, in view of the great financial costs of the American political system. Moreover, the foundation of different parties—being representatives of different interests—would in Fang's view have led to the deepening of social inequalities in China, while the Chinese one-party system would instead have leaned towards what he refers to as 'harmonization.'

Over the last ten years some authors believed that the push for democratization was exploited as a tool by Western powers—especially the USA—to interfere in the internal affairs of other countries. Liu Xirui, professor at the National School for Public Administration e.g. believed that China had in a sense already established a democratic system with its own valuable characteristics (Liu 2007). On the contrary, for others, China is not ready for democracy in the present stage of its development, because this process would cause chaos and unrest with negative repercussions for Chinese economic growth and stability. Furthermore, according to Zhang Weiwei, professor at Shanghai Fudan University and at Geneva School of Diplomacy, the Western political model is not applicable to China or to other developing countries, since democracy is not a value, but only a tool of government (Zhang 2006).

The above-cited Chinese scholars all agree on one point: reaffirming the need for China to refuse the Western model of democracy and develop its own specific path to democracy, distinct from others. The rejection of the Western model is based on the belief that multi-party democracy is not the only valid kind of democracy. Denying the concept of the universality of values, it is a type of democracy very different from that of the West. A type of democracy with its very own characteristics different from any other type, encompassing China's unique features, drawing from the country's revolutionary and its reformist experience of the 1980s. This is once again a clear claim of autonomy and a nationalistic manifestation of pride in following a different path also towards democracy with what is referred to as 'Chinese characteristics' (*Zhongguo tese minzhu* or *Zhongguoshi minzhu*).[1] The result is a model of democracy that can be defined as 'contained' and 'caged.'

Among the proponents of this kind of democracy, Yu Keping, considered by many the rising star among the theorists of the CCP with profound knowledge of Western political thought, must be mentioned. He presents a kind of dual identity, both as a scholar and as a party official, since he holds academic positions at

[1]Among the various expressions officially used by the Party press, *Zhongguo tese minzhu* is an abbreviation for *Zhongguo tese shehuizhuyi minzhu*.

prestigious universities, such as Peking University, Tsinghua University and Fudan University and is at the same time deputy director of the Central Compilation and Translation Bureau of the Communist Party's Central Committee, which is an important point of reference for many Chinese government think tanks. As an insider in government circles—even if it is not shared by the majority within the Communist Party—his thinking reflects fairly liberal positions within the CCP and is particularly interesting because it introduces news ideas and concepts. His most well-known work, *Democracy is a good thing*, is the elaboration of an interview given by the author in 2005 and then collected in a volume (Yu 2006), which was also published in English (Yu 2009). One of Yu's central point is the conclusion that democracy is no longer 'dangerous' and therefore acceptable from an ideological point of view for the Chinese audience. Emphasizing the virtues of democracy seems to be in contradiction with the widespread (official) opinion in China that democracy is instead a 'bad thing' (Xie 2007a, b). In the context of the symbolism of the Chinese political language, in fact, affirming the positivity of a concept necessitates the need to disprove the negative idea of a previous concept. According to the author, supporting the virtues of democracy does not mean that everything is positive about it: it is a system with many internal inadequacies and contradictions, which cannot be considered a panacea for all ills. Yu also suggests to be cautious about accepting the concept of the universality of values at any given time, arguing that Western democracy is just one and not the only political system suitable for all countries. In his view, democracy would be less efficient than an authoritarian regime, since democratic procedures require time-consuming negotiations, consultations and compromises, which can slow down decision-making processes and reduce administrative efficiency. Eventually, however, democracy will prove to be superior, because it entails a stronger political legitimacy and greater stability in the long run. Democracy is a tool to effectively fight corruption, through popular supervision and balance of powers, he argues.

At the same time Yu warns that there will be in any case a price to be paid in terms of political, economic and social stability: it is possible that public order would no longer be governable, social contradictions would explode, and economic growth could slow down significantly. Such a situation could plunge China into chaos and undermine national unity. Divisions within the Party, the country and among different ethnic groups preoccupy the current ruling class, which wants to preserve a united and strong China. Therefore, trying to minimize the perceived negative consequences of democracy is a great challenge. The key concept for Yu is gradual, incremental democracy (*jianjin minzhu* or *zengliang minzhu*). Democracy that cannot be achieved through a hurried process, accelerated by radical measures, but instead on the basis of three key steps: reducing risks, gradualism and dynamic stability (*dongtai wending*) (Yu 2002, 2003). This concept challenges the idea of stability at all costs, a static stability that has been pursued so far by the CCP. Instead, Yu advocates 'dynamic stability', aimed at channeling tensions, necessary to give the people a chance to express themselves through petitions, public interpellations and protest. Dynamic stability maintains order not by repression, but through negotiation with social forces. In this way, authority will be firmly legitimized which in turn will result in generate greater stability. Without verifying the existence of adequate social and cultural preconditions, a hasty as opposed to gradual introduction of democracy could have disastrous consequences for the country.

By avoiding a multi-party electoral competition and a Western-style division of powers, the introduction of incremental democracy will not 'westernize' China. It should be achieved through governmental reforms, elections at the grassroots level of administrative units and the development of civil society. Only Chinese people can decide on their own path to democracy, which must take into account Chinese realities and adapt to them. Yu's theses have secured support within the Party and were not censored. On the contrary, they were reproduced and re-proposed in various versions (Yan 2009). However, it is worth noting that, approaching the 18th Congress of the Party, Yu partly changed his view in his latest book, published almost six months before the opening of the meeting. The topic of this volume was not democracy but governance: *Jingwei Minyi: Zhongguo de Minzhu Zhili yu Zhengzhi Gaige* (In Awe of the People's Will: Democratic Governance and Political Reform in China) (Yu 2012). This can be considered a considerable change of course for the Xi era. Yu suggests that it is necessary to move towards good governance (*shanzhi*) and not towards what Western social scientists refer to as 'democracy'. For Yu good governance is the process of social management aiming to maximize the interest of the public, which can be achieved through good governance and the involvement of civil society. Good governance's defining feature is the cooperative supervision of public life between state and citizens, a new relationship and interactions between state and civil society.

With a certain degree of vagueness, as noted by some authors (Wang and Guo 2015), Yu emphasized the importance of the rule of law, civil society and citizens' civil and political rights for China's political development. Popular will as expressed in public opinion would be the only true basis for the legitimacy of political leadership in China and is regarded as a basic consensus on the government, in order to supervise public officials and administrative affairs. However, in my view, the peoples' will is not necessarily to be understood in the same way as in Western representative democracies, but rather it is a populist way of expressing opinions, adequate for one-party systems.

4 The Evolution of the So-Called 'Deng Xiaoping Model'

As discussed above, the prospects for any meaningful political reforms are all but inexistent in Xi Jinping's China. This seems in line with the so-called 'Deng Xiaoping Model': an almost exclusive focus on economic growth and development with at the same time a static and unreformed political system. These characteristics are the building blocks of the country system developed by Deng in the 1980s and were inherited with some adjustments by China's current leaders. The model evolved and was revised when a new important element was added to it: China's rising position in international politics. This process originated in the Hu Jintao period and is now further progressing in the Xi Jinping era. It is noteworthy that China's increasing role in and impact on global politics was accompanied by an inner-Chinese ideological discourse, which started with the concept of China's 'Peaceful Rise' (*heping jueqi*). That concept was officially put forth in April 2003 by Zheng Bijian, a well-known scholar of the Central Party School, who defined China's rise a mutually beneficial for China and for the world: "China's Peaceful Rise, in particular, will contribute to the creation of a win-win situation and common prosperity" (Zheng 2005). Although the slogan 'Peaceful Rise' flourished in China's political debates, it encountered criticism, because of the of unsettling nuances of 'rise.' (Zheng and Tok 2005). As a consequence, in order to remove the negative connotation of the word 'rise', the original slogan was replaced by a more reassuring one: 'Peaceful Development' (*heping fazhan*). The decision to replace 'Peaceful Rise' with 'Peaceful Development' can be considered a sign of China's increasing sensitivity towards the international audience (Glaser; Medeiros 2007).

Furthermore in order to deflect criticism of China's international rise and further rebut the so-called 'China Threat' concept, CCP authorities have resorted to the reassuring theory of a 'Harmonious World' (*hexie shijie*), which suggests that sustainable peace and common prosperity are part of a wider global 'harmony' (*hexie*) (Wu 2006). In fact, next to 'Harmonious World' outside China, a twin slogan was used for domestic politics: a 'Harmonious Society', which was claimed to be built inside the country, in order to oppose social inequalities and support regime survival. The concept of 'harmony', which has strong roots in traditional Chinese philosophy, has been promoted as a model for the world, advocating China's alternatives of the ideas of freedom and democracy, opposing Western liberalism (Callahan 2015).

Conflicting with the Western model, China proposed the concept and vision of the so-called 'China Dream' (*Zhongguo meng*). This is the new idea that Xi Jinping has introduced during the first months of his tenure in 2012. The 'China Dream' is accompanied by the concept of what Xi calls the 'Rejuvenation' (*xing*) of the Chinese nation. Arguing that the nation's 'renewal' is the biggest dream of China today, the 'China Dream' Xi propagates is aimed at 'revitalizing' the nation, achieving a rich and powerful country and the people's happiness (Xu 2013). These concepts were promptly taken up by the aforementioned Zheng Bijian: in his view, the 'China Dream' would be the best suited formula in order to address China's problems, through the realization of objectives such as greater social justice, less corruption, a better life for the majority of the population (Yifeng Wang 2012). In the international field, 'rejuvenation' should be pursued within the framework of the above-mentioned 'Peaceful Development' and on the basis of China's new global position going along with a more active global Chinese role and impact. China, Xi urges, should return to the position it occupied before the advent of modernity and the clash with the Western powers. Relying on the historical importance of its culture and civilization and what is in China referred to as 'glorious past', the idea of a Great Chinese empire and China's centrality in the international system is thus to be revived.

In this undoubtedly nationalist celebration, the cultural factor marks the superiority of the 'China Dream' over the American dream, which had great appeal in China in the 1980s, but which is now rejected by China's new contemporary nationalism (Miranda 2012). With the denial of Western values and in opposition to them, the leadership of the Party has sought to create a national prototype, adopting a development path in conformity with the characteristics of China and one that is based on the cultural heritage of the country and on the uniqueness of China's national conditions. In this alternative model, new factors of uniqueness, characteristics and national conditions (*guoqing*) are highlighted. They are to be recovered in a journey back through the history of China, its philosophical and cultural traditions, stressing as much as possible the peculiar elements of the unique and unrepeatable Chinese civilization.

The political and diplomatic rhetoric of the Hu Jintao era is similar to that of the Xi Jinping era in some respect. Rhetoric that emphasizes contrasts with and opposition against the West, stressing China's sense of alleged cultural authority and civilizational supremacy. These factors were originally not included in the model attributed to Deng Xiaoping, but made it into in the 'China Dream', which projects the image of what China strives to be and become in the future. Instead of concluding that the 'China Dream' has completely replaced the above-mentioned 'Deng Xiaoping Model' it is probably more accurate to argue that in political terms the Deng model is still in place, since China's political system remains largely unreformed. However, Deng's model evolved and new elements were added in the eras of Hu Jintao and Xi Jinping. The evolution of and changes to the Deng model became particularly evident in the 'China Dream' concept. Given that the new 'China Dream' concept emphasises the strength and impact of both Chinese domestic and international policies, it becomes consequently difficult to explain and advocate reforms of China's political system.

Moreover, in addition to the political rhetoric accompanying the 'China Dream', it is necessary to take into account the realities of what is happening in Xi Jinping's China today. It is clear that not only reforms moving towards liberal democracy can be counted as political reforms, since this understanding hardly captures the concept of political transformation in China nowadays. Given that political reform can represent a much broader spectrum in the Chinese context, in my view, it is not necessarily useful and relevant to take into consideration village-level elections, although they are officially regarded as the core often advertised so-called 'basic-level' program of political reforms (Li 2003; O'Brien and Han 2009). In fact, for reasons related to structural policy choices and priorities, the village-level elections experiment is currently restricted to rural areas, and absolutely does not affect the nature of the overall and national political system. Basic and essential changes to China's political system could e.g. be the introduction of political and institutional checks and balances and the introduction of a transparent and sustainable system of the rule of law. However, Xi Jinping's policies do not point into such a policy direction and do not take any unambiguous stand against the worst aspects of the current political system. A set reform are necessary before being able to introduce and maintain the rule of law in China: the separation of powers between the Party and the state, because of the overlap of the two in many fields of competence and even in the tenure of offices. The intervention on this overlapping of powers was invoked by Zhao Ziyang in the 1980s, but it was never resumed later.

Conversely, Xi Jinping has set in motion a process, which goes into the opposite direction and is accompanied by a certain institutional regression of the system. This has allowed Xi to consolidate and increase his political power base (Miranda 2016). In fact, the Party increased its powers and authority at the expense of the power of the state. The primacy of the party over the state is almost a return to the revolutionary period of the 1950s and 1960s when the CCP completely controlled the state apparatus. The Party's predominance over the state was accompanied by the establishment of three major agencies in the central administration: they supervised matters of strategic importance for the country and they are bodies of the Party not of the state. They are in charge of domestic issues, not related to the management of the CCP. The first of those offices is the 'National Security Commission' (*Zhongyang guojia anquan weiyuanhui*), established in January 2014. It closely connects internal security with the international context, it deals with terrorism, sovereignty and territorial disputes, problems of the Internet and with all perceived threats from outside, including issues such as the status of Hong Kong, Tibet and Xinjiang (Lampton 2015). The chairmanship of this agency enables Xi to control the security forces, police, special forces, secret services, as well as indirectly the courts and prosecutors' offices. This provides Xi with the possibility to better coordinate policies related to internal security, using a more centralized control of the public order system. Another recently established office is the 'Central Leading Group for Internet Security and Informatization' (*Zhongyang wangluo anquan he xinxihua lingdao xiaozu*). Through that agency Xi coordinates the existing bodies in charge of the censorship on the web, such as the cybernetics section of the Ministry of Public Security and that of Industry and Information Technology (Tiezzi 2014).

The third agency is the 'Central Leading Group for Comprehensively Deepening Reforms' (*Zhongyang quanmian shenhua gaige lingdao xiaozu*), established in December 2013 (Huang 2013). Its task is to define the guidelines for economic, social, and cultural reforms ethical issues, while at the same dealing with obstacles posed by the bureaucracy. The control over this agency allows Xi to consolidate his power over the vast apparatus of the government, including the State Council, which is formally controlled by the Prime Minister. Accordingly, some observers began to argue that Xi significantly reduced the role and power of Premier Li Keqiang, obliging him to operate in Xi's shadow (Huang 2015).

The tendency of a regressive course is also evident in the way Xi conducted the battle against corruption, one of the major tasks he is engaged in since taking over power in 2012. In fact, the anti-corruption campaign is entrusted to another organ of the Party (opposed to the state): the 'Central Commission for Discipline Inspection of the CCP' (*Zhongguo Gongchandang zhongyang jilü jiancha weiyuanhui*), the highest internal control body of the Communist Party, which has the task to strengthen and enforce internal regulations to combat corruption and malfeasance (Becker 2008). However, it enjoys little autonomy with respect to the apparatus of the Party, which affects its ability to efficiently fight corruption. It is therefore confronted with strong political interference in areas where it should be operating independently. Instead, the fight against corruption should be conducted by the judiciary, supported by institutional checks and balances.

5 Conclusions

The current regressive above-mentioned policies adopted by China's leader are not a good omen for future developments and for an enlargement of the Chinese political agenda that could include, if not sweeping measures of political reform, at least the start of a process of institutional evolution: rebalancing of the state apparatus, eliminating the 'rule of man' and advancing the rule of law. In addition, another element is to be considered, i.e. the slowdown of the Chinese economy.[2] This will be a major challenge for Xi's administration, since previous rapid economic growth has in the past been a guarantee for stability for the regime. All these factors are likely, in the long run, to lead to a far-reaching transformation of China's economy and politics which is still influenced by the above-mentioned 'Deng Xiaoping Model' of economic and political governance.

References

Becker J (2008) Tackling corruption at its source: the National Corruption Prevention Bureau. J Chin Political Sci 13:287–303

Béjà JP (2004) À la Recherche d'une Ombre Chinoise -Le Mouvement pour la Démocratie en Chine (1919–2004). Éditions du Seuil, Paris

Callahan WA (2015) History, tradition and the China Dream: socialist modernization in the World of Great Harmony. J Contemp China 24(96):983–1001

Chan M (2011) Wen in renewed plea for wider political reforms. South China Morning Post (Internet edn, 29 29.04.2011)

Fang N (2009) Wo guo jue bu neng gao xifang de duodangzhi (My country cannot accomplish the Western multiparty system). Renmin Ribao 09(02):2009

Glaser B, Medeiros E (2007) The ecology of foreign policy-making in China: the ascension and demise of peaceful rise. China Quart 190:291–310

Hu J (2007) Segnali positivi e calde speranza: il 'socialismo democratico' in Cina (translated from Chinese by Chiara Romagnoli), Mondo Chinese, vol 132, pp 60–67

Hu P (2010) Tantan dui Wen Jiabao jianghua de ruogan zhengyi – jian yu Yu Jie shangque (Some controversial points of Wen Jiabao's speech—a simultaneous discussion with Yu Jie), Beijing zhi Chun, n. 10 (internet ed)

Huang C (2013) Xi Jinping to head reform panel, taking another role from premier, South China Morning Post (internet ed., 31.12. 2013)

Huang C (2014) China's Xi Jinping supports 'democracy'… but not in the Western sense, South China Morning Post (internet ed., 24.06.2014)

[2]This chapter was completed in April 2016.

Huang C (2015) Chinese premier Li Keqiang steps out of president Xi Jinping's shadow, South China Morning Post (internet ed., 24.06.2015)
Jiang H (2010) Sanfang jibian Wen Jiabao zhenggai lun (The heated debate on three fronts on the theory of Wen Jiabao's political reform), Zheng Ming, vol 11, no 397 (internet ed)
Kwok K (2009) Congress chairman rejects calls for reform based on western models, South China morning post (internet ed., 10.03.2009)
Lampton DM (2015) Xi Jinping and the National Security Commission: policy coordination and political power. J Contemp China 24(95):759–777
Li L (2003) The empowering effect of village elections in China. Asian Surv 43(4):648–662
Liu X (2007) Zhongguo de minzhu moshi yijing queli (The democratic system has already been established in China). Renmin Ribao (25.04.2007, internet ed)
Miranda M (2011) I discorsi di Wen Jiabao sulla riforma politica: alcune interpretazioni. In: Miranda M (ed) Il Modello Cina: quadro politico e sviluppo economico. L'Asino d'Oro Edizioni, Roma, pp 79–90
Miranda M (2012) La questione dell'identità nazionale in Cina e il nuovo nazionalismo contemporaneo. In: Miranda M (ed) L'identità nazionale nel XXI secolo in Cina, Giappone, Corea, Tibet e Taiwan. Editrice Orientalia, Roma, pp 45–56
Miranda M (2013) La Democrazia in Cina: le Diverse Formulazioni dagli Anni '80 a Oggi. Editrice Orientalia, Roma
Miranda M (2014) Wen Jiabao alla fine del suo secondo mandato: ancora sul problema della riforma politica. In: Bulfoni C, Pozzi S (eds) Atti del XIII Convegno dell'Associazione italiana di studi cinesi, Milano 22–24 settembre 2011. Franco Angeli, Milano, pp 249–259
Miranda M (2016) Il veloce consolidamento della posizione politica di Xi Jinping all'inizio del proprio mandato. In: Miranda M (ed) Politica, società e cultura di una Cina in ascesa - L'amministrazione Xi Jinping al suo primo mandato, Cina Report 2016. Carocci Editore, Roma, pp 27–48
Naughton B (2015) Is there a 'Xi model' of economic reform?–Acceleration of economic reform since Fall 2014, China Leadersh Monit Online 46:1
O'Brien KJ, Han R (2009) Path to democracy? Assessing village elections in China. J Contemp China (Special Issue: State of the Field: Assessing Village Elections in China) 18(60):359–378
Ribao R 15.09.2004, Hu Jintao: Renda hui zhidu xianshi qiangda shengmingli he juda youyuexing (According to Hu Jintao, the system of the National People's Congress reveals formidable vitality and great superiority) (internet ed)
Song L (2009) Wo weishenme renwei minzhu bu heshi Zhongguo (Why I believe that democracy is not suitable for China), 27 Jan 2009. http://blog.ifeng.com/article/2099462.html
Tanner MS (2016) China in 2015—China's Dream, Xi's Party. Asian Surv 56(1):19–33
Tiezzi S (2014) Xi Jinping leads China's new internet security group. The Diplomat (28.3.2014, internet ed)
Wang Q, Guo G (2015) Yu Keping and chinese intellectual discourse on good governance. China Quart 224:985–1005
Wang Y 3.12.2012, Zheng Bijian jiedu 'Zhongguo meng': bu zuo 'Meiguo meng Ouzhou meng Sulian meng' (Zheng Bijian interprets the "Chinese dream": do not realize the 'American, European or Soviet dream'). http://news.ifeng.com/mainland/detail_2012_12/03/19765705_0.shtml
Wen J (2010) Zhiyou jianchi gaige kaifang, guojia cai you guangming qiantu (Only by persisting in the opening up and reform [policy], the country will have a bright future), Renmin Ribao, 22.08
Wu J (2006) 'Harmonious world' helps rebut 'China threat'. People's Daily online, 20.3
Xie M (2007a) Minzhu bu shi ge huai dongxi (Democracy is not a bad thing), Zhongguo Jingji Shibao (15.01, internet ed)
Xie T (2007b) Minzhu shehuizhuyi moshi yu Zhongguo qiantu (The model of democratic socialism and China's future). Yanhuang Chunqiu (February 2, internet ed)
Xin Z (2013) Xi Zhongxun kaipi de daolu (The road taken by Xi Zhongxun). Kaifang zazhi 11:33–36

Xu H (2013) Zhongguo meng: Xuexi fudao baiwen (The China dream: 100 questions for study and guidance). Yanjiu chubanshe, Beijing

Yan J (2009) Rang minzhu zaofu Zhongguo - Yu Keping fangtan lu (Let's make democracy beneficial to China—Interview with Yu Keping). Zhongyang Bianyi chubanshe, Beijing

Yu K (2002) Toward an incremental democracy and governance: Chinese theories and assessment criteria. New Polit Sci 24(2):181–199

Yu K (2003) Zengliang Minzhu yu Shanzhi – Zhuanbian zhong de Zhongguo Zhengzhi (Incremental democracy and good governance: Chinese politics in transition). Shehui Kexue Wenxian chubanshe, Beijing

Yu K (2006) Minzhu Shige Hao Dongxi (Democracy is a good thing). Shehui Kexue Wenxian chubanshe, Beijing

Yu K (2009) Democracy is a good thing—essays on politics, society and culture in contemporary China. Brookings Institution Press, Washington D.C

Yu J (2010) Wen Jiabao quefa Hu Yaobang de zhen jingsheng (Wen Jiabao lacks the true spirit of Hu Yaobang). Zheng Ming, 9(395)

Yu K (2012) Jingwei Minyi: Zhongguo de Minzhu Zhili yu Zhengzhi Gaige (In awe of the people's will: democratic governance and political reform in China). Zhongyang Bianyi chubanshe, Beijing

Zhang W (2006) The allure of the Chinese model. International Herald Tribune (November 1, internet ed)

Zheng B (2005) China's 'peaceful rise' to great-power status. Foreign Aff 84(5):18–24

Zheng Y, Tok SK (2005) China's 'peaceful rise': concept and practice. University of Nottingham, Discussion Paper, China Policy Institute, p 1

Zhu X (2010) Wen Jiabao de dianfu xiaoying (The subversive effect of Wen Jiabao). Dongxiang, 10(301) (September, internet ed)

From 'Chinese Characteristics' (*Zhongguo Tese*中国特色) to 'Chinese Dream' (*Zhongguo Meng*中国梦)-The Chinese Political Discourse Today

Alessandra C. Lavagnino

Abstract Which have been the most significant changes in the official Chinese communication over the last 30 years, i.e. the years from the beginning of the *gaige kaifang* 改革开放 ('Reform and Opening') era up until today? How far has the Chinese political discourse moved away from Maoist slogans? The principal events that marked the fundamental phases of this process will be retraced through some of the main catchphrases used in Chinese official discourses in order to better contextualize meanings and recurring themes and changes over time. In other words, the chapter will examine how some of the important changes in China over 30 years have been expressed and described with keywords and slogans in Chinese past and present political language and documents.

1 Introduction

The reflections that follow are the results of long years of contacts with the Chinese official press: I started reading Chinese newspapers more than 40 years ago, when, together with the few other Chinese language students at the University of Rome, we were supposed to study only classical Chinese (Confucius and Mencius etc.). However, we created an alternative course in newspaper reading, obviously the *People's Daily*, the official organ of the Chinese Communist Party that was supposed to indicate the 'correct political opinion'. During that period—we were at the end of the 1960s—the language with which the Chinese authorities expressed themselves was formulated in a monotonous *langue de bois* of official rhetoric, built of simple slogans that everyone had to enunciate: repetitive formulas of elementary linguistic structure that the omnipresent propaganda repeated with obsessive constancy without granting possible alternatives (Gunn 1991). However, this expressive poverty meant for us young Italian students, unaware of what was taking place

A.C. Lavagnino (✉)
Department of Sciences of Linguistic Mediation and Intercultural Studies, University of Milan, Milan, Italy
e-mail: Alessandra.Lavagnino@unimi.it

S. Beretta et al. (eds.), *Understanding China Today*, Understanding China,
DOI 10.1007/978-3-319-29625-8_17

in the 'revolutionary' China at the time, that the reading of the Chinese press became apparently simple. There was only one newspaper, and it always repeated the same words and sentences. Therefore today, more than 40 years later, when I read the comments and the analyses of some Western observers on the current situation in the Chinese press, I recall those years in order to assess whether in terms of China's political language and rhetoric progress has or has not been made until today.

The fact that in China's biggest cities today one can purchase a copy of a daily paper in Chinese or in a foreign language at any newsstand seems to be 'normal' only to those who don't know what China was once like: it was only fairly recently in fact, that the Chinese postal service opened newsstands, which were authorized to sell the national daily and weekly newspapers and magazines published in China. The current 'normality' of this development for any Chinese citizen or foreigner is a clear indication of the significant changes that have taken place in China over recent years: until the 1990s, in fact, the direct purchase of newspapers and magazines in places outside government post offices was practically impossible, as even apparently harmless buildings such as newsstands were simply unthinkable in a country where large parts of the press was charged with the task of responding to the demands of politics, and the divulgation of information still had to conform more or less rigidly to the directives of the Chinese Communist Party (CCP). On-street distribution was authorized only for some local newspapers, while official newspapers and the entire periodical press was delivered directly to subscribers—public or collective structures—single copies of magazines could only be bought in post offices, and the names of subscribers were registered and checked (Zhao 1998, pp. 129–138). This was the case in large cities, while in the countryside the local distribution of any type of periodical took place via post and was always handled via and thanks to the mediation of the local party secretary. The secretary handled the administration of the appropriate number of copies of the publications on a rotational basis, from which the contents of the so-called 'political study', obligatory for all members of the local structures of the CCP, were drawn. In fact, when I first went in China more than 40 years ago I found a country in which it was almost impossible to read, look at, or see anything other than what the omnipotent party decreed, produced, selected and published. That meant, obviously, a pervasive atmosphere of control, mistrust, and silence in daily life. Scholars working on the effects and impact of Chinese political language of that period observe "…a bifurcation between official and unofficial language", where the control of the formalized political language by the state was very strict (Link 2013, p. 13). This intense control of the state over the language which comprised publications of all kinds, provoked also a severe limitation of the daily linguistic communication—referred to as 'linguistic impoverishment' by Michael Schoenhals in 1992.

The reform process put in place at the end of the 1970s after the Third Plenum of the 11th Central Committee of the CCP (December 1978) triggered a chain reaction. As far as the system of the Chinese media was concerned, changes have been very substantial. It has been noted by Professor Li Xiguang, director of the Center for International Communications Studies at Tsinghua University that at the end of

1990s "…if a Chinese thinker, a Marxist orthodox, would today wake up after twenty years of sleep, he would surely think he was living on another planet. Reading the Chinese press today he would find more than half of the words completely strange to him, almost impossible to understand" (Li 2001, p. 388). And Professor Li Xiguang goes on by showing that from the end of the 1970s up the end of the 1990s in the Chinese official press there has been an increase of about 800 new words per year, which it means that almost 5000 new words have been accepted in the official Chinese press" (Ibid.).

When Professor Li Xiguang wrote these sentences roughly 15 years ago the Internet and the new media were not yet playing the important role that they have today, but we can nevertheless agree with his reflections and apply it to today's situation. In the last 30 years the Chinese media have seen what prof. Li calls a 'quiet revolution'.

2 Past and Present

Drawing from my personal experience as a longtime reader of Chinese press—mostly *The People's Daily* and other official, and unofficial media—I had the opportunity to see how the language of the Chinese media, and also ordinary language among the Chinese people have changed over these years. An example: 40 years ago, a mass movement called 'Criticizing Lin Biao and Confucius' (*Pilin pikong*, 批林批孔) was going on all over the country and one of the strongest criticism addressed to Lin Biao was that he was 'double-faced' (*liangmianpai* 两面派), and that he was 'ambitious' ('ta you ye xin', 他有野心, literally: 'He had a wild heart'). At that time 'to be ambitious' was a very negative attribute, because it was the expression of 'subjectivism', 'bourgeois thinking' and 'reactionary thinking.' Today, the term *yexin* in the very competitive China has become entirely positive, as we can see from a report in the following quotation from *The Economist*: "The Visitor to China soon discovers that the Chinese people are being transformed both materially and psychologically. They are developing new hopes and new ambitions. The Mandarin word for ambition, *yexin*, partially tells us the story. It means literally 'wild heart' and as the translation suggests it has traditionally been a negative trait, reserved for wild boys and trouble-makers and ne'er-do-wells. Now bookshops are full of titles like 'How to have wild-heart in your Twenties' (Economist 2014).

Dictionaries and linguistic studies are booming with research and studies about linguistic transformations, new words and discursive practices, field research and taxonomies on how much today's language reflects and describes the reform process in China.[1] The following will concentrate only on some particular aspects of

[1]See the dictionary recently published in Shanghai: Song (2015).

the recent communication strategies through which the CCP has built up, consolidated and guaranteed its internal consensus.

3 Slogans and Watchwords

As a Leninist party, the CCP has always placed a strong emphasis on propaganda. It has a very long history of issuing slogans, *kouhao* 口号, and it often turns to mass mobilization to achieve its political objectives. The formalized political expressions used by the CCP are known as *tifa* 提法, a term which has been translated by the China specialists at the China Media Project in Hongkong, (http://cmp.hku.hk) as 'watchword'. Covering relevant political matters, *tifa* are always used deliberately and they are commonly seen as political signals or signposts. To outsiders, the political 'watchwords' used by China's top leaders can sometimes seem nonsensical: what do Chinese policymakers mean when they speak about the 'Four Basic Principles,' or the 'Three Represents'? But understanding what the CCP is saying, the lexicon it uses and why, is fundamental for anyone who hopes to make sense of the complex world of Chinese politics. As Michael Schoenhals has argued in 1992, it is very important for Western scholars to have an advanced and nuanced Chinese reading ability—in particular, a reading ability that enables scholars to understand the above-mentioned *tifa*. And this is most important if we want to avoid generalizations and stereotypes, which are still now very common when talking about China in general the Chinese political discourse in particular.

As we can recall from the extraordinary amount of written and visual material at our disposal (http://chineseposters.net/index.php), during the 1970s Chinese slogans and images were very assertive and authoritative. In fact, already in 1962 Chairman Mao issued the famous slogan 'Never Forget Class Struggle' (*Qianwan bu yao wangji jieji douzheng* 千万不要忘记阶级斗争, www.people.com.cn/GB/historic/0924/3144.html). Since then 'class struggle' became something more and more relevant, dramatically marking those difficult decades along with a complete set of very 'martial' slogans which were soon spreading all over the country through the powerful CCP propaganda instruments. Over the last 30 years, from the beginning of Deng Xiaoping's 'Reform and Opening' era, there have been great changes in the Chinese official communication, and the Chinese political discourse moved from Maoist slogans to a more complex communication strategy.

As the Chinese writer, Yu Hua 余华, has recently pointed out in an article for the *The New York Times*: "…China has, over the last 30 years, gone through tumultuous changes. Its abnormal development has generated a huge gap between rich and poor, and pervasive corruption has ignited conflict between officialdom and the population at large. These days, Chinese society is riddled with contradictions, but 'Never forget class struggle' has been replaced by 'Harmonious society' and 'Stability overrides all other considerations'. That earthshaking slogan of 'Never forget class struggle' has vanished from the scene, absconding to another world and seeking refuge with Mao. For our current leaders even to mention class struggle would be tantamount to their digging their own graves. Therefore, it is that during these last 64 years, China has written an absurd history of class struggle. In the past, class was eliminated, but our rulers decreed that the people must 'never forget class struggle'. Now class has returned, but our rulers demand that class struggle be forgotten" (Yu 2014). In fact, the 1980s were years, which Chinese intellectuals still remember as 'fabulous.' These were the years of hopes and expectations that the world of culture and information had been entrusted to the more reformist wing of the CCP.[2] A series of new publications was issued which, although still dependent on government organizations, also found in the topics they covered, certain *niches* of—if not true independence—of at least a certain autonomy.

Throughout the whole country by now there was a broadly accepted need for diversified information, of higher quality and depth when speaking about themes that were once absolutely 'forbidden' such as science, technology, arts and entertainment, daily life and leisure time. The greater political openness favored the founding of new periodicals that immediately had great commercial success, becoming also important sources of profit for the organizations of the CCP and government that owned them (Wu 2000, pp. 45–57). And the irrepressible impetus of economic development started with reforms made the establishing of a new relationship between the power and the media system inevitable, and the old system of circulating information from the center, of propaganda, of political censorship, had to learn to deal with new demands driven by economic considerations. A very subtle, difficult negotiation between the objective laws of economics (newspapers have to be sold, to earn a profit!) and the control by the central power has been ongoing since then, evolving according to the changes of politics. In such a context, the truly new element that entered with greater importance into the Chinese media system, was the first appearance in daily newspapers, then also on radio and television, of commercial advertising, an aspect of public life that until 1978 had been rigidly prohibited as an iniquitous expression of the capitalistic world. This new development rapidly began to have a profound influence on the discursive practices, and considerably modified the social behavior of the Chinese people. This long and complex process involved in a substantial way not only the sphere of economic policies and politics, but also that of the entire social system. A process that was reflected in the reform of the media in general and the print press in particular. We will now briefly retrace this process by analyzing some of the keywords, which in the Chinese official media have been the best indicators of those changes.

---

[2]On this subject see Zha (2006).

4 'Crossing the River by Feeling the Stones'

We can start by recalling that in the first years of reforms, one of the sentences which best represents this crucial period of new economic and social experiments is the expression 'Cross the river by feeling the stones' ('*mozhi shitou guo he*' 摸着石头过河). This sentence it is commonly attributed to Deng Xiaoping but it seems that it had been pronounced for the first time by another great revolutionary of that time, Chen Yun, on Dec. 16, 1980, at the work Conference of CCP "The economic situation and the lesson of our experience" (*Jingji xinshi yu jingyan jiaoxun* 经济形势与经验教训). Back then, Chen Yun had just re-entered politics and government affairs after the end of the 'Cultural Revolution.' The expression was referred to the complicated situation China found itself in at the time, and how the new politics was in his early stages, and tentative, like crossing a river. And it is said that Deng Xiaoping was enthusiastic about the slogan and used frequently in his own speeches (http://www.baike.com/wiki/摸着石头过河). Deng Xiaoping said that the slogan "Cross the river by feeling the stones," meant that even though China was moving forward into new directions it needed to stay with both feet on the ground and advance prudently according to its economic means and abilities. And the set of *tifa*, which emerged from these years show clearly the fact that China wanted to remain, in the dawn of reforms, firmly rooted on the orthodox path of socialism. We will take as an example what has been called 'The mixed bag of socialism'.

5 Socialism with 'Chinese Characteristics'

In China, Qiang Gang writes: "There is a popular phrase people use when referring to the seemingly whimsical world of the political slogan. 'It's an open basket', they'll say of this or that watchword, 'Anything can be thrown in there'. … And it is certainly true of one of the most central phrases now in use by the Chinese Communist Party—'Socialism with Chinese Characteristics' (*Zhongguo tese shehuizhuyi* 中国特色社会主义)". The 'patent rights', so to speak, of 'Socialism with Chinese characteristics' go back to Deng Xiaoping. He first used the term in his opening remarks to the 12th National Congress in 1982, which were printed in the *People's Daily*. For Deng, this was a reform slogan, and the obvious target of his reform was the Mao-style socialism that had been practiced to great detriment in China for 30 years. By the time the congress started 1982, the Party had already dissolved the 'People's Commune' system in China's countryside, and market reforms were adopted. However, the changes Deng initiated were already drawing opposition from conservatives in the party ranks. Deng had to proceed cautiously. He could not force a break with the political orthodoxy without losing important allies needed to push reforms" (Qian 2012).

We can agree with Qian Gang saying that Deng's introduction of the term 'Socialism with Chinese characteristics' was a sort of … "stratagem or, to return to the popular Chinese phrase, it was a 'basket.' On the outside, it seemed ideologically acceptable to conservatives, but inside it could accommodate Deng's vision of change. The crux of the term is not 'socialism' but "Chinese characteristics." The term 'Chinese characteristics' enabled Deng to qualify and adapt the term socialism to the country's economic and political situation at the time. This was Deng's great 'magic trick', i.e. the 'trick' of making people believe socialism was still there even though it had disappeared right before their very eyes. In 1982, 'Socialism with Chinese characteristics' became the central watchword of Chinese political and economic development. It had not yet appeared in General Secretary Hu Yaobang's political report to the 12th National Congress, held in September that year. The term rose to prominence only after Deng Xiaoping, Hu Yaobang and Zhao Ziyang laid out their blueprint for further reform" In fact the real shift of the meaning of the term 'socialism' started a few years later initiated by Zhao Ziyang. At the 13th Congress of CCP (1987), Zhao not only pointed out the 'special colors' (*tese*), or 'characteristics' of socialism in China: he went on to launch the 'primary stage' (*chuji jieduan* 初级阶段) of Chinese socialism. And this was a further development of the so-called 'initial stage' of socialism already mentioned by Mao in 1958 (Li 1995, p. 400). Zhao advocated to develop what he called a 'Planned commodity economy on the basis of public ownership', acknowledging the private economy's new role in the development of China. In this initial stage, Chinese socialism can and must go along new paths, have new experiences and go against past dogmatism, it was argued. As Deng Xiaoping said in 1978: "Emancipate your minds" (*jiefang sixiang* 解放思想) and "Get rid of superstitions" (*pochu mixin*' 破除迷信). Deng was courageous enough to go against the past Maoist dogma and according to Deng Chinese socialism shows his own 'special color' through giving space to new possibilities emerging from the new situation China itself in at the time. It is a 'special' new project, never attempted before, and courageously proposed by Deng, and the metaphor of 'crossing the river feeling the stones', was the image, which stood for the experimental spirit of those first years of reforms. To be sure, it was a Chinese model applicable only in China and not elsewhere. It was a completely new plan for the country, never experimented before: China was going to travel on a completely new path, which had to be found through new experience, and the image of a road (*daolu* 道路) is the metaphor employed by Zhao Ziyang in his political report to XIII Congress of CCP (Sept. 1987) (http://news.xinhuanet.com/ziliao/2003-01/20/content_697061.htm). It was emphasized that such Chinese model is unique and that the country's efforts were focused on identifying and defining the path to be taken. And this political line had been applied and developed even if the political career of its first promoter, Zhao Ziyang's life ended abruptly in 1989. In fact, the expression was applied from the 13th Party Congress in September 1987 until the most recent one, the 18th in November 2012. And it is still relevant today: each Congress report would add its own interpretation, but the fundamentals remained. Each CCP Secretary-General left his own distinguishing mark, but the expression 'Socialism with Chinese characteristics' remained well radicated in the official discourse. 'Firmly march on the path of socialism with Chinese characteristics and strive to complete the building of a moderately prosperous society in all respects' is the title of the last official report delivered by Hu Jintao before passing the baton of the political power on his successor, Xi Jinping (http://cpc.people.com.cn/n/2012/1118/c64094-19612151.html). The objective of this chapter is not to elaborate on the ideology which characterized Jiang Zemin and his 'Three Represents' (*sange daibiao* 三个代表) or Hu Jintao's 'Harmonious Society' (*hexieshehui* 和谐社会) Instead, the objective is to highlight that the past leadership of Jiang Zemin and than Hu Jintao both stressed the fact that China wanted to remain into the mainstream of socialism, albeit socialism with its own 'special colour' (*te se*)".

6 From Characteristics to Model

A vivid debate developed among Chinese intellectuals in the 1990s, when the focus on reforms shifted from whether or not to adopt reforms, to how to make better reforms. Cheung (2008, pp. 163–184) highlights that this debate reflects a process of re-defining the Chinese identity through a kind of 're-narrating' interpreting the Chinese past in various ways to create a concept and narrative of the Chinese nation on the path of modernization through reforms. This debate became an integral part of the new paradigm of reforms, which was eventually summarized in the expression 'Socialism with Chinese characteristics.' In other words, starting from the 1990s the Chinese public discourse "… has experienced a narrative shift from the discursive boundary of 'socialism' to the boundary of Chinese Characteristics" (Guo and Guo 2008, p. 8). In fact, throughout the 1990s reforms were adopted rapidly and the country's economic development was fast and impressive. The set of words describing this process is slowly but firmly shifting from 'special color/uniqueness/experiment/tentative' to a more solid and firm 'model/example', i.e. a model for economic development, that can be followed by others as a sort of new 'prototype'.

In 1991, the term 'China Model' appeared for the first time in *People's Daily*. It had its origins, apparently, in praise of China from some unspecified commentators in Romania (People's Daily 1991). The Berlin Wall had fallen. The Soviet Union and socialism in Eastern Europe had all but disintegrated. And yet, China avoided the collapse many Westerners were predicting at the time. China took another path, promoting privatization and reforms on the economic front while maintaining a tight CCP monopoly on power. This path of political tightening and economic opening became the kind of 'Chinese characteristics' that many people spoke about. Commemorating the 20th anniversary of economic reforms in 1998, the *People's Daily* wrote that "When you search the four corners of the earth, you find that the prospects here [in China] are particularly fine. International public opinion has accoladed China's development path, and the fruitfulness and effectiveness of the 'China model'" (People's Daily 1998).

At the beginning of this century, the term 'moshi' 模式, ('model'), became more and more often used in the economic context, meaning 'model of growth.' And one of the main text of reference on this tendency is 'The Choice of China Growth Model' (*Zhongguo zengzhang moshi jueze*中国增长模式抉择), published for the first time in 2005, and revised in 2007. The author of this book is one of the most important experts on China's economy during the reign of Deng Xiaoping, Prof. Wu Jinglian 吴敬琏, one of the most authoritative supporters of the positive role of the market for the development of the Chinese economy. The frequency of the term *moshi* as recorded by the Chinese search engine Baidu peaked in the period between 2007 and 2009. At the same time, the word took on new meanings, in a more broad political context.[3] Either way, in March 2011, during the so-called 'Two Sessions' (*Liang hui* 两会), the annual Chinese Parliament meeting, Chinese Premier Wen Jiabao affirmed that China does not consider its development a model for others: "All countries can have their own development paths which are suitable for their own national conditions and we respect the choice of their people" (http://2011lianghui.people.com.cn/GB/214392/14135967.html). At the time the formula 'China model' began to appear in the headlines of newspapers and in the titles of books: a whole new set of terms emerged to describe the country's growing national power. "Taken together, these form what might be called a 'discourse of greatness', or *shengshi huayu* (盛世话语). China's discourse of greatness includes such terms as 'China in ascendance' (*shengshi Zhongguo* 盛世中国), 'The China path' (*Zhongguo daolu*中国道路), 'The China experience' (*Zhongguo jingyan* 中国经验), 'The China pace' (*Zhongguo sudu* 中国速度), 'The China miracle' (*Zhongguo qiyi* 中国奇迹), 'The rise of China' (*Zhongguo jueqi* 中国崛起)" (http://cmp.hku.hk/2010/02/23/4565/). This shows how far the Chinese political discourse had then shifted from identifying itself as a peculiarity within the Marxist-Leninist orthodoxy, to becoming a discourse, which describes a Chinese way of development, which eventually can be adopted as a model by others.

7 From Model to Dream

Ever since Xi Jinping came to power (2012), he quickly brought the political and institutional agenda up to date and has given priority to a significant change of direction. This change—even if appears to be couched in the consolidated language of continuity—stands for a significant change of ideas and practices-ideas and concepts different from those propagated by the country's previous leadership. In fact, the 'Scientific Vision of Development' which was proposed by his predecessor, Hu Jintao, was as opaque, as Xi's new vision is brilliant: the stream of sparkling quotations and anecdotes which flow from the official media have given Xi an increasingly reassuring and optimistic image (Jacobs and Buckley 2015). His new 'Chinese Dream' generates and encourages a feeling of 'belonging', forges

[3]See the frequency of the term "China Model" in the People's Daily. http://cmp.hku.hk/2012/09/10/26667/.

links even across boundaries and offers an alternative vision of China's future. It no longer advocates the previous 'Scientific vision of development' consisting only of 'Looking at things with new eyes' or building what was vaguely defined as a 'Harmonious Society'. This new 'Chinese Dream' advocates and defines a project with a definite aim, a path which all Chinese can aspire to and along which they can all travel. And yet the 'dream' is still the ancient one: a dream of a country that is 'rich and strong', a dream which has now become part of everyday life. In short: China's new 'national' watchword.[4] We can therefore without any doubt maintain that from the time when Xi Jinping became the undisputed leader of the of the Fifth generation in 2012 he has displayed from the very beginning his ability of combining some of the key formulas of the past Maoist rhetoric with expressions and slogans inspired by Chinese tradition, using these with language which perpetuates the glories of the pre-revolutionary past and foretells the crowning fulfilment of long cherished dreams. This seems to be part of a culture, which has traditionally looked to its past in order to build its future: even the official objective of achieving a society which is 'moderately prosperous' (*xiaokang shehui* 小康社会) uses an expression which belongs to ancient Confucian literature.

In recent years we have been witnessing the emergence of a series of 'national' themes, which are rooted in Chinese tradition. An example of this is the expression 'rich and strong' which refers to the ancient saying 'Rich country, strong army' (*fuguo qiangbing* 富国强兵), the origins of which can be found in the writings of Han Feizi, an influential political philosopher of the Warring States period 'Chinese Legalist' school. His philosophy was seen in direct antagonism to Confucian ethics: he was decidedly in favour of the strict application of the law, the importance of the state and of military power. These theories seem to have gained a new popularity in recent days: they are seen as a possible inspiration for Xi's policies against corruption and in support of the laws emanated by Xi Jinping (Hilton 2015). This orientation, which is becoming more and more explicit in the contemporary Chinese political discourse, is focused on a re-discovering and highlighting 'Chineseness.' Everything gravitates around the theme of the 'Chinese dream', a theme which has been used constantly to describe the renewal of the country and its prosperity and prestige in the international arena.

Both the Chinese leadership and the media have previously used the word 'dream' (*meng* 梦) metaphorically to describe the country's re-emergence as a major power and other contemporary national aspirations. They celebrated the 2008 Beijing Olympics, for example, as realising a century-old dream using the slogan was 'One World, One Dream' (*Tong yige shijie, tong yige mengxiang* 同一个 世界 同一个梦想). Even before the Xi Jinping took over power in 2012, the dream metaphor had already been introduced in different contexts and was the subject of numerous studies and publications of varying importance. However, Xi is the one

[4]It is worth reading the recent: Chen (2014) on the 'discursive power of Xi jingping', as the heading of the book writes. See also Bandurski (2015).

who has given the official definition of what this metaphor means and what its objectives are. The official records show that the slogan was first used in November 2012 when Xi visited the Chinese National Museum in Beijing: the occasion was an exhibition called 'The Road to the Renewal', which displayed a large number of historic photos and documents of modern contemporary Chinese history from the time of the first Opium War in 1839. On that occasion, recently appointed members of the new permanent Committee of the Politburo were also present. The 17th Party Congress had just been completed and the visit therefore took on a powerfully symbolic significance as a legitimation of a shared historical perspective.

"Nowadays, everyone is talking about the 'Chinese Dream'", Xi Jinping said. "In my view, to realize the great renewal of the Chinese nation is the greatest dream for the Chinese nation in modern history" (Xi 2012). He thus made a point of stating very clearly that a bridge had been crossed from the attainment of communist ideals, now consigned to an improbable future, to a more pragmatic, achievable dream, which in his view would reflect the true spirit of China. A few months later, in March 2013, Xinhua Press Agency records that he referred no less than nine times to the 'Chinese dream' in his first speech to the National Assembly of the People (Xinhua 2013). From that day onwards, the theme would become the leitmotif of official political discourse. Although Xi Jinping calls for the 'Great Renaissance of the Chinese Nation' (*Zhonghua minzu weidade fuxing* 中华民族伟大的复兴) the core aim of the country's twenty-first century dream has featured in official rhetoric for over a decade (and in Taiwan for many decades). Related exhortations urging national revitalisation such as 'Revive China' (*Zhenxing Zhonghua* 振兴中华) have been part of the official political rhetoric far longer. "Its historical antecedents include the revolutionary Sun Yat-sen's 'Revive China Society' (*Xingzhonghui* 兴中会). Founded in Hawaii in 1894, the 'Revive China Society' played a central role in the 1934 Republican-era New Life Campaign. While the CCP promoted a consensual vision for China in terms of a 'national dream', from the end of 2012, independent writers and thinkers on the other hand want China to achieve something else first: governance according to the country's constitution (*xianzheng* 宪政)" (Barme 2013).

8 Conclusions

We have seen how skillfully Xi Jinping's leadership is in constructing a complex web of texts and speeches in which allusions and quotations to past tradition alternate with evocations and references to the established Maoist revolutionary legacy. Xi Jinping's aim is to create a reassuring vision of the future, in which the guiding role of the party acquires a constant and solid legitimization. With this in mind, even the old slogans and obsessively repetitive formulas of the Maoist past will re-gain, in ways which may seem paradoxical, a new vitality. Within this clever combination of past and present slogans and concepts, the previous revolutionary discourse is dismantled, only to be patiently reconstructed so that it strikes a distinctly reformist note. In no way does this provoke an obvious break with past Maoist orthodoxy, which on the contrary will continue in alliance with Confucius and a thousand glorious ancestors to be the luminous face of the ever changing prism which is the China of today.

References

Bandurski D (2015) Meeting Mr 'Hot Phrase'. China Media Project, 02/06, http://cmp.hku.hk/2015/02/06/38107/

Barmé GR (2013) The China Dreams. In: Barmé GR, Goldkorn J (eds) The China story yearbook 2013. Civilizing China. Australian Centre on China in the World, The Australian National University, Canberra. http://www.thechinastory.org/yearbooks/yearbook-2013/forum-dreams-and-power/chinese-dreams-zhongguo-meng-中国梦/

Chen X 陈锡喜 (ed) (2014) Ping Yi jin ren (平易近人) ([Xi Jin] Ping is close to people). Shanghai Jiaotong Daxue Chubanshe, Shanghai

Cheung K (2008) Modernity, history and the negotiation of Identity: revisiting the liberals/New left debate. In: Guo B, Guo S (eds) China in search of a harmonious society. Rowman & Littlefield, Lanham, pp 163–184

Gunn E (1991) Rewriting Chinese. Stanford University Press, Stanford

Guo B, Guo S (eds) (2008) China in search of a harmonious society. Rowman & Littlefield, Lanham

Hilton I (2015) Ancient origins of President Xi's harsh brand of justice in China. The Financial Times, August 15

http://chineseposters.net/index.php

http://cmp.hku.hk

http://cmp.hku.hk/2010/02/23/4565/

http://cpc.people.com.cn/n/2012/1118/c64094-19612151.html

http://2011lianghui.people.com.cn/GB/214392/14135967.html

http://news.xinhuanet.com/ziliao/2003-01/20/content_697061.htm

Jacobs A, Buckley C (2015) Move over Mao: beloved 'Pa pa Xi' Awes China. New York Times, March 08

Li G (1995) A Glossary of political terms of the PRC. Chinese University Press, Hongkong

Li X (2001) Creeping freedoms in China's Press. In: Brahm LJ (ed) China's century, the awakening of the next economic powerhouse. Wiley, New York

Link P (2013) An anatomy of Chinese. Rhythm, metaphor, politics. Harvard University Press, Harvard

People's Daily (1991), October 29

People's Daily (1998), November 22

Qian G (2012) The mixed bag of socialism. China Media Project. http://cmp.hku.hk/2012/10/04/27771/

Schell O, Delury J (2013) Wealth and power. Random House, New York

Schoenhals M (1992) Doing things with words in Chinese politics: five studies. Institute of East Asian Studies University of California, Berkeley

Song Z 宋自然 (ed) (2015) 100 nian Hanyu xinci xinyu da cidian (100年汉语新词新语大辞典) (100 year's Dictionary of Chinese new words). Shanghai cishu chuban, Shanghai

The Economist (2014) Wild at heart, May 31. http://www.economist.com/news/books-and-arts/21602978-how-countryand-peopleare-changing-wild-heart

Wu G (2000) One head, many mouths: diversifying press structures in reform China. In: Lee Chichuan (ed) Power. Money and media. Northwestern University Press, Evanston (Illinois)

Xi J 习近平 (2012) Inheriting the past looking toward the future: let's bravely march forward with the aim of rejuvenating the Chinese nation (Chengqian qihou jizhu kailai jixu chaozhe zhonghua minzu weida fuxing mubiao fengyong qianjin) (承前启后 继往开来 继续朝着中华民族伟大复兴目标奋勇前进). http://news.xinhuanet.com/politics/2012-11/29/c_113852724.htm

Xinhua (2013) Special correspondence: Xi Jinping mentions nine times the 'Chinese Dream' (Texie:Xi Jinping jiu ti 'zhongguo meng') (特写:习近平九提'中国梦'), March 17. http://news.xinhuanet.com/2013lh/2013-03/17/c_115054547.htm

Yu H (2014) China's struggle to forget. The New York Time, March 16. https://www.nytimes.com/2014/03/17/opinion/chinas-struggle-to-forget.html?_r=1

Zha J 查建英 (2006) Bashiniandai caifang lu (八十年代 采访录) (Interviews on the 1980s). Sanlian shudian, Beijing

Zhao Y (1998) Media, market and democracy in China. University of Illinois Press, Chicago

'Disclosure Is the Norm, Non-disclosure Is the Exception'. A Genre-Based Analysis on Institutional Discourse on the Government Information Disclosure in China

Bettina Mottura

Abstract Government information disclosure in China is a set of procedures, tied to the public institutions, aimed at generating a steady and timely flow of information between the state and the citizens. From 2007 to 2016, the scope and the procedures of this policy have been codified by a number of official documents, and these texts can be considered expressions of the Chinese institutional discourse on government information disclosure. The policy on open government information has led to a scholarly debate on the concrete goals the Chinese central government is pursuing through the implementation of information disclosure. In this chapter, a corpus of texts on government information disclosure (including all of the relevant official documents published from 2007 to 2016) will be analysed through a genre-based approach, in order to contribute to the discussion on the implementation objectives and their development. Finally, the statements stemming from genre analysis will be examined taking into account a variety of lexical features of the corpus documents.

1 Introduction

In China, the open government information system is a set of procedures, tied to the public institutions, aimed at generating a steady and timely flow of information between the state and the citizens. A government capable of guiding the circulation of news within national borders through the publication of selected information on the executive bodies' work, supporting the official statements with documented

B. Mottura (✉)
Department of Language Mediation and Intercultural Communication, University of Milan, Milan, Italy
e-mail: bettina.mottura@unimi.it

B. Mottura
Contemporary Asia Research Centre, University of Milan, Milan, Italy

S. Beretta et al. (eds.), *Understanding China Today*, Understanding China,
DOI 10.1007/978-3-319-29625-8_18

opinions of eminent experts, acquires a strong position in the communications landscape. Thanks to the effective strategy of spinning the news, the government can reinforce its credibility and prestige.

The effort to strengthen the influence of institutions on news production is not new in China. In the contemporary history of the country the control on information and the leadership of the masses were constantly exercised by the Chinese Communist Party through the mechanisms of censorship and propaganda. However, the legal framework regulating the government information disclosure activities was first consolidated in 2008 with the enforcement of the 'Regulations of the People's Republic of China on Open Government Information' (Guowuyuan 2007) issued by the State Council.

The emphasis that pervades the regulations seems to highlight the persuasive intent of the author. It seems as if, through the normative text, the central executive organs were attempting to demonstrate the usefulness of the government information disclosure system and should convince the lower level offices to abide by the new rules. This allows us to believe that the implementation of this policy is not perceived as a simple reworking of established mechanisms.

From a national perspective I believe that the innovative quality of the policy resides first in attributing directly to the state administration bodies a responsibility in shaping the news, rather than to those of the party. Secondly, it is equally innovative to affirm that a dominant political position is better consolidated through an accurate dissemination of information, which partially limits the arbitrariness of secrecy in the government work. Finally, this norm creates the possibility for citizens to access relevant information from the administration, thereby strengthening the relationship between the public and the executive offices.

Over time, the policy development progressively took into account a growing awareness of the citizens regarding the importance of certain aspects of social life, often accompanied by a greater critical capacity in evaluating relevant events and assessing the quality of a related communication flow. These abilities contribute to shaping the collective representation of a situation, primarily because the people directly participate in creating the news through social media.

In a comparative perspective, the Chinese institutional discourse on the disclosure of information by the public administration organs and the citizens' right to access it do not diverge from the standard of the international policies on these matters. The lexicon of the policy documents, for example, is coherent with the international and worldwide discourse on information disclosure. Nonetheless, due to the above-mentioned characteristics of news management in China, the concrete formulation of the policy caught the interest of several scholars. One of their main concerns was to verify what, since 2008, the concrete goals of the open government policy in China had been, and to analyse how those objectives have subsequently evolved. The problem of the scope as well as the aims of the open government information policy will be further discussed in the third section of this chapter.

2 Information Disclosure

The Regulations (Guowuyuan 2007) define 'government information' as information distributed or obtained by administrative organs in fulfilling their responsibilities, and data that should be recorded and stored in a given form. Since the publication of the norm, the executive organs at all administrative levels must disseminate information on their work or on any relevant event that happened in the areas under their jurisdiction. A piece of information is to be considered particularly relevant if it involves the vital interests of citizens or if it concerns the structure and functioning of the public administration organs. Any significant fact should be disclosed within 20 working days from the event's occurrence. State secrets and news that may endanger national security or destabilize society must be considered as exceptions to the policy of open government information (Horsley 2009).

The policy implementation has created a network of decentralized actors committed to ensuring that the citizens receive an accurate and timely dissemination of news, with truthful and complete information. When disclosing government information, administrative organs should observe the principles of justice, fairness, and convenience to the people.

Official gazettes, government websites, press conferences, newspapers and periodicals, radio, and television (and other media) are considered key communication channels for news circulation. Moreover, the public can also access administrative documents through state archives, public libraries, or dedicated desks in the administrative offices.

Each administrative organ in charge of policy implementation must first draft an open government information guide, a catalogue, and an annual report on their respective performance. The guide indicates the categories of content to be delivered, the classification system in use, and the rules for public access. The catalogue will organize the information in different categories and keep a record of previously published materials. Insofar as single institutions have to define and regularly update both their guidelines and a catalogue of relevant issues for the policy implementation, there appears to be a certain degree of local autonomy in each organ's activity.

The process of information disclosure shows a very strong top-down orientation, emphasising the commitment of state institutions in disseminating information and data. Nonetheless, the policy, as described in the Regulations (Guowuyuan 2007), also entitles the citizens to access information detained by administrative bodies in order to protect their personal interests. Every citizen's demand for information should be submitted in written form, and the applicant is entitled to receive a response within 15–30 working days. Even if the request is rejected, the administration is bound to provide an answer explaining the motivation for refusal.

From 2008 and 2016, several documents have been issued by the State Council (or other state organs) in order to better define the scope and the procedures of the open government information policy implementation.

In parallel, the institutional discourse on the possibility of accessing documents produced by the public administration widened its scope by granting Chinese citizens the right to be informed. The right first appeared in the section on Civil and Political Rights of the 'National Human Rights Action Plan (2009–2010)' and again three years later in the 'National Human Rights Action Plan (2012–2015)'. Both plans explicitly emphasise the existing tie between the government's transparency effort and the right to be informed. The protection of this right is considered strictly dependent on a successful open government information policy implementation, but this assumption is expressed in slightly different ways in the two texts.

The 2009 Action Plan document addresses the issue of the right to be informed by claiming a full and effective application of the existing norms on the open government information, requesting a further development of these rules, indicating transparency as a target at the national and the local levels, and pointing out specific matters to focus on in disseminating the news.

In the 2012 document, the scope of the commitment of the state in the protection of the right to know is wider. The open government information policy in this case is mentioned only once, and the disclosure of the information is assumed as a general principle, which should inspire all of the government's actions. In particular, a selection of priority issues is published. For example, the circulation of information on the appointment or dismissal of officials in leading positions is required, with the aim to promote the institutionalization and standardization of procedures for appointment. Another target is the dissemination of information on the work of enterprises or institutions providing public services (hospitals, schools, public transport, etc.), to ensure greater public control over their activities. The project also encompasses access to information on company business conceded to the employees of public or private firms.

With the shift from opening government information to the protection of the right to know, the role of the citizen changed from people being the target of a unidirectional flow of information issued by the institutions (liberally published or disclosed upon request), to every single person becoming a right holder.

Two years later, The Fourth Plenary Session of the 18th Central Committee of the CPC approved a 'Resolution on Certain Major Issues Concerning Comprehensively Advancing the Law-Based Governance of China' (Zhong Gong Zhongyang 2014). The resolution endorsed for the first time the principle that disclosure of executive bodies' information should be the rule and that non-disclosure should be the exception (Horsley 2016). This statement paved the way for the possibility to draft a "negative list" on open government affairs, clearly defining the kind of information that should not be divulgated, and therefore opening news from any other sector to lawful diffusion (Zhong Gong Zhongyang Bangongting/Guowuyuan Bangongting 2016).

In the last decade, the institutional discourse has shown an evolution from a perspective mainly centred on the government and its responsibility to disseminate information on its work, to a panorama in which the state is the protector of the right of the citizens to access information even when the demand is presented to other organizations. In recent documents, the state is also represented as a gatekeeper on transparency in sectors such as public finance and procurement, public housing, food and drug safety, environmental protection, production safety, expropriations and demolitions with forced relocation, and education. In regulating the news circulation flow, the state organs have to verify the trustworthiness of the news and ensure that the most important pieces are expressed in an authoritative manner. Every office should also try to foresee the potential impact of a specific item of information on society in order to be able to cope with the reactions of the public, should it be necessary. Overall, there seems to be a partial loss of relevance of the open government information activity as it becomes just one aspect of a broader political project on governmental participation in shaping the news.

3 The Open Government Information Policy and Its Objectives

Article 1 of the 'Regulations of the People's Republic of China on Open Government Information' of 2007 outlines the aim and the scope of the information disclosure policy:

> Article 1. In order to ensure that citizens, legal persons and other organizations obtain government information in accordance with the law, enhance transparency of the work of government, promote administration in accordance with the law, and bring into full play the role of government information in serving the people's production and livelihood and their economic and social activities, these Regulations are hereby formulated.

This formulation had been used since 1987 in documents jointly issued by the Chinese Communist Party Central Committee and the State Council, when they called for the 'three openings' (*san gongkai* 三公开): to enhance further transparency in business, in the villages, and in the government. In addition, a number of experimental open information strategies had been carried out by administrative bodies at the village and provincial levels since 2000 (Xiao 2012; Liu 2011; Horsley 2007; Carter and Lü 2007).

In discussing the open government information policy objectives, some authors affirm that we should go beyond the statement of Article 1 of the Regulations (2007). The declared objective is to systematize transparency mechanisms within executive bodies. This effort would bring two further advantages: on the one side, an efficient circulation of information on the work of the government would protect people's rights despite their vertical and hierarchical relationship with institutions; on the other hand, it would grant the bureaucratic centre the possibility of exercising more stringent control on the local apparatus.

The first perspective would place the Chinese information disclosure policy under the influence of the European tradition of the freedom of information defined as allowing the general public to access data held by the national government through a set of standardized procedures.

The second point of view is based on the assumption of an existing adversarial relationship between the central government and local authorities, where granting the public regular access to working news would be a tool for top-down supervision within the public administration (Hubbard 2008).

In a previous article, I identified the last aspect of the implementation of information disclosure mechanisms as the predominant view and this was confirmed by other authors' publications (Mottura 2014; Burns 2014). This perspective seems to be challenged by the positions published in a recent document jointly issued by the Chinese Communist Party Central Committee and the State Council (Zhong Gong Zhongyang and Guowuyuan 2015). In the 'Implementing Outlines for Building a Government Under the Rule of Law (2015–2020)' there is a paragraph which discusses the strengthening of checks and controls over the power of the administration. Interestingly enough, this text explicitly links control over the executive bodies' work and sanctions on illegal actions by the administration with an effective protection of the rights of information, participation, expression, and supervision exerted by the people. It seems, therefore, that the two previously mentioned hypotheses are not in conflict, but, instead, work in synergy.

This chapter will attempt to contribute to the discussion on the policy objectives starting from an analysis of the institutional discourse on information disclosure displayed in official documents. Through a genre-based approach an attempt will be made to verify the coexistence of a need for tighter control on the administration and the aspiration to the protection of rights in the institutional discourse on information disclosure in China. The results of the analysis of the texts as genre realizations will be discussed by taking into account some of the lexical choices made by the authors of the examined documents.

In the next section, I will give an account of the collection of a corpus focused on institutional discourse on information disclosure as well as describe the main characteristics of the selected texts.

4 Institutional Discourse on Information Disclosure Policy: Three Sub-Corpora

As previously stated, the 'Regulations of the People's Republic of China on Open Government Information' established the legal foundations of the open government information policy in 2007. In the text, the reader can find the definitions of key concepts, policy objectives, and general procedures for its implementation.

Since then, these basic tools have been enhanced by a number of different measures issued by the State Council, published either to lead the concrete work of administrative organs in the field of news circulation or to widen the scope of the policy. These texts represent—to this author's knowledge—all of the available primary sources of the administrative discourse on the open government information policy. It has therefore been possible to collect a set of sixteen texts published in

Chinese from 2007 to 2016, aimed at structuring the policy and orienting its implementation at the national level. The selection criteria applied to the corpus exclude the local level documents and any text that represents a product of the implementation work (such as the information guides, catalogues, or annual reports).

Furthermore, in 2009, the People's Republic of China published its first 'National Action Plan for Human Rights (2009–2010)' and three years later a second Action Plan (2012–2015) was issued. The enactment of the action plans led to the publication of an 'Assessment Report on the Implementation of the National Human Rights Action Plan (2012–2015)' in 2016. In light of the Action Plans' content and the aforementioned importance of the 'right to be informed', I argue that these three documents are relevant for the collection of a corpus on the institutional discourse on the information disclosure policy.

Consequently, in the analysis of institutional discourse on government information disclosure in China, the corpus considered relevant for this paper consists of the nineteen texts mentioned above—sixteen of which are measures for the design and implementation of the policy and a further three texts promoting the right to know.

Due to the basic criteria chosen for the corpus collection, all of the texts have been drafted and published by central government organs from 2007 to 2016, and most of them have been released by the State Council. The corpus can be divided in three sub-corpora focused on different specialized languages: legal language, bureaucratic language, and political language. The ascription of each text to one of the three sub-corpora is based on genre analysis (Swales 1990; Bhatia 1993). The basic definition of this approach is (Swales 1990):

> A genre comprises a class of communicative events, the members of which share some set of communicative purposes. These purposes are recognized by the expert members of the parent discourse community and thereby constitute the rationale for the genre. This rationale shapes the schematic structure of the discourse and influences and constrains choice of content and style. Communicative purpose is both a privileged criterion and one that operates to keep the scope of a genre as here conceived narrowly focused on comparable rhetorical action. In addition to purpose, exemplars of a genre exhibit various patterns of similarity in terms of structure, style, content and intended audience. If all high probability expectations are realized, the exemplar will be viewed as prototypical by the parent discourse community. The genre names inherited and produced by discourse communities and imported by others constitute valuable ethnographic communication, but typically need further validation.

Swales links the identification of a genre to the awareness of a discourse community using specific texts in their professional activities in order to reach an intended communicative purpose. His original definition has been further developed by Bhatia (1993) and successive literature. The communicative purpose as a primary criterion to place a piece of text in a particular generic category has been widely discussed (Askehave and Swales 2001).

The generic categories applied in order to analyse the corpus and identify each text as the concrete realization of a genre will be based on existing classifications formally codified in China. Over the last decades, there has been a strong drive toward standardization in text production and the definition of draft creation procedures in many public sectors. Two examples of this effort are the amended version of the 'Legislation Law' (Quanguo Renmin Daibiao Dahui 2015) regulating the production of legal texts, and also the 'Regulations on Party and Government Organs Document Processing Work' (Zhong Gong Zhongyang Bangongting and Guowuyuan Bangongting 2012), which focuses on administrative documents. Drawing from the law, regulations, and the copious amount of literature on the subject, the nineteen documents of the corpus on the information disclosure policy can be identified as concrete realizations of specific textual genres which appear to be deeply embedded in given specialized languages.

Document type	Specialized language	Number of occurrences
Regulations 条例	Legal language	1
Notice 通知	Bureaucratic language	11
Opinions 意见	Bureaucratic language	4
Action Plan 行动计划	Political language	2
Report 报告	Political language/bureaucratic language	1

Notices and opinions are genres identified by the 'Regulations on Party and Government Organs Document Processing Work' (Zhong Gong Zhongyang Bangongting and Guowuyuan Bangongting 2012) as different types of official documents (*gongwen* 公文). In addition, as previously mentioned, the corpus includes other kinds of texts: regulations, a legal discourse genre, and actions plans and reports, which are expressions of the political discourse genre. However, genres borrowed from political or legal discourses in the corpus do belong to the genre system (Bazerman 1993, 1994) of public administration, in the sense that these texts are used by members of the discourse community of the Chinese bureaucrats to communicate with people outside of their professional group, such as, for example, the ordinary public (Bhatia 2002).

The sub-corpus of official documents shares a common feature: all of the texts are regulatory measures, although their scope is limited to the jurisdiction of the organ that emanates them. In addition, each genre within the corpus has a communicative purpose established by the 2012 regulations on document processing (art. 8). Notices (*tongzhi* 通知) may be used by administrative organs to announce and transmit information or directions to subordinate offices or other working units; to approve for distribution official documents written by lower level offices; or to forward texts published by higher level agencies. Opinions (*yijian* 意见) serve to express a view on relevant problems and suggest a way to solve them within the public administration.

Legal texts outline norms. In particular, regulations (*tiaoli* 条例) are legal texts on specific topics promulgated by state or lower administrative organs in the framework of relevant policies or laws with the aim of structuring concrete actions to execute them.

The sub-corpus of political documents is composed by two Action Plans on Human Rights and a Report on their implementation. The existence of the codified genre of Human Rights Action Plan (*renquan xingdong jihua* 人权行动计划) is affirmed by paragraph 71 of Part II of the 'Vienna Declaration and Programme of Action of the World Conference on Human Rights' (1993) discussing the content that such a plan should encompass. The intended purpose of the genre is stated in a manual for the preparation of these documents published by the Office of the United Nation High Commissioner for Human Rights (2002):

> The fundamental purpose of a national human rights action plan is to improve the promotion and protection of human rights in a particular country. It does this by placing human rights improvements in the context of public policy, so that governments and communities can endorse human rights improvements as practical goals, devise programmes to ensure the achievement of these goals, engage all relevant sectors of government and society, and allocated sufficient resources.

Finally, the report (*baogao* 报告) has been considered here as being a genre belonging to both the administrative and political languages. Within the state administration, these texts are written by lower level offices for their superiors in order to present an account of the work done, report on the state of affairs, and respond to an enquiry. In the political context, public reports are issued by institutions to account for policy implementation.

5 Corpus Features and Strategic Objectives of the Information Disclosure Policy

The hypothesis outlined in the second section is that in China the institutional discourse on information disclosure by the government is targeted to strengthen top-down control within the public administration and, by this means, enhance people's rights protection. The question then becomes how can one validate this hypothesis starting from the institutional discourse on information disclosure?

To discuss this hypothesis, one possible tool is the analysis of genre distribution within the selected corpus. As shown in the intended purpose descriptions of all of the genres described earlier in this chapter, the administrative and the legal genres displayed in the corpus are all produced by state organs and addressed to other governmental agencies. As far as the genres of the political field are concerned, the author is the government, while the targeted audience is ideally composed nationally by the citizens and internationally by other states.

Overall, more than 80% of the corpus is composed of administrative and legal texts. Therefore, the institutional discourse on information disclosure is mostly composed by an internal flow of communication between different actors all belonging to the public administration. On the basis of these findings, the open government information policy seems essentially designed to enhance control capacity.

In this context, what is the position given to the citizen in the documents? Lexical choices are useful to highlight the text orientation on this topic. To reflect on the respective roles attributed to the state and the citizens in the documents examined, it is noteworthy to pinpoint the selection of words having as extra-linguistic referent the recipients of the information flow. On the basis of a frequency analysis in the administrative sub-corpus, these words, listed by decreasing number of occurrences, are: the 'public' (*gongzhong* 公众, 94 occurrences), the 'citizens' (*gongmin* 公民, 52 occurrences), the 'masses' (*qunzhong* 群众, 35 occurrences), and 'public opinion' (*yulun* 舆论, 12 occurrences).

In discussing this data, it is relevant to highlight that the most frequently used word, the 'public', generally identify a large part of society. 'Public opinion' stems from the language of the media. Meanwhile, 'citizen' comes from the legal language, and 'masses' is clearly characterized as belonging to the political language, and carries a heavy burden of historical meanings.

Therefore, 'public' refers to society as a collective actor and is linked to concepts such as common interests and shared values. The use of 'citizens' gives much more importance to the rights and duties the people are entitled to when dealing with the state authorities. The 'masses' refer to an indistinct group of political actors with a highly asymmetric hierarchical relationship with the institutions. Finally, when the documents employ 'public opinion', they emphasize the relevance of the communication flow generated by the government and its possible impact in strengthening political legitimacy. These lexical choices seem to confirm the centrality conferred to the government action in the field of information disclosure.

However, analysing the corpus lexicon in a diachronic perspective, we should note that new words appeared in institutional discourse on disclosure after 2012. First, we can mention 'public opinion', followed by 'public sentiment' (*yuqing* 舆情, 33 occurrences). As a result of introducing these concepts as relevant, the government acquires new tasks such as 'to monitor public sentiment' (*genzong yuqing* 跟踪舆情), 'to guide public opinion' or public sentiment (*yindao yulun/yuqing,* 引导舆论/舆情), and to face and fight any public doubts about the trustworthiness of the institutional news or statements.

These lexical choices demonstrate the growing attention granted to the recipient of the information flow, as compared to the one provided to the authors of the above-mentoned 2007 Regulations. This orientation confirms a renewed centrality of the citizen already highlighted in the action plans. In addition to that, the very identity of the people is increasingly defined in terms of their ability to benefit from the information received, and less in terms of a hierarchical relationship between state and citizens.

In light of these lexical findings, it is possible to infer that the idea of an open government information policy mainly targeted to strengthen top-down control within the government administration is challenged by a growing necessity of dealing with a highly demanding public.

The keyword of this new perspective is 'government credibility' (*gongxinli* 公信力, 13 occurrences), which starts to appear regularly in the documents in 2013. On the basis of the selected corpus, an effective implementation of the information disclosure mechanisms requires a stronger commitment to transparency and openness and wider participation and control of the masses over the administration; this is based on the concrete knowledge of the details of any relevant situation, which is associated with the right to enquire (*shenqingquan* 申请权). These elements could strengthen the credibility of the government by demonstrating its accountability and effectiveness in crisis management.

The attention devoted to crisis management is particularly relevant in 2014 with the appearance of expressions such as the 'right to assistance in case of emergency' (*jiujiquan* 救济权, 2014). The texts contain a precise description of how the administrative offices must behave when a relevant topic strikes the interest of many people and is liable to arouse social concerns or protests. The first institutional reaction should be an assessment of the impact the event could have on public sentiment, followed by an information campaign aimed at containing the risk of social discontent through the refined use of communicative tools (for example, the microblogging channel). The news flow produced by the state organs should encompass a detailed analysis of the situation and accurate explanations of its effects. The campaign to neutralize any rumours and guide public opinion should involve experts who express their views, and it requires a profound and complex understanding of society based on a long-term preventive monitoring mechanism and the optimal use of available communication channels.

Between 2015 and 2016, the documents expand their scope to broader concerns such as promoting public participation in government rulemaking and decision-making alongside improving the feedback-delivery mechanism on public comments regarding the actions of the government.

The rights mentioned in the previous section confirm a greater centrality attributed to the citizen in stimulating the executive bodies to publish reliable and useful information. The public takes on an active role in the concrete policy implementation. On the basis of the lexical findings, information disclosure is represented as a tool for dealing with the risk of expansion of social discontent; it seems therefore evermore useful in consolidating both the political legitimacy of the government as well as social stability.

6 Conclusions

In light of the analysis of the corpus, government information disclosure in China is a relevant channel for hierarchical supervision and control within the public administration. Consider, for example, the emphasis placed on transparency in public finances and the management of funds. However, some elements of the lexicon used in the documents throughout the years highlight the fact that the effectiveness of the information flow in reducing the risk of social conflict is a matter of growing concern for the Chinese government. This perspective emphasises the relevance of the public as a conscious and proactive target of the communication process. Therefore, both the state organs and the citizens are now considered relevant stakeholders in policy implementation, along with private companies, which are considered important as guarantors of the people's right to know. Nonetheless, the involvement of these categories of actors in the information disclosure system is still embedded in the context of a highly asymmetric relationship in terms of power distribution. It is the government that is entitled to spreading the news of its work, supervising the companies' commitment to transparency, and, finally, guiding public opinion.

In conclusion, the information disclosure system appears to be an instrument to consolidate the legitimacy of public institutions to rule the country, either through the administrative control of the central apparatus on the local authorities or through the skilful management of the emotions and sentiments within Chinese society.

References

Askehave I, Swales JM (2001) Genre identification and communicative purpose: a problem and a possible solution. Appl Linguist 21:195–212

Bazerman C (1993) Foreword to. In: Blyler NR, Thralls CS (eds) Professional communication: the social perspective. SAGE Publications, London, pp VII–VIII

Bazerman C (1994) Systems of genres and the enactment of social intentions. In: Freedman A, Medway P (eds) Genre and the new rhetoric. Taylor and Francis, London, pp 79–101

Bhatia VK (1993) Analysing genre. Language use in professional settings. Longman, London

Bhatia VK (2002) Applied genre analysis: a multi-perspective model. Ibérica 4:3–19

Burns JP (2014) Looking west: the impact of western ideas on public sector reform policies in China. In: Brødsgaard KE (ed) Globalization and public sector reform in China. Routledge, Abingdon, pp 23–37

Carter M, Lü Y (2007) Access to government information in Europe and China: what lessons to be learned?. EU-China Information Society Project, Beijing

Guowuyuan 国务院 (2007) 中华人民共和国政府信息公开条例 (Regulations of the People's Republic of China on Open Government Information). http://www.gov.cn/zwgk/2007–04/24/content_592937.htm

Guowuyuan Xinwen Bangongshi 国务院新闻办公室 (2009) 国家人权行动计划 (2009–2010年) (National Action Plan for Human Rights 2009–2010). http://www.scio.gov.cn/ztk/dtzt/2015/33423/33432/Document/1448652/1448652.htm

Guowuyuan Xinwen Bangongshi 国务院新闻办公室 (2012) 国家人权行动计划 (2012—2015年) (National Action Plan for Human Rights 2012–2015). http://www.scio.gov.cn/zxbd/nd/2012/Document/1172889/1172889.htm

Guowuyuan Xinwen Bangongshi 国务院新闻办公室 (2016) 国家人权行动计划 (2012–2015年) 实施评估报告 (Assessment Report on the Implementation of the National Human Rights Action Plan 2012–2015). http://www.gov.cn/xinwen/2016-06/14/content_5082026.htm

Horsley JP (2007) Toward a more open China? A Florini (2007) The right to know: transparency for an open world. Columbia University Press, New York, pp 54–91

Horsley JP (2009) 关于政府信息免予公开典型条款的几点思考 (Some Thoughts on Typical Exemptions for Government Information Disclosure) 政治与法律 Issue 3, pp 37–41

Horsley JP (2016) China promotes open government as it seeks to reinvent its governance model. Freedominfo.org, 22 Feb 2016. http://www.freedominfo.org/2016/02/china-promotes-open-government-as-it-seeks-to-reinvent-its-governance-model/

Hubbard P (2008) China's regulations on open government information: challenges of nationwide policy implementation. Open Gov J Freedom Inf 1

Liu W (2011) Approaching democracy through transparency: a comparative law study on Chinese open government information. Am Univ Int Law Rev 4:983–1007

Mottura B (2014) Il governo cinese informa: strategie discorsive sul rapporto tra stato e cittadini. In: Dossi S et al (a cura) L'Asia tra passato e futuro. Scritti in ricordo di Enrica Collotti Pischel. Giuffrè, Milano, pp 63–76

Office of the United Nation High Commissioner for Human Rights (2002), Professional training series, vol 10. Handbook on national human rights plans of action, New York, 29 Aug

Quanguo Renmin Daibiao Dahui 全国人民代表大会 (2015) 中华人民共和国立法法 (Legislation Law). http://news.xinhuanet.com/politics/2015lh/2015-03/18/c_1114682142.htm

Swales JM (1990) Genre analysis. English in academic and research settings. Cambridge University Press, Cambridge

World Conference on Human Rights (1993) Vienna declaration and programme of action. Vienna, 25 June

Xiao W (2012) Gradual legislative process for FOI reforms in China. In: Xiao W (eds) Freedom of information reform in China: Information flow analysis. Routledge, Abingdon, pp 70–79

Zhong Gong Zhongyang Bangongting/Guowuyuan Bangongting 中共中央办公厅、国务院办公厅 (2012) 党政机关公文处理工作条例 (Regulations on Party and Government Organs Document Processing Work). http://www.gov.cn/zwgk/2013-02/22/content_2337704.htm

Zhong Gong Zhongyang Bangongting/Guowuyuan Bangongting 中共中央办公厅、国务院办公厅 (2016) 关于全面推进政务公开工作的意见 (Opinions on Comprehensively Promoting Open Government Affairs Work). http://news.xinhuanet.com/politics/2016-02/17/c_1118075366.htm

Zhong Gong Zhongyang 中共中央 (2014) 关于全面推进依法治国若干重大问题的决定 (Resolution on Certain Major Issues Concerning Comprehensively Advancing the Law-Based Governance of China). http://news.xinhuanet.com/politics/2014-10/28/c_1113015330.htm

Zhong Gong Zhongyang/Guowuyuan 中共中央、国务院 (2015) 法治政府建设实施纲要(2015–2020年) (Implementing Outlines for Building a Government Under the Rule of Law 2015–2020). http://www.gov.cn/xinwen/2015-12/28/content_5028323.htm

A Portal or A Mirror? The Reporting of Foreign Countries in 'China Daily'

Riccardo Puglisi

Abstract In this chapter I undertake a systematic investigation of the coverage of the main foreign countries in the Chinese newspaper China Daily, a state-run newspaper English (during the period from 2002–2009). The available empirical evidence allows for the conclusion that a country obtains significantly more coverage the higher its GDP and the geographically closer it is to China. The second finding is that 'bad news' are more newsworthy than 'good news': China Daily is found to devote more coverage to a country when its unemployment rate is high. In fact, how coverage of a given country does increase with higher unemployment does not in turn depend on its economic power and geographical proximity to China.

1 Introduction

One of the main functions of the mass media is to provide citizens with information about public affairs: the task of gathering and selecting news is delegated to media outlets, since it would be extremely costly for citizens to perform this task by themselves. But it is also true that—in a less immediate fashion—media outlets provide information about the views of those who publish them. This is the case, because editors and journalists enjoy some degrees of freedom in the choice of the issues and events they deem as 'newsworthy'. The way these degrees of freedom are systematically exploited might provide valuable cues about the opinions of those journalists, editors, and owners.

An expanding literature, which is mainly focused on the U.S., aims at obtaining some replicable measure of the ideological position of media outlets. In fact, the agenda setting behaviour of media outlets—i.e., the choice of newsworthy issues—can be fruitfully analysed in order to obtain this kind of measures (Puglisi 2011;

R. Puglisi (✉)
Department of Political and Social Sciences,
University of Pavia, Pavia, Italy
e-mail: riccardo.puglisi@unipv.it

S. Beretta et al. (eds.), *Understanding China Today*, Understanding China,
DOI 10.1007/978-3-319-29625-8_19

Larcinese et al. 2011; Puglisi and Snyder 2011). Other researchers have proposed other measures of the partisan leaning of media outlets, which are instead based on the 'similarity' of those with political actors of known ideological positions, namely members of the U.S. Congress. This has been done by looking at patterns of think tank quotes or at indicators of overall language similarity (Groseclose and Milyo 2005; Gentzkow and Shapiro 2010; Puglisi and Snyder 2015 for a survey of empirical methods to estimating media bias).

A salient feature of the most recent contributions on this topic is that they exploit the availability of online news archives, on which automatic keyword-based searches are performed. One advantage of this procedure is that, by definition, it is not intensive in the usage of human capital. Its low cost means that it can be used to gather data on a large number of news outlets over a long time span, restricted only by what is available in digital archives. More importantly, an automatic search is easily replicated, as it is based on a known set of words and/or sentences that are used as classifiers.

To date, these data-gathering techniques have been largely applied to media outlets—and especially newspapers—that are U.S. based. But there is large room to extend the analysis to media outlets that are located in other countries. A notable exception is the extensive analysis of Chinese newspapers in Chinese language by Qin et al. (2016). This type of analysis is of course feasible, if a newspaper has a news archive that is available online. In this chapter I will focus on China Daily, which is a China newspaper written in English. It is state-run, and is probably the most widely cited China-based media source in foreign countries. Against that background, it is particularly worthwhile to focus on the newspaper covers international relations: more precisely, this chapter provides a preliminary but systematic analysis of how the China Daily has covered the main foreign countries during the 2002–2009 period.[1] Not surprisingly, I find that a country is systematically more covered on the China Daily the higher its GDP and the geographically closer it is to China. Moreover, 'bad news' regarding a given country are more newsworthy than 'good news'. In fact, when exploring the time variation in the coverage of the various countries on a monthly basis, it turns out that the China Daily systematically assigns more coverage to a country when its unemployment rate happens to be higher than its average during the time period.

This chapter is organized as follows: in Sect. 2 I will describe the dataset and provide some summary statistics. Section 3 is devoted to the discussion of the results of the empirical analysis, while Sect. 4 concludes.

[1]For an empirical contribution that is close to the present one see Wu (2000): this is a cross-country analysis of the determinants of other countries' coverage on domestic newspapers. Also see Qian and Yanagizawa (2016) for an analysis of the coverage of human right violations in foreign countries on U.S. newspapers, as a function of the status of the diplomatic relationships between the U.S. government and that country's government.

2 Data Description

The website of China Daily (http://www.chinadaily.com.cn) allows to perform searches on the archive of its paper edition, dating back to 2002. In order to gather data on the coverage of the main countries of the world, I have run automatic searches of this archive, and obtained the monthly count of articles mentioning each country. The countries under consideration are the following: Brazil, Canada, France, Germany, India, Italy, Japan, (South) Korea, Russia, UK and USA. The last month in the sample is December 2009.

Since the size of the paper edition of China Daily might change over time, I divide the monthly count of articles mentioning country *c* by the monthly count of articles mentioning 'China'. Since the name of the newspaper (China Daily) is included in each article, this ratio should give a measure of the relative frequency of articles mentioning country c. Summary statistics of the variables under consideration are shown in Table 1, where I separately report figures for each country. Not surprisingly, the U.S. are the most frequently cited country on China Daily, with an average of around 15%. The second one is Japan (with almost 10% of articles), while the third one is Germany, narrowly preceding France. It must be also noticed that for almost all countries (except for France, India and the United Kingdom) the distribution of mentions is positively skewed, as witnessed by the fact that the average is larger than the median.

Table 1 Summary statistics

Variable	No of obs.	Mean	Median	Std. Dev.	Min	Max
Relative frequency of hits on China daily						
Brazil	96	2.154094	2.124254	0.9589242	0	5.339266
Canada	96	2.514963	2.417615	0.8266165	0.9646302	5.898876
France	96	5.465977	5.521118	1.832804	2.572347	14.40129
Germany	96	5.534072	5.239806	1.863264	2.310231	12.68076
India	96	3.632922	3.672965	0.9923897	0.4672897	6.930693
Italy	96	2.915011	2.72683	1.440796	0.660066	8.934517
Japan	96	9.6067	9.216846	2.749821	5.91829	20.22654
Korea	96	3.707601	3.28716	1.443457	1.659751	11.00324
Russia	96	4.835401	4.740886	1.223534	1.581028	10.19417
UK	96	1.65214	1.690432	0.8071712	0	3.253119
USA	96	14.68057	13.95858	4.738634	8.547718	37.21683

Notes Relative frequency of hits about a given country are calculated as the ratio between the monthly number of articles where the name of the country appears, divided by the monthly number of articles where the word "China" appears. Relative frequencies are expressed in percentage terms, i.e. "1" stands for one percent

Table 2 Country coverage on China daily, cross sectional analysis

Dependent variable	Relative frequency of hits on China daily	
2008 GDP, billions of PPP dollars	0.001***	0.001***
	[13.13]	[16.70]
Distance from China (thousands of km)	–	−0.206*
		[2.09]
R squared	0.81	0.87
Observations	11	11

Notes The table displays the output of OLS regressions with the average relative frequency of articles mentioning each country as the dependent variable. Standard errors are robust against heteroskedasticity, with t-statistics reported under each coefficient
*Significant at 1%
**Significant at 5%
***Significant at 1%

3 Results

In this section I will explore the correlates of country coverage in China Daily. Firstly, it is worthwhile to explore the simple cross-sectional variation in the coverage of the different countries. To do so, for each sampled country I compute the average relative frequency of mentions during the time period. I thus end up with 11 observations, which I match with reasonable proxies for their relative newsworthiness. More precisely, I use as explanatory variables the GDP of each country in 2008 (expressed in PPP-adjusted billions of U.S. dollars), and the air distance of each country's capital to Beijing (measured in thousands of kilometres).[2] The rationale for these proxies is straightforward: one can approximately get a sense of the economic relevance of a given country by looking at its overall GDP, which in turn should be made comparable across countries by taking into account the purchasing power of each currency. On the other hand, a country is likely to be more relevant to the readers and journalists of any given newspaper, the closer it is to the country where the newspaper is based. From a statistical viewpoint, I run 'ordinary least squares' ('OLS') regressions with the average relative frequency of country mentions as the dependent variable. Table 2 shows the output of this simple exercise.[3] In the first column I solely monitor a country's GDP, which is a very significant predictor of country coverage. The coefficient on this variable is positive and statistically different from zero at the one percent confidence level. Moreover, the magnitude of the correlation is sizeable: a coefficient of 0.001 would imply that

[2]The source for country GDP is the World Bank. The source for the air distance measures is the Google Maps-based calculator by Daft Logic: http://www.daftlogic.com/projects-google-maps-distance-calculator.htm.

[3]Standard errors are robust to heteroskedasticity, i.e. heterogeneity in the variance of the error term.

a country with a GDP that is one-trillion dollars larger than another one would on average obtain an additional one percent of articles on China Daily.

In column 2 I add as a control the air distance measure. The positive correlation between media coverage and GDP, as it turns out, is very robust to this change in the specification, albeit within a very small sample made of 11 observations only. Moreover, distance from China is negatively correlated with the dependent variable, and the correlation is mildly significant at the 10% confidence level. In terms of magnitudes, a coefficient of −0.206 implies that a country that is one thousand kilometres closer to China as compared to another one would on average obtain around 0.2% articles more on China Daily.

One might also be interested in exploring the correlates of the time variation in media coverage for the different countries in the sample. This is feasible, since for each country there are 96 monthly observations. The main focus of this analysis is on whether China Daily would change the coverage of the sampled countries as a function of their time-varying economic conditions. As mentioned above, I proxy those conditions with the quarterly level unemployment rate. A working hypothesis here is that 'bad news'—namely an increase in the unemployment rate—are more newsworthy than 'good news', i.e. a decrease in the unemployment rate. This would translate into a positive correlation between newspaper coverage and the unemployment rate. An additional concern here is that the sensitivity of coverage to the economic cycle might itself depend on the newsworthiness of each country, as proxied by the GDP and distance variables that I have included in the previous cross-sectional exercise. In other words, it might be the case that a higher unemployment rate in a country is more newsworthy the bigger the country's economy is and/or the closer it is to China geographically.

The standard methodology to look into those issues consists of implementing a fixed effects analysis, i.e. a multivariate linear regression which allows for separate averages for each unit of analysis, in our case for each country. According to this framework the coefficient on the unemployment rate would capture the so called 'within' correlation between newspaper coverage and the unemployment rate itself, i.e. whether a country systematically gets an amount of coverage that is above its average coverage when its unemployment rate happens to be above its average. Again within a fixed effects specification one can also include country-specific time trends, so that the coverage of each country on China Daily is allowed to have a different mean *and* follow different trends, which would typically depend on long term factors.

The outcome of this exercise is shown in Table 3, whereas the country-level unemployment rate during the past quarter is used as the main explanatory variable. Throughout the table standard errors are clustered at the country level, in order not to overstate the precision of the estimates when the error term could be correlated within each cluster, i.e. within each country (Bertrand et al. (2004). Consistently with the discussion above, across all specifications I include country fixed effects and country-specific time trends. In column [1] I only include the unemployment rate, which is positively and strongly correlated with newspaper coverage, so that one cannot reject the hypothesis that 'bad news' about a given country's economic

Table 3 Correlates of country coverage on China daily, panel specification with fixed effects

Dependent variable	Relative frequency of hits on China daily			
	[1]	[2]	[3]	[4]
Country-level unemployment rate, past quarter	0.517***	0.459*	0.447**	0.45
	[5.40]	[1.84]	[2.99]	[1.80]
Unemployment rate * distance from China	–	0.007	–	-0.0003
		[0.33]		[0.02]
Unemployment rate * 2008 GDP	–	–	0.00001	0.00001
			[1.30]	[1.62]
R squared	0.89	0.89	0.89	0.89
Number of countries	11	11	11	11
Observations	874	874	874	874
Country fixed effects	Yes	Yes	Yes	Yes
Country-specific time trends	Yes	Yes	Yes	Yes

Notes The table displays the output of fixed effects regressions with the monthly relative frequency of articles mentioning each country as the dependent variable. Standard errors are clustered at the country level, and the corresponding t-statistics are reported in brackets under each coefficient. Country fixed effects and country-specific time trends are included in each specification
*Significant at 1%
**Significant at 5%
***Significant at 1%

cycle are relatively more newsworthy than 'good news'. The size of the coefficient is non-negligible: a point estimate of 0.517 implies around half of a percentage point more articles about a given country when the unemployment rate is one percent higher. In fact, this result is quite consistent with what found by Larcinese et al. (2011) in the case of U.S. newspapers, which assign more coverage to the issue of unemployment when the unemployment rate (both at the federal and at the state level) is higher.

In column [2] I expand the specification by controlling for an interaction term between the unemployment rate of a given country and the air distance measure. The interaction term is estimated to be positive but it is very far from being statistically significant. On the other hand, the coefficient on the unemployment rate is still positive, but now it is only mildly significant at the 10% confidence level. A relevant caveat here is that the inclusion of an interaction term within a fixed effects specification is likely to create problems of approximate multicollinearity, i.e. it is statistically hard to tell apart the correlation of the dependent variable with the unemployment rate and with its interaction with the distance variable, since the latter are by definition strongly correlated one with the other.[4]

[4]The presence of approximate multicollinearity within this type of specification is also signalled by the fact that an F-test of the joint significance of the unemployment rate and its interaction with air distance strongly rejects the null hypothesis. This is true for columns [3] and [4] as well.

By the same token, in column [3] I monitor the interaction between the unemployment rate and the GDP: in this case the estimated coefficient on the interaction is positive, but not significant, while the coefficient on the unemployment rate is again positive and significant at the 5% confidence level. Finally in column [4] I add both the interaction with air distance and with GDP. In this case the interaction with the GDP variable is positive and not far from statistical significance at the 10% level, while the interaction with air distance is estimated to be negative but not significantly so. In this specification the coefficient on the unemployment rate is positive but not significantly so at ordinary confidence levels. Again, the most likely reason for this is the approximate multicollinearity stemming from the inclusions of variables that are very correlated one with the other.

4 Conclusions

As mentioned in the introduction, the use of automatic keyword-based searches of online news archives allows to gather coverage data in a cost-effective and replicable fashion. However, the present analysis is solely focused on the agenda-setting aspect of newspaper coverage, i.e. the amount of space devoted to the various news items, in this case a set of different countries. From this point of view, the next step on the intensive margin would be to try and obtain a replicable measure of the *tone* of stories regarding each country. One could also classify the specific issues that are covered when mentioning a given country, and explore the correlates of this variation. Of course, there is large room on the extensive margin as well. In particular, it would be especially interesting to compare the coverage on China Daily with the one on Chinese-written newspapers.

References

Bertrand M et al (2004) How much should we trust differences-in-differences estimates? Quart J Econ 119(1):249–275

Gentzkow M, Shapiro JM (2010) What drives media slant? Evidence from US newspapers. Econometrica 78(1):35–71

Groseclose T, Milyo J (2005) A measure of media bias. Quart J Econ 120:1191–1237

Larcinese V et al (2011) Partisan bias in economic news: evidence on the agenda-setting behavior of US newspapers. J Publ Econ 95(9–10):1178–1189

Puglisi R (2011) Being the *New York Times*: the political behaviour of a newspaper. BE J Econ Anal Policy 11(1), (Contributions), Article 20

Puglisi R, Snyder JM Jr (2011) Newspaper coverage of political scandals. J Polit 73(3):931–950

Puglisi R, Snyder JM Jr (2015) Empirical studies of media bias. In: Anderson S et al (ed) Handbook of media economics, vol 1B, North-Holland, pp 647–667

Qin B et al (2016) Media bias in China. Mimeo, IIES, Stockholm University. Available here: http://perseus.iies.su.se/~dstro/Media_Bias%202016Nov21.pdf
Qian N, Yanagizawa-Drott D (2016) Government distortion in independently owned media: evidence from US cold war news coverage of human rights. J Eur Econ Assoc (forthcoming)
Wu DH (2000) Systemic determinants of international news coverage: a comparison of 38 countries. J Commun 50

Part IV
Italian Views on China

Confucianism, Communism and Democracy: A 'Triangular' Struggle in China-Reflections on Italy's Historical Experience with Cultural Reform

Lihong Zhang

The prosperity of a country depends, not on the abundance of its revenues, nor on the strength of its fortifications, nor on the beauty of its public buildings; but it consists in the number of its cultivated citizens, in its men of education, enlightenment, and character; here are to be found its true interest, its chief strength, its real power.

– Martin Luther King

Abstract At the beginning of the 20th century, democracy and communism were introduced in China to counterbalance Confucianism and in order to overcome the deep social crisis and strive for the modernization of Chinese traditional culture. The contemporary history of China is the history of struggle between Confucianism, democracy and communism. No foreign ideology can survive in China unless it has capacity of harmonizing itself with Confucianism. Learning from the Italian experience of the development of culture in order to successfully modernize the country's traditional culture, China needs to recognize and protect more the individual rights and freedom and build up a society in pursuit of the truth by the elimination of the traditional bureaucracy-oriented mentality and money-worship idea. A political order modelled on the Roman Principate, characterized by the centralization of powers in a head of state and rule by law, can be a realistic and interim solution for China to realize at low cost the passage from totalitarianism to republicanism. Before reforming successful its traditional culture, it is convenient for China to implement continuously Deng Xiaoping's so-called '24-character strategy'.

L. Zhang (✉)
East China University of Political Science and Law, Shanghai, China
e-mail: lihong111@gmail.com

L. Zhang
European Center for International Affairs, Brussels, Belgium

S. Beretta et al. (eds.), *Understanding China Today*, Understanding China,
DOI 10.1007/978-3-319-29625-8_20

1 Introduction: Qichao Liang's Perplexity Regarding Chinese Traditional Culture

After the first 'Opium War' (1839–1942) China was dramatically reduced into a semi-colonized country. With the invasion of Western powers and the domestic rebellion of the Taiping Heavenly Kingdom (太平天国 1851–1864), the Qing government survived even for more than 70 years, thanks to the 'Self-Strengthening Movement' (洋务还,动 1861–1895) promoted by the famous ministers of the so-called 'Resurgence' in the late Qing Dynasty such as Guofan Zeng (1811–1872) and Hongzhang Li (1823–1901). Believing firmly in the superiority of China in terms of traditional culture, civilization, the capacity of production and good customs, they attributed the weakness of China to its technical backwardness and attempted to overcome the crisis and revive the national prestige by improving Chinese technologies, instead of modernizing its political system and traditional culture.

The complete annihilation of the 'Beiyang Fleet' (北洋水师) in 1895 by Japan, the conclusion of the 'Treaty of Shimonoseki' in 1985 and the 'Boxer Protocol' in 1901 marked the definite failure of the 'Self-Strengthening Movement', which limited itself to introducing and using foreign technologies without neither reforming the political system nor modernizing Chinese culture. Two months after the 78-year-old Hongzhang Li, the most important figure of China at that time, passed away in 1901, the 29-year-old Qichao Liang, the most prominent Chinese historian of the 20th century, wrote a biography about Hongzhang Li and pointed out that "Li is a man with talent and experience but without modern knowledge and courage. He is only a hero created by history, even if he could have created history. His tragic ending is caused by the fact that he has never understood in his entire lifetime that the victory of a country in the international competition mainly relies in the quality of its citizens, but that of its government" (Liang 2009).

Liang's idea to renovate the people's thoughts in order to strengthen the power of a country was expressed more clearly in his famous article called 'On Trends of Competition between the Peoples and the Future of China' in 1899: "The motivating force [of modern international competition] stems from the citizenry's struggle for survival which is irrepressible according to the law of natural selection and survival of the fittest. Therefore the current international competition is not something which only concerns the state, it concerns the entire population. In the present day international struggles in which the whole citizenry participate (and compete) for their very lives and properties, people are united as if they have one mind. The international competition of the past, which was the concern of the rulers and their ministers, would subside after a period. But the current international struggle will last forever because it is constantly a matter of concern for the life and property of the people. How dangerous it is! How will we, who bear the brunt of this international struggle, stave it off?"[1] (Liang 1899). In Liang's view, after the

[1]The translation is cited from Mishira (2012), p. 160.

second half of 19th century, the results of military wars became almost totally foreseeable before they even began. The holder of the real power, he argued, wins the war in any case. The closer to a civilized society and the more established the rule, the fittest and most powerful survive.

2 Modernization of Chinese Traditional Culture and the Development of Struggles Between Confucianism, Democracy and Communism

Liang's idea of modernizing China through educating its people is nothing else but the continued application of Confucianism, which was created in the fifth century B.C. According to Confucius, the basis of a stable, unified and enduring social order can be found in the traditional rituals (Li) (礼), which consists of the ceremonies and civilized and cultured patterns of behaviour developed through generations of human wisdom (Berling 1988; Cheng 1997; Littlejohn 2011; Yao 2000). Pursuant to the canonical interpretation of the philosopher Zhongshu Dong (179–104 B.C.), Confucianism is essentially the observance of the so-called 'Three Gang and Five Chang' (三纲五常). The 'Three Gang' denote the most fundamental human relationships: that between a ruler and his subjects; that between a husband and his wife, and that between a father and his sons. The 'Five Chang' on the other hand refer to five enduring ethical rules: (a) benevolence towards others (Ren); (b) righteousness (Yi); (c) practice of the traditional ritual and propriety taught by the ancestry (Li); (d) wisdom (Zhi); (e) honesty and trustworthiness (Xin). Therefore, for the realization of a peaceful and civilized society, moral education (Li) plays a much more important role than strict punishment by law (Fa), which constitutes norms legitimizing criminal and administrative punishment.

In other words, in the Confucian view, the rules by education (德育) prevail always over the rule by (or of) law (法治) and "the interest of the country shall go first, then that of family, at last that of an individual". The Western motto '*Educatio et disciplina mores faciunt*' ('Education and discipline form morality') was well-understood and intensively applied by the Chinese for many centuries. Confucianism revolves around the pursuit of the General Unity (大一统), which consists in the unity of the 'Self' with the 'Heaven' (天人合一) and the unified relationship of humanity with the 'Heaven', as well as the harmonization between all the people (Adler 2014). It is therefore easily understandable that as a result from the practice of Confucianism, the bureaucracy-oriented mentality was firmly established and the protection of individualism and personal freedom were indeed very limited in the Chinese traditional society.[2]

[2]"The state was neither the embodied product of free will nor an impersonal encroacher upon individual autonomy. Instead, at least in theory, the relationship with the state was far more one of trust, modeled after the family, in which the Emperor and his representatives were conceived of more as senior than public figures .... As was the case the Chinese family, those in position of

At the beginning of 20th century a fundamental question emerged in China: what kind of modern thought should be introduced into the country to educate the people and reform China in order to overcome the country's crisis? To be sure, it was not Confucianism, which was considered an obstacle standing in the way of reform. Modern thought, it was concluded, must be introduced from foreign countries. At this point, Qichao Liang argued that Confucianism can be modernized only through the idea of so-called 'democracy', namely, the establishment of a democratic political order aiming at the protection of the civil rights of the people (民权) and the development of modern science in China. Together with other reformists, he helped the Chinese emperor Guangxu (1871–1908) realize the so-called *Hundred Days' Reform* (百日维新) in 1898. Unfortunately, that attempt to adopt democratic reform ended in *a coup d'état* conducted by powerful conservative opponents. After the Russian Revolution in October 1917, communism, according to which the struggle between classes constitutes the main force for the development of history, was introduced into China in an attempt to end the country's deep-rooted socio-economic crisis.

In the view of both democrats and communists,[3] Confucianism was completely obsolete as a traditional ideology and had to be reformed or indeed even eliminated. Consequently, during the 'May 4th Movement' in 1919 (五四运动), the so-called 'New Culture Movement' (incorporating both democratic and communist forces) strongly criticized Confucianism as an anti-revolutionary and feudal ideology. That was the first time that Confucianism became the object of open criticism in almost two thousand years after it became China's official ideology and spiritual instrument to govern the country in Dynasty Western Han (202 B.C.–8 A.D.). From 1919 until today, the political history of China is a history of the struggle between Confucianism, democracy and communism. Its development can be divided into four phases:

(1) The initial phase (from 1912 to 1949—the year of the founding of the Republic of China), during which democracy and communism, advocated respectively by the Chinese Nationalist Party and the Chinese Communist Party worked together against Confucianism. Those two parties even formed an alliance from 1923 to 1927 to overthrow Confucianism, in their eyes a feudal philosophy. In 1939, Mao Tse-Tung created the theory 'New Democracy or New Democratic Constitutionalism' (新民主主义), which replaced the 'Old Democracy' introduced by the Chinese Nationalist Party, at the time aimed at the realization of a liberal capitalist and parliamentary democratic system. In Mao's view, 'New Democracy' in China would be guided by the Chinese Communist Party to adopt communism through the creating of a coalition of four classes: proletarian

(Footnote 2 continued)

power owed an enormous, fiduciary-like obligation to those over whom they exercised power". See also Alford (1986), p. 945.

[3]At the beginning, some promoters of democracy were also the spiritual leaders of Communism and even the founders of the Chinese Communist Party, for example, Duxiu Cheng (1879–1942) and Dazhao Li (1889–1927).

workers, peasants, the petty bourgeoisie, and the capitalists. He insisted that Chinese 'New Democracy' must take a decisively distinct path, very different from the one taken by the Western world or by the Soviet Union (Mao 1960).

By launching the slogan "To overthrow the local despots and distribute land' (打土豪分田地) (Mao 1977) Mao promoted a populist movement fighting against its political rivals in the countryside. Mao, opposing the classic Marxism doctrine, launched communist propaganda among the peasantry and the working classes and adopted the so-called strategy 'Surrounding the cities from the countryside' (农村包围城市). In 1949, the Communist Party took over power in Mainland of China.

In June of 1949, Mao put forward a new concept which he referred to as 'People's Democratic Dictatorship'[4] (人民民主专政) by combing two classic communist political doctrines: the 'Dictatorship of the Proletariat' (无产阶级专政) and the 'People's Democracy'(人民民主). By creating this seemingly contradictory term 'People's Democratic Dictatorship', Mao aimed at conciliating communism with democracy in opposition to feudalism with Confucianism at its ideological and spiritual core.

In conclusion, it is accurate to conclude that Mao's sinicization of Marxism was a process of transplanting a foreign dictatorship ideology in form of democracy into a Chinese traditional totalitarian culture.

(2) The phase of total victory of communism over democracy and Confucianism (from 1949 to 1979). The founding of the People's Republic of China (PRC) in 1949 marked the triumph of communism over democracy. The main reason for the Chinese Communist victory was the extraordinary capacity of the Chinese Communist Party to modify Marxism according the needs of the Chinese people, who under the strong influence of Confucianism, called for a savoir against the corrupt and incompetent government of the Chinese National Party. Hence, after the failure of democracy in China, the political governance of the Chinese Communist Party in Mainland China from 1949 onwards can be defined as an experiment of communism on the original 'soil of Confucianism'.

Soon after the founding of the PRC, Mao Tse-Tung found that Confucianism continued to be a cultural obstacle for the realization of Communism. With the intention of eliminating completely Confucianism, Mao in 1966 launched the 'Cultural Revolution', arguing that "To build up a new world, it is necessary to annihilate the old one" as a declaration of a total anti-Confucianism war. From 1973, Mao became even more explicit and started the so-called 'Criticize Lin, Criticize Confucius' campaign. Throughout the ten years of the Cultural Revolution (1966–1976), not only all of the Confucian sculptures, the building and books on Confucianism but also almost all of Chinese traditional cultural relics were completely destroyed. However, even if the material things related to Confucius or

[4]Mao (1950), pp. 1–45. The 'People's Democratic Dictatorship' is embedded in China's constitution of 1982 as the form of government in the PRC.

feudalism were destroyed at the time, the attempt to erase in several decades an ancient 2000-year-old philosophy of life turned out to be futile. As a matter of fact, as a Chinese traditional ideology, Confucianism continued to be practiced spontaneously by the Chinese common people, even during the 'Cultural Revolution'.

(3) The phase of decline of communism and the re-emergence of democracy and Confucianism (from 1979 to 2012). Due to the kind of pragmatism adopted by the Chinese political leadership after the 1979 opening-up of China,[5] in particular, under the influence of the theory of soft-power, the Confucian role is emphasized and used by the Chinese Communist Party as an instrument of China's soft power to strengthen the influence of the country in the rest of the world (Bell 2008; Yeung et al. 2011). Many Confucius Institutes were set up all over the world and Confucianism revived in contemporary China.[6]

Also, over the latest three decades, democracy increased significantly in China. On one hand, Chinese intellectuals have been demanding more and more political democracy, economic liberty and freedom of speech. A civil society in pursuit of the private autonomy, which should be free from the political interference in individual freedom, emerges in China today. On the other hand, legally speaking, China has been gradually recognizing some modern democratic and constitutional rules and principles. For example, under the 1998 'Law of Organization of Village Committee', the rural citizens have the right to elect directly the heads of their villages. In 1999 and 2004 amendments of China's constitutional law, the rule of law (art.5) and the protection of human rights (art. 33) were consecrated as constitutional principles.

After 1979, the development of the Chinese economy followed the Western capitalist model, for example, but it lacks the protection of labour rights and environment.[7] Today's Chinese society has become overwhelmingly consumption-and-money oriented. Many Chinese are evaluating everything and everybody in terms of money, believing that "Money is not everything, but it is only the thing".[8] Furthermore, interpersonal relationships, so-called Guangxi (关系), governed by the ethical rules are playing a more important role than law.

[5]Deng Xiaoping's famous motto " No matter if it is a white cat or a black cat,a cat that can catch rats is a good cat!" is a perfect manifestation of the pragmatism applied by the Chinese political leadership in that period.

[6]For the renaissance of Confucianism in China and the related debates and problems see e.g. Fan (2011), p. 1 et seq., p. 17 et seq., p.33 et seq.; Billioud and Thoraval (2015), p. 3 et seq.

[7]For details, see Coase and Wang (2012), p. 175 et seq.

[8]This widespread thought in China is tellingly expressed by a girl with her famous declaration "I prefer to cry in a BMW car than to laugh on a bicycle" during a Chinese popular television show 'If You Are the One' (非诚勿扰) in 2011. For related analysis, see also Zavoretti (2016), pp. 1190–1219.

In fact, the 'burocratic and consumption' oriented idea has already infiltrated in almost all fields, such as bureaucracy, economy and culture.

In this context, the importance of communism in contemporary Chinese daily life has already been reduced significantly and has been replaced by the re-emerging Confucianism and democracy.[9]

(4) From 2012 until today. On December 15, 2012, President Xi Jinping was elected as the Secretary-General of Chinese Communist Party and took over political power in China. Obviously, as a pioneer of the 'Red Generation of the Chinese Communist Party', Xi is aware of the decline of Communism in today's China. Consequently, soon after taking over power, he started attempts to revive communism in opposition to democracy by e.g. intensifying arrests of lawyers fighting for the protection of human rights and the political dissidents. Moreover, he is taking use of Confucianism to raise rapidly his personal prestige among the common people, especially by conducting an anti-corruption campaign on a large scale.[10]

The appointment of Chinese judges by the Communist Party in contradiction to the concept of Western judicial independency demonstrated clearly that the rule of law interpreted by the Chinese current leadership is not based on the separation of powers and the judicial independence and is therefore fundamentally different from how democracy is interpreted and understood outside China (Hornby 2017).

Currently, there is increasing antagonism between communism and democracy in China and the question is whether communism or democracy will be the prevailing ideology as the basis for the modernization of culture in today's China. As the Communist triumph in 1949 proved, only the ideology capable of utilizing Confucianism to realize its political purpose in China can be the final winner. Consequently, the ability of seeking harmony with Confucianism has become a key point in the present struggle between Communism and democracy.

3 Usefulness of the Study of the Italian Experience for the Modernization of Chinese Culture

(1) Why does China need to learn from Italy?

Both Communism and democracy are the cultural products of modern European civilization, which is formed essentially by Renaissance and originates from the

[9]The 1989 Tianan Men Square Accident, the 1990 collapse of the Berlin Wall and the 1991 dissolution of the Soviet Union alarmed the Communist Party in China.

[10]For the change of Xi Jinping's administration on Chinese political policy, see Ross and Bekkevold (2016), p. 155.

classical Greek and Roman civilizations, as well as the medieval Christian civilization.[11] As the successor and practitioners of Greek philosophy, the birthplace of Roman civilization, the centre of the Catholic world, the cradle of the renaissance, in terms of time and space, Italy is the only European country that has incessantly experienced all of these civilizations.

China and Italy started their cultural exchanges in 166 A.D., when the Roman emperor, Marcus Aurelius sent delegates to China to give presents to the Han dynasty emperor. In the entire history of cultural exchanges between Italy and China, both countries refer to each other as reference. Thanks to the publication of Marco Polo's (1254–1324) book *The Travel* in 1298, China was considered by the Italian and other European people as a 'role model country', with peace, economic prosperity, good government and advanced technology. Orientalism was worshiped all over Europe over many centuries. It is Matteo Ricci (1552–1610), an Italian missionary, who introduced for the first time not only Western science to the Chinese but also the Confucian and Chinese classic literature to the West. Only after Matteo Ricci's visit to China, the Chinese began studying European technology and striving for modernization through science.

Just like China, Italy has a very rich and complex history, full of success and failure, love and hate, pain and joy. Both of these two peoples have many astonishing similarities, in terms of not only character of people, but also in terms of history. There is a saying: "The Italian are the Chinese in Europe, the Chinese are the Italian in Asia." Qichao Liang, during his exile in Japan after the failure of the *Hundred Days' Reform Movement* in 1898, studied three great figures of the founding period of Kingdom of Italy (Giuseppe Mazzini, Giuseppe Garibaldi and Camillo Cavour) and published a paper entitled '*The Biography of Three Heroes of the Founding of Kingdom of Italy*' (《意大利建国三杰传》) in 1901, affirming that "As to the situation before the founding of the Kingdom of Italy, only Italy of that time was the same as today's China. As far as patriotic ambition and behaviour are concerned, only Italian patriots of that period ought to be modelled by the Chinese" (Liang 1936). In particular, for the ongoing modernization of Chinese culture, the Italian renaissance has an extremely important significance as role model. Before the renaissance, Italy experienced the splendid Roman civilization. After the end of the West Roman Empire in 476 A.D., the whole of Italy and Europe went through the Middle Ages for almost one thousand years. In this period, the Catholic Church sought to restrain freedom of thought and intellectual exchanges. It is the renaissance that set the Italian and European people free from ignorance and spiritual persecution. The renaissance, as the greatest culture revolution in European history, exerts still a tremendous influence on the contemporary Western world, among others as the cultural basis for the achievement of the Western political, economic and military superiority in successive centuries.

[11]The American civilization and the Latin American civilizations are an extension of European (or Christian) civilizations outside Europe. For this conclusion and the conflicts between civilizations. See Huntington (1993), pp. 22–49, (1996), p. 47.

(2) What can Italy provide to China?

Culturally speaking, today's China is very similar to Italy in the eve of renaissance and the Chinese people are confronted with the same socio-political and cultural perplexity and problems the renaissance pioneers were confronted with. The successful experience of the renaissance as engine of cultural and socio-political reform is very important for China today. It could be argued that it can provide the following useful and relevant ideas for the present modernization of Chinese culture:

a. Enhancing the protection of individual freedom and civic and 'humane' behaviour towards others in general

According to humanism, the guidance principle of renaissance, the human being is the centre of the universe and individual rights, freedom and creativity are the wealth of the whole community, and hence they are worthy of being protected. In today's global digitalized world, the insufficient protection of individual freedoms in China—as a result of the influence of Confucianism—continues to stand in the way of the country's socio-economic development.

b. The spirit of pursuing truth

Veritas lux vita mea! ('The truth is the light of my life!'). That is the philosophy and mantra, which many great Western scientists and thinkers practiced in the period of renaissance. They searched the truth by the independent exercise of their own capacity and proved it through experiments and logic reasoning, as opposed to blindly following the ideas of political authorities or those rigid doctrines. In pursuit for the truth in this way, many remarkable Italian talents such as Gaileo Galilei and Leonardo Da Vinci, made extraordinary scientific discoveries and inventions.

Under the strong influence of Confucianism, the Chinese people have since the ancient been attaching importance to the study of the philosophy of life for many centuries, the skill of ruling the people and the harmonization of human interrelationship by means of ethical education. As a result, politicians ascribed often their power and authority over the truth while the common people have developed a strong bureaucracy-oriented mentality as opposed to an interest to conduct scientific research or question the 'truth' as established by authorities. Today, to a large extent, these problems exist still in Chinese society. Without encouraging its people to pursue the truth and eliminating their bureaucracy-oriented mentality, China cannot overcome its present cultural crisis.

c. to abandon gradually the totalitarian form of government and build-up a political system based on the rule of law and the separation of powers

As we know, Roman civilization started from the 'Kingdom' and then moved on to the 'Republic', the 'Principate', the 'Tetrarchy' and ended with the 'Monarchy'. Rome flourished in the republican period and experienced its peak of development during the period of the 'Principate'. From the republican period onwards, the Roman political system underwent a process from the separation of powers to its complete centralization in the hands of the monarch. Since the institution of the republican constitution, as a tool of safeguarding the Roman prosperity, is the best allocation of political powers to resolve the conflicts between fairness and efficiency, its decline ultimately resulted in Rome's decay.[12]

Owing to the various factors, such as e.g. a closed geographical location, the so-called 'General Unity' (大一统), the Confucian idea aiming at keeping social stability at any cost and the application of economic policy 'Stimulus to Agriculture and Suppression against Commerce' (重农抑商), China basically remained an autocratic monarchy in its five thousands years long history. It is different from the Roman Principate (from 27 B.C. to the end of third century), the system in which the heads of state were eventually restrained constitutionally by the senate. China's republican history began with the founding of the Republic of China in 1912, even if in reality, the republican system was carried out effectively only for very few years.[13]

Compared with thousand years of imperial dynasties, the decades when the Chinese people were in pursuit of a republican political order and the introduction of constitutionalism are obviously very short. It needed a long time and a lot of efforts to change old feudal thoughts in China. From the point of view of human and social development, the stabilization of political order in China after 1979, which re-emerged from the previous political and economic crisis through Deng's economic reforms, paved already a useful path for the Chinese people towards the establishment of constitutional democracy.

However, the deep-rooted bureaucracy orientation formed in the millennium of Chinese feudal society cannot be eliminated in such short period of time. The impetuous accomplishment of a classic democratic constitutional order, in conformity with different parties holding power on a rotational basis, as suggested by many Westerners and radical democrats within China would, with high probability, lead to inefficiency of decision-making, an enormous waste of social resources, political chaos, national secession, and in the case of out-of-control application of democracy, would risk China's collapse—the same way it happened to ancient Greece in the past.

A relatively practicable and interim form of government, which is taken as reference in China, is the Roman Principate, in which the aristocratic class (from a Chinese perspective the political party in power) elects a head of state as the

[12]Montesquieu (1689–1755), the creator of the theory of separation of powers, after studying with accuracy the history of Roman Empire, concluded that one of the main reasons for the decline of the Roman Empire is the formation of the totalitarianism. See Montesquieu (1734), p. 62.

[13]In 1915, as the first formal president of Republic of China, Shikai Yuan (1859–1916) restored a very short-lived monarchy (3 months). After his death, China was divided in warlord factions known as Beiyang Cliques from 1916 to 1928 and after that China was governed by the Chinese Nationalist Party until 1949 under Chiang Kai-shek. From 1949 to 1976, especially in period of Culture Revolution, the Mainland China was ruled practically by Mao Tse-Tung alone. Only in the last 30 years—gradually and with difficulties—have the people in Mainland China begun to demand the introduction of democracy. Even in Taiwan, the real practice of democracy started from year 2000.

ultimate political decision-maker and the people grant him *autoritas*, i.e. the absolute power to decide on important issues. The exercise of his power in turn should be under control of the senate (today's parliament and the self-control system of the party in power) and governed by law (today's so-called rule by law). By law, the people and some public organs have the power to supervise and investigate any of his political decisions made in office, even impeach him and sue him before the court.

Actually, to some extent, China's political leaders from Deng Xiaoping onwards have adopted this kind of Principate system and its effectiveness has been prove successful over the last 30 years.[14] It helps China to carry out smoothly a transition from an autocratic monarchy, which exists for more than three thousands years, to a mature and sound republican government. It also helps China to realize the right balance between democracy and autocratic monarchy, as well as between efficiency and fairness.

Governing a state is like living one's own life. Compromise is a necessary skill for the survival and development. It is easier for most of us to use extreme speech and thought, but only a person with great wisdom is able to resolve the conflicts on the basis of reality and balance, and by means of compromise to identify and adopt practicable solutions, in which the advantages outweigh the disadvantages.

The great Chinese ancient philosopher Lao-tzu (around 7th century B.C.) says that 'Governing a large nation is like cooking small fishes' (治大国如亨小鲜). It means that only with the right temperature, the punctual stir-frying and the grand patience, can a delicious dish of small fishes be made. In other words, we need to respect and follow the laws of nature on the ruling of a country. Never overdo it nor interfere in it too frequently.

4 Conclusions

China remains in the initial stage of the modernization of its traditional culture and it needs to reform Confucianism. In the past, the Chinese Communist Party achieved great success in China, thanks to the sinicization of Communism and the realization of its harmonization with Confucianism. However, the complete abandonment of Confucianism by the Chinese Communist Party led to disaster during the 'Cultural Revolution'. The great socio-economic progress accomplished by China after its opening-up in 1979 was also a result of the respect for and promotion of Confucianism. Recently, democracy has entered more and in conflict with

[14]In four generations of Chinese political leadership after 1979, all leaders, Deng Xiaoping, Jiang Zemin, Hu Jintao and Xi Jinping, exercised unchallenged authority and maintained control over the army and the final decision-making for all most important national issues. Each of them was (in the case of Xi Jinping still is) the core Chinese political leader of their respective generation. At the same time, formally, the exercise of their power is always under the control and supervision of the parliament and the politburo of the Chinese Communist Party.

communism. Which ideology will prevail in China in the future: communism or democracy? That will also depend on the ability of harmonization with Confucianism (both in the case of democracy or communism). Learning from the European historical experiences, in particular those of Italy and the Roman Empire, the reform of Confucianism became necessary and China needed to strengthen gradually the protection of individual rights and freedom, promote the scientific development, thereby replacing the former traditional bureaucracy-orientation and today's money-worship mentality. Last but not least, China established a political order modelled on the Roman 'Principate', as a practicable and pragmatic interim solution towards the final realization of democracy. No matter what kind of foreign ideology is transplanted into China, it needs to be sinicized to be able to function well and it needs to be modified to the extent that it becomes suitable for Confucianism.

Only through cultural modernization, China's overall and systemic renovation of its politics, economy and technology can take place in the future. Since this cultural reform is still at an early stage, as far as its international strategy is concerned, in the long term, China still needs to carry out conservatively the so-called "24-Character Strategy" put forward by Deng Xiaoping in the early 1990s: "Observe calmly, secure our position, cope with affairs calmly, hide our capacities and bide our time, be good at maintaining a low profile, and never claim leadership" (冷静观察、站稳阵脚、沉着应付、韬光养晦、善于守拙、决不当头). Only in this way, China can avoid its self-destruction caused by excessive self-confidence.[15]

References

Adler JA (2014) Confucianism as a religious tradition: linguistic and methodological problems. Kenyon College, Gambier Ohio, USA, p 10

Alford W (1986) On the limits of grand theory in comparative law. Washington Law Review 61 (975), p 945

Bell DA (2008) China's new confucianism: politics and everyday life in a Changing society. Princeton University Press, Princeton (USA), p. 20

Berling JA (1988) Confucianism. Focus on Asia studies, vol II(1), Asian Religions, p 6

Billioud S, Thoraval J (2015) The sage and the people: The confucian revival in China. Oxford University Press, Oxford, New York, p. 3 et seq

Cheng A (1997) Histoire de la pensée chinoise, Le Seuil Presse, Paris, p. 62 et seq

Coase R, Wang N (2012) How China became capitalist. Palgrave Macmillan Press, London, UK, p. 175 et seq

Fan R-P (ed) (2011) The renaissance of confucianism in contemporary China. Springer Press, Heidelberg, London, New York, p 1 et seq., p 17 et seq., p 33 et seq

Hornby L (2017) China's top judge denounces idea of judicial independence. Financial Times, 17 Jan

[15]This is also Deng's concern as cited by Kissinger (2011), p. 438. In the Chinese official version, Deng's 24-charter strategy was further developed into 28 character one, by adding other four character 'Strive to make achievements' (有所作为).

Huntington SP (1993) Clash of civilization? Foreign affairs, vol 72(3), Summer, pp 22–49
Huntington SP (1996) The clash of civilizations and the remaking of world order. Simon & Schuster Press, New York, London, Toronto, Sydney, p 47
Kissinger HA (2011) On China. Penguin Press, New York, p 438
Liang Q-C (1899 reprinted 1999) On trends of competition between the peoples and the future of China (论近世国民竞争之大势及中国前途). In: Qichao Liang's complete works (1999). Beijing Press, vol 1, p 949
Liang Q-C (1901 reprinted 2009) Biography of Hongzhang Li (<<李鸿章传>>). Shanxi Normal University Press, Xi'an, p 288
Liang Q-C (1936) Collection of works of Yinbing Room (饮冰室合集), vol 11. Zhonghua Book Press, Beijing, pp 1–2
Littlejohn RL (2011) Confucianism: an introduction. Palgrave Macmillan Press, New York, p 20
Mao T-T (1977) On agricultural collectivization and the transformation of capitalist industry. In: Selected works of Mao Tse-Tung, vol 5. Foreign Language Press, Beijing, p 212
Mao T-T (1960) On new democratic constitutionalism. Foreign Language Press, Beijing, pp 1–15
Mao T-T (1950) On people's democratic dictatorship. Foreign Language Press, Beijing, pp 1–45
Mishira P (2012) From the ruins of empire: the intellectuals who remade Asia. Farrar, Straus and Giroux Press, New York, p 160
Montesquieu (1734) Considerations on the Causes of the Greatness of the Romans and their Decline, Translated by Lowenthal D (1965). The Free Press, New York, pp 91-93
Ross RS, Bekkevold JI (eds) (2016) China in the era of Xi Jinping: domestic and foreign policy challenges. Georgetown University Press, Washington, DC, USA, p 155
Yao X-Z (2000) An introduction to confucianism. Cambridge University Press, Cambridge, p 30
Yeung A, Fung CH-H (2011) The soft power in the confucian 'kingly way'. In: Fan R-P (ed), cit., p 109 et seq
Zavoretti R (2016) Is it better to cry in a BMW or to laugh on a bicycle? Marriage, 'financial performance anxiety', and the production of class in Nanjing (People's Republic of China)'. Mod Asian Stud 50(4), pp 1190–1219

Italy's Policies Towards and Relations with China from 1937 to 1945

Guido Samarani

Abstract Starting from late 1936 to early 1937 Italy's policies towards and relations with China became more and more complex while at the same time Rome and Tokyo had begun to move towards rapprochement. From 1937 to 1945 Italy-China relations were marked by some important historical and political trends and questions. In this chapter I will focus on two of them. Firstly, Italy's choice to support Wang Jingwei's decision to collaborate with Japan (late 1930s-early 1940s), which led to crisis in relations with Chiang Kai-shek's China. Second—within the larger context of the new Italian anti-fascist foreign policy—the resumption of Italy's contacts and relations with Chiang Kai-shek's China in the final part of the war.

1 Introduction

When Italy invaded Ethiopia on October 3, 1935, China fully supported the international sanctions imposed by the *League of Nations*, which led to a cooling of bilateral relations. International sanctions against Italy were rescinded in 1936, and Rome tried to make up for lost time by renewing assistance to and cooperation with China: it was immediately clear that it would be an impossible task for Italy to regain its former position, as American and German suppliers had moved into filling the void. Thus, through late 1936 and early 1937 the scope for collaboration between Rome and Nanjing decreased, even if there remained the possibility of improvement (Borsa 1994; Fatica 2014; Moccia 2014; Serri 2015). At the same time, however, starting from late 1936 Rome and Tokyo had begun to move towards rapprochement. This was spurred by the Japanese decision to cease

G. Samarani (✉)
Department of Asian and North African Studies,
University of Venice Ca' Foscari, Venice, Italy
e-mail: samarani@unive.it

S. Beretta et al. (eds.), *Understanding China Today*, Understanding China,
DOI 10.1007/978-3-319-29625-8_21

opposition to the Italian invasion of Ethiopia: Japan's change of heart was mainly due to its fears being put to rest that the Italian conquest would threaten its economic interests in Ethiopia (exports of cotton fabrics, rayon, glassware, etc.).[1] It was also the result of a strong conflicting debate in Tokyo between, on the one side, popular anti-colonial feelings and, on the other side, "those politicians, ideologues, and bureaucrats who were waiting for the moment to consolidate Japan's 'independent foreign policy'" (Hofmann 2015, p. 102; Strang 2013). The Japanese signaled their change of policy being the first power to recognize (November 1936) the Italian annexation of Ethiopia; Italy reciprocated by setting up a consulate in Mukden (Shenyang), a first step towards recognition of Manzhouguo (Ferretti 1983).

In this chapter I will discuss some trends and aspects of Italy's policies towards and relations with China from 1937 to 1945. In particular, I will focus on two main periods and questions; first, Italy's choice to support Wang Jingwei's decision to collaborate with Japan (late 1930s-early 1940s). Second, the resumption of Italy's contacts and relations with Chiang Kai-shek's China in the last part of the Sino-Japanese war, within the larger context of the new Italian anti-fascist foreign policy. In my analysis I will rely mainly on Italy's political and diplomatic documents and sources, together with more general relevant sources to better understand the overall historical and political context of those years.[2]

2 Playing the 'Wang Jingwei Card'

Rome's adherence to the *Anti-Comintern Pact* of November 6, 1937 followed by the recognition of *Manzhouguo* on November 29th of the same year stood for a major shift in Italy's policy in favor of Japan. The improvement of relations between the two countries was reflected in Italian diplomacy and the press coverage of bilateral relations. However, in the first half of year 1937, the emphasis had been on Italian's friendship towards China and opposition to Japan's imperialistic drive. Italian Foreign Minister Ciano,[3] in his speech at the Fascist Chamber in May 1937, clearly emphasized that "Mutually cordial relations exist between our nation and the Chinese Republic [...] Our interests in this great country, with its infinite rice fields and limitless possibilities, are growing at a most satisfying rate" (*La politica estera dell'Italia* 1941, p. 69). In late 1937, however, emphasis was more and more laid on the fact that while Japan was not formally a fascist country, its policies and people clearly should be included within the bloc of Fascist states. In June 1938, Ciano

[1]In the first half of 1934 Japanese products in Ethiopia outsold those of Western countries (Hofmann 2015, p. 99).

[2]Translations from Italian sources and documents into English are the author's.

[3]Galeazzo Ciano (1903–1944) had become Minister of Foreign Affairs in June 1936.

himself in a speech expressed Italy's concerns over Nanjing's rapprochement with Moscow (*La politica estera dell'Italia* 1941, p. 85):

> It is not premature to state here and now that the conflict currently ablaze in East Asia has its roots in the dissolute actions of Bolshevism, with which the Chinese government has imprudently fraternized, not realizing that a nation's cause is misplaced if linked to a state that has proclaimed itself the champion of international leftism.

In fact, relations between Italy and China had begun to deteriorate soon after the outbreak of the Sino-Japanese war in July 1937 and the Chinese rapprochement with the Soviet Union in August of the same year. On several occasions, Ciano expressed strong skepticism about China's capacity to deter a Japanese offensive for any length of time: the rapid Japanese advance into China during the first year of the war and Ambassador Taliani's reports from China seemed to have proven Ciano correct in his assessment (*La politica estera dell'Italia* 1941, pp. 83–87; MAE/DDI 1957/2, doc. 263; 1957/2, doc. 332; 1959/3, doc. 237; 1959/3, doc. 426). Mussolini himself was skeptical about China's prospects in the war. On November 19, 1937 he told a Chinese government delegation that Japanese military superiority would soon prevail and that the Chinese would be deluding themselves if they thought the Western powers would offer any help. He suggested that China should immediately open negotiations with Tokyo, and to this end he offered Italian and German mediation: an initiative, which did not succeed (Mussolini's talk is quoted in Ciano 1990, pp. 57–59). It was within such a historical and political context that Italy became increasingly interested in Wang Jingwei's so-called 'Peace Movement' following Wang's sudden departure from Chongqing in December 1938. As a result of Japan's relentless military advance into China, Wang Jingwei had concluded that Japan was undefeatable: the capture of Wuhan in October 1938 convinced him that the war must be ended; some months before, Hitler had recalled all German advisers and put an end to arms sales to China (Barrett and Shyu 2001; Mitter 2013).

The appeasement policy toward Germany and Italy adopted by both the European democracies and the Soviet Union also influenced, if indirectly, the Chinese situation. In September 1938 Britain and France agreed in Munich to the cession of the Sudetenland to Germany; and in August 1939 Germany and the Soviet Union signed a ten-year non-aggression pact. These events dealt a blow to Chiang Kai-shek's hopes of an anti-Japanese coalition including the United States, Britain and the Soviet Union, which would assist him in resolving what he referred to as the 'Japan question.' On the opposite side, European developments gave the Japanese more leeway in their China policy. Through sustained military pressure and continued diplomatic maneuvering Tokyo intended to force Chiang to negotiate. However, Chiang Kai-shek refused to yield despite continuing military setbacks, and held on to his belief that the Western powers would eventually come to China's assistance. Thus the Japanese had to search for a new strategy if they were to end the war with China on their terms. They now began to play the so-called 'Wang Jingwei card': threatening the establishment of a rival Chinese government under Wang in order to bring Chiang to a peace settlement.

The progress of Wang's 'Peace Movement' was followed in the Italian print media. On October 12, 1939, the *Corriere della Sera*, one of the country's largest newspapers, carried a short but revealing interview with Wang Jingwei conducted by very well-known journalist Vittorio Alessi. Entitled *'Meeting with the Future Head of the Chinese Government'* the article first noted that Wang was only now prepared to speak publicly about his new political role. Alessi quoted Wang as indicating that his aim was to bring China and Japan to find an *entente* and bring about an improvement of their relations (Alessi 1939). According to the Italian journalist, Wang Jingwei reaffirmed his position toward Chiang Kai-shek and stated that (Alessi 1939):

> It is unfortunate that Chiang Kai-shek refused the peace mediation offered in January 1938 by the German Ambassador. We can only condemn the Generalissimo for refusing to avail himself of the Duce's sympathies for China or of Count Ciano's friendship in offering mediation. In the latter instance, I spoke with the Generalissimo about the possibility of mediation, but he did not want to ask for the intervention of Count Ciano, whom I recommended as the best mediator possible, or of the Duce. This was indeed a serious mistake.

A longer analysis of the Far Eastern theater appeared at the same time in *Relazioni Internazionali*, one of Italy's most authoritative foreign policy publications. It gave considerable weight to Wang's activities, though it admitted that their ultimate impact on the war between Japan and China could not be overestimated (Incognite nell'Estremo Oriente 1939, p. 746):

> The situation appears to be moving substantively, if not uniformly, in Japan's favor. This is attributable to recent international events, in particular Soviet Russia's change of course of its Far Eastern policy. The resumption of military operations [by Japan against China] is to be seen in such a favorable light, while Wang Jingwei's continuing efforts to establish a new Chinese government in direct opposition to Chiang Kai-shek are extremely important. Chiang Kai-shek has recently declared that "one of the results of the [outbreak of the] European war is that China will struggle even more vigorously against Japan, as we are convinced that final victory is ours, and that we will occupy our deserved position in the new world order once it is established.

It is difficult to say on what basis Chiang Kai-shek based his optimism at the time. The fact that military developments have been to Japan's advantage certainly does not support Chiang Kai-shek's claims. However, it was yet to emerge how the pro-Japanese, and therefore anti-Chiang Kai-shek moves of Wang Jingwei and his followers unfolded, as these were to determine China's future course. Reports from Ambassador Taliani from China were less positive in assessing Wang's role in shaping the events. He first of all noted the many rumors circulating in Shanghai diplomatic circles about a 'secret agreement' between Wang and Chiang, whereby Wang was to use his contacts with Tokyo to secure an honorable peace with Japan. Taliani had met Wang a number of times in Shanghai, and had been told by the latter that he was encountering many difficulties in obtaining Tokyo's cooperation in forming a new Chinese government. On January 31, 1940 Taliani wired Ciano (MAE/DDI 1959/3, doc. 237):

> Speaking to me about the recent conference in Qingdao,[4] Wang told me he was satisfied with the results obtained. He further confided that in the course of it he had to deal with all sorts of obstacles caused by constant changes in Tokyo's position. He finally managed to get Tokyo to give up its plan to appoint political advisers [to his intended government] and to send instead only technical advisers.

In the following weeks, Taliani drew on his personal contacts with Japanese diplomats in Shanghai to report on the progress made by Wang in his negotiations with Tokyo. He also mentioned the frosty response of Britain and France to the announcement of the new government (MAE/DDI 1959/3, doc. 329; 1959/3, doc. 361; 1959/3, doc. 372). Summarizing the current Chinese situation on March 2, 1940, Taliani emphasized Chiang Kai-shek's determination not to surrender, and then considered Wang Jingwei's impact on developments (MAE/DDI 1959/3, doc. 427):

> The Nationalist Chinese fight on, and will continue to fight on, staking everything on Tokyo's presumed war-weariness and the as yet unforeseen outcome of the European conflict. They do not regard Wang Jingwei as credible: they minimize his importance as they are convinced that he will never be able to drum up support from Germany and that he will definitely encounter barriers to his government on the part of the United States [...] Iron statues have been set up in the squares of all the main centers of Nationalist China, depicting Wang Jingwei and his wife on their knees, branded as traitors to their eternal shame. But in many places there are people who maintain that relations between Chiang Kai-shek and his former collaborator [Wang] have not been completely severed, and that some invisible thread continues to link the two: that one day when circumstances are more favorable Chiang might strike an agreement for a nation-wide peace settlement in order to curb Soviet penetration.

However, as the months passed after the establishment of Wang's regime on March 30, 1940, hopes within the Italian government and press for a last-minute '*entente cordiale*' between Chiang and Wang began to fade. Meanwhile, on June 10, 1940 Italy declared war on France and Great Britain, thus linking its fortunes in Europe with those of Germany; and on September 27 Italy, Germany and Japan signed the *Tripartite Pact*, which declared the common interests of these nations in opposition to those of the Western democracies. Finally, on November 30, 1940 Japan extended official recognition to the Wang government; this opened the possibility of more direct Italian support for the Nanjing-Tokyo relationship. On July 1, 1941 Rome (and Berlin) formally recognized the Wang Jingwei Nanjing government and few days later Chongqing severed its diplomatic relations with Rome. Re-visiting those years, Giuliano Cora—who had served as ambassador to China in 1937–1938—observed however in a pamphlet published in 1941 on the 'Chinese question' that some hopes remained still alive in Rome and other European capitals for a compromise peace between Tokyo and Chongqing. Cora summarized Chiang Kai-shek's position as follows (Cora 1941, p. 50):

---

[4]The reference is to the meeting held in late January 1940 in Qingdao between Wang and leaders of the Japanese-sponsored governments in North and Central China, with the aim to create a national unified government.

> It is openly admitted that Chiang Kai-shek, while beaten in battle, has not been vanquished in war, and that his prestige in China has not been diminished by the events of the last three years. It is Japan, in fact, that has modified its former position, by which it regarded the Guomindang Government as a purely regional administration... with which it refused to negotiate.... Some of Japan's most important people in China have already spoken of [contacts between Tokyo and Chongqing], and I myself have more than once heard them say that a lasting and realistic peace can only be negotiated with Chiang Kai-shek.

Italy's relations with the Wang Jingwei government span over a period of two years from the recognition of Nanjing on July 1, 1941 to the fall of the fascist regime in Italy and its replacement by the Badoglio government on July 25, 1943. During this period, Italy's main efforts in the Far East were devoted to exerting pressure, albeit cautiously, on Tokyo to grant greater autonomy and powers to the Nanjing government. These efforts ran up against vested Japanese interests in China, as Tokyo was reluctant to see Nanjing given genuine autonomy. They were further complicated by growing tension between Germany and Japan, arising from German concerns that Japanese companies, with the support of Japanese authorities, were systematically undermining German economic interests in China (on these questions, see MAE/DDI 1989/9, doc. 515; 1989/9, doc 603).

The reports sent by Taliani to Ciano and Mussolini during 1942 and early 1943,[5] together with Ciano's memoirs, are very illuminating in this regard. Taliani spoke many times of Wang Jingwei's frank comments to him about the evasive and inexplicable behavior of the Japanese. Taliani also noted that Wang was concerned about the possibility that Japan had not yet entirely abandoned hope of an agreement with Chiang Kai-shek. Taliani reported frequently to Ciano how the discouragement and pessimism he had noted earlier in the Nanjing government was becoming more evident and he conveyed Wang's own admission that his work had come to a halt. According to Taliani, the original optimism on the part of the Japanese about the prospects of the Nanjing government was slowly yielding to doubt, and in fact some Japanese now admitted to having made policy mistakes in not giving Nanjing more autonomy. Taliani's impressions were largely shaped by his frequent meetings with Japanese political and military experts, among them Lieutenant General Yokoyama Isamu, at that time Commander of the 4th Manchurian Army, and Shigemitsu Mamoru, Ambassador to Nanjing before becoming Japanese Minister for Foreign Affairs in early 1943 (see MAE/DDI 1989/9, doc. 18; 1989/9, doc. 27).

In Rome, Ciano seemed to be experiencing similar doubts as to Japan's ability to end the China war, either on its own terms or through the intermediacy of the Wang regime. This is revealed in an unusual diary entry on August 10 (Ciano 1990, pp. 642–643):

[5]In February 1943, after an extensive government reshuffle, Mussolini had also become Minister of Foreign Affairs, while Ciano became the Italian representative to the Vatican.

> No forecasts can be made here, especially as [Nationalist] China […] refuses to bend its rigidly anti-Japanese stance, and even Wang Jingwei, that Nanjing Laval,[6] is pessimistic about being able to bring about a rapprochement between the two peoples. My opinion is that the struggle between China and Japan is destined to be eternal: there will be pauses, there will be ups and downs, but it will never completely subside. More than a political fact, it is a biological fact. And, biologically, China is very strong.

In late October Taliani sent another long telegram to Ciano, stressing the differences increasingly apparent between Nanjing and Tokyo. He noted the emergence of two Japanese camps on the Nanjing question comprised of political-diplomatic experts on one side and military authorities on the other. Taliani referred specifically to a plan, drafted by the military and strongly opposed by the civilian experts, which involved the reorganization of the Nanjing government in order to reduce its already limited powers (thus further reducing Wang Jingwei's role and authority), and the augmentation of the authority of the military command in China at the expense of the Japanese ambassador, who would be reduced to a purely formal presence. These proposals appeared to have been motivated by the increasing lack of confidence on the part of the military in Wang, who, in Taliani's words, "has lost vitality and is incapable of holding his greedy followers in check and controlling the situation" (MAE/DDI 1989/9, doc. 258).

Considering the situation extremely serious, Italy stepped up its diplomatic efforts towards the end of 1942 in order to convince Japan to agree at least in part to Nanjing's requests. Rome greeted with great satisfaction to the announcement on January 9, 1943 that Nanjing had declared war on Great Britain and the United States. The official Italian statement stressed the political implications of Nanjing's move, stressing that Nanjing's military potential was extremely limited. Nevertheless, Italian military experts saw Nanjing making a certain contribution to the war effort, as its forces presumably would be used "fight against the rampant guerrilla forces, thus freeing an equal number of Japanese troops for other purposes" (MAE/DDI 1989/9, doc. 424). On July 25 1943, however, Mussolini fell from power, to be replaced by the Badoglio government, which signed an armistice with the Allies on September 8. This latter event prompted the establishment on of the *Italian Social Republic* (*RSI*) September 23, which was nominally under Mussolini but in reality was a puppet regime of the German army in northern Italy: this regime remained linked with Japan in the Axis Powers until the end of the conflict.

3 Liberated Italy and Chiang Kai-Shek's China: Moving Towards New Friendly Relations

Even if it had achieved the status of a co-belligerent nation, Italy was nonetheless regarded as a defeated enemy country by victorious powers. During the negotiations that would lead to the drafting of the Italian peace treaty, a punitive approach

[6]The reference is here to Pierre Laval, prime minister of the Vichy collaborationist government.

had prevailed and in February 1947 and the adoption of The *Paris Peace Treaty*) the Italian government had been compelled to accept a sort of diktat: territorial losses (Dalmatian territories and the Istria peninsula, African colonies, Dodecanese islands), heavy reparations to pay, severe limitations as regards armed forces and military capabilities (Lorenzini 2007, p. 169). From the end of the war and for more than two years Italy was thus subject to the armistice terms and to foreign occupation, and foreign troops (in essence American troops), who would leave the country only at the end of 1947.

Italy's international status sharply contrasted with the aspirations nurtured by the Italian anti-fascist political class, by the diplomatic corps and by many Italian opinion makers: in their opinion, Italy had to recover the role of a middle-rank power which would exert its influence in the two traditional areas of Italy's foreign policy: the European continent and the Mediterranean. Thus, the recognition of the nation's international status and the revision of the most severe clauses of the peace treaty became the main goal of Italy's foreign policy after the end of the Second World War and especially after the signing of the *Paris Peace Treaty* in early 1947.

In liberated Italy it was the first De Gasperi government (10 December 1945–12 July 1946) that began the process of normalizing relations with Nationalist China, even if first preliminary steps were taken by the Parri government (21 June 1945–1949 December 1945), with De Gasperi as foreign minister (MAE/DDI 1992/2, doc. 334; 1992/2, doc. 354). The first negotiations toward reestablishing diplomatic relations were conducted through Moscow, but these proved less fruitful than expected. Consequently, Italy's ambassador to Moscow, Piero Quaroni (on the role of Quaroni within Italy's foreign policy see Monzali 2014, pp. 39–50), who had good Chinese contacts there,[7] told Rome in late 1945 that it would have to begin direct talks with the Chinese government. The first step was the appointment of a diplomatic mission to China charged with that task. The normalization of relations was soon achieved, with the accreditation in early 1946 of Enrico Anzilotti to Chongqing as interim *chargé d'affaires*. He moved then to Nanjing when the Nationalist government returned to its prewar capital. Finally, in the summer of 1946 the new Italian ambassador, Sergio Fenoaltea, arrived. At the same time China accredited a new ambassador to Rome.

Sergio Fenoaltea (1908–1995), a leading politician within the *Partito d'Azione*, discussed with Chinese foreign minister Wang Shijie and Chinese diplomats problems related to the future of China-Italy relations. Two main problems were raised and discussed during the last months of the war and the first post-war period: first, Italy's possible entry into the war against Japan; second, the contents of the Italy-China treaty peace to be defined at the *Paris Peace Conference* scheduled for 1947. During the last months of the war, before Japan's surrender, the issue of Italy's possible entry into the war against Japan was raised: a participation which was seen basically as symbolic by many countries, including the United States (which was

[7]Quaroni seemed to have good relations with the Chinese Ambassador in Moscow, Fu Binchang. On Fu's diplomatic rolc scc also Foo (2011).

nonetheless supportive of Italy's choice), but which was regarded as important by Italy in order to demonstrate its complete break with its past and confirm its position as a now democratic and anti-fascist country. Various sources maintain that the US Department of State clearly indicated to the Italian ambassador in Washington, Tarchiani, that Italy's declaration of war against Japan will surely enhance Italy's international profile and facilitate Italy's passage from a co-belligerent to an allied country (on Tarchiani's role in Washington see Fracchiolla 2012). It must be also said that such a choice was also welcomed by China, which was obviously supportive of a further strengthening of the anti-Japanese front (Borzoni 2004, who stresses the role of Renato Prunas, the powerful general secretary of the Italian Ministry for Foreign Affairs from November 1943 to November 1946, in particular pp. 455–469; MAE/DDI: 1992/2, document 304; 1992/2, document 332; 1994/4, document 85; 1994/4, document 93).

However, eventually this option turned out to unrealistic. As for the problem of the contents of the peace treaty between the two countries within the larger context of the *Paris Peace Treaty* (Italian colonial legacy in China, repatriation of Italian citizens, Italian properties, etc.), after many meetings and talks at the end, within the above mentioned *Paris Peace Treaty* of February 1947, a special section (Section V), articles 24, 25 and 26 concerned "Italy's Special Interests in China". Articles 24, indicated that "Italy renounces in favour of China all benefits and privileges resulting from the provisions of the final protocol signed in Peking on September 7, 1901 and all annexes, notes and documents supplementary thereto, and agrees to the abrogation in respect of Italy of the said protocol, annexes, notes and documents. Italy likewise renounces any claim thereunder to an indemnity". Article 25 stressed that "Italy agrees to the cancellation of the lease from the Chinese Government under which the Italian Concession at Tientsin [Tianjin] was granted, and to transfer to the Chinese Government of any property and archives belonging to the municipality of the said Concession"; and Article 26 maintained that "Italy renounces in favour of China the rights accorded to Italy in relation to the International Settlement at Shanghai and Amoy [Xiamen], and agrees to the reversion of the said Settlements to the administration and control of the Chinese Government" (text in UNTS 1950, pp. 18–19; Italian text in Lorenzini 2007, p. 169; see also MAE/DDI: 1993/3, document 372; 1993/3, document 610).

4 Conclusions

In the second half of the 1930s, the so-called 'golden years' of Sino-Italian relations were basically over and Rome–from late 1936-early 1937 on—had started, however gradually and rather ambiguously, to look more and more to Japan. Italy's adherence to the *Anti-Comintern Pact* and the recognition of *Manzhouguo* at the end of 1937 stood for a major shift in Italian policy towards China and the Far East in general. Soon after the outbreak of war between China and Japan in July 1937, Sino-Italian relations further deteriorated and Italian naval and air-force missions, established in the 1930s, were pushed to the sidelines after the summer, due to expanding Italian-Japanese ties and Italian disapproval of the non-aggression pact between Nanjing and Moscow. Japan's relentless military advance into China in 1937 and 1938 and the strengthened international position Tokyo now enjoyed through its adherence to the *Anti-Comintern Pact*, convinced Italian diplomacy more and more that the initiative in international politics now belonged to the Rome-Berlin-Tokyo axis and that Wang Jingwei's 'Peace Movement' should be carefully followed and actively supported. Such a support was basically assured to the Nanjing government after the establishment of Wang's regime on March 30, 1940, by supporting the regime's quick recognition by Rome and Berlin (in July 1941) and by pressuring Tokyo to give more autonomy and power to the Wang regime. This in turn damaged Chongqing diplomatic relations with Rome.

The period from 1943 to 1945 was a highly complex one in the East Asian political and military theater. Chiang Kai-shek's participation in the *Cairo Conference* (November 1943) and Wang Jingwei's participation, in the same period, in the celebrations of the *Greater East Asia Conference*, stood for a fundamental step towards a new post-war order in East Asia. Events in Italy and Europe complicated Italy's alliance with Wang Jingwei: on July 25, 1943 Mussolini fell from power, and was replaced by the Badoglio government, which signed an armistice with the *Allied Forces* on September 8. This latter event prompted the establishment on September 23 of the *Italian Social Republic* (*RSI*), which remained linked with Japan in the *Axis Powers* until the end of the war. The process of normalization between democratic and anti-fascist Italy and Nationalist China started during the last months of the war and in the first post-war period, especially through the arrival of new Italian ambassador Sergio Fenoaltea in China in the summer of 1946. At the same time, China accredited a new ambassador to Rome. With the signing of the peace treaty between Italy and China in Paris in 1947, by which Italy renounced all former colonial rights and interests in China, a new chapter was opened in the history of bilateral relations.

References

Alessi V (1939) A colloquio col futuro Capo del Governo cinese, Corriere della Sera, 12 October 1939

Barrett D, Shyu L (eds) (2001) Chinese collaboration with Japan, 1932–1945. The limits of accomodation. Stanford University Press, Stanford

Borsa G (1994) Tentativi di penetrazione dell'Italia fascista in Cina: 1932–1937. In: Borsa G (ed) Europa e Asia tra modernità e tradizione. Franco Angeli, Milano, pp 239–290

Borzoni G (2004) Renato Prunas diplomatico (1892–1951). Rubbettino, Soveria Mannelli

Cora G (1941) Uang Cing wei e il nuovo ordine in Cina. Firenze: s.n

Fatica M (2014) The beginning and the end of the idyllic relations between Mussolini's Italy and Chiang Kai-shek's China (1930–1937). In: Marinelli M, Andornino G (eds) Italy's encounters with modern China. Palgrave Macmillan, New York, pp 89–115

Ferretti V (1983) Il Giappone e la politica italiana: 1935–41. Giuffrè, Milano

Foo YW (ed) (2011) Chiang Kai-shek's Last Ambassador to Moscow. The Wartime Diaries of Fu Binchang. Palgrave Macmillan, New York
Fracchiolla D (2012) Un ambasciatore della "nuova Italia" a Washington. Alberto Tarchiani e le relazioni tra Italia e Stati Uniti 1945–1947. Franco Angeli, Milano
Hofmann R (2015) The fascist effect. Japan and Italy, 1915–1952. Cornell University Press, Ithaca, London
ISPI (1941) La politica estera dell'Italia nei discorsi e scritti di Galeazzo Ciano, Milano
Lorenzini S (2007) L'Italia e il trattato di pace del 1947. Il Mulino, Bologna
MAE/DDI [Ministero Affari Esteri; *Documenti Diplomatici Italiani*] (1957), Ninth series, vol 2, vol 3 (1959), vol 9 (1989), Tenth Series, vol 2 (1992), vol 3 (1993), vol 4 (1994), Istituto Poligrafico e Zecca dello Stato, Rome (online edition: http://www.farnesina.ipzs.it/home/)
Mitter R (2013) China's war with Japan 1937–1945. The struggle for survival. Allen Lane, London
Moccia V (2014) La Cina di Ciano. Libreria Universitaria, Padua, La diplomazia fascista in Estremo Oriente
Monzali L (2014) Pietro quaroni e la politica estera italiana (1944–1947). In: Baldi S (ed) Un ricordo di Pietro Quaroni. UNAP Press, Roma, pp 39–50
Relazioni Internazionali (1939) Incognite nell' estremo oriente, 39 settembre 30
Serri N (2015) Fascist imperialism and the Italian arms trade to Nationalist China 1929–1937. Nuova Rivista Storica 99(2):435–457
Strang GB (ed) (2013) Collision of empires. Italy's invasion of Ethiopia and its international impact. Routledge, London, New York
UNTS [United Nations Treaty Series] (1950) Treaty of peace with Italy, 49, pp 18–19, http://treaties.un.org.doc/Publication/UNTS

Human Resource Management in China: An Italian Perspective

Maria Cristina Bombelli and Alessandro Arduino

Abstract Human resources management (HRM) in China requires a different approach from the ones commonly implemented in Europe or the United States. For the casual observer, what stands out are the difficulties that Chinese workers are accustomed to facing, such as overtime work, extreme working conditions due to hazardous materials, a lack of safety regulations, and an increasing unemployment rate in low technology energy-intensive industrial sectors that is casting a shadow over the near future. The Western media tends to focus on the negative consequences such as environmental and social degradation after three decades of China's so-called 'economic miracle' accompanied by double-digit GDP growth. However, it is imperative to contextualize these and other related issued within the country as a whole. While China has been evolving at breakneck speed, this fast-changing process has led to China becoming the 'world's factory', it was able to reinvent itself during past and current global economic and financial crisis. This chapter introduces some case studies of Italian businesses operating in China, analyzing different phases of HRM, starting from the past financial and production crises that have led to the bankruptcy of thousands of small and medium—sized companies to the most recent collapse of Chinese stock markets. The analysis will take account of the different categories of Chinese companies such as state-owned companies (SOEs), companies that operate with other companies through joint ventures and wholly foreign owned enterprises. China's historical and cultural background and cultural information too are considered in order avoid a mere Western interpretations of phenomena and realities that need to be understood in a local context.

M.C. Bombelli (✉)
Wise Growth, University of Milan Bicocca and Bocconi School of Management, Milan, Italy
e-mail: bombelli@wise-growth.it

A. Arduino
Security and Crisis Management Program, Shanghai Academy of Social Sciences—UNITO, Shanghai, China
e-mail: ardualex@gmail.com

S. Beretta et al. (eds.), *Understanding China Today*, Understanding China,
DOI 10.1007/978-3-319-29625-8_22

1 Introduction

In organizations that function in a global context beyond their geographical and political borders, human resources management functions need to operate in a cross-cultural dimension (Sparrow et al. 2004). Understanding different cultures requires an attentive and cautious approach. While it is easy to fall victim to cultural biases and ethnocentrism, it is nonetheless almost unavoidable to compare different cultures in order to truly understand and localize individual actions and social dynamics (Geerz 1987; Hall 1966, 1976; Hannerz 1996; Hofstede 1980, 1991; Samovar and Porter 2000; Schein 1996). Stereotypes of different cultures may reduce or even block cross-cultural effects (Bombelli and Arduino 2005). As Osland and Bird (2000) emphasize, there is a risk that some management literature may even contribute to developing new and more sophisticated forms of stereotypes and biases.

However, the role of cultural information is gaining importance within management tool kits, and there is an increasing differentiation between cultures, serving as a base for the Italian and Chinese contexts. As Turner (1993) points out, "We run the risk of reifying cultures as separate entities by magnifying their diversity, and overestimating the impenetrability of their boundaries. We also risk assigning too much value to internal homogeneity in such a way that could be used to legitimize repressive measures to instill group conformity. In short, (…) we run the risk of turning cultures into fetishes that have been extracted from critical analysis". If this is the case each time we superimpose cultural boundaries over geographical ones, classifying people as American, Italian or Austrian, then the risk becomes even greater for a vast and complex country such as China. The turbulent developments that took place in this country over the last fifteen years, further add complexities that render attempts to define and classify cultures more difficult. The same risks apply in Italy. In this chapter, we will look at some of the prevalent stereotypes of the Chinese people and culture prevalent within Italy's managerial class. The recent wave of Chinese merger & acquisitions (M&A) in Italy that started with the Chinese company buying Cefla as well as Benelli, Ferretti and Energy resulted in a new breed of stereotypes. These were similar to the ones that we have witnessed in our many years of working in academia and consulting. To be sure, when looking at stereotypes it needs to be pointed out that we are confronted with generalizations. In Italy, as in any other country, there are people who are capable of taking into account the changes and complexities of cultures, just as there are individuals who do not venture beyond superficial appearances and flashy articles often prioritized by the general press.

2 An Italian Point of View of the Chinese Work System

During the public presentation in Italy of our research on organizational development and human resources management in China, we became accustomed to two common questions that were repeatedly posed to us. The first question sought a better understanding of China's working environment. This arises from the fact that, in Europe, despite the profound chances that the Chinese production system has undergone in the last decade, we are used to associating China's working environment with harsh conditions, such as long working hours, scarce safety and security measures high rates of pollution and health risks. What is more, the massive explosion of a chemical warehouse in Tianjing in 2015 and the alarming rise of pollution rates increase in Beijing and Shanghai continue to provide the media with material to paint a gloomy picture of the Chinese social and natural environment degradation. The second question, which attempted to focus on worker's rights and interrelated labour laws, stems from a desire to understand how workers can be protected, and who they will be able to enforce their rights. In short, there is an urge to know how Chinese workers can improve their harsh working conditions.

In our responses, we attempted to emphasize the complex situation and circumstances in China, as well as the fact that the majority of factories, either foreign-owned or joint venture companies, offer working conditions that are very similar to those found in the countries of companies working with Chinese partners in joint ventures. For instance, as for the question of pollution, there are laws in effect that have become increasingly restrictive and conscious of the importance of an eco-sustainable development in China. Regarding the problem of workers' rights, there is the possibility of appealing to a labour union—albeit a single union—but nevertheless, one that is capable of carrying out its functions. To be sure, alongside these realities, there are other less regulated ones, where working conditions are severe and in need of improvement. However, this is also the case in Italy, where to avoid degradation of working conditions, it is necessary to pay close attention to these issues and to be prepared to come up with new solutions.

The stereotypes on Chinese labour, which contribute to shaping Italy's perspective on this topic, very often stem from the media's reporting on the Chinese communities in Italy: in many Chinese small factories and workshops based in Italy, you see families working and living in the same quarters, children growing up next to mothers bent over sewing machines, and people who seemingly work without interruption, sleeping only a few hours a day on a mattress in the factory. However, such unregulated and non-monitored realities also exist in Italy today, even if they are the very exception. The images of above-mentioned unregulated Chinese working environments help to create a negative impression of the way the Chinese work and interact with their co-nationals. This current picture is corroborated by another impression among Italian business people, which is one of unfair competition, resulting from low wages and what is criticized as undervalued Chinese currency. In reality, however, the overall situation is more complex than that, and in order to better understand the evolution of Chinese personnel management we need to look back to the past of China's economic development in China to overcome a perspective, which is often distorted by flawed and one-sided information.

3 The 1970s

The Italian view of China's working environment during the *Chinese Cultural Revolution* is rather biased, also due to reports by some writers and journalists who tended to present either an idealized vision of the country at that time, or an extreme criticism of it. The role of the so-called 'Working Unit' e.g. (*Gongzuodangwei*) has been exaggerated without taking its peculiarities and core problems into proper account. One camp describes the 'Working Units' as pure and harmonious habitats, where everyone had the chance to contribute to and benefit from according to his or her means in accordance with Marx and Engel's manifesto for the Communist Party. The other camp presents the 'Working Unit' not as an entirely functional unit, but rather as a social experiment that had resulted in economic failure (Maciocchi 1971).

Few people are able to gage the actual working conditions of the time and, specifically, the effects of the state-organized diaspora, which forced people to periodically abandon their cities and move to the countryside, where they would undergo 're-education'. A factor that has been overlooked but needs to be remembered today to understand the situation in Chinese factories, was the closing of universities during the *Cultural Revolution*. For roughly ten years, schools and universities had ceased its role in building the necessary knowledge base for steering the course of the country. It was also during this period that the function of the welfare state was idealized, wherein so-called 'barefoot doctors' were portrayed as medical experts dedicated to curing the poorest of the population, using adequate resources and producing notable results. China thus became an often-cited example among intellectuals worldwide, a mirage that needed to be achieved, and wherein people can reach their full potential for self-fulfillment. This critical vision is still often used today to sanction developments that some consider being a betrayal of the original spirit of the Maoist revolution.

4 Opening up to the World

Recent history in China, starting from the 1980s, combine a series of characteristic and somewhat contradictory events that are doubtlessly difficult to understand at first glance in the West (Clissold 2005). Entrepreneurs and managers who operate in China bring with them different backgrounds. Not many of them have the patience to familiarize themselves with Chinese contemporary history, or sometimes even the culture, of their host-country as a way to understand the events that immediately surround them. Thus, they are confronted with difficulties in organizing a coherent working situation within the local context. The Italian perspective was also conditioned by the accumulated experiences that result from first-hand interaction with China. The following case study is one example of many Italian companies that set-up joint ventures with Chinese partners during the period of China's economic opening-up, which usually resulted in benefits of all involved parties (Arduino et al. 2007).

5 Bracco in China

Bracco SpA produces prescriptions goods, over-the-counter pharmaceutical products, and is a global leader in the production of radio contrast agents. Its presence in China dates back to 1999, even if its products have—via Hong Kong—been sold on the Chinese market, throughout the 1990s.

The new management that took on the leading HR functions a few years ago refocused the group strategy. Its entrance strategy, via Singapore, was to establish a joint venture with the Shanghai Sine Pharmaceutical Company, a so-called 'Collectively Owned Enterprise' (COE), thereby becoming part of a holding of the Shanghai Municipal Government. Together they formed a company that specializes in radio contrast agents. Bracco's joint venture choice was not based on any criteria of non-intervention on the part of the Chinese partner in the activities of the mother firm. On the contrary, the partnership between Bracco SpA and the Sine Pharmaceutical state colossal in the medical sector (Shanghai Bracco-Sine Pharmaceuticals) implied that the Chinese partner assumes an active role, through its supply of structural edifices, the land for the construction of plants, and logistical services. Bracco thus made use of Chinese utilities and services and, at the same time, underwent relatively mild bureaucratic procedures, due to the nature of the partnership.

Their choice is based on a desire to gain local market presence, rather than to take advantage of low labour costs. Since 2012, China is Bracco's sixth biggest market and in the same year an Italian has been appointed as General Manager. The company's philosophy is to be truly 'glocal', in order to have the general guidelines, but then to leave locally the freedom to apply the guidelines.

Mr. Canepa, the new General Manager argues that the Chinese culture requires a very open minded approach. "We must dispel the myth that the Chinese are inscrutable, you just need to pay attention to body language", he argues. Furthermore, he maintains that there is the need for greater importance to listening to the local necessities and differences. He tries to avoid what he refers to as the common 'expatriate mind sets', starting with the choice not to live in compound designed for foreigners to the daily use of the metro and sharing free time with both foreign and Chinese friends. In Bracco many of the key people are returnee Chinese, who are back in China after a period of study and work overseas. Several of his retention strategies encompass a mix of bonuses after 3 years of employment, regular job training and activities to project a positive and appealing corporate image. Furthermore, pride of belonging to the company is promoted daily with regular meetings and involvement in corporate social responsibility projects in the suburbs as well as the 'Bracco family day' and the green summer campus for the children of the employees.

Presently, there are more than 350 employees at Bracco-Sine's Chinese headquarters in Pudong (Shanghai). Non-specialized workforce is supplied directly by Sine Pharmaceutical, while skilled employees are selected directly by Bracco-Sine, which also oversees the organization of periodic training programs. In an attempt to counteract the increasingly diffuse phenomenon of job-hopping, Bracco adopted a policy to retain skilled employees based on short and long-term annual incentives, award systems, life annuities and child benefits, social responsibility programs and other benefits. Furthermore, top-level positions are filled by choosing from local personnel pool to guarantee opportunities for growth. From an operational standpoint, an ad hoc organization chart was developed for China, wherein the general director was given discretionary authority within the realm of budgets approved by Bracco SpA. In general, the directors of Bracco SpA do not provide official guidelines for the area of network direction and rather than importing Italian cultural paradigms into China, they tend to adopt parameters of Chinese methodology.

Bracco's management success lies in some key points: the ability to choose and trust the right partner, give credit to management that is assigned to the Chinese the leading functions, and interact with employees locally, rather than globally, thus leaving autonomous space to the management (Bjorkman and Xiucheng 2002). Alongside such success stories there are also many failed ones, situations wherein the Chinese partner turned out to be unreliable, performing side deals with other Western companies, or stealing know-how to set up analogous firms using only Chinese capital (Chee and West 2005). Contrasting the aforementioned model, there are also large multinational companies, which operate exclusively on a global level, wherein personnel management and other branches of company operations are carried out by headquarters and imposed, without any distinction, onto all company branches around the world (Fernandez and Underwood 2006).

6 Job Hopping and Labour Market Contradictions

Turbulent developments in China characterized the 1990s. Alongside a flood of foreign direct investments and the establishment of small and large Western multinationals, Chinese firms began to consolidate, forming conglomerates of small and medium-sized family companies and enterprises overseen by an ever-changing state (Studwell 2005). The job market exploded: demand for personnel exceeded supply, and the phenomenon of job-hopping began, as people moved from one position to another within short periods of time (Waldkirck 2004).

For Westerners, it is hard to reconcile the idea of more than a billion people looking for work, with the difficulty that companies faced in locating qualified workers to take on positions in their organizations. During these years, the phenomenon of so-called 'overselling' gained ground, i.e. the tendency to exaggerate one's experiences and qualifications in order to obtain high compensations and substantial benefits. When the worker's inability to do the job properly emerged, he or she would move on to another company, since there were always businesses in difficulty that were ready to believe what was written in a 'polished' curriculum. The damages resulting from this phenomenon were immediate and visible; not only did the company lose time and money in recruiting and training managerial employees who, after a short period of employment, abandoned the firm. Workers meanwhile, who came to consider their supervisors as mentors and leaders—an attitude stemming from a still-existing Confucian mentality—lost faith in, and loyalty to their employers.

During this phase of development, stereotypes of unreliable Chinese employees took shape- the same employees who underwent successful management training in companies like Bracco, as well as other Italian and European firms. Companies such as Bracco understood that job-hopping could be counteracted by focusing not on quality, but rather on the building-blocks of quality: instilling a rapport with one's own employees, nurturing what is referred to *guanxi* in Chinese (meaning 'personal relationship'), and promoting growth that involves education and personal development. It was aimed to establish solid and profound relations between workers and the management, the kind of relations prevalent in family firms suiting expectations of many Chinese people (Chan et al. 2002).

When university graduates were confronted with the consequences of the 2008 global economic and financial crisis, some of them opted to apply for a public service or government position or for seeking employment in a state-owned enterprise (SOE) in order to avoid the uncertainty of private companies in general and IT startup companies, which experienced bankruptcy at an alarming rate, in particular. However, the 'safe' choice of opting for public service jobs did not stop the job hopping rate-it rather created graduates that 'hop' on the one and graduates that don't on the other hand.

7 Linguistic Borders

A question that has been generally overlooked by many Italians and Europeans is the management of 'linguistic borders'. In general, multinational companies go to China not so much with the exclusive goal to reduce labour costs, but rather with the long-term objective of establishing a stable presence on the Chinese market. They invest conspicuously through the number of expatriates, and by filling important posts with people who already have long company experience, and who would bring work methods that have already been tried in the mother firm or in other tested countries. In such cases, English is the designated language, and the linguistic border is only one. Managers and employees, whether they are expatriates or Chinese, use English, while office workers and on-site labourers use Chinese. Here, companies offer English language courses, involving increasingly lower levels of the corporate hierarchy in order to widen and improve the potential for communication. This process is analogous to the situation in Italy, where English, rather than Italian, is the most commonly used language in the offices of many foreign multinational companies.

Barring some rare exceptions, Italian companies operate with a rather different linguistic model. The use of English is uncommon, which often leads businesses to hire, and place in the major positions, bilingual speakers of Italian and Chinese. Compared to the previous model, expat employees constitute a low number, and in some cases even only one. Two linguistic borders commonly characterize this structure: a manager who speaks both English and Italian. English is also used by some locals, usually in the area of sales in order to communicate with non-Chinese clients inside and outside of China.

8 The Inghirami Company

Inghirami is a textile company that produces and distributes quality clothing. Representing several clothing lines, including Inghirami, Reporter and Pancaldi, it possesses know-how that runs from top to bottom, and its products are found in many countries around the world. The decision to open a plant in China was a strategic choice that saw China's open door policy of the most populated country in the world as an opportunity not to be missed. Thanks to an acquaintance who had good relations with the textile office of Shanghai, and who advised the company that the department was interested in establishing an agreement with an Italian company, they started to make plans for the new plant. It was the early 1990s, and China was in the process of promoting and expediting its policy of opening its doors to the world. The company was founded in 1993, in the district of Pudong in Shanghai. What was once a farmland area is today the home of the financial center of Lujiazui and the location of the Universal Exposition/EXPO in 2008. It used to take more than an hour to get to the city center. Today, however, as a result of investments into the infrastructure it takes only 25 minutes by car, and one can choose between three underground tunnels, metro lines, and four new bridges. Sanremo Garment Company is a joint venture with 65% of the company belonging to the Italian company and 35% to the Chinese state. Its products are sold predominantly on the Chinese market, through single-brand stores and exports to other countries. Because of logistical costs and negative reception on the part of consumers, especially in Italy, the company decided not to introduce their products into Europe. There were around 400 employees at the time the company was founded, including Italian expatriates with families back home. The pivot of the entire company's operations was its managing director Zhang YingZi. Her story is emblematic of some personal development paths and company policies. She arrived in Italy from Shanghai when she was 14 years old and attended an Italian school, where she earned a degree in accountancy. In 1992, she started interpreting for Giovanni Inghirami. Her profound understanding of the two cultures, Italian and Chinese, greatly helped the company in its initial stage developing reciprocal trust between the Italian and Chinese partners. Her active presence in meetings and negotiations allowed her to quickly understand the stages and details of the production process, as well as technical and management issues. Shortly after the company was founded, she learned to fully comprehend all aspects of management in the field (Black and Gregersen 1999). During her work, Zhang does not speak Mandarin with her employees, but instead, the everyday dialect of Shanghainese. This way, she works not only as a manager, but also as a mediator between two cultures. Zhang is not surprised when some workers ask for her advice on private matters, such as domestic issues between husband and wife. She knows that this takes place against the background of the *gonzuo danwei*, the *workplace unit*, which often was the first and only reference point between institutions and individuals. She also knows that there are different approaches towards questions of safety and security, and that Chinese workers are used to coping with existing situations slowly and reluctantly, ignoring to follow official procedures: some points to realize and keep in mind. The Italians in the company did not learn Chinese, so they use interpreters for their work. English is used in the commercial sector only for external communications (Cragg 1995).

9 Crisis and Change in the Job Market

The global economic crisis and the 2015 crash of Chinese stock markets have had repercussions on the Chinese job market, which are at times difficult for the Western world to understand. Firstly, it is hard to comprehend the notion of the cultural concept of 'collective, i.e., the general prioritization of group over individual well-being. Clearly, this is an across-the-board issue in cross-cultural relations between Italy and China and, in general, between Western and Asian societies. Between 2007 and 2008, the collapse of the textile market especially hit those sectors linked to exports to Europe and the United States when demand fell sharply. As a consequence, more than 20 million people lost their jobs and were forced to return to villages that lacked enough land and, in some cases, even sufficient food reserves, to be able to receive them (Arduino and Bombelli 2009).

In response, the Chinese government adopted an economic stimulus package worth approximately 4 billion Yuan to be allocated into three macro groups. The first group supported a monetary policy that helped economic initiatives, including fiscal breaks and bank interest rate cuts. The second supported industries planning to enter high-tech sectors. The third group aimed at the promotion and increase of domestic consumption (Arduino 2009). The last two points are integral parts of China's 11th five-year program for economic planning, and the effect of the stimulus should fundamentally accelerate its implementation. Against this background, the government had already made an important choice, by renewing the foundations that had supported Chinese economic development from its early stages: commerce, direct foreign investments, and industrial production. With this last five-year plan, the 'world's factory' has demonstrated an awareness of its own weaknesses, as well as a willingness to take action by expanding the domestic market and promoting investments that move from mass production to high-tech production.

This structural intervention has allowed China more than most OECD countries to successfully counter the repercussions of the recent financial and economic crisis, However, still today, the Chinese economic stimulus package is associated with Western stereotypes that view a wholly state-controlled approach under a negative light and criticize what is referred to as ‘creative statistics’, i.e. official statistics and economic indicators, which e.g. exaggerate economic growth rates. At the same time, other problems of a structural nature seem to have become more evident to China’s leaders, even if solutions to these problems will require more work, and the results will only become visible in the long run. These problems include imbalances between urban and rural areas, the development of an efficient welfare system that is capable of rendering health services accessible for the poorest of the population, and providing pension for the elderly population, which has risen dramatically as a result of China’s *One-Child Policy*. There have undoubtedly been repercussions on the job market, but they are being countered by the above-mentioned economic stimulus measures. Indeed, Chinese workers in general and migrant workers in particular have paid the price for the crisis. Apart from the millions of migrant workers who did not return to their workplaces in southern China after their traditional trip home for Chinese New Year at the time, young graduates without specialized skills and experiences had difficulties finding work during the global economic and financial crisis in 2008/2009. The same job-hopping phenomenon, which was considered a norm just a few months before, has shown signs of a reversal since 2008.

10 Conclusions

In conclusion, the following issues need to be emphasized. Cultural distance cannot be bridged without reciprocal understanding. To minimize stereotypes that have unfortunately taken root, it is helpful to encourage travel, training periods, and projects that allow direct cooperation between Italians and Chinese (Letta 2003). For Italians and Westerners in general it is hard to understand China’s strategy of so-called ‘market socialism’, which undoubtedly has its merits and is becoming increasingly popular in developing countries. The term itself sounds like an oxymoron and it appears to be irreconcilable in reality. Whereas capitalism—despite its extreme weaknesses and vulnerability—seems to work for the time being, it becomes increasingly associated with the negative term of the Italian “mercatismo”, i.e. the notion that market forces prevail over all other considerations. As the starting point for managing a nation, China’s ‘market socialism’, with its 5-year plan, reminiscent of Soviet agendas, prioritizes the local sector, and values a temporal outlook that is in line with programming long-term structural development.

From the perspective of human resources management, the Chinese system of production is returning to a model that was once the backbone of pre and post-communist development: one of the extended family, viewed as an indistinct mass of personal and professional relations. Especially from 2008 to the present, it seems that state-owned companies, whose privatization and amalgamation plans date back to the 1990s, are retracing their paths towards a state management of resources, as well as a dominance of the public over the private.

In this model, there is the risk that interfamily relations will overshadow meritocracy. Private medium-sized Chinese companies, which are located mainly in the coastal areas of the country, possess an entrepreneurial model that is similar in many ways to Italian small and medium-sized family businesses. Against that background, it is possible to imagine some instances of reciprocal exchanges (Pierce and Robinson 2000). However, what appears to be problematic is the often indiscriminate adoption of personnel management models that stem from global multinationals, especially American ones. Characteristics and peculiarities of societies—Chinese society as well as other societies—are completely overlooked and there is a very strong focus on duplicating management systems that aim at enforcing oversimplification. Much remains to be done in this field. Some so-called ‘pocket multinationals’, as many Italian companies have come to be defined, can offer a single contribution, by adapting their own characteristics to a context that is very different from their own., As such, it is possible to locate areas that unite rather than divide. A Chinese proverb that we have used as the title of one of our books describes such a concept rather well: *tian xia yi jia* (*beneath the sky we are all one family*). Turning this auspice into a reality requires a cosmopolitan mentality and a project outline that sees Italians and Chinese working together on new paths, even if these paths represent an alternative to those management models that appear to promote only one concept: the one made in the USA.

References

Arduino A (2009) Il fondo sovrano cinese CASCC, O Barra O Edizioni

Arduino A, Bombelli M C (2009) The year of the Ox, lived dangerously. European Asian Strategies, EAST Dossier n. 26

Arduino A et al (2007) Cina: sotto il cielo una famiglia. Gestire le persone e le organizzazioni nel paese più grande del mondo, Guerini e Associati

Black JS, Gregersen HB (1999) The right way to manage expat. Harvard Business Review, March–April

Bombelli MC, Arduino A (2005) Comunicare tra Italia e Cina. Sviluppo & Organizzazione, September–October

Bjorkman I, Xiucheng F (2002) Human resource management and the performance of Western firms in China. J Hum Resour Manage 13:853–864

Chan RYK et al (2002) The dynamics of Guanxi and ethics for Chinese executives. J Bus Ethics 41:327–336

Chee H, West C (2005) Myths about doing business in China. Palgrave, London

Clissold T (2005) Mister China. Constable & Robinson, London

Cragg C (1995) Business on the orient (Chinese business ethics). Accountancy Age, 11 May, pp 20–22

Fernandez JA, Underwood L (2006) China CEO. Voices of experiences. John Wiley & Sons, Asia

Geertz G (1987) The interpretation of cultures. Basic Books, New York

Hall ET (1966) The hidden dimension. Doubleday, New York
Hall ET (1976) Beyond culture. Garden City, New York
Hannerz U (1996) Transnational connections. Routledge, London, New York
Hofstede G (1980) Culture's consequences: international differences in work-related values. Sage, Beverly Hills
Hofstede G (1991) Cultures and organizations: software of the mind. McGraw Hill, London
Letta CGM (2003) EA EU partnership. The future dynamics of East Asia-European union relationship. The Senjong Institute
Maciocchi MA (1971) Dalla Cina. Feltrinelli, Milano
Osland JS, Bird A (2000) Beyond the sophisticated stereotyping. Academy of Management Executive, February
Pierce JAII, Robinson RB (2000) Cultivating Guanxi as a foreign investor strategy. Business Horizon, January-February
Samovar LA, Porter RE (2000) Intercultural communication. A Reader, Wadsworth, Belmont CA
Schein EH (1996) Culture: a missing concept in organizational studies. Adm Sci Q, June
Sparrow P et al (2004) Globalizing human resource management. Routledge, London
Studwell J (2005) The China dream. The elusive quest for the greatest untapped market on earth. Profile Book, London
Turner T (1993) Anthropology and multiculturalism: what is anthropology that multiculturalists should be mindful of it? Cult Anthropol 8:411–429
Waldkirck K (2004) Job hopping and his reasons. Asia Bridge, March Postrel V, Silicon Valley: job hopping contributes to innovation, New York Times, 1 Dec 2005

Fa Versus *Guanxi*: Legality with Chinese Characteristics and Implications for Italian Business in China

Renzo Cavalieri

Abstract The distinctive features of the Chinese concept of legality, as established and developed through the years in the People's Republic of China and further defined by constitutional amendments in 1999, give the cue for some reflections with regard to the existing dialectic between legal norms and 'alternative' systems of rules and norms, in particular between what is referred to as *fa* (*law*) and *guanxi* (*personal relations, personal connections*). This relationship has implications also for Western operators conducting business in China: differences between knowing and applying law as formulated in text books together with the difficulty on moving on unknown ground in business operations in China, where history, politics and culture are intertwined, leading to a notion of a 'fluid' and pragmatic concept of business ties in general and a contract in particular. This chapter concludes with the analysis of some of the reasons why Western business operators have difficulties negotiating contractual relationships with Chinese counterparts.

1 Introduction

Italian business operators often wonder whether the law and contracts have the same value and meaning in China they have in the Western world. It is a generally accepted belief that Chinese businesses—either partners or competitors—do not take into consideration legal aspects related to their business activity, while relying more often on alternative systems: in China political and personal relationships count more than rules and contracts, and in the case of dispute, mediation and conciliation and political and personal relationships are preferred to rules and

An Italian version of this chapter has been published under the title: *Fa* vs *Guanxi*: la legalità 'alla cinese' e l'operatore italiano. In: Barbatelli and Cavalieri (2015), pp. 46–55.

R. Cavalieri (✉)
Department of Asian and African Studies,
University of Venice Ca' Foscari, Venice, Italy
e-mail: cavalieri@unive.it

S. Beretta et al. (eds.), *Understanding China Today*, Understanding China,
DOI 10.1007/978-3-319-29625-8_23

contracts. Such an assessment reveals an underlying idea: law, and therefore legal obligations, play in China a far less significant, or at least less central, role than in the West. Such idea, in turn, is based on two of the main characteristics of the Chinese political and institutional system.

The first characteristic consists in the centuries-old tradition, which considers law not as a scientific, technical and professional system, independent from other branches of the public administration, but a mere instrument in the hands of government. Such tradition bestows priority to harmony and social stability and the Western legal mechanisms and instruments are deemed inadequate in the Chinese context. Rather, a constant, flexible and dynamic balance of interests is preferred in China. The highly hierarchical concept of social relations—part of the Confucian legacy and traditions—plays a significant role in limiting the scope and importance of individual rights: the same idea of full and absolute rights recognized by law and protected by courts against a superior or the public interest is considered an expression of antisocial individualism. The second characteristic is the socialist nature of the People's Republic of China, which has grafted on to such traditional substratum some principles and institutional mechanisms equally scarcely compatible with concepts of legality, such as the principle of unity of state powers and the leading role of the China's Communist Party of China (CCP). Also the interaction between economic and political actors and between businesses and the administration prioritises relational forms over legal ones.

2 Legality with Chinese Characteristics

Thirty years of reforms transformed and modernized Chinese institutions and freed them, at least to a large extent, from the Soviet legacy and Maoist ideology (Peeremboom 2002). Chinese law today is expressly founded on the principle of (socialist) legality: "The People's Republic of China governs the country according to law and makes it a socialist country under rule of law" (Article 5,1 Constitution). Legality with Chinese characteristics means, first of all, that the state organs must abide by the law. On the other hand, the separation of legislative, executive and judiciary powers is not recognized and therefore there are neither bodies, which control constitutionality of laws nor judicial independence is recognized with regard to judiciary considered as a separate state body. Legality means that today in China there is a modern and well-structured system of legislation, which resumes and adapts Western, especially European models. After thirty years of developing a legal apparatus, disrupted by the Mao era, laws, decrees and regulations govern almost every field of social relations. There is a sophisticated technical language and a remarkable professionalism among jurists, both in public administration and in the private sector. In large law firms in Beijing or Shanghai Chinese lawyers' education, experience, work and practice are similar to the work of their Western counterparts. Legality in China means therefore that the enormous discretion of the bureaucracy is being more and more reduced and being replaced by laws. The administration still has enormous weight and great power, but its hand today is less 'visible' (Mazzei and Volpe 2010): while still controlling the market, the state and the CCP do not have a direct and complete control over businesses. What has enormously changed over the years is the governing method, which today is founded upon law and legality much more than in the past: party politics and party guidelines have become formal norms and even laws. Nevertheless, it should be remembered that in China laws remain something different from the expression of the legislative will, democratically formed and subject to the constitution: today laws approved by the National People's Congress (NPC) are almost always approved by majorities bigger than 90% and, as mentioned above, there is no control over their constitutionality.

Rights (and freedoms) are still interpreted in a relative and not absolute way and always must go in accordance with what the authorities define as 'public interest.' Over the years, owing to a freer movement of goods, capitals, persons and ideas, Chinese citizens and businesses have achieved greater—mainly but not only economic—autonomy and freedom than in the past. However, even today Article 51 of the Chinese Constitution states: "Citizens of the People's Republic of China, in exercising their freedoms and rights, may not infringe upon the interests of the State, of society or of the collective, or upon the lawful freedoms and rights of other citizens". Rights' certainty and accountability in China, are therefore less complete and less clear than in Europe (Groppi 2015). Laws are still often uncertain and in their interpretation and execution authorities operate with great flexibility: in China the exercise of freedoms, autonomy and rights is made possible only in so far as such conditions, defined and protected by law, are tolerated by the political authorities. Moreover, this is true especially for foreigners.

There is another aspect to consider. While written laws and propaganda point to legality as the cardinal regulatory principle on which society is founded, in practice, in addition to law (*fa*, 法), regulatory force is attributed to alternative systems of rules, which can be described as 'meta-legal' and are much more opaque and informal than the legal system. Such systems are essentially two: that of political rules, based on the so-called 'leading role' of the CCP, and that of 'personal relations'/'personal connections') (*guanxi* 关系) ('relational rules on which foreign businessmen so often rely (So and Walker 2010). The coexistence of legal and meta-legal rules brings with it numerous problems leading to difficulties of enforcing laws. Among them, the most serious are those deriving from the subjection to political power of judiciary and control authorities, which are not independent in China, but eventually controlled by the executive, i.e. the government.

The Chinese judicial system, in particular, is now overall well organized and efficient, and obtaining justice is in many respects quicker and less complicated than in Italy. However, the judiciary remains a very weak category, poorly paid and little recognized professionally (Song 2007). While depending entirely on local political organs, which appoint, control, revoke and sanction them, judges do not have guarantees and are organized in a strictly hierarchical way. They belong to a unitary power system and tend to take into consideration *guanxi* at least as much as laws. In this regard, they do not differ from officials, businessmen and managers: in the

Chinese system, economic and political interests interact intertwined and even a judicial decision is not a merely technical decision, but also a political and, *a fortiori* in the most relevant or politically sensitive cases: when the strict application of law leads to solutions not approved by politicians, even the judge often avoids applying it, trying instead to replace it with a 'soft exhortation' to settle disputes through an amicable mediation. Always in the name of 'harmony' and economic and social 'stability' concepts and their meaning can change greatly depending on circumstances and parties involved.

The unitary power system and the double track upon which judicial practice develops are complex, especially for foreigners. Generally speaking, in relations with the public administration, foreign citizens and companies do not always have full access to rights that the law grants them in theory. Using a metaphor borrowed from sports, in China—particularly in provinces—the referee, either a judge or an official, often sides with one of the teams.

3 Drawbacks in Business

There are many criticalities deriving from such unbalanced condition to foreign business operators, in every type of business relations, ranging from mere sales contracts to more complex trade relations, but it is mainly in relations with partners and public administrations in joint ventures that they become a serious structural problem. Both during the establishment and in ordinary governance and, especially, in some extraordinary moments in the company's life (capital increase, shares assignment, liquidation, etc.), formal and informal linkages existing between the Chinese partner and the local public administration organs can prevent the foreign partner from the full exercise of his rights. This is maybe the main reason why, after several disappointments and problems over the years, the preferred vehicle chosen for direct investment by foreigners in order to structure their own business in China, unlike in the rest of the world, is not the partnership with a Chinese business, but instead the wholly foreign owned enterprise (WFOE). Problems deriving from unfair treatment are noticeable also in the public procurement system, in market access conditions, in the attitude of authorities in controlling actions (certifications, customs, antitrust, taxation), but especially in every stage of judicial activities: from the process (e.g. when in court cases regarding international contracts judges decide a priori not to respect the contractual autonomy and apply with no exception Chinese law) to the enforcement of verdicts, when, despite of having won the case, the foreign party often decides to retire from the game in view of impeding further bureaucratic obstacles. In all these cases, law as defined in text books usually turns out to be inadequate and insufficient: in China the recognition of a right by the law does not mean necessarily that it is always enforceable. Knowing the law in China is not enough: understanding how law in action works in a certain context is also required.

4 The Power of *Guanxi*

The foreigner as well as the businessman and the practitioner who operate in China therefore have to try to secure and expand their *guanxi*, not only in order to intervene in the administrative or judicial action, but in order not to find himself too disadvantaged with regard to those who have and use *guanxi* (Schramm and Taube 2003). However, such practice does not replace knowledge and the respect of laws: foreigners move with much difficulty on the ground of unwritten rules in a linguistic and cultural context so different and this implies a number of risks, especially when a heedless management of such 'parallel' rules exceeds in corruption cases, relevant also under European legislations, including the Italian D.Lgs 231/2001 (Bonelli and Mantovani 2014).

The *guanxi* system has a further negative impact on foreigners. They are inclined to blindly rely on the power of such personal connections without really understanding them. Incited by the local modus operandi, foreigners—Italians in particular, who pretend to feel at ease on this ground—trust their partner, intermediary or supplier, who boasts about a fabulous patronage network, political protection or powerful relations, and follow him in rickety business projects, sometimes on the edge of legality without being able to exercise any control. Deficiencies of the system alone but also poor knowledge and preparation of foreigners doing business are to blame when failing to successfully conduct business in China. That leads us to a central subject in trade relations between foreign and Chinese businesses: contracts.

5 *Fa* and *Guanxi* in Contracts

Simplistic conclusions and statements that Chinese people have a fundamentally different attitude towards written contracts than Westerners are not supported by empirical evidence. At times—even by Sinologists—it is argued that Chinese business people do not respect contracts as much as their Western counterparts. However, that is not or at least no longer true. To be sure, rather only recently, have Chinese businessmen begun respecting contracts as a fundamental, if not the only means for regulating relations between economic operators. And only recently have Chinese businessmen and their lawyers and consultants obtained the technical expertise to master such instrument. Chinese history, politics and culture are intertwined even here. Like for legal norms, indeed, also in business relations there is a natural inclination in China to overlap and use simultaneously different systems of rules: written agreements are only a part of a dynamic trade relation, on which factors not included in the formal agreements have a role. According to pragmatic Chinese thinking the contract is a commitment, but also a declaration of intent, which is placed in a fluid relational framework and to which it is neither convenient nor appropriate to strictly refer. Is this concept somehow contradictory? According to our Western approach that is the case: agreements are either respected or they are not. However, the Chinese civilization is quite indifferent to the idea of contradiction and, on the contrary, is still characterized and defined by a number of oxymora: China is both a socialist and capitalist country, meritocratic while inclined to patronage, unitary while locally fragmented. Therefore it is not surprising that agreements are meant both as commitments to be respected and intents to be adapted when circumstances and balance of power change, exactly as traditionally *yin* and *yang* interact in the celestial diagram: they are antinomies that may confuse Western people (while being perfectly understood by Chinese people).

The fact that the Chinese concept of contract does not correspond with that of the Western legal tradition should not lead us to underestimate the importance of written documents when doing business in China (Zhou and Xu 2012). Indeed, not only carrying out a careful legal and fiscal planning for each business is fundamental, but investing time and human and financial resources in order to know the market and its rules and devoting attention and skills to the negotiating and drafting of contracts are essential too.

In so far as his own ability to negotiate allows so, the foreign operator shall always find solutions that can reduce the negative impact of some characteristics of Chinese law, for instance trying to delocalise contracts and avoid using Chinese courts, by including some specific clauses on the settlement of disputes. Therefore, for instance, for cases arising from contracts, derogation to ordinary justice will be foreseen to submit to arbitration, which is an independent and quick kind of dispute resolution. Moreover, arbitration leads to decisions easily enforceable—especially but not only at the transnational level—or at least more easily than judicial decisions. When the negotiating power of the foreign party is not sufficient to wring from the Chinese counterpart the agreement on an independent international arbitration commission, the former will have to content himself with an arbitration administered by Chinese institutions (often the 'China International Economic Trade Arbitration Commission' 'CIETAC'), which however hasn't yet established a reputation of professionalism and credibility at the global level.

6 Western Weaknesses When Negotiating with Chinese Counterparts

In most contractual relationships, the Western—especially Italian interlocutors—find themselves in a constant condition of weakness when dealing and bargaining with Chinese counterparts. What determines such weakness? Rather, what determines the extraordinary ability of Chinese parties to be always in a strong negotiating position? Determining factors are mainly three and act jointly. The first one is time: usually Chinese can afford developing strategies over a very long time, while having the ability to make coexist perfectly such strategies (another oxymoron that works well) with tactical reasoning of very short time. The second one is size, actual and potential. The size both of Chinese businesses and of the market and of the single markets on which they operate is indeed bigger than that available to Italian businesses. Partly owing to objective reasons, partly due to China's ability to market itself, such difference in size is generally supposed to grow in parallel with the constant growth of the Chinese economy. The third one is the Chinese ability to network: Chinese businesses can always count on the integrated support of their own political, financial and legal national system, whereas this does not always the case for foreigners and never for Italians. In this regard, the distinctiveness of the Chinese law and its way of functioning, which is somehow a harbinger of problems at the internal level, at the international level represents an element of competitive advantage for Chinese businesses.

References

Barbatelli C, Cavalieri R (eds) (2015) La Cina non è ancora per tutti. Edizioni Olivares, Milano

Bonelli F, Mantovani F (eds) (2014) Corruzione nazionale e internazionale. Giuffrè Editore, Milano

Groppi T (2015) Il perimetro delle libertà e dei diritti nel sistema costituzionale cinese, Sulla Via del Catai, Rivista semestrale sulle relazioni culturali tra Europa e Cina, vol 12, pp 43–58

Mazzei F, Volpi V (2010) La rivincita della mano visibile. Egea, Milano

Peeremboom R (2002) China's long march toward rule of law. Cambridge University Press, Cambridge

Schramm M, Taube M (2003) The institutional economics of legal institutions, Guanxi and corruption in the P.R. China. In: Kidd J, Richter T (eds) Fighting corruption in Asia. World Scientific, Singapore, pp 271–296

So YL, Walker A (2010) Explaining Guanxi: the Chinese business network. Routledge, New York

Song J (2007) China judiciary: current issues. Maine Law Rev 59(1):141–148

Zhou KZ, Xu D (2012) How foreign firms curtail local supplier opportunism in China: detailed contracts, centralized control, and relational governance. J Int Bus Stud 43(2012):677–695

Printed by Printforce, the Netherlands